Fashioning the Eighteenth Century

Sharon Diane Nell, Series Editor

The book series Fashioning the Eighteenth Century embraces works focusing on the century's social history, material culture, and literature, toward the end of illuminating the cultural fabric itself.

NAPOLEON AND THE WOMAN QUESTION

NAPOLEON AND THE WOMAN QUESTION

Discourses of the Other Sex in French Education,

Medicine, and Medical Law

1799–1815

June K. Burton

Foreword by Susan P. Conner

Texas Tech University Press

This book is typeset in Garamond, Cochin, and Nuptial Script. The paper used in this book meets the minimum requirements of ANSI/NISO Z39.48–1992 (R1997). ∞

Designed by David Timmons

Library of Congress Cataloging-in-Publication Data
Burton, June K.
   Napoleon and the woman question : discourses of the other sex in French education, medicine, and medical Law, 1799–1815 / June K. Burton; foreword by Susan P. Conner.
      p. cm. — (Fashioning the eighteenth century)
   Summary: "Examination of predominantly primary sources focuses on discourses of women and women's issues in light of the prevailing view of the relationship between the physical and the moral in feminine bodies and minds. Burton discusses France's first national system of midwifery education, women's medicine and surgery, and medical law"—Provided by publisher.
   Includes bibliographical references and index.
   ISBN-13: 978-0-89672-559-1 (hardcover : alk. paper)
   ISBN-10: 0-89672-559-6 (hardcover : alk. paper)
      1. Women—Health and hygiene—France—History—19th century. 2. Medicine—France—History—19th century. 3. Medical jurisprudence—France—History—19th century. I. Title. II. Series. [DNLM: 1. Women's Health—history—France. 2. History of Medicine—France. 3. Jurisprudence—France. 4. History, 19th Century—France. WA 11 GF7 B974n 2007]
   RA564.85.B87 2007
   613'.04244—dc22

                                                                            2006013489

Printed in the United States of America
07   08   09   10   11   12   13   14   15   /   9   8   7   6   5   4   3   2   1

Texas Tech University Press
Box 41037
Lubbock, Texas 79409-1037 USA
800.832.4042
ttup@ttu.edu
www.ttup.ttu.edu

For my mentors,
Malcom M. Wynn and Lee B. Kennett

Contents

Illustrations

Foreword

BY THE END OF THE EIGHTEENTH CENTURY, woman was no longer a misbegotten or mutilated male as Aristotle and Galen had first proposed. Debates had moved beyond whether she was made at the first instance, whether all of her body had come from the essence of Adam's rib, and whether or not she had a soul. But, at the same time, woman's nature was not yet clear. She had been made for man's delight, if one consulted Rousseau. She had carried weapons and threatened the Assembly in the early years of the Revolution, but she was still the weaker of her species. She was "the other sex."

While a thriving historiography of French Revolutionary women exists, women under the Napoleonic regime have, for the most part, been invisible and ignored in historical scholarship. The French Revolutionary period was so fertile with the continuing *querelle des femmes* and its visible manifestation in family law, pamphleteering, and political persuasion that the post-Revolutionary period has seemed bland and uninteresting for historians of gender. Not surprisingly, there has been a temptation to ignore the period from 1799 to 1815. Historians have suggested that the *Code Napoléon* placed women squarely in the private sphere, and Napoleon's rebuffs to women of the court society have been quoted and requoted. If the finest woman was the one who had the most children and if a woman did not have the right to speak because her speech might be construed as her husband's opinions, then Napoleon had said it all. His language created reality and controlled discourse.

Napoleon and the Woman Question: The Other Sex in French Education, Medicine, and Medical Law, 1799–1815 takes a very different tack. June Burton's book, using Napoleon's own words, posits that the emperor did not consider women the weaker sex. In fact, they were strong, perhaps too strong. With their tears or their allure, they could control a man. Even physically they were the dominant of the species. In some cases, they were "queen bees in the Bonapartist hive," a phrase that also might be a subtitle for this volume. In other cases they were autonomous beings who could move around the system, interject themselves into it at the right moment, and further the cause of women without being unduly noticed. For woman's nature, what mattered was *la différence*.

June Burton's book is part of a series on "fashioning the eighteenth century." Readers should note that the series intentionally uses the word *fashioning* in its title to give rise to a higher understanding of the cultural fabric of the eighteenth century. Works in this series explore and challenge assumptions about social history, material culture, and literature. In this vein, Burton's book recognizes that the *ancien régime* may have been less restrictive for some women than the Napoleonic years, but she is not nostalgic. She is comfortable in ferreting out the women who found ways to adjust the public sphere to include them or simply, against odds, to take charge of their lives.

Napoleon and the Woman Question is not a theoretical work, nor does it strive to be. It does not join the works of Joan Landes, Dorinda Outram, Antoine de Baeque, and Geneviève Fraisse, but it is informed by them. When Landes noted that "the 'unrestrained' public women and their sexuality threatened the harmonious community of the gendered republic," Burton looked for the strategies that Napoleonic women employed to control their lives.[1] When she is concerned that the discourses might not have played themselves out fully in reality, she turns to the living actors in the drama of Napoleonic France. Burton goes to the heart of the period— to the women who found their lives in the balance. She provides the personal, the anecdotal, and the case study. She, as she notes in her Preface, has begun her study by working from the sources to the topic, not the reverse. Her book is an archive and a treasure of stories that ultimately undergird theory.

Napoleon and the Woman Question also provides a nuanced approach to late-eighteenth-century and Napoleonic studies. If Poullain de la Barre had noted in 1673, "*l'esprit n'a point de sexe*," most late-eighteenth-century minds had not reached the same conclusion.[2] *La différence* was imbued in women's bodies just as in men's. Mind and body were not separate; they were ineluctably bound. Napoleon and those who surrounded him had endorsed the "average shallow opinion" of women, as Burton describes them. They espoused the post-Jacobin rescission of women's rights and the family values that replaced revolutionary liberalism. They were men around whom materialism swirled, and they viewed the Revolution of 1789 as anomalous. Conventional and conservative to a fault, Napoleon was simply concerned about the preservation of France, and he fully believed that France's population was declining. Much of what he did, therefore, revolved around his misplaced belief that depopulation was threatening the empire.

To him, marriage and motherhood had to be brought back into the pantheon of French belief.

The unifying theme of Burton's book is discourse, and there are three, as her subtitle suggests: discourses by and about women in French education, medicine, and legal medicine, i.e., medical practice and disclosure as used in the judicial system. But underlying all of the discussion, Burton concludes, "in real life . . . daughters, wives, mothers, female patients, and working women were individual subjects who had to navigate the social structure and institutions to survive, moving carefully between the public and private spaces." They had lost the collective power that they briefly held during the Revolution, but they were not powerless as individuals.

The book begins with an analysis of Napoleon's personal attitudes about the nature of women. If his beliefs had been honed from his Roman Catholic paternalism and Corsican origin, he had also been radically influenced by the Revolution. "We have spoiled everything by treating women too well," he remarked, and he committed himself to *la différence*. Women had beauty, charm, and seductiveness. Men had power and supremacy. Women's obligations were dependence and submission. The latter obligations were important to Napoleon because, unlike some of his contemporaries, he did not view women as weak vessels and frail members of the human species, as classical philosophers had described them. They were industrious and strong, but they needed to be shown their place in the hierarchy of life. They were, he noted, "baby-making machines."

Among the most significant arguments of Burton's book is her creative analysis of the mechanistic language that informed the period. Writers of the Scientific Revolution and eighteenth-century materialists had removed the layers of language that clouded scientific discourse. There was a certain obsession with the mechanics of the body, and neither women nor men were excluded from that preoccupation. Napoleon, who was equally enamored by the new practices of science and concerned about what he believed to be a declining population, defined a significant and primary position for women in society: marriage and maternity. They were, in the language of the late eighteenth century, machines like men. But *la différence* was that they were responsible for the procreation of the species. They could not fail at this crucial task.

While most historians of the Napoleonic era have used Napoleon's memoranda conclusively to determine practice, Burton's analysis of imperial women's education goes behind his mandates into the realm of the schools themselves. While Napoleon founded five schools for girls, surpassing the educational initiatives of the Sun King Louis XIV, most girls and women did not feel the largesse of the Napoleonic state. More important was homeschooling, consistent with the emperor's belief that good mothers taught their daughters to be good women, wives, and mothers, as well. The industrious woman, who might be both feared and admired, should learn to read so that she could care for the household, which ultimately would be her domain.

When Burton turns to the discourses of medicine, her sources are midwives, surgeons, and Georges Cabanis, whose "science of man" dominated the medical profession. She questions how women carved out their space in midwifery, as doctors professionalized medicine. Questioning historiography, she posits that there was no official line that kept women from the public sphere when it came to maternity. There were extensive debates on nymphomania and cesarean sections, for example, but Napoleon did not engage in them. What mattered was his legion of soldiers and the women who would bear and rear them. Philosophically naïve, he simply adopted the prevailing theory that anatomy was destiny.

Napoleon and the Woman Question splendidly opens new discussion, because it unabashedly takes on the ambiguities of the Napoleonic period. It provides faces to the otherwise anonymous women whose educational and medical experiences have been overlooked, yet whose experiences were significant and often liberating. Further, there is something very current about Burton's book. How does a society address abortion and infanticide? Does life begin at conception? How does one choose between a mother and a child when a difficult pregnancy requires such a decision? The questions that Burton raises are just as critical and poignant today as they were under the Napoleonic regime.

Susan P. Conner
Florida Southern College, 2007

Preface

Napoleon and the Woman Question: Discourses of the Other Sex in French Education, Medicine, and Medical Law, 1799–1815: a great deal of thought went into this title. When I was in graduate school, the focus of history was shifting away from the "great man theory" to the study of *mentalités* and "history from below." Nevertheless, it seemed logical to start my manuscript with a chapter on Napoleon's ideas in order to establish a benchmark by which to compare the ideas of his administrators. This manuscript then reaches below the emperor in search of realism. My inclusion of *filles mères* and foundlings, the nannies as well as the nanny goats requisitioned to feed them, and the sheepdog and the family pig that the woman of the house was given instruction on how to wash, is by no means elite history.

Originally, I thought of calling the manuscript *Napoleon and Woman Nature* because I was trying to reflect women's unequal status during the Napoleonic era as a subset of *human nature*. Others suggested use of the better-sounding term *womanhood*, but this is not synonymous with *woman nature*, because *womanhood* has a direct opposite that is totally equivalent—*manhood*—while *woman nature* does not. Furthermore, Napoleonic women also were viewed as being "different" from males (not mirror images, though); and, therefore, while elevated and sometimes protected, their difference justified the fact that in France women were not entitled to political rights until they had "earned" them, which in the minds of Frenchmen turned out to be after World War II.

Eventually, I arrived at the present title, *Napoleon and the Woman Question,* which better suits the language of the period of 1799–1815 and is not anachronistic. The "woman question" has a broad enough connotation to include the nature of women as well as their femininity, manners, roles, gender, and so forth. In the context of twentieth-century women's history, mentioning the "woman question" immediately makes us think of the woman's suffrage movement or "female emancipation." But in the context of late-eighteenth-century France, the term *the woman question* was used as an imprecise generalization. After all, as Karen Offen has pointed out, the French word *féminisme* was not even coined until the 1870s.[1]

The subtitle of *Napoleon and the Woman Question* is *Discourses of the Other Sex in French Education, Medicine, and Medical Law, 1799–1815.* That too calls for some explanation. First of all, notice that "Discourses" is plural, that there were many discourses going on at the same time among members of the various professions and the readers who participated in the print culture of the First Empire. Usage of the "other sex" is taken directly from the titles of the numerous textbooks of that era. Although some published research in feminist theory says that women were simply called "the sex," as if males had no sex, that is not the terminology used in titles of Napoleonic-era textbooks for women and girls. Whether it was an arithmetic for the *other sex,* a primer for the *other sex,* a history lesson for the *other sex,* or anything else, everyone knew for whom these books were designed: the *other sex* was women and girls, and textbooks with these titles were meant to bridge women's learning deficit.

Political and social historians have published a plethora of excellent research on the years 1789–1799, which served as historical background for the present manuscript with its focus on the post-1799 era. While the historiography on the age of Napoleon is immense, most of the recent research on the Napoleonic era continues to focus on military or political history, as it always has. When I started to attend conferences in the 1970s, I heard papers presented on the women's history of other European countries and eras, which started me thinking. The relationship between the evolution of feminism, literacy, and print culture led me to wondering whether there might have been some heated discourses exchanged behind the cool facade of neoclassicism under the French Consulate and Empire. Since the women's history of this age has not been examined exhaustively, I thought the best approach to take would be to work forward not from a topic to the sources, but from the primary sources to the topic.

I began by casting my net widely to see what came up. Initially, I searched for all the books published in France between 1799 and 1815 that might tell me something new about the "women's history" or femininity and feminism of that era. At the time, simply making such a list was a difficult task because the annual list of all books printed in France, *Bibliographie de la France; ou Journal Général de l'Imprimerie et de la Librairie,* only commenced with the year 1811, a date that is closer to the end of the First Empire than to its beginning. Moreover, the first volume of André Monglond's nine-volume bibliography, *La France Révolutionnaire et Impériale* (Grenoble: Editions B. Arthaud), appeared in 1930, but Monglond had not yet gotten as far as the Napoleonic era. Nevertheless, by following the good advice I once received from M. Marcel Dunan, I was able to build a bibliography of primary sources for the earlier years by consulting the *Journal Général de la Littérature de France ou Répertoire Méthodique des Livres Nouveaux, Cartes Géographiques, Estampes et Oeuvres de Musique Qui Paraissent Successivement en France, Accompagné de Notes Analytiques et Critiques* (44 vols. Paris-Strasbourg: Treuttel et Würtz, 1798–1841). The *Journal* also gave me authors' names, which I checked for other books and editions of books not listed. I added to my list anonymous works published within my time frame. After studying the list, I eventually conceived the idea of doing a study of the extant cache of rare manuals in the fields of education, law, medicine, and legal medicine published between 1799 and 1815, which in some way addressed the woman question.

The printed sources I located at the Bibliothèque Nationale, the Institut de France's Bibliothèque Mazarine, the Bibliothèque de l' Académie de Médecine, and the Bibliothèque Marmottan were supported by more books and papers in the Archives Nationales and the Archives de l'Assistance Publique. These sources showed how the Napoleonic government's administrators moved beyond mere discourse to actually implement some programs. The government's deliberate actions thus sought to reform ordinary women's lives by building institutions that aimed at improving, or possibly saving, the lives of women and children who previously would have died miserably from neglect.

I also was struck by the fact that the simultaneous discourses ranging from the naïve to the sophisticated, which were going on in the fields of education, medicine,[2] and legal medicine, seemed to be obsessed with women's bodies and minds, the connections between the two, and everything else about women's values and roles, and what modern American society calls "family values," as well as notions about femininity, masculinity, and gender. In other words, they were "gynocentric."

But why these three fields? Because at that time, educators (as well as branches of medicine in which this is obvious) had a different conception of the body's importance than we have now. We think of education as training for the mind or developing the intelligence and the intellect—all seated in the individual's brain. But they perceived "the mind" as being very much a part of the material body and its behavior and intentionality. For them, the body harbored the reasoning capacity of women in a different manner than it did for men. Depending on which male author was speaking, women's generative and reproductive organs were said at least to influence or, at most, to completely control an adult woman's reasoning capacity—a case of the material controlling the spiritual. This necessitated two completely different kinds of education for "the sex" and the "other sex," for males and females. Likewise, medical practice, which once had thought in terms of the special medical care efficacious for each social class, now began also to think in terms of women's medicine (gynecology) as a specialized practice appropriate for all of the standardized woman's softer, clammier, spongier, feebler parts.

Some historians see this from another point of view. During the Enlightenment, the Roman Catholic Church had lost its former hold on people's minds along with its role as arbiter of the body. Into the vacuum stepped the humanistic and scientific professions, and the debates began—and continued—nonstop down to the modern age. The thinking of these secular professionals converged quite naturally because they all were self-appointed guardians of the body, the family, and moral values, and/or of maintaining order in society through the controlling of women. Under Napoleon, these debates still aroused emotions and stimulated optimistic leaders to act, plan, and build new institutions for the *longue durée* and to enact new laws in pursuit of the dream of a better and stronger nation (physically as well as militarily) with a healthier economy than France's neighbors and competitors.

Another explanation for these imperial writers' choice of subject matter—the woman question—may be the fact that the official censorship machinery Napoleon put in place, and the zealousness of the secret police, conspired to preclude serious political discussion. But they did allow the public and, in private, the salons to talk about lighter subjects, such frivolous old ideas as the war of the sexes, the attributes of femininity versus masculinity, child rearing, good manners and etiquette, and housekeeping, in sum, all the superficially innocent, nonthreatening subject matter that filled these prescriptive manuals. It was well known that Mme Germaine de Staël, arguably the most famous French female author of the era, insisted on speaking and writing about politics; she also tried to influence politics through her salon. Even if Napoleon had been willing to forgive her for teaching people how to think, a talent that he acknowledged she had (to Mme Rémusat), he could not overlook treason. Since she could not be shut up, she was hounded by Napoleon's secret police in order to make of her an example for everyone else so inclined. Her tongue cost her ten years in exile, symbolically sending her beyond the anointed emperor's sacralized gaze, for expressing strongly anti-Napoleonic views as well as favorable opinion of the British style of monarchy. The chastisement of Mme de Staël was meant to send a loud and clear signal to the intelligentsia: to refrain from openly engaging in political quarrels and criticism of the regime, or be cut off from the source of power and authority, his elite social circle and all the other benefits of imperial patronage.

Another condition to consider in formulating an answer as to why educated women and male and female members of the helping professions focused on feminine concerns during the Napoleonic era was that the print culture of the Enlightenment had been better-established during the Revolution. A great quantity of literature was published and read in the Napoleonic era—a much greater amount than some historians have estimated by using the data from the receipts of the excise tax on paper without realizing that the tax was not levied by the *page,* but by the *feuille,*[3] which was how books were then made. (Each *feuille* was printed on both sides, then folded into several pages, depending on their dimensions.) The size of the reading public was growing as the population expanded, and more books and new journals were circulating than ever before. Some of the first French medical journals originated during the Napoleonic era and their contents stimulated discussions about the body and the mind and their interrelationship in both sexes.

Psychologists also tell us that eras that are socially disruptive, like the great French Revolution of 1789 and the Terror, cause a great deal of sexual anxiety, especially among males. If that is the case, these discourses suggest that their authors, of both sexes, were disturbed by the contradiction inherent within the political philosophy of the era that bore on the woman question. On the one hand, the promise of the Revolution guaranteed the Rights of Man to all persons regardless of sex, but then women were not given the right to vote or to speak in public. They had to be represented by men, a policy that made men superior and women inferior. Women were "domesticated," that is, put in their place and put in charge of their own lives only in the private space of the home. Thus, the political tension of democracy was troubling and went unresolved. Authors sought release from their anxiety, as well as solutions to the problem, in written discourses.

Regardless of their authors' fields of expertise, these works were characterized by a broad spectrum of overlapping ideas and values associated with the age of Enlightenment, along with a strong emphasis on domesticity (woman's traditional place is in the home, being a good wife and mother), and modernity (the nontraditional way we view women's nature and proper role at the beginning of the twenty-first century). As Carla Hesse has shown in *The Other Enlightenment: How French Women Became Modern* (Princeton University Press, 2001), the early-nineteenth-century "modernity" was consistent with liberal rather than radical feminist ideals. Hesse's working definition of women's "modernity" as their self-consciously leaning toward autonomy and being self-creating is a good one that works well in the Napoleonic context. By looking at these books from the perspective of feminist theory, some of them appear to be "feminist" as well.

While a devil's advocate might wish to argue that the collection of positive opinions vis-à-vis women's nature expressed by contemporary sources was the opinion of a minority and therefore of no real importance, examination of advances in midwifery education, medicine, and legal medicine tell quite a different story about what was in process. The Napoleonic era was foremost an age of glorious warfare supported by the pitiless conscription of males; but, concomitantly, it was characterized by progress in the building of social institutions and systems that improved the survival rate or lessened the misery of the humble masses left behind on the home front.

After a great deal of heady institutional and social history, Chapter 10 is the compelling, human story of two well-educated, strong women who reigned over their households and capably managed their families' domestic affairs—Adrienne Noailles Lafayette (wife of the "hero of two worlds") and Frances Burney d'Arblay, the latter an international celebrity herself. Both women had tragic medical histories that provide us with a look at how contemporary women interacted with the medical community and how their families handled their cases. Mme Lafayette, whose female relatives had been guillotined during the Terror, was treated for several years for chronic illnesses; and, Mme d'Arblay, a novelist of social commentary, became a surgical (mastectomy) patient. They squarely faced the daunting task of literally keeping body, mind, and soul together in a dignified way. These and other imperial women, such as the great midwifery teachers Mme Lachapelle and Mme Boivin, who perfected new surgical operations and were awarded German medical degrees, are as much the heros of this manuscript as Napoleon himself.

I would like to acknowledge the appearance of two enviable books on the late eighteenth century that encouraged me to continue working on women's history in the Napoleonic era. Notably, 1988 saw publication of Joan B. Landes's exciting *Women and the Public Sphere in the Age of the French Revolution* (Cornell University Press), which discussed the public sphere and questions of gender, such as domesticity versus equal rights for women, prior to the Napoleonic era. Then in 1998 came Nina Rattner Gelbart's *The King's Midwife: A History and Mystery of Madame du Coudray* (University of California Press), which is a brilliant biography of that great forerunner of Napoleonic midwives. Mme du Coudray provides a much needed point of reference for evaluating Mme Lachapelle's and Mme Boivin's careers.

After I finished most of my research, I was delighted at the appearance of Joshua Cole's monograph: *The Power of Large Numbers: Population, Politics, and Gender in Nineteenth-Century France.* Cole's findings were of great interest to me since the mission statement of Napoleon's La Maternité had identified the gathering of statistics related to childbirth and infanticide as part of its efforts to valorize and sanctify motherhood and childhood. In *The Power of Large Numbers* Cole showed how the philosophy of domesticity coupled with a focus on statistics was not doomed to become a political dead end. Instead, it eventually led to a widening of the franchise to include French women. Cole called attention to the fact that a host of twentieth-century French feminists "all attempted to use the pro-natalists' valorization of motherhood and family to further the cause of women's rights."[4] Consequently, the pursuit of domesticity as public policy did not necessarily mean that women had to continue to be deprived of political rights, as they had been in the Napoleonic era. After domesticity came to be really appreciated for contributing to population growth, women were ultimately granted the right to vote because they made an inestimable contribution to the nation's well-being, a different one that nature had designed for their sex alone. Without motherhood, French culture and civilization would have ceased to exist. Thus, Napoleon I's administrative regime institutionalized the antecedents of the twentieth-century welfare state and liberal (versus radical) feminist ideas.

Finally, in the twenty-some years I have been at work on this manuscript, the important field of feminist theory has also developed as an offshoot of woman's history, and although it was never my intention to write what could be called purely a book of feminist theory, a review of the most relevant literature in this emerging field can, nevertheless, help to situate and frame the present contribution.

Two fascinating books by Londa Schiebinger, *The Mind Has No Sex?* (Harvard University Press, 1989) and *Nature's Body* (Beacon Press, 1993), head this list. One of the themes that Schiebinger explored in her books was how gender shaped the development of European science and medicine and natural history. In the former, she used graphic images to make the point that in their anatomical drawings, scientific illustrators drew great distinctions between male and female skeletons, notably in the inverse relationship between the size of the pelvic basin and the size of the skull that harbors the female brain, drawings that reflected the illustrators' emotional biases more than rationalism or empiricism. Likewise, in *Nature's Body*, Schiebinger used illustrations that naturalists drew of primates before they had actually seen or studied these animals to show how they attributed typical masculine and feminine traits to these mammals: the male primates were taller and sexually aroused while the modest females demurely covered their private parts with their folded hairy hands and cast down their eyelids, which were edged

with seductive lashes. Schiebinger also found that while women participated in science in the early modern period, as science became professionalized and moved out of the home into the public space, women came to be
increasingly excluded. By the nineteenth century the reign of aristocratic
women was over and the newly powerless female intellectuals also were
excluded from attending universities and academies. Women, such as midwives, were accused of being ignorant, yet they were denied access to the
medical education that would have enlightened them and, thereafter,
allowed them to compete with the new male accoucheurs who seized control of the female body by monopolizing the practice of obstetrics and gynecology. What is an odd feature of Schiebinger's work, however, is that she
concentrates largely on the pre–French Revolutionary era and only picks up
the threads of her stories again around the 1830s, skipping ever so lightly
over the entire period of 1789 to 1815. She does claim that the debate about
"complementarity" (the notion men and women are not equal but that a
married couple, the smallest social unit of society, complete or complement
each other) ended before the French Revolution broke out. Since her argument was that complementarity and republican motherhood had already
won the day, she found nothing more left to say about the fifteen years that
I intend to investigate.

Geneviève Fraisse, a French philosopher, also has made significant contributions. In *Opinions des femmes* (Paris, 1989) she introduced five important female authors who went public as feminists between 1787 and 1801.
Fraisse also produced two important books relating to women's struggle: *La
Raison des Femmes* (1992) and *Muse de la Raison: La Démocracie Exclusive et
la Différence des Sexes* (1989) (in English as *Reason's Muse: Sexual Différence
and the Birth of Democracy* [1994]). The latter was a long essay merging philosophy, logic, literary criticism, and feminism in a historical context. It
focused on notions about the question of women's reasoning capacity, circa
1800–1820. Her opening chapters examined two public discourses or quarrels that attacked exceptional women: one centered around the satirical
polemic of Sylvain Maréchal who proposed a "law" prohibiting women to
read (1801) and the feminists who answered him, Mme Marie-Armande-
Jeanne Gacon-Dufour and Mme Albertine Clément-Hémery; and, an earlier poetic controversy between Ponce Denis Ecouchard Lebrun, Gabriel
Legouvé, and Constance Pipelet, princesse de Salm, which centered on the
issue of whether women could be poets. The substance of these quarrels was
about the war between the sexes: namely, women's ability to reason and to
acquire knowledge; whether women can, or should, become writers and
poets, and if so, can they ever produce anything better than mediocre
pieces; whether women can invent and create like men have done through-

out history; and whether women have a right to an education and to perform salaried work. Her third chapter discussed the single discourse among six selected medical philosophers (whom I will be discussing later), whose goal was to write a natural history of the human race. But the doctor-philosophers all thought women were physical weaklings whose lame brains could not grasp theoretical knowledge. She argued that they feared the prospect that the exceptional women might become the rule. Fraisse's final chapter was devoted to two issues: the debate over democracy's exclusion of women and dating the moment when things started to change for the better for women. She pinpointed the historical break between the Enlightenment's "war between the sexes" (antifeminism) and the birth of feminism—women's movement for liberation and emancipation—not at 1789, but at 1800. She ended with a call for more feminist research because, as she declared in her final line: "We do not yet know whether or in what way reason is sexed."[5]

Before moving on, I need to call attention to some interesting observations that Fraisse made, which I plan to return to in the conclusion to this manuscript. The context for this was how at the birth of democracy, the relation between political and sexual difference was always fueled by anxiety about confusing sexual identities; or, that sexual difference was inherent in democracy. Fraisse became explicit: "the historical period, the Empire, did not seem to reassure them."[6] I hope to shed some light on the question of what was happening that could possibly have made imperial men feel that they needed assurance that the sexes were not being confused.

The fourth volume of *A History of Women in the West,* edited by Geneviève Fraisse and Michelle Perrot, subtitled *Emerging Feminism from Revolution to World War* (Belknap-Harvard University Press, 1993), followed in the wake of Harvard University Press's earlier multivolume work, *A History of Private Life,* edited by Michelle Perrot (1990). This new collection was an interesting mix of articles drawn mostly from fields other than history, such as philosophy, sociology, art, literature, and anthropology, with translations of excerpts of primary sources prefaced by excellent but short introductions the editors have written. Because they saw feminism coming from many points of view, Fraisse and Perrot claimed to be presenting a volume of "plural history" that offered no single answer to the mystery of the woman question. The framework they superimposed on the nineteenth century is simple: after the brief period of feminism during the French Revolution was spent, in the first half of the nineteenth century women were idealized as the bearer of feminine values at the same time as they were being "standardized." They were restricted to the practice of domesticity. By the end of the bourgeois century, however, women began to venture out once again into public space in order to make use of their feminine values and virtues, which were antithetical to the masculinity of business and industry. But instead of going in public to seduce men (as coquettes and courtesans had done during the Enlightenment), late-nineteenth-century women moralists again ventured into public space to join reform movements hoping to eradicate social ills. They also claimed that times of political crisis, like the French Revolution and the World War I era, are apt to be characterized by intense sexual anxiety.

Dorinda Outram's *The Body and the French Revolution: Sex, Class, and Political Culture* (Yale University Press, 1989) attempted to merge the history of the French Revolution with the history of the body. Outram said that the French Revolution failed to create a state, rather it created a new public space where none of the many discourses in play ever won decisively. Outram also emphasized the important role of the medical profession whose new philosophy and the creation of a scientific language (known only to themselves) was a precondition for the crisis. During the Revolution, as a reaction to crisis, middle-class men role-played Stoic heros of classical antiquity, even to the point of electing heroic suicide or the guillotine, in lieu of running away in fear, in order to control their own deaths. Ironically, those who practiced Stoic dignity colluded with the Terror by not resisting. Energetic reaction was displaced onto the furies of society—women, the working class, and the peasants who responded actively, displayed emotion, and empathized with the suffering of others. Middle-class men justified the exclusion of women by condemning their emotion and passions, which to them were neither Stoic nor dignified.

The guillotine cut across all class lines and made execution of batches of people bearable because it was quick technology and actually concealed more rather than fewer details from the audience's line of sight. Doctors like P.-J.-G. Cabanis objected to the fact that the crowds became apathetic to the violence of death. Also, the whole process was devoid of religious comfort. Yet, the guillotine had the capacity to generate myths, such as the "Charlotte Corday myth" whereby witnesses claimed that Corday's severed head responded miraculously by blushing when it was slapped.

Outram shifted her focus from the construction of male bodies as arenas for public authority to the construction of a female body in Chapter 8 when she focused on the life and death of Mme Manon Phlipon Roland, the best-documented woman of the late eighteenth century. Roland was an avid reader—especially of erotic novels whose heroines she imitated. Outram showed how through her writings Mme Roland created a fractured self-image that shifted poles as she blurred boundaries between masculine and feminine space, engaging in quite a variety of public and private roles. Her experience of childbirth and breast-feeding caused her tensions as well. Like Marie Antoinette and Charlotte Corday, Mme Roland's virtue disappeared because she intruded into public space and for that she was falsely accused of engaging in "boudoir politics" or uncontrolled sexuality.

Outram maintained that the feminization of the public realm that had existed before 1789 was totally reversed five years later. But these austere Stoic practices, which included heroic suicide, were short-lived after Thermidor, 1794, and were virtually gone ten years later because Napoleon stabilized politics so that individual bodies were no longer in such crisis that they needed to role-play. Outram concluded that the deep determination, of all political groups during the Revolution of 1789 and in the nineteenth-century replays of that Revolution, to retain the patriarchal character of French society was paradoxical, yet more characteristic of it than the class conflict Marxist historians saw occurring.

Finally, most recently, Karen Offen's *European Feminisms, 1700–1950: A Political History* (Stanford University Press, 2000) attempted to move gender away from being considered a subset of other "-isms" to being the center of a reconceived European political history as she compared the emergence of French feminism, which entailed mostly political not philosophical claims, with other distinctly nationalistic forms of feminism. The metaphor Offen chose to describe the sporadic emergence of feminism in history was a geologic or volcanic one; whereas Gloria Steinem had spoken in terms of two "waves" of feminism; in 1975, in her charming book *The Reign of Women in Eighteenth-Century France* Vera Lee spoke of it as a "patchwork quilt"; and Madelyn Gutwirth, in *The Twilight of the Goddesses* (1992), spoke of "one long festering." Offen also saw feminism rising necessarily out of female literacy and the advent of print culture in all nations—this is how she accounts for the emergence of feminism occurring much later in slower-developing nations.

Offen's most important contribution, however, was to construct a definition of feminism so cosmopolitan and timeless that it is applicable to all cultures, even twentieth-century Africa, Asia, and Latin America. She set forth this definition briefly in *European Feminisms,* but she initially published it twelve years earlier in "Defining Feminism: A Comparative Historical Approach," an article that has been translated into many languages (*Signs Journal of Women in Culture and Society,* 14, no. 1 [Autumn 1988]: 119–157).

Offen arrived at her final definition after establishing that historically two modes of discourse have been put forth by feminists. She called these the "relational" and the "individualist," and either one or both of these have been appropriated to some degree by French feminists.

Relational feminists are advocates for complementarity and companionate marriage, and view the male-female couple as the smallest basic unit of society. Relational feminists, therefore, seek women's equal rights without abandoning their womanliness and sexual difference, as Mary Wollstonecraft did. They made claims on society as recompense for women's significant contributions to society. (Relational feminism is a term that Joshua Cole could have used to define French feminism in his manuscript. Offen and Cole's books were both published in 2000.)

By contrast, Offen considered individualist feminists as characterized by their quest for female independence and absolute equality with men. They discounted the value of all socially defined roles and sex-linked contributions of any kind. For them, it was the individual who was the primary unit of society, not the married couple or the family. Twentieth-century U.S. suffragettes and supporters of the Equal Rights Amendment are examples of legalistic persons who sought the protection of a "sex-blind" legal system and a society stripped of protections for sexual differences.

After delineating these two historical modes of argumentation for feminist goals, Offen was ready to enunciate her definition of feminism, which had to be supple enough to encompass both. Feminism, she said, has been a critical ideology in which women resisted male dominance and superiority in the family and society and sought to redress the sexual imbalance of social, economic, and political systems. Yet, respect for the differences between the sexes was maintained. Offen saw this challenge to traditional cultures as being "transformational." Given this definition, Offen defined a feminist by three criteria, which can only be briefly summarized here: anyone, male or female, who (1) acknowledges the validity of women's interpretation of their lived experience; (2) demonstrates consciousness of inequities or injustices in a given society between men and women as groups; and (3) challenges coercive practices and institutions that preserve male domination of culture and society. At the end, Offen's agenda for the future of feminism was to combine both forms of feminist argumentation—relational and individualist—in order to preserve women's womanliness and sexual differences while bringing an end to male dominance and thereby achieving equality. I shall be using Offen's definitions of relational and individualist feminism throughout my text.

No gendered history of women can be written today without bowing to the authors of these seminal works, which have added a fresh impetus to what was becoming (it can only now be admitted) a rather stale and flat field. This new composite of research on the body should impel future research on the social and intellectual aspects of the French Revolutionary/Napoleonic era to become more prismatic.

A host of historians, archivists, bibliographers, and other colleagues helped in large and small ways to bring this research slowly to fruition—foremost, in Paris, Mmes Ulane Z. Bonnel and Nicole Villa-Sébline; in Heidelberg, Theodore Mackiw; and in the United States, the late Boris Blick, Shelly Baranowsky, Keith Bryant, Ruth Clinefelter, Susan P. Conner, Mary Durham Johnson, and Karen Offen. In 2002 Harold T. Parker honored me (three months before his death) by painstakingly reading the entire first draft and offering his suggestions. Lafayette scholar Robert R. Crout set me to work on the subject of Adrienne Lafayette as a medical patient; and pharmacology professor emeritus J. Leon Lichtin (University of Cincinnati) contributed his expertise to my analysis of her prescribed medications. Earlier versions of some materials in this book were presented as papers at annual meetings of the Southern Historical Association, the Western Society for French History, and the Consortium on Revolutionary Europe, 1750–1850.

I am especially indebted to the latter for allowing me to share the original version of Chapter 3 (on the contents of humanistic manuals of sex and home economics) at the 1983 Consortium of Revolutionary Europe program in Athens, Georgia, and publishing it in the *Proceedings* (681–96) as well as Chapter 9, "The Nineteenth-Century Discourse of Napoleon's Program to End Infanticide" on its 1997 program and in its *Selected Papers 1997* (Florida State University Press, 1997, 234–50). Chapter 10 was likewise launched at the 1999 CRE held in Charleston, South Carolina, and published by FSU Press; in the *Selected Papers 1999*, 83–92, under the title "Adrienne Noailles Lafayette (1759–1807) and Fanny Burney (1752–1840) as Medical and Surgical Patients under the First Empire." I am also indebted to the American Friends of Lafayette for publishing "Adrienne Noailles Lafayette (1759–1807) as Medical Patient: Lafayette's 'Better Half' in the Worst of Times" in their pamphlet series (1999).

I owe an expression of esteem and gratitude to Garnette Dorsey, whose secretarial assistance and encouragement meant a great deal at the beginning of this project, which was a physically challenging period of my life. I am greatly indebted as well to a multitude of anonymous staff members who brought me materials that I never would have found myself, or placed my chair near a warm radiator on a rainy day in Paris. I owe a lot to just plain "good fortune" for stumbling accidentally on many interesting sources that happened to be bound with other titles; this was especially true at the Institut de France. For recent courtesies, I wish to thank James Edmonson and Laura Travis at the Dittrick Medical History Center and Karen Medlin, Claire Carpenter, and Sara Schroeder at Texas Tech University Press for their assistance with the illustrations and indexing.

Finally, I am indebted to the libraries of the University of Akron, Kent State University, Cleveland State University, the Allen Library and Dittrick Medical History Center at Case Western Reserve University, as well as to the Cleveland Museum of Art for their assistance and access to their collections, especially since my retirement from teaching at the University of Akron in 1994.

Akron, Ohio
2007

NAPOLEON AND THE WOMAN QUESTION

Ah! qu'il est cruel d'être femme,
Et de ne pouvoir pas créer.

Mme Marie-Victorine Perrier, 1807

1

Napoleon and Woman's Nature

THE FRENCH REVOLUTIONARIES had failed to meet the needs of families for public primary education for girls to augment and replace the religious schools that had been closed. Consequently, the Napoleonic regime inherited this problem in 1799. Of course, this failure was due in part to the patriarchal culture of the Convention and the Directory, which valorized domesticity, and put women and girls where men thought women's "rightful place" was—in the home—under the direction of their husbands and fathers. But there was more complexity to the issue than that. No one voice framing a practical plan for women's education could be heard above the din of competing ideologies. A mélange of enlightened philosophical ideas of the seventeenth and eighteenth centuries had challenged the traditional ideas of the Old Regime, and when the cult of antiquity came into vogue, even the revived ideas of pagan antiquity competed with the status quo. The effect these opposing ideas had on education was to make almost all pedagogical theory ever known in the history of Western civilization contemporaneous. The resulting climate of opinion among imperial educators was, as François Guizot phrased it, a "conflict of still-confused ideas." "How to distinguish, how to choose that which can be of real utility? How to take what is already good, whatever is new, in order to combine it with what is still true even if it is old?"[1] These were the questions Guizot posed to readers of the official journal of education in 1811. This superabundance of ideas represented an impasse in itself.

Nor had the Revolutionaries arrived at philosophical agreement about an understanding of basic human nature, especially about the connection between the physical and the moral, a topic in which there was great interest on the part of anthropological physicians as well as educators and the literate reading public. For many, the philosophical issues forming the foundation of education, which still needed to be solved, overrode all else.

Imperial educators, administrative officials, and Napoleon, initially as first consul and later as emperor, engaged in a similar discourse about the nature of women and, following logically from that, what should be women's proper role in French society. The planners needed to arrive at some sort of consensus before they could begin to create new public institutions to prepare young women to fill their modern societal role. This approach made sense to them in terms of providing the rationalized and stable government the French people needed after enduring so many years of crisis. Naturally, Napoleon's own opinions about these issues would have the most importance in determining the sexual politics of the consulate and the empire.

Napoleon's Personal Attitudes about Woman's Nature

In addition to traditional Roman Catholic paternalism, Napoleon's personal attitudes about womankind in general reflected early on the Corsican origin and later the cynicism of the aging hero. As first consul, Napoleon invited the French-Swiss woman of letters Mme Germaine de Staël[2] to a reception at his newly purchased home, the château de Malmaison, where he engaged in a cordial conversation with her. "Who would you say is the most meritorious woman in all of France?" she is reputed to have asked him. "Madame," he answered simply, but with heart, "it is she who has the most children." Moreover, Napoleon always respected the care that mothers of large families ideally provide for their offspring, despite their terrible struggle for survival in times of scarcity. He liked to point to his own family's history as a perfect example: "Consider," he was fond of saying, "how poor we were and my widowed mother had eight children to raise." In time, such expressions of his humanitarian concern for motherhood and the protection of children would become cardinal ingredients of Napoleon's plans for enlightened projects, and they eventually became enshrined in the Napoleonic legend[3] that grew after his exile and death on Saint Helena.

In spite of Napoleon's insistence that in the public sphere women ought to be submissive, he realized how much power they exercised within the household, as had his own mother. "A wife who sleeps with her husband," he said, "always exercises great influence over him." And again, "Sleeping together is a very moral act that has a remarkable influence on the household, assures the influence of the wife, the dependence of the husband, maintains intimacy and good manners."[4] True to his words, he moved his bed upstairs to the second floor. Napoleon thus recognized the psychological power of women to manipulate their spouses by clever use of the conjugal bed inside the home, which seemed to him to be their proper place to exercise power.

In contrast to his more charitable and thoughtful comments about female nature, as he grew more successful and increasingly cynical, he occasionally, in the handling of routine administrative matters, let slip quick, more ven-

Napoleon Bonaparte as a young officer. Photo-etching after a painting by Zanerio. From William Hazlitt, *The Life of Napoleon.*

omous remarks, as in 1807 when he spoke of the "feeble-mindedness of women" or of their "fickleness."[5]

Later at Saint Helena and in a pensive mood, he likewise remarked to the Napoleonic war hero Baron Gourgaud, one of his companions in exile and formerly general aide-de-camp:

> In France women are too highly esteemed; they should not be regarded as the equals of men and are, in reality, just machines to make babies. During the Revolution, women rose in rebellion, set up assemblies, wished even to form battalions; men were obliged to check that idea. Disorder would reign entirely in society if women came out of the state of dependency where they ought to remain. There would be continual fights. One sex ought to be submitted to the other; women have made war like soldiers; then, they are coura-geous, worthy of much exaltation, capable of committing unparal-

leled atrocities. . . . If a battle between the sexes occurs, it will be
quite different from what we've seen between the grandees and the
lesser people, the whites and the blacks. . . . In a combat situation
pregnancy is the only thing that could give inferiority to the woman.
The women of the market places are as robust as the majority of
young men.[6]

It must be recalled that Napoleon's exile was embittered by the disaffec-
tion of the Austrian princess, Marie Louise, his young second wife. He had
empowered Marie Louise far more than he ever had his older first wife,
Josephine, yet she kept their young son, the King of Rome—his only legitimate child—from visiting him during his captivity. On another occasion he
rambled on to his companions-in-exile in a vein similar to the above: "We
have spoiled everything by treating women too well. We have brought
them, very wrongly, almost to equality with us. . . ." He thus credited himself with advancing the position of women too far, before he specifically
addressed his female companions, in an affected show of philosophy and
logic:

> And of what do you complain after all, ladies? Have we not recog-
> nized that you have a soul? You know that there are some philoso-
> phers who have weighed it. You lay claim to equality? But that is
> folly: woman is our chattel and we are not hers; because she gives us
> children and man does not give them to her. She is, therefore, his
> property just as the fruit tree is the gardener's.
>   It is, therefore, ladies, and you must admit it, only lack of judg-
> ment, common ideas, and lack of education that could bring a
> woman to believe herself equal to her husband in all things. More-
> over, there is nothing discreditable in *la différence;* each has his char-
> acteristics and obligations. Your characteristics, ladies, are beauty,
> charm, seductiveness; your obligations, dependence and submission.[7]

Thus Napoleon had spoken like a dictator. Napoleon's line of reasoning
resulted in defining women as chattel and circumscribed their place as
being under the control of their husbands. However lovely they might be,
they ought never dream about claiming human rights, least of all, voting
rights, which were so unspeakable they were not even under discussion.

From these typical examples of Napoleon's conversations and letters
about the female sex it becomes clear that he did not make them in jest—he
was deadly serious about his convictions. Moreover, they are important
beliefs relating not only to woman's nature and political rights but to medi-

cine, law, and legal medicine. And once more his references to the authority of Nature and disdain for theology stand out in his conceptualization of femininity and gender. To the end, he believed in male supremacy, which he came to justify by what he perceived to be the social necessity of keeping society orderly following the French Revolution and the Terror. But now, the outbreak of the potentially atrocious war between the sexes was his worst nightmare. While he stated bluntly that he viewed women as "baby-making machines" designed by Nature for this purpose, he also recognized women's great physical strength, which he equated with that of soldiers' (certainly a role he respected, perhaps more than any other occupation). In other words, women were the hardier, productive queen bees in the conceptual recesses of Napoleon's mind. It is well to remember that the golden bee was the heraldic symbol of his family; and to a man with his classical education, the bee symbolized three things: agriculture, industry, and fertility.

Napoleon and La Mettrie

The reader, however, needs to exercise caution about misconceiving precisely what Napoleon meant when he stated his conviction that women are "baby-making machines" designed by Nature for this purpose. In prior centuries the metaphor connoted quite a different idea than it does in the modern English of postindustrial society. Originally, the metaphor of man as machine came from an exaggerated reaction to iatro-chemistry on the part of those who espoused the mathematical approach to medicine at the end of the seventeenth century. Descartes led the way in 1664 with the publication of his *Traité de l'Homme,* which described the human body as a machine formed by God; that century's definition of "machine" was simply all the organs making up the body of man or an animal.[8] Furthermore, it has not been appreciated until recently that Descartes the physicist was also a sensitive medical theoretician whose contribution to the Enlightenment was to connect medicine and politics, thereby foreshadowing the social medicine movement of the mid-nineteenth century. In fact, Descartes's primary interest was not physics, mechanics, or optics, but "the conservation of health," a practical philanthropic design.[9] Descartes the parent, for example, responded to those who said that his daughter should not do anything besides have babies with the warning that if her "pretty little machine" was not given a respite between pregnancies, she would be enfeebled and destroyed.[10]

Descartes was not alone in his obsession with the mechanics of the body. Closer to the Napoleonic era, a practitioner of elite medicine and materialist philosopher, Julien Offray de La Mettrie (1709–51), penned the popular work *L'Homme Machine* (1748).[11] This treatise greatly influenced early-nineteenth-century language. Initially, his anonymously published work embodying the man-machine concept caused such a stir that after his authorship was discovered he was at risk for his life. Fleeing from Leiden (where he was studying with Herman Boerhave), he sought refuge at the Prussian court of Frederick the Great at Berlin. La Mettrie's solution to the riddle of body-mind nexus was to break with the theologians and members of the metaphysical tradition by saying that Nature and Man are ultimately unknowable but that mental life probably has physical causes, which in turn result from the irritability of body fibers and nerves that stimulate responses from the brain. La Mettrie believed that the body therefore governed the mind and not vice versa; consequently, he was humane toward criminals. Furthermore, he somehow avoided choosing between the extremes of God or Chance as Creation by opting for belief in a creative Nature concept. Likewise, his belief in instincts as well as reason helped him to avoid the excesses of the Enlightenment but resulted in his view of man as being so hardly distinct from higher animals that he once tried to teach an ape to speak. Nevertheless, La Mettrie's appreciation of the role of instincts led his psychology to stress the inborn temperament of each individual. Unlike most of the philosophes, the sensually exuberant La Mettrie emphasized imagination as the most important mental faculty. Fittingly, when he spoke about the brain or the universe, he thought in terms of musical analogies: metaphorically, the brain was a clavecin (a sort of compact harpsichord) listening to itself, while the universe was a grand opera being performed. So the ramifications of his man-machine concept were far from being Orwellian. Instead, when correctly understood by contemporaries, La Mettrie's mocking of traditional canonical thought was conveyed in a light and witty manner. Although La Mettrie was the object of ridicule and they tried to distance themselves from him, his man-machine concept was carried on in the last half of the century by such revered thinkers as Diderot and D' Holbach, and, during the age of Napoleon, by Dr. Pierre-Jean-Georges Cabanis.[12]

Just as Descartes was remembered more for his physics than for his greater interest in public health, La Mettrie's emphasis on medicine and medical philosophy was neglected until the publication of Kathleen Wellman's monograph, *La Mettrie: Medicine, Philosophy, and Enlightenment* (Duke University Press, 1992). She contended that La Mettrie's "entire philosophy applies his scientific knowledge to philosophical questions such as the nature of matter and human beings and the relationship of human beings to nature and society" and that he was motivated by zeal for "humanitarian reform, especially . . . the alleviation of human suffering."[13] She concluded her study thus:

> [H]e was avant-garde in his recognition of the role physiology would play in the social sciences. La Mettrie . . . seems to be the most modern of the philosophes. He was convinced that medicine and science would replace religion as a way to understanding all human behavior, including rationality and morality, and he assumed that physiology was the crucial determinant of all human behavior, including rational and moral behavior. His fundamental premise was that physiology might produce at the least some toleration for deviants and, more optimistically, some real benefits for mankind. His ultimate hope, and one the nineteenth century assiduously sought to fulfill, was that physiology might yield a realistic understanding of human nature.[14]

Thus, we find in the works of La Mettrie several currents that swirled into the mainstream of Napoleonic intellectual debate over the nature of women, women's roles, their proper education, and medicolegal issues such as criminal responsibility in infanticide cases.

As we shall see shortly, these recurring themes appeared frequently—in all kinds of imperial medical treatises when physicians, surgeons, and *officiers de santé* (a third category of less-educated healers, licensed by the Napoleonic government to practice in the countryside since military conscription had created a serious shortage of doctors) speak specifically about women's nature and seek rationally to justify unequal treatment of women politically.

The mechanistic conceptualization of women put forth by Descartes and La Mettrie linguistically went beyond words and entered visual imagery. Nina Rattner Gelbart's study of Mme du Coudray's midwifery manual makes the point that then, even medical illustrations of the female body made women look mechanical and unreal.[15] This mechanistic trend continued in imperial medical illustrations as well.

Regardless of intellectual protests about how outmoded La Mettrie's ideas were supposed to have become by the post-Revolutionary era, the 1835 edition of the Académie Française's dictionary still sanctioned use of the figure of speech that "Man is an admirable machine,"[16] a generic remark that, of course, could correctly apply to women as well as men. Given the enduring popular use of the man-machine phrase, whether coming from the emperor or contemporary surgeons, the use of the phrase "baby-making machine" circa 1799–1815 to describe women's natural (re)productive capabilities did not mean they necessarily were perceived solely as sex objects. A stronger case can be made that women were thought of as sexual subjects whose *primary* but not *only* physical function was generation, and that this was such a marvelous and awesome ability and role that men were envious of it. The problem arises not from men saying that women are fitted by Nature to have babies; but, if they go further and say that women ought to be limited to having babies, then it becomes problematical.

With this warning about the need for interpreting quotations in context, let us move on from summarizing how Napoleon expressed his understanding of the nature of women in general and the meaning of that to considering the kinds of relationships he formed with individual women who were important in his life.

Napoleon's Female Relationships

Undoubtedly, the formation of Napoleon's personality and values were influenced by his associations with individual women. None influenced him more than the first woman in his life, his mother, Letizia Ramolino Bonaparte (1750–1836). Thanks to research by two Corsican authors, the British-born ethnographer Dorothy Carrington and revisionist historian Jean Defranceschi, today we know much more about eighteenth-century Corsican women in general and about Letizia in particular.

One cannot read any of Napoleon's descriptions of strong women who fought beside their husbands without remembering the character of his mother, a bride at the age of fifteen who married a man four years her senior. At the age of eighteen she supported her husband in the Corsican struggle for independence (1768–1769), during the months before Napoleon's birth. Consequently, as Defranceschi wrote in *La Jeunesse de Napoléon*:

> . . . la mère de Napoléon avait toutes les qualités des femmes corses qui firent les guerres de l'indépendence. Elle était capable de marcher des heures durant avec un fardeau sur la tête, gravir une montagne, se frayer un passage à travers le maquis, traverser un torrent en crue, dormir à même le sol roulée dans son manteau en poil de chèvre (pelone), endurer la faim et la soif, monter à cheval, faire le coup de feu. Sur ce point Napoléon disait vrai: "Les pertes, les privations, les fatigues, elles supportait tout, bravait tout, c'était une tête d'homme sur un corps de femme."[17]

By the end of her pregnancy on August 15, 1769, Letizia was so exhausted from the dangers she had shared with her husband Charles (Carlo) (1746–1785) that when she gave birth to her second son, he was a scrawny

Napoleon's mother, Letizia Bonaparte, who became "Madame Mère" when her son became Emperor Napoleon Ier. This is an unusual portrait of his attractive mother wearing fashionable court dress. From William Hazlitt, *The Life of Napoleon*.

infant. To compound matters, her milk failed and she could not feed him herself, as Corsican women normally did. Fortunately, Napoleon's parents were soon able to find a wet-nurse—a young housewife, Camilla Ilari, who was known for her piety and whose own son (her third child) died on the twenty-seventh of August.[18] Under her loving care, the infant Napoléon thrived, and he established a bond with the good seaman's wife that lasted throughout his life. Having Mme Ilari as a surrogate mother may have contributed to the emotional gulf that existed between Napoleon and his birth mother throughout his life: he never said that he "loved" her, but he respected her. Moreover, the memory of his own mother's inability to nurse him herself gave the emperor personal insight when he had to solve grave social problems such as how to lower the infant mortality rates of foundlings and orphans and how to reward and regulate wet-nursing in France.

Napoleon's father, Carlo, whose intellectual abilities have recently been reassessed[19] as being far better than previously thought by historians, died in 1785. Letizia was widowed and left alone to rear her large family, standing by them in good times and bad and wisely preparing for the unfortunate eventuality—the fall of the Napoleonic Empire—about which she had a premonition. Undoubtedly, she had a strong influence on the formation of her son's personality, as Harold T. Parker has observed so well.[20] In fact, the newest research of Dorothy Carrington, which was published a month after her death in January 2002, suggested that while Napoleon may have grossly undervalued his father's intellectual ability, he always credited the ambitions of his mother for all his success. Although we really don't know whether Letizia was literate, it was she who had insisted that the acquisition of a superior education, even for her daughters, was the key to the family's upward mobility and fortune.[21]

Besides Letizia Bonaparte, some other women whose associations influenced Napoleon's thinking were noted by Frédéric Masson among the amorous adventures recounted in his *Napoleon: Lover and Husband* (1894), the book that applauded the superior human quality of the emperor's sexual experiences.

The first of these encounters that can be related to the legal position and wifely role of women was with his first mistress, a "modest" young prostitute from Brittany, who solicited the eighteen-year-old military student after a theatrical performance at the Palais-Royal. In the conversations that this woman struck with her client circa 1786, she explained to him how she would certainly have preferred having the security of a husband and a home of her own over her actual means of livelihood as a public woman, a cycle of poverty that she had fallen into after taking up with and being abandoned by three military officers.[22] Another of Napoleon's early relationships was with Mlle de Lauberie de Saint-Germaine, the cousin and future wife of Count Montalivet, prefect and later Minister of the Interior (1809–14). As emperor Napoleon elevated de Lauberie to the position of lady in waiting to Empress Josephine (1806), with the lady's stipulation that this appointment was never to interfere with her higher duty to her own family as wife and mother.[23] Hence, Napoleon accepted these women's arguments because they reinforced his own strongly held view that a woman's proper destiny and safeguard was marriage, and that was to be valued above all else.

The Corsican revolutionary Carlo Bonaparte. Napoleon's ambitious father arranged scholarships for his children's educations in France to secure their futures. From William Hazlitt, *The Life of Napoleon.*

Masson also described the legal aspects of Napoleon and Josephine's marriage contract wherein the couple had no common property, separated their financial responsibilities, and allowed Josephine to retain complete authority over her own children.[24] Napoleon's personal experience with revolutionary family law foreshadowed the provisions of the Civil Code of 1804 that allowed enough flexibility for the continuance of such arrangements.

Stories are legion, of course, supporting the emperor's desire for an heir, dating this as early as the Egyptian campaign. Masson included an interesting one about an occasion at Malmaison when Napoleon proposed to organize a game hunt in the park of the château. Josephine reportedly changed her husband's mind when she protested tearfully that at that season of the year all the animals in the park were with young. But Napoleon did not abandon the idea of going hunting without making a barbed reply: "Well, then, I suppose it must be abandoned; everything here seems to be prolific except the mistress!"[25] If he was insensitive to his wife's feelings, he did express compassion for wild animals that were newly born or were in the family way, although it is really impossible to know how much of his

Empress Josephine in court dress. She never showed her teeth in portraits. Her friends knew her by the name of "Rose," and she planted a rose garden at Malmaison, where she continued to live after the divorce. From Frédéric Masson, *Napoleon: Lover and Husband.*

concern was actually motivated by sympathy for these young creatures or was merely motivated by his desire to increase the size of the game reserve of his estate.

While that hunting story may be apocryphal, we know with certainty that publicly Napoleon threw all the blame for the royal couple's childlessness upon Josephine even if he harbored private doubts about his own fertility (before his mistresses produced his illegitimate children).[26] While in all probability he may have been correct since the empress truly was in poor health and reaching menopausal age, his casting the blame on the woman reflected his generally chauvinistic beliefs. But the emperor's accusation raises the question: What actually was medical opinion about the cause of marital infertility, and was the husband or wife usually more responsible for conception? In fact, how conception itself was defined was of great importance to the practitioners of legal medicine of the First Empire who needed to know exactly when life begins not only for the prosecution of abortion and infanticide cases but also to establish paternity in bastardy cases. Like most eighteenth-century men of science, Napoleon also believed that the mothers of his children determined their sex and not he, the father.

One physician and one accoucheur (male midwife or obstetrician) who figure in Masson's narrative sought to prove that Napoleon was as wonderful a lover as he was a husband. It was taken as a sign of Napoleon's affection for Marie Walewska, the blonde Polish countess whom he had met in Warsaw in 1807, that when she came to Paris with their son, Alexandre-Florian (Walewski), in 1810, he charged his Court physician Jean-Nicolas Corvisart to attend to her health. After Napoleon's first abdication in 1814 it was also Corvisart who advised Empress Marie Louise to take the baths at Aix when Napoleon was relocating his retinue to Elba.[27] Antoine Dubois was the official accoucheur who delivered the King of Rome. After the heir apparent's difficult birth, Dubois was of the opinion that a second pregnancy would imperil the empress's life. Her lover Count Adam Albert von Neipperg, whom she married morganatically in 1821 after Napoleon's death, ultimately proved that Dubois's medical opinion was overly cautious by siring several children. Napoleon nonetheless respected Dubois's admonition concerning his wife's delicate health and made no further sexual demands of her.[28] Thus Napoleon hired medical specialists to look after the health and hygiene of the mothers of his sons.

Masson also went on at length about how the role of motherhood sanctified Marie Louise in the emperor's eyes and led him to downplay her treachery in 1814 and infidelity thereafter.[29] Actually, the birth of the King of Rome is very significant from the perspective of women's history and warrants more detailed coverage than Masson gave it. This unique occasion offers real insight into Napoleon's opinions regarding the complications of childbirth.

A Royal Husband in the Labor Room

Three variations of the story of the birth of the King of Rome have come down to us. Masson used Emmanuel Las Cases's account that in some instances corroborates that of Dr. Barry O'Meara, the Irish naval surgeon who served as Bonaparte's personal physician during the exile on Saint Helena. Although Las Cases had been present at the "blessed" event at the Tuileries Palace, both he and O'Meara took dictation or made the notes from conversations with Napoleon, which would form the basis of the Napoleonic legend. A third version, published by Fréderic Dubois in 1864, from among the elegies presented at public *séances* of the Academy of Medicine since 1845, is enriched with the information and medical statistics known to doctors Dubois and Corvisart that informed their thinking during the crisis. So rather than having only the recollections of one parent (the father) recorded by the makers of the Napoleonic cult, we also have available for comparison and analysis the contemporary medical insight from

Marie Louise's medical records, which were preserved for posterity by the French medical elite.

In the autobiographical account, Emmanuel Las Cases recalled being summoned along with the other chamberlains to witness the lying-in of the empress on the night of March 19, 1811. The troubled scenario became legend. Napoleon, playing the role of the dutiful spouse, offered moral support to his wife during the long period of labor. Her cries could be heard in the anteroom by all the dignitaries assembled to witness the birth, who passed the time by enjoying refreshments. In the middle of the night the emperor left his wife to prepare his bath, but almost immediately the empress's discomfort resumed so severely that Dubois hurried to find the emperor. A memorable exchange reportedly occurred:

> "Calm down," Napoleon reassured the accoucheur, "proceed as though you were delivering a bourgeoise from the rue Saint-Denis."
>
> "But Sire, the situation is dramatic. It is necessary to choose between the mother and the child."
>
> "Very well, opt for the mother; I will have another child."

Due to the great excitement everyone went into the birthing chamber. The doctor removed his coat and laid it aside while the empress, who by then thought she was about to be killed, writhed in agonized fear. Twenty-two horrified people observed the frightful scene. The apparently lifeless infant was received by Dubois and placed down on the parquet floor while the mother was revived. It was not until after Corvisart arrived on the spot and the child was worked on that the small body showed signs of life.[30] Finally, infant Napoleon-Francis-Joseph-Charles cried and the signal went forth to sound the cannon for the 101-gun salute (rather than the 21 guns that would have signaled the birth of a girl). Thus began the great public celebration whose high point was a balloon ascension by none other than the dare-devil performer of the regime—the thirty-three-year-old female aeronaut, Mme Marie-Madeleine Blanchard, an exceptional woman who was a childless widow and who had learned the science of flight from her late husband and continued to advance the science of pyrotechnics on her own.[31]

One line especially leaps forward in the foregoing account presented by Las Cases—that Napoleon chose to opt for the mother when the right to life of mother and child conflicted. What we would probably call his "pro-choice" rather than "pro-life" stance is interesting since it was coupled, as we know, with the prevailing contemporary belief, which had been institutionalized by the Church and reinforced by the legal and medical establish-

Napoleon's second wife, young Empress Marie Louise with roses in her fair hair. An ironic choice of flower since the rose was used (in addition to the swan) as an emblem for Empress Josephine. From Frédéric Masson, *Napoleon: Lover and Husband.*

ments, that life begins at conception. The scales of canon justice were not yet tipped in favor of the child when the rights of mother and offspring were weighed. The sacrifice of the woman was not required and certainly made little sense when infant mortality rates were so high—even if life was perceived to begin at conception. Theologically, baptism of the infant would save its soul and start its onward journey to heaven. Only later, as modern people became more "this-worldly" and medical technology had improved did legal systems add weight to arguments favoring the position of opting for a potential child since its chances for survival had increased so dramatically.

A somewhat different version of the birth of the King of Rome was the one Napoleon gave to Dr. Barry O'Meara in February 1818, when the news finally reached Saint Helena about the death in childbirth of Princess Charlotte of England. Being far less fortunate than Marie Louise, whose older husband was worldly, the twenty-one-year-old British princess was in labor fifty hours before a nine-pound child was stillborn. Forceps were never applied because the obstetrician believed in natural childbirth. Afterward

Charlotte hemorrhaged and died five and a half hours after giving birth. The autopsy indicated that she had bled to death. O'Meara said that Napoleon was shaken by the tragic news and remarked to him that it seemed bizarre that everything had been handled as badly as possible. Some older women who had borne many children themselves, such as her grand-mother Queen Charlotte (the consort of George III), should have been present, Napoleon thought, to insist that the princess be given assistance when she needed it. It was public knowledge by then that Princess Char-lotte was not permitted by her father to have close relations with her popu-lar mother, the Princess of Wales, Caroline of Brunswick, because he intended to divorce her in order to marry his Catholic mistress. So, under these complicated circumstances, Queen Charlotte might have prevented her granddaughter's death. Napoleon did not blame Charlotte's husband, Prince Leopold, whom he thought was just a boy who had no idea what to do in such a crisis. Napoleon then proceeded to tell O'Meara that he, the husband and head of the household, personally had safeguarded his spouse Marie Louise during labor to prevent her from dying in a potentially dan-gerous situation:

> All the time that she was in labor I was in a nearby apartment from which I went to her chamber at regular intervals. After several hours of labor and when I was stretched out on a sofa, Dubois, the accoucheur, came to me, visibly upset, and said:
> "The empress is in great danger; the infant is not presenting itself as it should." I asked him if he had seen such a presentation before. Dubois responded that he had seen it, but very rarely, perhaps less than once in a thousand cases, and that he was extremely vexed that such an extraordinary case should be the empress's fate.
> "Forget," I told him, "that she is the empress, and imagine that she is the wife of a small merchant from the rue Saint-Denis. That is the only favor I ask of you."
> Then I accompanied Dubois to the bedside, encouraged and soothed the empress as much as possible, and held her while the for-ceps were applied. The child seemed to be stillborn, but by employ-ing frictions and other means it was vitalized.

Thus is Napoleon's version—that of a husband who had been present in the labor room—depicted, seven years after the fact, of how he had dealt coolly and courageously with obstetrical complications, like a general under fire. First of all, he assessed the critical situation, made his battle plan, and saw it through to a happy conclusion. Dubois, in spite of his vast experience, was depicted as unnerved by the dilemma posed by the unusual fetal position that threatened Marie Louise's life combined with the fact that his aristocratic patient was Empress of France and the child at risk none other than the long-awaited heir to the Bonapartist dynastic throne. But the masterful emperor calmly asked Dubois if he had experience with such a case and then relied on the professional to do his best after offering him a universally valid maxim—whatever the social position of the *accouchée*, treat her following good obstetrical principles.[32] In this description there was no "opting for the mother," but a critical detail has been added: Napoleon held his wife while the forceps were used to extract the fetus.

The doctors in the Academy of Medicine provided their own case history[33] for Marie Louise, which was written from Dubois's professional viewpoint rather than Napoleon's. It went straight to the heart of the matter by indicating that Dubois, who had seen the empress previously, was summoned to her side on March 20, 1811. Since he worked at La Maternité where the research on medical statistics was done, he arrived armed with the knowledge that of the 20,357 births that had occurred there since 1797, 20,183 had occurred naturally. In other words, intervention was necessary only in about 2 percent of the cases. When Dubois arrived, he found his friend, Dr. Corvisart, already present and learned from him that labor had commenced hours earlier. He soon discerned that the fetal presentation was a breech by the *hanche*, or buttocks, an unusual position that happened in fewer than .25 percent of births (42 times out of 18,000).

When Dubois ushered Corvisart aside to a window area to tell him to fetch the emperor so that the patient's husband could be informed, Corvisart insisted that it was Dubois's duty as royal accoucheur, and not his, to find as well as to inform His Majesty. In any case, Dubois found Napoleon in the bathtub. Scarcely had he begun to explain the complication when the emperor interrupted him and cried: "Save the mother." Dubois claimed that the thought of such a choice being necessary had not yet crossed his mind, that he had said nothing about choices, so that it was Napoleon who appeared to have overreacted to protect Marie Louise's life. Instead of thinking (as his enemies might have expected) like an ambitious politician out to stabilize and perpetuate his throne at any cost, including the sacrifice of his wife's life, Napoleon exhibited human qualities of tenderness and compassion for his young bride of less than a year. So, in this account then, it was Dubois who reassured Napoleon that while the uncommon presentation was serious, he did not believe it would be fatal. Under such circumstances, however, the custom was to call in several consultants. But Napoleon exhibited faith in Dubois alone: "If you were not here, it is you whom they would be going to search for; return near the empress and treat her as you would a shop-keeper's wife from the rue Saint-Denis." The emperor's confidence made Dubois feel even more pressured because he knew very well that Marie Louise was not just any average woman. It was her first pregnancy, the fetus was full-term, and it had to be turned because spontaneous version was impossible from this position.

While the dignitaries waited in the salon, the emperor alone knew that a dangerous maneuver had to be performed. As he encouraged his wife, he assumed the same serene aspect that he characteristically did under stress on the battlefield. Without delay, Dubois turned the fetus and began the process of parturition. Although he saw the sex of the child before he extracted the feet, he kept silent[34] until one by one he disengaged the hips, the trunk, and the arms; finally, instead of pulling on the throat, he applied forceps to the head. But the child remained lifeless for seven minutes before it seemed to take a single breath. "He breathed!" cried one of the assistants. "Yes," answered the emperor, "but was it not for the first and last time!" Suddenly, the child began to breathe normally and cry.

Then Napoleon, overwhelmed by some poetic spark, as he often was, picked up his son by the underarms and raised him up in his powerful hands and carried him to the salon to present to the amassed dignitaries: "Messieurs, this is the King of Rome." Then he retraced his steps to Dubois and handed back the infant. "Baron Dubois," he said dramatically, "here is your child." Thus the detail of Dubois's sudden elevation in rank—to Baron of the Empire—became a heroic stage scene meant to be engraved into the historical memory of a grateful French nation.

Nor was the question of Dubois's fee omitted. According to this version, Corvisart had proposed an annual salary of 15,000 francs, although Napoleon had generously promised in advance to augment that with 15,000 francs per delivery. But in the actual situation, Count Daru was ordered to increase Dubois's compensation by remitting 100,000 francs. Also, Napoleon made Dubois a chevalier of the Légion of Honor, which meant that he would not only be honored and compensated with a one-time bonus, but he would be pensioned annually for life and "covered with glory" by this distinction of knighthood.

Some details of varying importance can be reconciled in these accounts of the advent of the King of Rome, while others cannot; concomitantly, some differences have more importance than others. For example, it matters little whether Dubois found Napoleon on a sofa or in the bathtub. Two accounts, however, did state that Napoleon said to opt for the mother—Las Cases's and the Academy of Medicine eulogy; and all three speak of treating Marie Louise like any middle-class wife, that is to say, the same as the wife of any ordinary citizen. But the last one implies that any elite doctor in such

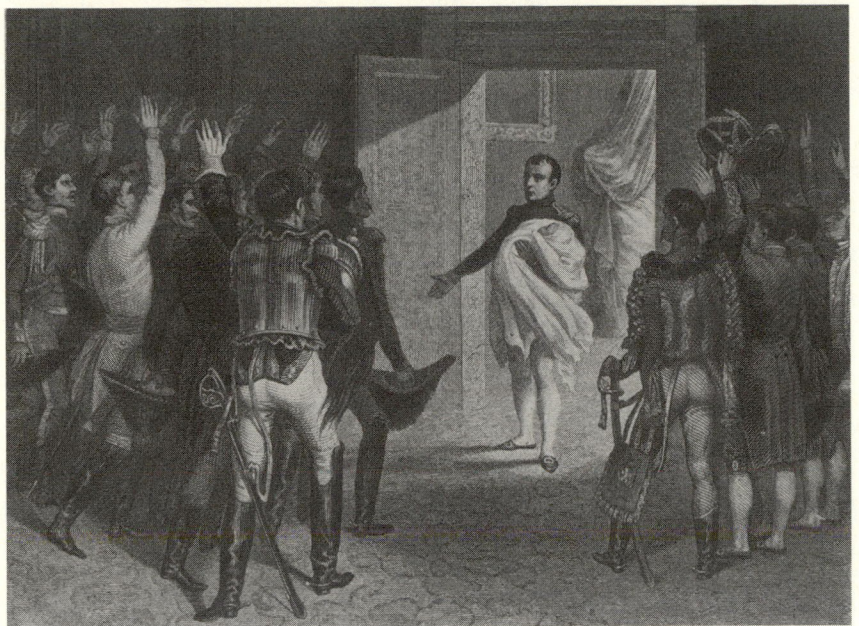

Originally published with the title, "The Birth of the King of Rome engraved by Coterelli after a painting by Raffet," this portrait serves as a frontispiece for the memoirs of Madame Junot. However, the painting actually depicts Napoleon's presentation of the newly born King of Rome to the dignitaries of the empire—an all-male event. From *Memoirs of Madame Junot (Duchesse d'Abrantès)*.

Empress Marie Louise and her son, the infant King of Rome. Motherhood exalted her in the eyes of her husband and the nation for bearing a male heir to the throne. From H. A. Guerber, *Empresses of France*.

a situation would be too aware of this patient's special status to be able to heed such advice. It also tells us the contemporary protocol between Corvisart and Dubois, the official court physician and the official ob-gyn: consequently, while the surgeon-accoucheur had to take greater risk, he ended up with a greater reward from the appreciative father for producing the much-desired happy denouement. More importantly, it also suggests that Napoleon was less in control than Dubois, and that the doctor had to calm and reassure the father, rather than vice versa. In fact, it has Dubois categorically denying that he ever told Napoleon that he had to choose between wife and child, but that he was just trying to play it safe by bringing in outside accoucheurs for a second opinion.

Thus, we are presented with a sentimentalized portrait of a human, if not a weak Napoleon, an older husband with tender feelings for a younger bride, and far less feeling for the much-wanted heir apparent than we traditionally associate with Napoleon's desire to perpetuate his dynasty. It seems almost as if Napoleon were trying to rebut accusations that he divorced Josephine and married the innocent young Marie Louise merely to produce an heir, using her only as a breeder. It tells us, too, that neither man allowed his worst fears to prevent him from doing his duty. Ultimately, Dubois's skill, expertise, and patience won out against all odds so that he delivered the heir to the throne alive and without having to resort to performing an unnecessary cesarean section, which probably would have proven fatal for Marie Louise and/or the child.

The medical case history was more precise about details, such as the fact that it was exactly seven minutes before the baby breathed or what the statistics were pertaining to this fetal presentation. So in Napoleon's versions, he saw himself as the hero and person in control; whereas, in the Academy of Medicine version published in the midnineteenth century, as one might expect, the real hero of the story was the more scientifically minded, technically knowledgeable, statistically armed, and skillful accoucheur, Antoine Dubois, who symbolized the improvements in modern medicine that were achieved during the First Empire and mark the ascendancy of French medicine to a predominant position internationally in the nineteenth century.

By all accounts, the only female mentioned—the terrified Empress Marie Louise—received no credit for her role in what seemed like an all-male event; nor did she ever have a voice.

What's more, all-male accounts of the birth of the King of Rome fail to mention that another Marie Louise played what possibly was a pivotal role in all of this—Mme Marie-Louise Dugès Lachapelle, the premier midwife of Paris's La Maternité, the central national normal school for the training of midwives. By following the biography of Mme Lachapelle (see Chapter

4) we learn that she was consulted several times for her opinion about these events, but that she allowed her male colleague Dubois to take all the credit and reap all the rewards for his success since it was considered more prestigious for the imperial family to employ a male midwife. Mme Lachapelle was reluctant to promote herself beyond the semi-private space of La Maternité over which she ruled. It may be that Napoleon's decision to use a male accoucheur instead of a female midwife to deliver his heir explains why historians have written that it was the official policy of the First Empire to replace women, who traditionally had played this social role, with men; but, as we shall also see in Chapter 4, Napoleonic administrators did not intend for the public to emulate the court's extraordinary behavior. Besides, very few people could afford to pay such high fees for the services of an obstetrician.

Several observations can be deduced from this brief overview of Napoleon's recorded generalizations about female identity and sex roles and specific experiences stemming from his sexual relationships with women. First of all, Napoleon's thinking about sexuality was modern, since he was not so simplistic as to see women merely as the opposite of men, that is as mirror images of men, but as different. They were the "other sex." However, his discussion about the existence of the soul of a woman was so old-fashioned that it belonged in pre-Revolutionary discourse. No one any longer questioned the existence of woman's soul, because women were accepted as belonging to the human race, which advanced the argument to the question of woman's reason and reasoning ability and questions of gender. His perception of the strength of women was a constant theme that is noteworthy because few philosophers shared it. He also believed in woman's "difference," that women had a uniquely necessary and useful biological role to play in increasing the population of his empire as well as in improving the rural economy, especially during wartime.

Consideration of his comments about "woman as machine" within the linguistic context of the time, however, suggests that his materialistic, mathematical, and secular discourse marked him as a man of the Enlightenment. Although the Concordat (of 1801, with Pope Pius VII) should have signaled the political condemnation of such radical Enlightenment ideas and a return to traditional scholastic thinking, the sway of modern science proved irresistible to Napoleon, who had always been its patron. He even continued to subscribe to the philosophy of the Ideologues after he fell from power and was in exile.

That Napoleonic educators, authors of manuals of housekeeping and sex, humanistic physicians, surgeons, and experts in legal medicine all shared La Mettrie and Napoleon's obsession with understanding human nature, and especially woman's nature, will become increasingly obvious as this manuscript unfolds. It is in their writings and in the Napoleonic State's activities in the arena of public health that La Mettrie's ideas finally became integrated, albeit ephemerally, into the final phase of the Enlightenment, before being subsumed by the reaction of the Bourbon Restoration.

Moreover, Napoleon was keenly aware of the natural forces that operate, govern, and join the biological activities of animals and humans in this world. Any improvement in the quality of life for individuals and society, he believed, can only be achieved through cooperation with Nature. Because population is important to the state, children are important, and the sex that produces them therefore has great importance, too; but to nurture women for this primary responsibility, the bourgeois state has to protect them from counterproductive exploitation and activities since, admittedly, the male sex is sometimes unreliable and weak. Motherhood, therefore, officially became an elevated position, and imperial women were envisioned, in terms of the heraldic symbol selected by the regime, as thriving in the golden role of queen bees in the Bonapartist hive. As we shall see, nowhere was this more evident than in Napoleonic manuals of sex and home economics.

Regardless of which account of the birth of the King of Rome is more exact, Napoleon realized after that close call that the angel of death has no respect for the social status of the mother or child in need of medical assistance. Good obstetrical principles transcend the boundaries of social class, he believed. While women played no apparent role in publicized accounts of the birth of his son, according to Dr. O'Meara, the Corsican-born emperor did believe that in order to prevent senseless tragedies, older, more-experienced women should help family members through childbirth, especially when the couple was young and having a first child. This notion was compatible with his philosophy of socialized medicine and would have great importance for the development of midwifery education for the masses in the grand empire.

Finally, Napoleon's opinions about the "war of the sexes," the characteristics of femininity and gender issues under the consulate, do not seem quite as reactionary when compared to two volatile public literary quarrels that were contemporaneous. The first discourse had been initiated by Ponce Denis Ecouchard Lebrun when he published an ode, "*Aux belles qui veulent devenir poètes*" (To lovely ladies who want to be poets) (1796), the gist of which was that women should inspire men to be poets but not be poets themselves because they "should leave no written trace of themselves . . ." and poetry written by a woman could only be mediocre.[35] The second quarrel, which overlapped with the earlier one, was set off by the anony-

mous publication of Sylvain Maréchal's polemic. Maréchal (1750–1803) was
a former radical Babouvist and atheist who wrote a serious pamphlet entitled *Projet d'une Loi Portant Défense d'Apprendre à Lire aux Femmes par S****
M*** (Proposed law prohibiting women from learning to read) (1801), a
proposal in which Maréchal was provoking women, making fun of them.[36]
Both initiatives did elicit discourses that included some moderate and liberal feminist responses, which were so brilliantly argued and stated with
such finesse that they have become famous in the annals of modern feminist
thought as well as in the history of women's education. Participants in these
discourses included Mme Marie-Armande Gacon-Dufour, Constance
Pipelet (later the princess de Salm), Olympe de Gouges, Mme Albertine
Clément-Hemery, Fanny Raoul, and the poet Gabriel Legouvé.[37] Fine
books and articles have been entirely devoted to the analysis of these discourses and comparisons have been drawn between these and other philosophical and educational writings of the time, with people like Mme de
Staël and Mary Wollstonecraft. The point that needs to be made here is that
in the context of the time, Napoleon's patriarchal musings about women's
nature, femininity, and gender were very much average, shallow opinions
that lacked the luster of stylistic presentation and deeply philosophical
intelligence of the literary elite. No wonder Bonaparte's liberal followers
were so disappointed in him right from the start. His holding of such ordinary conservative ideas regarding women's reasoning did not seem to por-
tend well for the future development of progressive programs for women's
betterment of any kind. Consequently, historians have shown little interest
in investigating whether he surprised his nay-sayers by accomplishing anything of the slightest significance for women.

2

Imperial Women's Education

Theory and Practice

NAPOLEON'S PERSONAL BIASES about woman's inherent nature had important implications for education designed for women and girls. The emperor immediately saw the need for higher education for boys—and excluded female education completely—when he later created the Imperial University, the state monopoly over education beginning at the lycée level. But initially he left girls' education at every level to individual families and religious and privately operated schools. Given the volatility of the unfinished theoretical discourses about the woman question, which was engaging the literary elite at the beginning of the Napoleonic era, it is not surprising to find disagreement among professional male and female educators about the basic purpose of women's education. In fact, women's education was in the air, and quills and ink were flying.

Many pedagogical authors were bubbling over with ideas about how to improve female education. The growing number of textbooks designed especially for the "other sex" also attested to the genuine interest and need for these. There was definitely a market for such manuals because prior to the Revolution larger numbers of women had learned how to read. Women, the middle class, and tradespeople had been drawn into what had become a thriving print culture. Now mothers who had their own educations interrupted by the events of the Revolution faced the daunting task of having to learn along with their daughters. Specialized textbooks on specific subject areas were published to help parents homeschool daughters. After the government showed signs of being interested, an official journal of education appeared from 1811 to 1814. Finally, some writers addressed the need for instruction for lower-class women to ameliorate the shortage of educated servants, lay nurses to staff the public hospitals, and home nursing aides. These aspects will all be surveyed in turn.

Male Pedagogues' Ideas

We have seen the emphasis that Napoleon himself placed upon the strength and great influence of women. His thinking was echoed by that of other men. For example, in the preface to his *Essai Générale d'Éducation Physique, Morale, et Intellectuel* (1808), Marc-Antoine Jullien included a long poem that eloquently elaborated upon this theme.

De l'Influence des Femmes

Des femmes ici-bas la suprême influence
Doit devenir pour l'homme une autre Providence:
L'ordre de la nature a soumis à leurs lois
Et les humbles bergers, et les superbes Rois.
Le farouche guerrier vient, d'une main sanglante,
Déposer ses lauriers aux pieds de son amante;
Le philosophe austère, inflexible, orgueilleux,
Qui bravait la douleur, la fortune et les dieux,
Sous le joug amoureux sent fléchir son courage;
Une femme a dompté cette vertu sauvage . . .

Amante, épouse, mère, à des titres si doux,
Chaque femme a le droit de dominer sur nous;
Mais qu'elle sache user d'un pouvoir légitime,
Sans vouloir sous le joug dégrader sa victime.
Qu'un amant, qu'un époux, qu'un enfant adorés
Au culte des vertus soient toujours consacrés . . .
Que l'amour conjugale et l'amour maternelle
Vers la gloire toujours soit un guide fidèle . . .
Mère tendre, ton fils doit puiser dans ton coeur
Le noble sentiment du devoir de l'honneur;
Le généreux besoin de servir l'innocence,
D'être le protecteur et l'appui de l'enfance;
D'offir à l'orphelin un bras consolateur,
De haïr les méchans, d'honorer le malheur.

Ainsi, de nos destins arbitres souveraines,
Femme! par vos vertus annoblissez nos chaînes;
Honorer votre empire, en nous rendant heureux:
Quand vous l'ordonnerez, nous serons vertueux;
Et nos coeurs, enflammés d'un sublime courage,
Des viles passions secouront l'esclavage.[1]

Other male authors also emphasized the superior qualities of the "other sex" in prose. Louis Dubroca wrote in the preface to his book on famous women of the Revolution that while women may be physically feeble and lack the brute strength of males, they, nevertheless, in times of extreme emergency "find delicate and ingenious ways" to "resist evil by the forces of their souls." He also believed that women are resourceful, resolute, courageous, and ready to suffer anything for the sake of their loved ones. He considered the best traits displayed by Revolutionary heroines, and the ones that all women should try to develop: to be maternal; to practice fraternal and conjugal love; to show parental respect and devotion; to demonstrate hospitality and fortitude in time of misfortune; to feel gratitude and selflessness; and to display courage inspired by the horror of crime and patriotism.[2] Another male author, Catherine-Joseph Girard de Propriac, while designing sexually segregated textbooks, wrote that "women are inferior to men neither in courage, heroism or virtue; and if they would give their education the same care, they would follow literary careers."[3]

The highly critical opinions that Georges Jouard expressed in his *Nouvel Essai sur la Femme Considérée Comparativement à l'Homme sous les Rapports Moral, Physique, Philosophique, etc.* (1804) are noteworthy because he challenged men, in no uncertain terms, to initiate the amelioration of women's condition in society. While female babies are no longer killed at birth, he commented, women are persecuted in more subtle ways by Frenchmen whose free society makes it easy to be hypocritical or more gallant than elsewhere. "We wait for them to be ours," he observed about marriage, "in order to make them feel our sovereign authority."[4] He condemned female education in the new public *pensions*, or boarding schools, and insisted that girls should be educated at home by *both* parents with the mother teaching her daughter how to conduct herself as a good wife and the father teaching her about members of his own sex.[5] He also viewed it as the mother's responsibility to include teaching her sons how to respect women. But any improvement in the relationship between the sexes, he concluded, had to begin through male initiative.[6]

Female Pedagogues' Ideas

While many imperial men shared these beliefs about the superior morality and stronger character of the female sex and the need for improved treatment, some of the most important and highly respected women educators did not. For example, at her fashionable *pension* in Saint Germain-en-Laye that was patronized by Empress Josephine for the education of her daughters, Mme Campan counseled young ladies thus: "What is the first and foremost basis of the happiness of women?—It is the meekness of their character. What are the most precious qualities that a young girl can possess?—Sweetness, indulgence, and good manners." In addition to striving for these qualities, she told her pupils to "especially remember, my darlings, that the deportment most befitting our sex is that which gives the constant habit of being occupied with needlework. One should never be without embroidery, knitting, a strand of thread, or a piece of work."[7] Thus, Mme Campan believed that her aristocratic adolescent charges should develop submissive qualities and be what she believed Nature intended them to be—as industrious as bees.

Another outstanding woman educator was Antoinette Legroing La Maisonneuve, one of Mme Campan's competitors who refused the emperor's offer of a position as superintendent of the two Légion of Honor girls' schools.[8] In her manual on female instruction, which was reprinted and enjoyed great popularity during the First Empire, Mme Legroing discussed her views of "the gifts with which Nature endowed women":

> She [Nature] gives them rather generally a sweet gaiety, a cheerful imagination, and the facility to express themselves; that is why their conversation is interesting, even when they do not have cultivated minds. A woman whose instruction is mediocre speaks as well, sometimes better, than people who always lived with books; and the art of conversing well is surely the one which contributes the most to amiability.[9]

Moreover, Mme Legroing had a definite opinion of the kind of atmosphere in which females thrived best:

> Freed to the most peaceable, the gentlest, the most unvarying occupations, women can count on passing their days tranquilly, and demonstrate this by a thousand virtuous deeds. As a matter of fact they will be carried out in the shadows and in silence; fame will not speak of them, and posterity will not remember them; but does virtue need the daylight? Does she not resemble the flowers whose brilliancy is better conserved by the aid of a favorable obscurity, than when they are exposed to the burning rays of the sun?[10]

Mme Sophie de Renneville, a prolific writer of pedagogical manuals for girls, reinforced the ideas of Campan and Legroing. For example, her volume entitled *La Mère Gouvernante ou Principes de Politesse Fondés sur les Qualités du Coeur* (1812) and her three volumes of stories that taught morality (1813)[11] all emphasized the cultivation of meekness, humanity, and *bien-*

faisance (charity). Little girls, she said, should be taught to walk and wait without raising their eyes.[12] The quality of meekness "is above all the lot of women" and should be evident in their thinking, in their daily activities, and in their public and private lives. "Blessed are the meek for they shall inherit the earth," she reminded them of the words of Jesus Christ from the Beatitudes.[13] Moreover, she advised her readers to pity animals,[14] to be humane and indulgent with elderly people (especially grandmothers),[15] to not be influenced by people's clothing,[16] and politely to say "Monsieur" and "Madame" to rich and poor alike.[17] In keeping with their position, little girls also should dress simply—only in white dresses—and have clean hair: "That is what is appropriate for your age; what neither attracts envious looks nor criticism; what does not wound the poor by making them notice their own misery."[18] Compared with the more modern and enlightened male authors, these three women writers who sought to cultivate meekness in young girls were indeed, "weak sisters." In fact, their zeal in this regard far exceeded that of the emperor.

Besides these manuals, women's journals were a vehicle for the expression of the female mentality. However, the contents sometimes suggested that the cultivation of meekness and the exercise of powerlessness could be a frustrating life script for the women who were forced to act it out. The *Petit Magasin des Dames* for 1807 contained a long, unsigned article entitled "*Des Femmes fortes*," which argued that since "the soul has no sex," the only difference between the sexes is "the limits of the great deeds of which both sexes are equally capable."[19] The contemporary understanding of the difference between male and female characteristics ascribed the power to create only to males. The same issue also carried a song, with lyrics by Mme Perrier written for the melody "Du Petit Matelot," speculating about what it might be like for a woman to play the role of the male Creator:

> *La Nouvelle Création ou Le Monde comme je le voudrois.*
> air: *Du petit matelot*
>
> Si je créois un nouveau Monde,
> D'abord, moi, je ne voudrois pas
> Que cette machine fût ronde;
> Tout en iroit mieux ici bas.
> Pourquoi voit-on chaque minute
> Des choses déranger le cours?
> C'est qu'il faut bien que tout culbute
> Dans un lieu qui tourne toujours.
> En unissant la femme à l'homme
> Je ne leur donnerois qu'un coeur . . .

Et ne voudrois qu'une pomme
De leurs enfans fit le malheur.
A leurs traits ôtant la grimace,
De leur sein arrachant le ciel,
Leur âme seroit une glace
Qui réflechiroit un beau ciel.
Je voudrois pour prix de ma peine,
Au lieu de cent cultes divers,
N'en voir qu'un seul, de qui la chaîne
Me soumettroit tout l'Univers.
Sublime idée! elle m'enflamme;
Tout devant moi viendroit plier . . .
Ah! qu'il est cruel d'être femme,
Et de ne pouvoit pas créer.[20]

Imagine contemporary readers singing this song, whose final line is an expression of shared frustration as they rocked cradles or busied themselves by imperial hearths. Such literary discourse emphasizing mind, salvation, and soul reflects the earlier eighteenth-century preoccupation with non-physical human attributes; yet, a new longing for this-worldly political empowerment had come across the horizon.

Justifying Domesticity as the Official Ideology

While all these references show that there were jarring differences of opinion about whether the female sex was naturally as weak as a delicate flower or as strong as a warrior, reproductive machines or soul creatures capable of feeling emotions, more virtuous or simply compatible, quiet or loquacious by nature, or the unhappy product of repressiveness training, there was a general consensus that coincided with Napoleon's personal opinion: a woman's proper role in society was being a wife and "worthily fulfilling the majestic functions of motherhood."[21] Educators, more notably women educators, endorsed the emperor's pronouncement in the Council of State: "Little girls all have the same goal when they come into the world, that is marriage."[22] It was accepted by both sexes that, usually, men worked outside the home as breadwinners who served their country as soldiers and civil servants, or pursued careers to advance their private fortunes and tried to achieve the various degrees of social position that had been made accessible by the Revolution.

At the same time, as sex roles diverged and the male professions developed, the duties of women as wives and mothers increased, especially in urban areas, so that the imperial woman became the actual head-of-household.[23] In spite of his talk about submission and self-denial, Napoleon himself recognized this: "The mother, in a poor household," he said, "is the person in charge of the house."[24] Like their husbands, wives had special obligations to fulfill: being good companions able to discuss the family's business and legal problems with their spouses, rearing children and giving them their first education, managing the home, and being ready in the eventuality of the husband's death to assume his affairs.[25] These were all challenges his own widowed mother had faced.

Regardless of the woman's social status, her duties included being able to manage finances well, for as Mme Campan remarked: "The fortune of families depends upon the economy of women."[26] Thus another female author wrote, a woman "could establish herself in the center of an empire of affection and trust, in which she would have all the ascendancy that this amiable benevolence gives, which scrutinizes hearts with a tender and enlightened eagerness, in order to increase its happiness or diminish its troubles."[27] Despite how high or low an opinion imperial educators held about the inherent nature of females, they generally thought that it was shameful to neglect totally the education of girls because of the important role women then performed as the real backbone of an increasingly modern society.

Many authors argued for change in order to help men rather than women. Several of them agreed with Hubert Wandelcourt who, writing in 1801, justified female education for man's sake following the line of reasoning that the education of women would somehow remedy all the vices of men.[28] Pierre-Louis Roederer, who was Director General of Public Instruction in 1802, also believed that women completed the education of men and that women's education would, therefore, accomplish much more than it might seem for the improvement of men. Thus, for the sake of both sexes, Roederer suggested that Napoleon follow the precedent set by Louis XIV and several Roman emperors by establishing boarding schools for orphan girls whose fathers had died in the military or civil service.[29] Robert le Jeune, a Lamarckian and student of ancient history, advocated the establishment of a national *athenée* at Versailles to train women who afterward would marry men educated at the Ecole Militaire and together would, in due course, generate an improved race of French people.[30] J. P. Gasc stated his belief that the happiness of the whole society rested in the hands of women and that the precious care mothers needed to give their children could not emanate from little minds. Moreover, he saw a corresponding relationship between the corruption of public manners and the degree of education of women. Women, Gasc opined, can never know too much and the higher their rank in society, the more they should know.[31] But the need for a modicum of education even for lower-class girls was noted by Boyveau-Laffecteur, who advanced a plan whereby women would adopt young girls who were born in the cities as a result of prostitution, illicit sex, and poverty, and educate them enough to perform household tasks in order to save the girls from resorting to prostitution—a practice, he maintained, that discouraged bachelors from marrying and repaying their debt to society.[32] In her moderately feminist refutation of Sylvain Maréchal's retrograde polemic, *Projet d'une Loi Portant Défense d'Apprendre à Lire aux Femmes* (1801), Mme Marie-Armande-Jeanne Gacon-Dufour (1753–1835), the forthright author of manuals of domestic science, expressed her belief in the necessity of female education when she bluntly stated her opinion that men could not be happy in the company of idiots.[33]

These various personal expressions were all ways of saying that indirectly men would profit as much as the obvious beneficiaries if schools were created for the "second sex." They also show no sympathy for women because of any perceived strength or weakness. Moreover, they seem to correlate education with happiness as well as link it with the abiding interest during this era in eugenics and increasing population as a form of patriotic duty.

In contrast to these ideas, Napoleon tried to justify his inattention to female education by pointing out that since marriage, not public life, was the single destiny of girls, they need only be educated in manners, something best performed by their mothers.[34] Hence, their education had to be practical enough to make them useful and nice as wives. Besides, Napoleon was wary of regular schooling and tended to agree with Mme Antoinette Legroing La Maisonneuve, who observed that the ordinary result of concentrated study was to isolate scholars from reality and make them economically unproductive members of society.[35] Napoleon and Mme Legroing's skepticism about the value of intensive, formal female education was shared by Wandelcourt, who criticized girls' schools, as they then were operated, for destroying all the rare qualities that Nature gave females for the purpose of enriching society because they made girls think about caring for their bodies more than for their hearts and minds.[36] Therefore, whatever was done for female education ought to be designed to correct these tendencies so that girls could be the better wives and mothers that France needed.

An 1803 Visit to Mme Campan's Saint-Germain-en-Laye Girls School

Taking advantage of the ability afforded by the Peace of Amiens (1802) to travel across the English Channel again, the British novelist who was the precursor of Jane Austen—Frances (Fanny) Burney d'Arblay—joined her husband, the former French emigré general, Alexandre d'Arblay, in Paris. Of course, Burney had no idea that she would be forced to remain there for a decade when shortly after her arrival the war resumed.[37] Burney was embraced by upper-class imperial society for a number of reasons. First of all, she had already earned her precocious literary status on both sides of the channel. Another fact in her favor was that prior to her recent-but-late marriage (in her early forties), she had served at the Court of George III as official "dresser" to Queen Charlotte, which had put her on intimate terms with the whole British royal family. Burney also had the good sense to keep a safe distance between herself and Mme Germaine de Staël when that socially unacceptable woman (unacceptable to the stuffy British aristocrats in Burney's circle)—she was, after all, French, a political writer, and a divorcée who dared to discuss politics with men in her living room, no less—had emigrated to England. Then there was her French husband's military service connections with the famous revolutionary figure, the *ci-devant* Marquis de Lafayette. When General d'Arblay returned to France in order to have his pension restored, he also succeeded in obtaining an official bureaucratic appointment to augment his wife's book royalties. For all of the above reasons as well as her own personal charm and wit, for almost a decade Burney found herself well received by all of France. General d'Arblay himself became widely known in Paris as the husband of a more famous wife who, for a living, penned lengthy novels whose underlying theme was the violence that contemporary British society inflicted upon women. In fact, Napoleon Bonaparte personally knew of her reputation, even the names of her novels, and was aware that she had followed her husband to France. Burney thereby became an important, critical, British observer of late consular and Imperial French cultural life and institutions.

Mme Jeanne-Louise-Henriette Campan (1752–1822) was the headmistress of a fashionable boarding school for girls, which was located at Saint-Germain-en-Laye, a suburb of Paris, beyond Malmaison, which had been the birthplace of Louis XIV. By the time of the annual examination and prize ceremony, the headmistress had learned of the recent arrival in the capital of the distinguished British author.

Mme Campan was an interesting personality herself. Her father had held a high post in the Ministry of Foreign Affairs. From 1774 to 1790, she was married to Barthollet Campan, master of the Garde royale of the comtesse d'Artois, but they both were preoccupied with their service to the Bourbons. For fifteen years Mme Campan was at Court, serving initially as the *lectrice* of the daughters of Louis XV then *femme de chambre* of Marie-Antoinette. She somehow managed to survive the Revolution despite her previous royal connections. To make a living, she turned to teaching, and

Frances "Fanny" Burney d'Arblay, diarist, novelist, and letter writer, par excellence. The wife of General Alexandre d'Arblay. Shy by nature, she chose to wear English-style clothing during the decade she spent in France. From *The Diary and Letters of Frances Burney, Madame d'Arblay,* frontispiece.

after the teaching congregations disappeared, she opened her own school at Saint-Germain-en-Laye. American President James Monroe and French General MacDonald's daughters were among the elite clientele, and their presence made other ambitious families want to send their daughters there as well—not just for the education but also to improve their marriage prospects.[38]

Apparently, Mme Campan thought it would be excellent publicity for her *pensionnat* if a woman writer as famous as Fanny Burney (and one who like herself had served a queen) were to attend the public event of the year—where so many notable parents would be present. To this end, Mme Campan shrewdly issued invitations to one of Burney's close friends, Mme d'Henin, urging her to bring the d'Arblays and other friends, including naval expert (later baron of the empire and chevalier of the Légion of Honor) Pierre-Victor Malouet, to the event.

Fanny Burney had been an excessively shy child and she continued this behavior well into adulthood whenever she was in the public eye. Interestingly, both her parents as well as her stepmother had discouraged her early education and development, although they had given her sister the advan-

Napoleon's step-daughter and sister-in-law, Hortense de Beauharnais (the daughter of Josephine), who married his brother Louis, temporarily King of Holland. The future Queen Hortense often revisited Mme Campan's fashionable school in Saint Germain-en-Laye, where she had been educated. From Frédéric Masson, *Napoleon: Lover and Husband.*

tages of schooling and education abroad. In addition to having weak eyesight, she may have been dyslexic. In any case, as a child and even a young woman she had to do much of her own writing secretly, although she was required to help her musicologist father prepare his manuscripts for publication. Later, she was pressed into taking the job at Court, whose title sounded prestigious but whose responsibilities amounted to being the queen's personal servant, so as not to be a spinster who burdened her family. Eventually, this position, which required her to stand still for hours beside the seated queen, ruined her health. Consequently, Burney could appreciate the advantages of women's education.

Burney was surprised and flattered by Mme Campan's gracious invitation and readily seized the opportunity to visit her *pensionnat,* perhaps to see how French education compared to that given to her siblings but which she herself had been denied. Always a careful observer of manners and personalities, Burney intended to take everything in so that she could later send an account home to the female members of the British royal family —Queen Charlotte and George III's five single daughters, the English princesses.

It was Burney's understanding that Mme Campan's school was designed for a limited although not small number of young ladies from childhood to about age fourteen—the age when it was then common for French women to be considered old enough to become wives, the mistresses even of large households, and mothers. She pointed out that this was the school where First Consul Bonaparte's youngest sister, Caroline Bonaparte Murat, as well as his step-daughter Hortense de Beauharnais, now Mme Louis Bonaparte, had been educated. Consequently, Bonaparte's patronage had made it fashionable for the other principal generals to enroll their daughters there.

On the appointed day, Mme d'Henin's party of six set out by carriage for the pleasant little journey that took them along the banks of the Seine and past the Château de Malmaison, the home of General and Madame Bonaparte. Burney observed that Malmaison looked like it must be too small a house to be such a big hero's personal residence, although the grounds were quite large enough and contained quarters for troops and adequate enough stables for cavalry. She also noted that the construction of the wall around the estate was progressing well. On a hill at the corner of the park, the party also saw the villa where Josephine's son Eugène de Beauharnais lived; and beyond that, on still another summit, they were impressed by the sight of the beautiful pavilion that had formerly served as a dwelling for the infamous (Burney described her as "wretched"), extravagant Mme Jeanne Dubarry, last mistress of King Louis XV, who had been guillotined in 1793.

Upon their arrival at Saint-Germain-en-Laye, the group presented their admission tickets and proceeded into the garden of the school, thence into the crowded *salle de compagnie*. Due to their tardy arrival, the youngest girls had already performed. The first thing they saw on the stage was twenty or so ten- to fourteen-year-olds seated around a large table. In an attempt to discourage vanity and competition among the girls, they all were dressed alike in a simple white muslin frock tied with a poppy-red sash and wore matching white shoes. Their hairstyle was uniform also: unadorned ringlets. Burney noted that the youngest girl was Mlle de Valence, a daughter of the general and granddaughter of the famous author, Mme de Genlis. At the corner of the stage, a box was cordoned off in case the first consul should arrive (although Burney thought he was not really expected to show up since this event occurred just before the Consulate for Life was going to be declared officially). Below the platform was seated the row of distinguished gentlemen who served as the judges. Among them, Burney easily identified the two who, in long dark coats richly embroidered with large green laurel leaves, were members of the Institut de France, over which she knew the first consul presided. The rest of the hall was filled to overflowing with rows of chairs for the audience.

Above the main floor, two galleries were filled with many of the most distinguished persons in attendance. Among them, Burney spotted Mme Louis Bonaparte, whom she admired: she observed that Hortense was not a beautiful woman but rather looked like a person of good character since she lacked coquetry or artifice. Burney praised her interest in learning and for being so fond of Mme Campan, the other girls, and the school routine itself. Since her marriage to Napoleon's younger brother, she often came to spend a couple of days at a time there, and whenever she visited the school, she still actively participated in the daily lessons as the regular students did and acted like a sister to all the girls. Seated next to Mme Louis Bonaparte was a sister of General Leclerc, who was then engaged in the ill-fated expedition to Saint Domingo. Two seats over, Burney also noted, was seated the young girl who was supposed to marry Napoleon Bonaparte's aide-de-camp and governor of the Tuileries palace, General Geraud-Christophe-Michel Duroc, in just three days—on her fourteenth birthday.

Burney first described how the pupils were engaged in writing a dictation, which one of the masters pronounced a phrase at a time, as the girls wrote it down individually in their best handwriting and grammatical style. At the end, each delivered her paper to the judges who examined it for orthography and correctness of accentuation and punctuation, with the winners to be announced later.

In the intervals between examinations, Mme Campan loudly greeted various personages in attendance, thus calling attention to their presence for all to see. Naturally shy in public spaces, Burney feared that Mme Campan would embarrass her by letting everyone know that she was there as well.

The next exam Burney observed was a test of grammar. For this, a grammar book was handed to one of the young ladies who was supposed to stand up and read a paragraph; as she went along, she indicated what part of speech each word was. Afterward, she handed the book to the next youngster to take her turn, and so on it went. Burney said that this process took so long that one of her compatriots became bored and started to whisper impatiently about how much longer it was taking for this than it ever would in England. Indeed, out of boredom one of her companions, Mr. Jerningham, began to behave rather outlandishly: whenever he spied any woman in the audience dressed in what was then considered to be the height of French fashion, he made terrible faces and bid Burney to look at the light drapery of her shocking attire. During the course of this day alone, Burney thought she saw more most-elegantly dressed women than she had yet seen in all her time in Paris because the assembly hall was filled with the real leaders of French couture. Nevertheless, there was a certain incongruity in the scenario. While the school girls dressed inconspicuously, as was fitting for sequestration here for training as France's future domestic goddesses, their mothers and other fashionable adult women in attendance showed individuality and exposed as much of their flesh as public women at the Palais Royal.

Eventually, the dull grammar exercise was followed by geography. For this, the stage was hung with large, framed sheets of paper on which the young ladies drew maps of all parts of the world, later marking longitude and latitude on them. They also mapped the heavens. Meanwhile, one young lady came forward to a completely drawn map at which she pointed out the names of the European countries and their chief cities, while another girl called out the longitude and latitude for each of the cities so named. (This complex exercise also challenged the attention span of the audience.) During this exercise, Mme Campan seemed to start toward Burney with a map of England for her approval; however, Burney was so afraid that people in the room would stare at her that, to Mme Campan's dismay, she melted into the crowd behind her to escape attention.

At this juncture, Burney's hostess, Mme d'Henin, decided she needed to get a breath of fresh air, so Burney accompanied her out into the garden. Getting away from the crowded hall gave them some relief until they were recognized by Mme Campan's first assistant who insisted they go upstairs to sit in the gallery with the other people of special distinction. When the ladies protested, the assistant ran off and returned with Mme Campan herself. Mme Campan dissimulated that she had not seen Burney previously, but now that she had, she insisted that Burney and her friends absolutely must pass along a corridor and emerge in the box reserved for the first consul (who it was now known positively would not be making an appearance that day). Burney was so embarrassed that she pleaded with Mme d'Henin to prevail upon Mme Campan not to announce to the crowd that she was present, which her friend did only reluctantly. Mme Campan, according to Burney, seemed surprised by her shyness and did not seem very gracious about her aversion to public notice. Apparently, the French women thought that the select few who had been invited to this prestigious social event had all come less to see than to be seen.

Meanwhile, the impressive geography exam was followed by that of history for which the members of the Institut de France asked the young ladies carefully formulated questions about the eras of Roman history. Burney appreciated the fact that the learned gentlemen took pains not to embarrass any of the youngsters: whenever a girl misunderstood a question or failed to answer properly, the inquisitors tactfully guided her toward the right answer. Moreover, the judges remembered to praise everyone's effort, despite how much help they needed to complete their answer. The audience endeavored to behave politely by applauding all the girls, and two girls who became so unnerved that they burst into tears and sat down were applauded the loudest.

After history came the final examination—*belles lettres* and poetry. For this exam, each girl recited criticism from Laharpe or another commentator before concluding with the recitation of a poem. Burney personally judged the best pupil in this category definitely to be little Mlle de Valence who, she thought, was so pretty and had such a lovely face. But Burney added a footnote in her journal, noting her surprise that little Mlle de Valence recited Rousseau's "Ode to Fortune" because the poem contains such vehement references against tyrants and blood-thirsty victors. She added that choosing to allow this reflected well on the headmistress's courage to teach such political virtue as well as paid honor to the first consul for permitting it to be heard so publicly at an elite gathering.

Toward the end of the recitations, Burney's loge received a party of prominent visitors—Napoleon's beautiful youngest sister Caroline Murat and her renowned husband General Murat, General Valence, and their entourage. Burney praised Caroline for the enthusiastic applause she gave all the girls as well as for her fair beauty and tasteful and stylish attire—the most superb gown she had ever seen, an open worked muslin gown with a long veil of Brussels lace draped over one side of her head and hanging down almost to its lace train. Burney thought that only Mme Louis Bonaparte (Hortense) showed more enthusiasm for the girls than Caroline did. Burney stood in awe next to Caroline for the rest of the program, hoping that she would not make any mistakes in French etiquette but felt that if she did, present company would merely attribute them to her "English barbarism." Burney felt great satisfaction when later she, Caroline, and Hortense were joined by the most famous female portrait painter of that era, Elizabeth Vigée-Lebrun, who had been the official portraitist of Marie-Antoinette in pre-Revolutionary days and having weathered the many successive political storms was also in attendance on this happy occasion.

In contrast to these stylish ladies, Burney said that she was "much surprised" to notice about that time, when the prizes finally were about to be presented, two other unattractive, older, hardy-looking women sitting opposite her party, who were dressed like her in English-style garments—except of a decidedly earlier era, which even Burney considered totally passé and inappropriate for this occasion. Mme Campan likewise noticed these two women, who although dressed in English style neither looked the part, nor made a very good impression. But when she asked whose tickets they had used to gain admission, she was surprised to learn that one of them was the Margravine of Anspach who had heard of the school and decided upon passing nearby to stop with her companion for a visit.

The next portion of the program was the selection of special awards and, finally, the long-awaited distribution of the examination prizes. The first special award was for *temper,* that is to say, sweetness of disposition; and the special prize, a rose. The winner, a seven- or eight-year-old, was so delighted at the announcement that when she came forward, she leaped into the arms of Mme Campan, embracing her, thanking her, and begging for permission to run to her mother in the audience to show her the rose she had won. After she "flew on the wings of joy to her enraptured Parent," Burney reflected that "this was a very pleasant part of the ceremony, and I thought it a happy idea that general good conduct should take precedence of every accomplishment."

The rest of the prizes distributed were books selected by the headmistress. The schools' masters picked the winners of the prizes for writing, music, French, Italian, singing, handwriting, and grammar, while the examining members of the Institut National chose the winners in the history, geography, and recitation categories. After receiving her book from Mme Campan, each girl bobbed forward happily, curtsied to the crowd, embraced Mme Campan, and curtsied again to the audience before returning to her seat. Burney observed this part critically: she thought all this bowing, although animating, made the event seem too much like a theatrical presentation.

The ceremony once concluded, Mme Campan's assistant gave Burney a guided tour of the gardens and whole establishment. She regarded both as elegant and functional. All of the foregoing she described immediately in letters she sent back to England, intended for the court of George III, and later commented about in her journal.

Although Burney only visited Mme Campan's school on this prize distribution day in the summer of 1803, she provided interesting and important information. Quite naturally she was struck by the early arranged marriages of these elite girls, marriages that contrasted so much with her own companionate one between two mature people. She showed how prudish English visitors viewed French couture as well. She also got to meet some

famous women, including Bonaparte's sisters, and even see the esteem in
which the portraitist Vigée-Lebrun was held by contemporaries. On a more
serious note, Burney presented a valuable overview of the ambience and values of Mme Campan's fashionable seminary, its curriculum, and the ages
and particular level of society for which this curriculum was intended. Burney's visit provided a basis for making comparisons with the new institutions Napoleon would create during his short reign as emperor. It also
showed Mme Campan in action, social climbing, engaged in self-
promotion and lobbying—skills that would carry her to an unusual position of influence under the imperial government.

Louis XIV's Saint-Cyr

The French monarchy had a history of involvement in education for
young noblewomen who came from poorer families. In 1685 Louis
XIV's second marriage was to Mme de Maintenon, the former governess of
the children of Mme de Montespan and the Sun King, whom Louis had
secretly married in a morganatic ceremony. Before her marriage, Mme de
Maintenon had been a Protestant educator; now, Louis made her the
patroness of his new girls' boarding school at Saint-Cyr. The school was
designed to educate two hundred and fifty girls from the eight thousand
poorer noble families and was located in a town near the royal palace at Versailles. (It later became even more famous as the French version of the U.S.
military academy at West Point, after Napoleon converted it into a military
school for boys in 1808.)

When the school was first created, the curriculum for women at Saint-
Cyr followed the educational ideas of Roman Catholic Archbishop Fénélon
(François de Salignac de la Mothe). He and Mme de Maintenon made
Saint-Cyr the most prestigious French school for girls under the Old
Regime. Fénélon disliked the way courtesans interfered in politics at the
Court of Versailles; but, he was equally concerned, and rightly so, about the
way the population of France had declined during the seventeenth century
due to famine, war, and disease. So he banked on training a significant
number of noblewomen to lead domestically oriented lives in order to
regenerate the manners and morals of the aristocracy while, at the same
time, producing more children for the nation. Naturally, religion still
played an important role in Fénélon's educational plans for women; but,
instead of taking religious vows upon matriculation as formerly would have
been expected after such an education, these young women in whom teachers were to inculcate the feminine virtue of modesty and family values were
destined for marriage and motherhood. Training at Saint-Cyr was supposed
to prepare them to reign over their own private space—the home—away

from the public space at the royal Court, which he believed should be reserved exclusively for men of noble birth.[39]

Napoleon Decides to Act to Create National Educational Establishments for Girls

Events early in the French Revolution had eliminated the functioning of the French royal Court at the Palace of Versailles, so Napoleon did not have to worry about noblewomen interfering in politics there as they had in Louis XIV's day. Even the prestigious school at Saint-Cyr, which counted Napoleon's sister Elisa Bonaparte (1777–1820), the future Grand Duchess of Tuscany, among its graduates, no longer existed since it had been suppressed in 1793. But the notion of decreasing population continued to be an issue for the emperor and his administrators—despite the fact that France's population had actually been increasing during the Revolutionary period and had not tapered off. Hence, the emperor shared Fénélon's natalism when he decided how he wished to educate the orphaned daughters of the military officers, who were his new nobility. He also expected properly educated women to transform manners and to stabilize society,[40] as had Fénélon.

The first sign appearing in his correspondence that Napoleon really became interested in educating girls in boarding schools occurred in 1804, when he asked his ministers to see if they could develop a reasonable proposal.[41] In December 1805 the emperor issued an announcement that in recompense for their supreme sacrifice, the fatherland would adopt the children, boys and girls, of the glorious officers lost in the Battle of Austerlitz, which occurred on December 2, 1805 (the anniversary of his coronation). After being educated, Napoleon said that the government would marry off the orphaned girls. He went as far as choosing the two sites for the separate boys and girls boarding schools—Rambouillet and Saint-Germain, respectively—before he abandoned the project.[42]

A few days later, however, Napoleon was thinking bigger when he announced the creation of boarding schools for the daughters of members of the Légion d'Honneur, an institution that had been organized by the law of May 19, 1802 (29 Floréal, year X). Consequently, on December 15, 1805, in the "Decree of Schönbrunn," which followed the French victory at Austerlitz, Napoleon awarded the cross of the Légion of Honor to 1,800 new legionnaires and envisioned bringing together four hundred to five hundred of their daughters, aged seven to ten, into three houses of education.[43]

The emperor's *Exposé de la Situation de l'Empire* of March 5, 1806, boasted that the legislature had established three houses of education for girls because that sex contributed so much to manners that in the interest of public morality their education had to be considered.[44] These *Maisons Impériales* originally were supposed to be located in existing state properties at Chambord, Saint-Denis, and Ecouen, which were then in various states of disrepair. Because Chambord required so much expensive work, Napoleon finally acquiesced to Grand Chancellor Lacépède's recommendation that late in the fall of 1807, Mme Campan move into Ecouen with the first fifty to sixty pupils while restoration continued.[45] As for curriculum, in January 1807, Napoleon had written from Warsaw that since he was too busy to spend much time on it, the organization of these institutions for girls would only be provisional until he could decide what the permanent organization should be. Finally, in May 1807 (a year and a half after first announcing them), the emperor wrote a long note on the direction of the school at the Château d'Ecouen.[46] This note on Ecouen of 1807 is usually treated by historians as the source for finding his intentions regarding women's education.

The Curriculum at Ecouen, 1807–1815

In his orders for Ecouen, Napoleon outlined the curriculum. Among the various subjects with which Napoleon then envisioned young ladies of modest circumstances being occupied, religion received priority because he believed that learning the Gospel would instill them with the resignation, indulgence, and charitable manner useful to persons destined for their station in life. To ensure the girls' religiosity, Napoleon gave instructions for them to spend part of their time in prayer, attending mass and learning the catechism. In addition, they were supposed to learn the three "Rs," some geography, history, and botany, and a smattering of factual physical science or natural history, just to keep them from being crass and superstitious. All of these activities were to take only one-fourth of their day while the other three-fourths of their time was to be spent making socks and shirts and doing embroidery or other sorts of handwork that poorer and bourgeois women normally must do in the home. He wondered, too, if it would be possible to teach them a little cooking and enough nursing skill so that they would be trained to care for their families in sickness and in health. In this plan, however, Latin and foreign languages were taboo, dancing (which he considered necessary for good health) should be restricted to a lively kind, and only vocal music (rather than the instrumental kind) should be taught.[47]

We have learned from Rebecca Rogers's solidly researched book, *Les Demoiselles de la Légion d'Honneur* (1992), that Mme Campan was a better educator than financial manager. Consequently, her private boarding school at Saint-Germain was experiencing financial difficulties in 1807. Early in the new year, she had written to her former pupil, the emperor's step-daughter Hortense, that she was most anxious to obtain the position available as headmistress at the first Maison Impérial to open at Ecouen. But she had to wait until the fifth of September to be appointed. Rogers says the sizable debt—60,000 francs—that Mme Campan left at her private Saint-Germain boarding school cast a shadow over her new appointment. While the emperor gave Mme Campan control of the curriculum, he wisely gave the financial and administrative powers to the first grand chancellor of the order, who from 1803 to April 1814, and again during the Hundred Days (March to July, 1815), was the naturalist Bernard de la Ville, comte de Lacépède. And after 1809, another layer of supervision, an administrative board, was also created to advise the scientist.[48]

Mme Campan was a determined person, however, with her own opposing ideas about female education. In spite of all the oversight Napoleon provided, the actual curriculum did not strictly conform to the emperor's note. Nor did the first three hundred girls who attended really come from families of modest means as he initially envisaged. Instead, the headmistress, Mme Campan, followed the curriculum, including the study of foreign languages by the older pupils as well as the learning of instrumental music, which she had used at her seminary at Saint-Germain-en-Laye that Frances Burney had visited in 1803.[49] In her book, Rogers stresses, however, that there was one real innovation at the Maison Impériale d'Ecouen: the democratization of the girls, who came from varied social origins with but one thing in common—their fathers had been decorated with the cross of the Légion of Honor.[50]

This is corroborated by a letter from young Nancy MacDonald to her father, the Maréchal duc de Tarente, telling how she sometimes spent her day reading Les Leçons de Littérature et de Morale by Noël, walking in the park, drawing, playing both piano and harp, embroidering, and having an English lesson.[51] Moreover, Napoleon was familiar with the regimen at the school through his official visits.[52] That he accepted the routine and curriculum indicates that he was not adamant or inflexible regarding the education offered by this state institution. During the Restoration, Napoleon's detractors unfairly pointed out that Ecouen failed to produce the modest, sensitive young ladies that the emperor said he wanted—unfairly because it was assumed that his original directives had been closely adhered to and that those courses had been aimed at making girls merely camp followers or housewives rather than cosmopolitan women who could discuss philosophy, converse in a foreign language, or skillfully pluck the strings of a harp.[53] Such was not necessarily the case, although sole reliance on Napoleon's previous correspondence might easily suggest that conclusion.

Pedagogy at Ecouen consisted mainly of memorizing, repeating, and copying lessons. The teaching corps of women at Ecouen, which had little contact with the outside world, showed no trace of feminism—not only during the Napoleonic era but throughout the entire nineteenth century.[54] The girls wore uniforms (initially long white dresses, later black woolen ones) and were disciplined like soldiers in a boot camp. Mme Campan was a stickler on punishment, and she produced some very dramatic forms of psychological punishment—for example, she orchestrated a public cere-mony to strip a naughty girl's ribbon from her uniform, which was so cruel it made many a girl faint from shame. Nevertheless, Rogers says, while they were socialized as a group, the graduates were still able to form a feminine identity.[55]

Saint-Denis

Another imperial decree of March 25, 1809, also assigned the Abbey of Saint-Denis, a State property since 1790, to the Légion of Honor for a second girls' school. This announcement outraged Mme Campan who thought that having a second location so close to Ecouen would cause enrollment problems for her school. She criticized this locale every way she could think of; yet, she still hoped to gain control of both schools. But Napoleon decided to hire Mme Bouzet, a widow whose husband had died at the battle of Jemmapes, to be the director of Saint-Denis.[56] A statute of March 29, 1809, envisioned six hundred girls boarding at these two schools—Ecouen and Saint-Denis. Two hundred of the girls would pay 1,000 francs annually to attend; another three hundred would receive a half-pension of 500 francs; and, the last one hundred, composed only of sisters and daughters of legionnaires, would be supported entirely by the Légion of Honor with a full pension.[57] In theory, the paying pupils were supposed to outnumber the scholarship students, but this did not work out at Ecouen. In fact, Mme Campan got herself into trouble for going over budget, whereas her counterpart, Mme Bouzet, had no difficulty at all staying within her budget at Saint-Denis. To reward her for this, Napoleon visited Saint-Denis on December 11, 1813, and elevated Mme Bouzet to the rank of "Baronne d'Empire" with an annual pension of 4,000 francs.[58] Given Mme Campan's cold and haughty personality, one can only imagine how jealous this made her of her female colleague's success.

The Maisons d'Orphelines

Besides creating the Maisons Impériales de la Légion d'Honneur to edu-cate the daughters and sisters of legionnaires, Napoleon created addi-tional boarding schools for orphan girls whose fathers came from all ranks of military service. This meant that needy girls from all social classes would be mixed together. These schools would welcome girls without resources, and the instruction would be aimed at assuring them a livelihood upon graduation. All this was initially outlined in a decree of July 15, 1810. A second official decree dated September 21, 1810, established the locations for the first four of these orphanages: the *marais* in Paris, Barbeaux (in the forest of Fontainebleau), Loges (in the forest of Saint-Germain), and Suresnes (the latter never was purchased, due to the fall of the empire). In contrast to the arduous start of the Légion of Honor boarding schools, three of the orphanages for girls were established and operating quickly. Rogers tells us that in the winter of 1811, Mme de Lézeau and forty-three girls moved into l' hôtel Corberon and in the spring Mme Dagoty, a former nun, moved into Loges. In July 1811, seventeen nuns and sixty pupils moved into Barbeaux.

The cost of running these girls' orphanages was far less than at Ecouen. We know for example that Mme Campan found it impossible to keep the cost of boarding each student within the seven hundred francs that Napoleon wanted to limit her to, in order to stay within budget. But these orphanages did with only four hundred francs per student. In the 1813 budget, Napoleon gave Mme de Lézeau an annual budget of 40,000 francs. Rogers says this was two and a half times less than it cost for a comparable number of girls to be educated at Ecouen and Saint-Denis. The fact that the curriculum of the orphanages only had three levels as opposed to the twelve levels at Ecouen, not to speak of further individualized enrichment opportunities Mme Campan provided exceptional youngsters, made these schools far less complicated to operate. Because the orphanages functioned so efficiently during their first three years of operation, Napoleon gave them supplementary money for the oldest girls. These schools for orphans were dissolved when the Bourbons first replaced the empire in 1814, but they were reorganized again in September 1814. At that time, girls were given a choice of staying, or leaving and being paid 250 francs a year until they turned eighteen.[59]

The disparity between what the emperor sometimes said and what administrators did in designing a proper education for girls was often tied to the budgetary problems of the empire; after all, during this period the French nation was intermittently at war on land and sea with most of Europe. But laying aside financial considerations, this divergence was partly due to the debate over "education" versus "training." It reflected the uncertainty among pedagogues throughout the Napoleonic era. Both sides believed that woman's destiny was marriage and motherhood. Agreement ended there. Moralizing educators were most concerned about a young girl's character and personality in preparation for assuming bourgeois housewifely duties and warned against the dangers of pedantry. Others emphasized the necessity of learning useful, domestic skills such as knitting, sewing, cooking, nursing, and gardening so that women would have alternatives to working in the fields and vineyards, should unforeseen misfortune in the form of another political revolution or the death of a husband befall them. As the primary purpose of female education, some intellectuals expressed a faith in the acquisition of academic knowledge, notably reading, writing, and arithmetic, but other subjects too, both for their own sake and for providing girls with pleasure and relief from the frustration of boring domestic routine. There were those, of course, who preferred a dual approach that taught girls practical subjects as well as academic ones so that women would be able to run their households and, concomitantly, participate in society and the sharing of their husbands' tastes. Also, if (heaven forbid!) they never married or were widowed, these young women needed to be made useful enough to be able to earn their own living. Within the dual approach, time could be scheduled in various proportions.

Regardless of where educators placed their emphasis, the need for cultivating girls' physical development and health was not overlooked because the prevailing climate of opinion was especially conscious of women's greater biological and physical ties to Nature. All of these opinions were set forth in the numerous manuals and textbooks of the period designed to aid parents, governesses, and teachers to educate and train girls by means of homeschooling,[60] thereby performing their duty to the nation.

The Official Imperial Journal of Education—Les Annales de l'Éducation

In 1811 an official point of view about the correct purpose, methods, and content of education for girls began to be disseminated in a new journal better designed to meet the need for guidance than occasional publications had provided parents. Napoleon granted the romantic historian and statesman François Guizot and his future wife, whom he would marry the following year (a novelist and critic for the *Publiciste*), the journalist Pauline de Meulan (1773–1827),[61] permission to edit the *Annales de l'Éducation,* which became the official journal of education. The articles published in this journal provided information about the ideas the government sanctioned during the last four years of the empire. Furthermore, the *Annales de l'Éducation* illustrated, in more detail, how some of the educational theories summarized previously were expressed in the thought patterns of the time.

An article in the first volume of this journal stated that the invariable and universal goal of education was the formation of a healthy body, sound mind, and a virtuous will.[62] Hence, articles were devoted to a wide range of subjects on the physical health and care of children, child psychology, new methods, and education in foreign countries,[63] as well as female education in particular. Mothers were advised about concerns ranging from simple methods of curing their daughters' constipation by feeding them prunes[64] to how to define learned and complex terms like "grandeur of soul."[65]

Several articles discussed how to cope with the behavior problems of girls. Parents were advised to look for the causes of them, then once the child understood why she did bad things she would desist.[66] Then there was the case study of twelve-year-old Rosine who was absolutely angelic in front of strangers, but exactly the opposite at home. Rosine learned to act better in private by reminding herself about what people would say if they only could see her there misbehaving like that![67] Parents were warned not to humiliate their children because it would lead to their offspring becoming apathetic or insolent.[68] Thirteen-year-old Elizabeth was a child who probably had been humiliated because she always said, "I can't,"—as an excuse for not trying to do her lessons anymore. Poor Elizabeth was afraid people would make fun of her because she danced and sang so badly; but then she learned to sew very well and this gave her such a real feeling of accomplishment that she resumed her other lessons. Immediately her whole appearance changed:

> Even her face changed. She was no longer that young girl walking with her arms hanging like pendulums, her head slung first on one shoulder, then the other, slumped down in all the arm chairs, and not knowing what position to take to relieve the malaise which caused her trouble. By learning to sew Elizabeth had gained self-confidence—something that every little girl needs.[69]

Other articles criticized Rousseau's theories of education. To illustrate how silly it would be for parents to give their children freedom to do whatever they wanted, Lord Kaim's story was repeated about a houseguest who overheard a family quarrel that resembled a situation comedy. Little Dick had decided that he wanted to play horsey on a large roast that the cook had just placed on the dining-room table. Father was about to stop him because he was afraid his son might be burned, but Mother was afraid that Dickie's personality would be ruined forever if he were denied the freedom to climb on the steaming roast. Parents were told that if they accepted Rousseau's exaggerated notions about personal freedom they were being overpermissive and forgetting the welfare of their offspring. In disciplining Dickie, making him get off the table, the father in the story knew he had to take charge in a dangerously hot situation.[70] It is noteworthy that this official journal criticized Rousseau for his idea that little girls should keep quiet and let boys do all the talking. Mme Guizot commented that Rousseau almost wanted women to be forbidden to talk; she, on the contrary, strongly felt that females needed very much to talk: because they spent so much of their time sitting and doing work with their fingers, she said, talking had great importance for them as their only outlet for expression and way of amusing themselves.[71] Consequently, if Rousseau's model of educational psychology were followed, it would harm not only individuals but also the family and society.

Some of the personal qualities that parents were encouraged to develop in their girls were docility,[72] sensibility, compassion, pity, and foresight.[73] They also needed to learn to sacrifice[74] and to suppress some of their desires and passions;[75] however, their desires should not be entirely suppressed because this would make Louise and Sophie develop slothfulness when they reached their twenties or thirties.[76]

From the standpoint of female education, probably the most interesting series of articles in the *Annales de l'Éducation* was written by Mme Guizot in 1812, under the guise of a diary written by a wife to her husband on the education of their two daughters. She said that, especially among the upper classes in a tranquil and idle society like theirs, women have an excess of vigor beyond what is required to run their homes. They, therefore, needed something to take their minds off themselves. To alleviate this frustration and restlessness she suggested that women turn to serious studies and learn things simply for pleasure. They might even study Greek as long as it did not become the foremost part of their lives. Regarding her studious daughter, she wrote that she wanted to see her engrossed equally in needlework and discussing history or analyzing stylistic matters in writing. Furthermore, the imaginary diarist told her husband that although instruction could fill the emptiness of their lives, their daughters should cede gracefully to the natural duties of life and not resist them.[77] Thus, upper-class women were informed from the pages of the official journal of education that they were to give their sex roles as wives and mothers top priority and were not even to think about becoming something that was quite unnatural for them—being parasitical intellectuals. But Mme Guizot also freely admitted that the life of a female in Napoleonic France was often empty, boring, and frustrating, and according to her, the higher a woman was in the social strata and the more intelligent she was, the more likely was the possibility of this happening to her.

By means of such literary formats as stories, anecdotes, and letters, the editors of the *Annales de l'Éducation* displayed a great deal of common sense. The emperor would probably have been in agreement with many of the articles, had he read them, especially with some of the criticism of Rousseau's free-spirited idea that boys should be undisciplined, since unruliness posed a potential threat to the social order and could not be tolerated in the military services under his command. But other articles, such as those about boredom and idleness or encouraging women to speak so much, certainly might have displeased him greatly had he not been too preoccupied with the pressing military and political affairs to which he assigned a higher priority after the Russian debacle. Overall, the education journal concentrated on pedagogical theory, child rearing and psychology, and entertainment for its readers. While focusing on the cultivation of young minds, it paid attention to bodily functions and needs, realizing the dual nature of humanness. Nevertheless, its theoretical emphasis tells us little about the actual curriculum in use during the last years of Napoleon's reign.

The Teaching of Traditional Academic Disciplines

Despite state neglect some girls did receive an education during this period, and the positive ideas of a number of educators concerning the specific subjects that should comprise the female curriculum can be deduced from examining the actual works, especially sexually segregated textbooks, published privately for use by women and girls. These indicate that Mme Campan was not the only school mistress who believed in teaching girls foreign languages. For example, Mme Legroing, who refused the emperor's offer of the position subsequently offered to and accepted by Mme Campan,[78] believed that the study of foreign languages, namely English and Italian, could develop women's reasoning ability and increase their knowledge of their native tongue as well. As a method of enhancing language lessons she recommended translating a book on the history of the country whose language was being studied. By the addition of appropriate comments, the teacher could fix the most important facts in female minds and help them to grasp knowledge of the epochs of national history. By following events on a map, these language lessons could also improve the pupil's geographical knowledge.[79]

The vogue in the imperial lycées for the teaching of history separately from language was also evident in women's education. Even educators who agreed with the emperor's statement that women's minds are usually more feeble than men's reached the conclusion that women should study history, an instructive and amusing subject. For these purposes Abbé Blanchard recommended that history, chronology, and geography be combined so that women would know whether an event occurred at the beginning, middle, or end of a century and whether it happened before or after the Christian era. Blanchard recommended the short geography by Buffier and corrected by Robert because its artificial verses were a good learning aid for girls with short memories.[80] As unenlightened as Blanchard's ideas about studying history seem in a twentieth-century context, for their own time they were still innovative, inasmuch as the study of history was not essential to the performance of housewifely duties and previously had been reserved as political training for future monarchs. Moreover, Blanchard was also critical of Rousseau's ideas as expressed in *Emile*, which he thought provided a bad model for educating children. Blanchard especially took exception to the "natural" role Rousseau prescribed for Emile's feminine companion—solely to please her male companion—because he intended for historical studies to be a liberating experience for the woman's mind.[81]

Some pedagogues went much further than Blanchard did to heighten female consciousness by writing books exclusively on women's history. That was the purpose of Dubroca's *Les Femmes Célèbres de la Révolution*,[82] P. N. Rougeron's *L'Historien des Jeunes Demoiselles* (1810),[83] and Girard de Propriac's two-volume *Le Plutarque des Jeunes Demoiselles* (1806). The author of the latter work thought women should memorize all the virtues and crimes of the women whose biographies were contained in the book so that they would not have to keep silent or display their ignorance whenever the names of celebrated women arose in conversation. Also, by really knowing their facts women could take pride in their sex and defend the reputations of heroines against jealous men who tried to keep women subjugated by denying their achievements.[84] After each of the lives in his women's history textbook, Girard de Propriac put a series of questions and answers, as was done in the officially adopted history textbooks boys memorized in the lycées, in order to simplify the teacher's job of preparing lessons.[85] Although the title specifically stated that this was a book for young ladies, the author commented at the end of his preface that it could also be used for teaching women's history to boys.[86] Although Rougeron's book concentrated on the virtues of famous exceptional women, it also pointed out how badly some of them have been treated; for example, he singled out the Native American princess Pocahontas as a prime example of a woman whose sacrifice was repaid by the worst sort of ingratitude.[87] In general, women's history was used to teach women two things: to accept stoically the traditional roles that they had filled in Western society for centuries and not to expect gratitude from society for their sacrifices.

At the elementary level, mothers were able to teach their girls the three "Rs" by adapting the methods of textbooks written as imaginary lessons being given by a mother to her child. Such reading manuals usually taught the vowels, consonants, syllables, grammatical rules, and exceptions to rules.[88] The form of writing manuals varied from being organized as an exchange of letters between two little girls[89] to songs that girls could sing to learn orthography and grammar.[90] Special arithmetic books for ladies appeared to teach the operations of addition, subtraction, multiplication, and division, and about complex numbers, progressions, square roots, interest and annuities, and comparison of the metric system with the pre-revolutionary system of weights and measures.[91] These primary works thus provide insight into teaching methods, content, and how far educators went to make learning fun.

In spite of the fact that some writers warned parents that a young girl's health would be ruined if she studied science,[92] books appeared whose purpose was to teach their daughters natural history, zoology, astronomy, and botany. For example, a book by Mme de Renneville, containing a conversation between a girl and her maid, told about Captain Cook's discovery of kangaroos complete with a picture of the exotic marsupial.[93] Jérôme de Lalande showed his interest in women's education by writing *Astronomie des Dames,* a book similar to Fontanelle's *La Pluralité des Mondes* (1686). Lalande began with a long essay about all of the women from the year A.D. 415 to the present who had distinguished themselves as astronomers. He wanted to encourage women to join the procession of exceptional women who had advanced this branch of science.[94] Other portions of his book explained how to identify the constellations, described the phases of the moon in relation to the calendar, and told how to measure the distance of planets from the earth. While botany was considered to be an important subject for the special pupils in the midwifery schools of the empire to study in relation to medicine,[95] its practical domestic applications were likewise especially important for women who planted kitchen gardens or who engaged in full-scale farming.

Grégoire's Vocational Training for Domestic Servants

Vocational education that would prepare lower-class women for domestic servitude, a notion that was neither new nor unique to imperial France, was seriously considered by Abbé Henri Grégoire.[96] The former abbot of Blois was an important Revolutionary politician (a member of the Convention) and thinker known widely for his egalitarian ideas regarding improvement of the social and political status of blacks, Jews, and lepers. He based his belief in the equality of women on his reading of the Bible: had not God created Adam *and Eve?* In his 1814 book, *De la Domesticité chez les Peuples Anciens et Modernes,* Grégoire opined that since an estimated one million domestics were currently employed in his country, it was important that they be honest, loyal, and moral. He regretted that during the Revolution servants had spied on their masters and sent them to the guillotine. He deplored the fact that lewd advertisements were being posted, and cited examples: "A *single* man would like to find for his household a young woman of eighteen to twenty." Or, "A young girl, having *agreeable talents,* wishes to place herself in the home of a *single* man."[97] The remedy for this corrupt behavior, he thought, was formal vocational training.

Grégoire revealed his inspiration—the works of Charles-Joseph, Prince de Ligne (1735–1814),[98] which had been published in Geneva in 1809. Ligne had outlined a plan for schools for domestic servants, which was designed to teach them to think, serve, and speak well. Interestingly, he asked that *collèges* be opened to teach servants morals, literature, music, and drawing as means of pleasing their masters, thereby assuring the former of steady work. The prince also thought such schools should serve as employment agencies where prospective employers could go to find good servants in place of the chancy practice of hunting randomly in the streets for servants to hire.[99] For his part, Grégoire thought the teaching of music, drawing, and literature to domestics was going beyond the appropriate boundaries of knowledge for their lowly social status. Instead, he recommended the sort of training provided by Père Sautier, an ex-Jesuit, at the school in Freiburg im Breisgau that he founded for the religious, moral, and industrial instruction of fifteen- to sixteen-year-old girls who were reduced to servitude.[100]

Grégoire was also impressed by several British efforts regarding poor girls' education. The former Roman Catholic *abbé* praised Sunday schools established there to teach religion as well as various training centers for learning the appropriate female skills of spinning, knitting, and sewing. Besides the Sunday schools, which were a legacy of the Wesleyan revival, Grégoire praised Lancaster's plan to educate the poor, as outlined in his book *Improvements in Education* (1805, 1807) and thought that Anglican clergymen like Trimmer had unfairly criticized the Lancaster plan merely because its author was a Quaker. However, Grégoire believed that Lancaster was being more influential in the United States, especially in New York state.[101]

Taking a cue from the British, Grégoire proposed that Sunday schools, which to date only operated in France at Strasbourg, ought to be set up all over the country because the children of the poor had no time for school when they had to work on weekdays. After all, Sunday schools had been introduced in Berlin with equal success, and these were supplemented by Mme de Krosik's institute for school teachers and chambermaids, which provided much more instruction for working-class women than was available in France. To remedy the paucity, Grégoire also called for the reopening of some exemplary French institutions for servants, such as the one established at Rheims by Nicolas Colbert's widow in 1635, the Petite Union established for chambermaids in Paris in 1679, the house of the Dames of

Sainte-Elizabeth, and l'Hôpital de Sainte-Catherine, all of which had been "devoured by the Revolution."[102]

As for existing French institutions, Grégoire praised Mme Cosway's school at Lyons, wherein she educated rich and poor girls together. At the Société des Jeunes Econemes, as it was called, the rich girls patronized their poor classmates as an act of *bienfaisance,* or charity. While the Société's curriculum included all housewifely skills, it also included reading, writing, French language, and a second living language. Whichever girls showed the most intelligence were rewarded for good behavior by being provided further instruction in geography, history, and drawing to enable them to become good governesses for children. But Grégoire noted that when Mme Cosway had attempted to teach the future governesses music, the piety of the school's female benefactors made them block her effort. He explained that the women feared that if the poor girls had their voices trained, they would be tempted to become showgirls in order to escape doing the useful employment, obviously very hard work, at which their training had been aimed.[103]

Rousseau's belief that a necessary correlation exists between the sciences and the arts and vice was rejected by Grégoire. Although he was well aware of the criticisms circulating regarding schools that allegedly turned girls into worldly women, rather than into mothers of families, he was confident that a balance could be struck between pushing women to develop to their utmost intellectually and helping them develop virtuously. He allowed that Rousseau probably had been correct in observing the ill effect of eighteenth-century education on upper-class women in that "age of refined barbarism," but Grégoire was more optimistic about the prospects for female education in the French society of 1814.[104]

Evidently, Grégoire's interest in practical training for lower-class women continued into the Bourbon Restoration. In 1819, he published *Des Gardes-Malades, et la Nécessité d'Établir pour Elles des Cours*, in which he expressed the sentiment that Providence had almost exclusively blessed the female sex with the talent to heal suffering, that women of equal intelligence, experience, and good will would always do a better job of nursing the sick than men. To solve the skilled-nursing shortage, he offered up again Marc Antoine Petit's *Essai sur le Médecine du Coeur*, which had first been published in 1806. Petit, in turn, had supported Dr. Morizot's plan to provide nursing lessons for rural women, after which they would have to pass a proficiency exam before being employed in hospitals. This practice would transform nursing from a poorly paid, unprestigious profession into an honorable one, according to Petit and Morizot.[105] Grégoire, too, emphasized the value of a nursing diploma as proof of capability and morality, especially of the latter.

While nurses' training ought to be religiously based, trained nurses nevertheless ought to treat patients of all faiths—even non-Christians, including Moslems and Jews, and Protestants or Anabaptists—the same because "Christian charity has no limits."[106] Additionally, a good nurse needs good health herself so she can stay up all night, plus an extraordinary measure of tactfulness. For the finest nursing textbook then available, he referred readers to the *Manuel des Gardes-Malades* by François-Emmanuel Fodéré, who had been a prominent professor of legal medicine, patronized by Napoleon I and to whom we shall return in Chapter 7.[107] Thus, ideas about vocational training for poor women that had circulated during the First Empire continued to be advocated after the fall of Napoleon. The need that enlightened thinkers such as Grégoire identified, continued to be unmet.

In summary, this review of Napoleonic education for the female sex indicates the richness and diversity of the ideas of that period. While it was generally agreed that women's societal role as wives and mothers was quite important and took precedence over everything else, there was disagreement about the kind of studies that best prepared girls for womanhood. This discord focused on several issues, including broad liberal arts education versus practical, vocational/technical instruction; how much of either kind of learning was appropriate to a woman's place on the social ladder; and how to discourage poor women from seeking less physically demanding vocations. Other ideas propagated also sound familiar, such as the offering of women's history to raise the level of female-consciousness and self-esteem and encouraging women to study the natural sciences that already were thought of as special preserves for men. There were prescribed limits for this, however. Bright women could study science so long as they did not allow this knowledge to turn into a career in which they would be competing with men for jobs. The emphasis on the importance of learning geography is also noteworthy because unlike the men who might be enfranchised or join the army or navy in some capacity, women in a traditional society were not apt to travel far from home, much less to foreign lands.

Of course, while some intellectuals and legislators largely theorized, parents and teachers acted to teach girls what knowledge they themselves had acquired from their own upbringing and what they were then learning from the numerous manuals being published and circulated for this purpose. Unfortunately, women, notably upper-class women, were not always the best advocates for developing the intellectual potential of their own sex when they expressed concern about the dangers of overeducation or directed pupils' curricula. Nevertheless, included in these books that formed the basic content of formal education are a concern about the child's personality and physical development, making learning fun, nostalgia, the cult of Nature, and the bourgeois values of equality, discipline, hard work, and economy. Agriculture, domestic science, home economics, and sex were not yet perceived as academic disciplines, although women were learning about these subjects as well.

Despite his preoccupation with warfare and other urgent matters, Napoleon made a commendable effort to match the achievement of Louis XIV, who had created one boarding school for the daughters of the nobility at Saint-Cyr. The emperor, instead, created five institutions for young women, and planned a sixth for relatives and survivors of the military. As limited as his achievement was from a modern point of view, his effort nonetheless far surpassed that of the Sun King. These schools represented a legacy for future generations of young women who would be privileged to benefit from the scholarships they provided. In time, they also would influence the curriculum and pedagogy of other educational establishments for girls.

3

Feminism and Domesticity in Humanistic Manuals of "Domestic Science," Home Economics, and Hygiene

*"Femme sage
Reste à son ménage."*

FOR THE IMPERIAL WOMAN who resided in the city or the country, this old but still popular French proverb[1] did not mean that while a wise woman stayed home, she was supposed to be ignorant. In fact, it was expected that girls would be trained by their mothers in all aspects of "domestic science," home economics, hygiene, and animal husbandry. In other words, in addition to the obvious housekeeping skills, this included physical education and sex education of children and adults, gardening and farming, forestry and soil conservation, caring for farm animals and their young, and the improvement of the species. Household management manuals, which incorporated a wide variety of scientific and practical knowledge, were available to assist the woman who wanted to further her own knowledge or who perhaps had been reared in another locale during the Revolution. Sometimes the education a young woman had received was not adequate under present circumstances in a society that expected much adaptability and versatility from women. These manuals were augmented by more specialized treatises containing essays on the female body, sexuality, and popular medicine that were written from a solely humanistic philosophical-anthropological viewpoint. An effort is purposely made to exclude from this chapter opinions of others with actual experience touching women's bodies, examining tissue, performing surgery or autopsies, and administering drugs in the process of forming and testing their professional, supposedly more "scientific" opinions about woman nature. Since such humanistic educational and philosophical essays focusing on women's health and physical characteristics provide special insight about the formation of female identity and gender differences for those who had to learn how to perform the housekeeping skills, these will be considered first.

Nature and Sexuality in Medical Treatises by Male Authors

The humanistic medical treatises that revealed the contemporary male mentality about the essential character and proper actions of women were replete with references to Nature and the natural. They stressed that the only way for a woman to be happy was to establish a harmonious relationship with the will and purpose of Nature. The first axiom they observed in this mysterious yet teleological universe was the unseverable connection between mind and body. Belief in the mind-body nexus allied education and medicine in a manner in which they had not been prior to the eighteenth century: both became holistic disciplines, if not really two aspects of a single discipline. Females were trained to behave and to use their newly important bodies in certain desired ways that were supposed to be dictated by Nature.

Writers often explored the physical difference between the sexes at various stages of life. For example, girls were thought to reach puberty sooner than boys. Likewise, adult women always aged faster than adult men. Some authors explained this by the smallness of female organs, being petite, fully developed within a shorter time frame.[2] Hence, girls became of marriageable age and reached their majority years ahead of boys. While some people said that the softness and suppleness of a woman's body were the results of education or manner of living, the radical innate difference between the sexes in every country had been determined by Nature itself.[3] Since women's bodies had less mass and more fluid humors than men's, they also had better coordination of their motor functions.[4] Women even had more facility for speaking, a fact proven by the greater number of actresses than actors of superior merit.[5]

Evidently, some writers could see right into the core of women's being to explain how this operated. We are told the organization of their bodies made "their existence consist more of sensations than in ideas and in body movements."[6] The flexibility of their organs was also what made them more capricious.[7] Reading novels did more damage to women's sensitive minds. But women's superior sensibility was also the faculty that enabled them to overcome the physical and mental handicaps of their natural constitution in order to perform heroic feats, such as braving flames or leaping into the waves of the ocean in order to save an endangered child. Thus, woman's nature developed and functioned in a special way, capable of neat explanation.[8]

Male writers especially were concerned about women's physical need for marriage. Costard's treatise refuting the notion that marriage is the "tomb of love, slavery, or a necessary evil," claimed that this "union of bodies and

souls" was the happiest and most desirable state.[9] Most authors agreed with
Jacques Moreau, who set the optimum age for women to marry at twenty to
twenty-five. Although age fifteen was the legal threshold, early marriage was
believed to bring on physical and mental illness, not to speak of loss of
youthfulness and beauty.[10] The warning that the first offspring produced by
teenage brides were effeminate weaklings who were unfit on the battlefield
obviously was designed as a deterrent against early teenage pregnancy.[11] But
marriage, nevertheless, was absolutely essential because the need for love
caused illnesses in unmarried women.[12] As Jacques-André Millot phrased
it, "girls must marry to extinguish their desire, keep their stomachs in order
and fluids from stagnating in their body, and to prevent general deterioration."[13] But a happy marriage had to be based on more than raw mechanistic desire or need. Marriage ought to be a love match between a man and a
woman only after the suitor has studied his fiancée's conduct well. To assess
her worthiness, a suitor should compare a woman to her mother.[14] Moreover, to assure happiness, both spouses should possess equal wealth.[15] Marriage should never be forced, and any man whose young bride is unable to
walk to the altar willingly "should not accept the sacrifice" because "if you
do not have her heart, you have nothing."[16] Ultimately, romantic love won
the day.

Humanistic manuals did not generally dwell on information about the
uniquely female bodily function menstruation. When one did, J. R. J.
Dubuisson's *Tableau de l'Amour Conjugal* (1812), an updated version of
Venette's seventeenth-century sex manual with drawings of male and female
internal and external sex organs, it was criticized by a medical journal for
being indecent for women to see.[17] While Dubuisson offered fathers the
acceptable advice to have their daughters examined at age nine so that any
discovered defects in their genitals could be corrected before puberty,[18] he
asserted that men are virile only between the ages of twenty to twenty-five
and sixty to sixty-five. Women, he claimed, are fertile from twenty-one to
fifty.[19] His, however, was the only manual by a layman that set these narrow
limits. In comparison, *L'Ami des Jeunes Femmes, ou Les Devoirs du Mariage
et de la Maternité* (1806)[20] consisted of childlike conversations between a
mother and her newly married fifteen-year-old daughter who needed to be
told the facts of life—only after she was married—since she could be
impregnated. However, neither book explicitly connected menstruation, or
rather the interruption of it, to pregnancy. Pierre Roussel, who died in 1802
but whose popular manual continued to be republished until the 1820s, in
fact, was so ill informed that he blatantly denied any connection at all
between menstruation and pregnancy. "Women in Brazil, according to trav-
elers, do not have periods; likewise in several savage nations." Closer to

home, he claimed that menstruation occurs later and less abundantly among women in the countryside because they are not subjected to the vices of urban society. These considerations led him to conclude that "there must have been a time when women were not subject to this incommodious tribute; and that menstrual flux, far from being a natural phenomenum, is on the contrary an artificial need acquired in the social state."[21] Thus Roussel thought menstruation was an unnatural process.

Conception, Pregnancy, and Fetal Development

By contrast, conception, pregnancy, and fetal development were topics that were frequently discussed at length. *L'Ami des Jeunes Femmes* broached the subject to innocent young brides by telling them that conception occurs in the "abdomen."[22] After this shocking revelation, the imaginary mother further explained that "procreation begins with eggs—yes, like a chicken's."[23] She hastened to add an aside to the effect that a chicken carefully hatches her eggs and a woman should too, in accordance with Nature. To continue, contact with the husband makes the eggs "fruitful" about three or four days after they are made. On the third or fourth day following conception, the then eight-day-old egg enters the womb. At that point the woman is pregnant and the fertilized egg the size of a cherry. On the sixth day in the womb, the egg becomes a fetus or embryo. At three weeks, the embryo is composed of cartilages.[24] A footnote to the text said that now that she knows the facts of life, the "young wife should no longer blush when she says the word *matrice* to her mother."[25] The only certain sign of pregnancy, the mother says, is the baby's movements because some women continue to menstruate until the end of pregnancy. Usually, however, pregnant women get morning sickness, headaches, and double vision ten days after conception as the first possible signs. During the second month, the woman vomits and has strange cravings; this continues and worsens during month three, and the fourth month produces general distress.[26]

L'Ami des Jeunes Femmes also gave advice on alleviating some of the discomforts of pregnancy. During the fourth month, cold compresses should be applied to the most extended and hardest part of the abdomen.[27] Pregnant women ought to avoid extreme temperatures. They can moderate hot flashes by drinking lettuce or poppy infusions, mild lemonade, orgeat (made from barley water flavored with almonds or orange blossoms), or lemon and violet syrups. During heat waves they should breathe into a sponge moistened with vinegar, and wrap their throats and necks warmly during cold spells. Spicy, heavy, and hard-to-digest foods should be avoided, as should *apéritifs* and smoked or salty things, which are poison for the expectant woman.[28] Animals, of course, do not suffer from these problems during pregnancy because "they live according to Nature's laws."[29] More-over, country women lead such frugal and well-regulated lives, breathing so much good, healthful air, that they can work during this time without harm.[30]

False pregnancies and miscarriage also were discussed. *L'Ami des Jeunes Femmes,* for example, explained that they are caused by leading an irregular lifestyle, drinking overly hot drinks, dancing all night, riding in carriages, and partaking in other similar abuses. The difference between a false pregnancy and a real one is that the former moves around while the latter remains in one place.[31] Other prescriptive literature claimed that miscarriage is an accident that occurs until the sixth month; after that what occurs is termed "birth." Ordinarily this is caused by great surprises, spasmodic illness, or excessively lively passions.[32] Women never should cut their hair or wear perfume during pregnancy.[33] Overly frequent intercourse, especially during the beginning stages, has the same ill effect as violent exercise. Animals have better instinct about the impropriety of intercourse at this time than men who are supposed to be rational. There is merit in sexual abstinence;[34] and if humans would follow the natural example set by stags and bulls, gestation would proceed with fewer accidents.[35]

The aspect of the birth process that most fascinated popular authors, however, was what might be called human engineering, that is, the problem of procreating better offspring and determining their sex. These theories were developed on the basis of some widely held assumptions. First of all, there was general agreement that the father transmits greater hereditary influence to the external parts of the offspring and to intelligence, while the mother contributes more to determining the "interior qualities," such as temperament, passions, and physical constitution.[36] In keeping with this belief was the idea, naturally, that "the degeneration of hereditary stock always is caused by the woman."[37] Moreover, the characteristics of maleness and femaleness of the future child are separated and preexistent inside the woman and not the man.[38] Hence, humanistic writers tried to explain the gender of the fetus by concentrating on the ovaries as the key to this mystery. Jacques André Millot provided the rationale for the intense interest in this subject in two of his works. "The moment is now for renewal and propagation, seeing that we have millions of men to replace," he wrote in 1802.[39] His purpose for writing *Médecine Perfective, ou Code des Bonnes Mères,* seven years later, also was to increase the population of the empire by one-third, he said, by serving as a handy reference and by providing husbands with sexual instructions that, if followed, would result in the production of a healthier new generation of Frenchmen.[40]

Millot's natalism was concerned about more than just the size of the population. Improving the characteristics of the race was equally important. A sickly woman understandably should never be impregnated because her children probably would be unhealthy, since the mother's physical condition determines that of her offspring.[41] People who live intemperate lives may produce robust children but of only mediocre intelligence.[42] Because the male sex has more intelligence, the child's intelligence is dependent upon the father, namely through "the excellence of the vital fluid that animates it [the egg] at the moment of fertilization." Therefore, it only stands to reason to procreate during the springtime when fluids are best, and when both sexes are most amorous.[43]

> Everything is allied to the return of the spring equinox, because hardly have the winter frosts fled before the first rays of a sun whose activity again makes us believe that the animal liquors somehow surge like the sap of vegetables coming out of their lethargy or apparent death, by a development and an increase; even our body again takes on the vigor that the frosts of winter had enchained; all the humors which circulate with the blood begin to purify themselves by the resumption of the breathing that was suspended by the North winds; then we feel a sense of well-being of which we had been deprived since the onset of lower temperatures in our climate. We counsel, therefore, men who want to know how to produce *healthy, vigorous, and intelligent* progeny to wait to fecundate their spouses until the arrival of spring, the time when Nature, revivified, speaks most energetically to our senses and when she makes us bring forth the greatest number of agreeable sensations; finally, it is the moment when certain temperaments enjoy an almost new existence.[44]

In addition to the most auspicious time of year, the optimum time of day for intercourse was discussed. Various opinions indicated that whether day or night was inconsequential if feeling dictated the need.[45] But since the sex partners should have digested their meals, be rested, and feel strong, probably the two best times of day are four to five hours after either lunch or supper.[46] Men needed to be careful so as not to ruin their health from intercourse—they were the ones who could be harmed by its sapping their strength.[47] Once male sexual prowess was lost, the loss was permanent, so men had to indulge in moderation.[48] Frequent intercourse was never excessive and could not harm the woman unless she was pregnant or nursing, and then it was not really she, but the effect on the fetus or her breast milk, that was the cause for concern.[49]

Theories on the Determination of the Sex of a Child

By the French Revolutionary era the question of sex was seen as simply being biologically determined. Manuals on the determination of human sexual development reviewed the history of relevant theories. One popular theory in the seventeenth and eighteenth centuries was Hippocrates's notion[50] that men had one testicle to produce sons and the other to make daughters. This led some peoples, they believed, to amputate one testicle; but infants of both sexes were born anyhow.[51] A modern surgeon, with the unlikely name of Dr. Michel Procope Couteau (Dr. Knife!), advocated amputation of the undesirable testicle. But Millot reassuringly advised imperial men: "Keep both of them: nature in her wisdom has made everything well; she has given us nothing in excess."[52] According to Dubuisson, Venette had predicated his seventeenth-century art upon the belief that girls are produced by the heat of youth and successive intercourses in one night. Hence, "Moderate your intercourse to produce boys," was his recommendation.[53] A third theory and the one that received the most discussion in all types of publications during the Napoleonic era was Millot's own ovarian theory, which happily would make it possible for rulers and sovereigns to choose the sex of the baby, to have the child of their choice.[54]

In defiance of Hippocrates, Millot claimed that in order to produce a male child, the man must fertilize an egg from the woman's right ovary; correspondingly, to have a girl, the left ovary's egg must be fertilized.[55] He reasoned that this was the case because the same fluid comes from both testicles and mixes together. Moreover, since the egg is constantly encased in membranes inside the ovaries, the sex of each egg is already predetermined before fertilization.[56] Under ordinary circumstances what determines which egg will be fertilized through intercourse is the woman's chance movement at the moment of fecundation. To counteract such unplanned parenthood, the female sex partner must refrain from all movement during intercourse and instead of lying perfectly flat, incline herself at about a 45-degree angle on her right side. If her tubes and ovaries are healthy on this side, the result is guaranteed to be a boy. Likewise, by inclining on her left side, a woman will deliver a girl. Millot wrote persuasively: "This method is neither hard nor painful to practice; try it, *Reader,* and you will be convinced."[57]

But everybody was *not* convinced. The reviewer of the third edition was dubious of his method and found his exposition of explicit details rather tasteless.[58] In 1812 Dubuisson wrote that there still was no proof of this well-known theory and that "Nature hides the secret from us."[59] Such preoccupation with the greater importance of the ovaries vis-à-vis the testicles did tie in with the general opinion, which Napoleon shared, that childlessness usually was caused by the woman's sterility and not the man's.[60] Also, if women were so important to the character of their offspring, then "men of spirit ought to be mated with women of spirit"[61] to produce the superior race—a belief that pointed to the need for female education to parallel that of men's in the Imperial University if such a mating scheme were to be practicable.

In any event, the obsession with the art of determining sex also had important implications for another current controversy—the very old one over the possibility of hermaphrodites and human monsters. As background, an extensive literature exists showing the evolution of notions about sex *from the Greeks to Freud* (to borrow the subtitle of Thomas Laqueur's much discussed book *Making Sex* [Harvard, 1990]).[62] In the Renaissance, Europeans could conceive of only one sex with male and female manifestations, which were mirror images of each other. One sex gave life, the other received it. In such a scheme, hermaphrodites could shift from one image to the other. The evolution of modern sexual theory changed that imagery. By perhaps the early seventeenth or mideighteenth century (depending on whether you believe Michael Stolberg or Laqueur and Londa Schiebinger's thesis is correct, respectively), sex had become polarized, that is, separated into two, the male sex and the "other sex." In political terms, the sexes were unequal; hence, the one with the penis was entitled to varying degrees of political rights, which were doled out according to a male's property, wealth, vocation, and social station, depending upon the traditions of the country where he resided. With very few exceptions, members of the other sex—the one with the vagina and uterus—had no political entitlements because as inferiors, they already were represented by their male protectors (whether father or husband) who could treat them like any other piece of property (chattel). Social convention dictated that males dressed and behaved like men, and females adhered to women's roles. To cross or transgress these social barriers was a taboo. Cross-dressing blurred the boundaries between genders. In any event, in the modern conception of sex, a hermaphrodite has to be of two sexes and possess two corresponding sets of sex organs simultaneously.

Obviously, if the sexes were separate and preexistent before conception in either the ovaries or the testicles, human hermaphrodites could not exist—an individual would have had to be one or the other sex depending on how he or she was conceived. Still, there was some disagreement among authors about this anyhow during the Napoleonic era. B. A. Richerand, for example, called belief in the birth of human hermaphrodites and monsters popular errors to be refuted along with many other examples of superstition and ignorance relating to physiology.[63] Millot conceded that hermaphrodism, though unnatural, was possible. Clearly, had his contemporaries generally accepted the possibility of hermaphrodism as physiological fact, they would logically have had to accept that it was sometimes Nature's course to blur the lines of gender, which in turn might logically cause a blurring of gender roles.

Moving on from speculations about the cause of human gender briefly to gender identity and sex roles in the age of Napoleon, one notion that was expressed very frequently by both male and female authors was condemnation of male midwives. Decency, they asserted, requires that an infant be born while the mother is covered;[64] and childbirth, they thought, ought to be secret and private with only two or three of the women's close friends lending a calm and cheerful presence at the event. Midwifery was an art that came as naturally to women as speaking prose came to Molière's *Bourgeois Gentilhomme*.[65] However, it was claimed that most midwives were better practitioners in ancient times than they are today.[66] Midwifery was thought to be a woman's job because women had the small, dextrous hands needed so as to conveniently penetrate to the source of the trouble and cure it without rousing dormant pain.[67] A man who had this same ability was ridiculed as a "midwife in trousers," playing a role counter to Nature's intentions.

Breast-Feeding

Thus, in the treatment of the preceding subjects, a Romantic appeal to Nature is strongly in evidence. But the topic about which popular authors went to the greatest extremes with this tendency was infant *cuisine*. For the newborn this meant that every infant should not only be breast-fed, but preferably be breast-fed by its own mother for as long as Nature required. Millot's concern was based upon his conviction that the human species was degenerating in Europe, especially in France more than in Germany and Switzerland, for three reasons: (1) inattention to marriage alliances, (2) the hiring of wet-nurses, and (3) child rearing customs that discouraged the physical development and strengthening of the body from earliest infancy through adulthood.[68] He thought about the greatest people in the world, the Chinese, whose men were the most robust, and attributed this to Chinese women always nursing their own babies.[69] From the standpoint of nationalism then, "women who refuse to breast-feed are ungrateful to the government and criminal in the eyes of Nature."[70] The publicist Michaud's review of Millot's book informed the public that his treatise was indeed the fullest account ever attempted of the real truth about breast-feeding and the proper diet for nursing women, improving upon the writings of Locke, Rousseau, Ballexserd of Geneva, and several English, Scottish, German, and French doctors.[71]

Other authors echoed Millot's grave concern through emotional appeals. *L'Ami des jeunes femmes* stated that "the first cry of the infant who comes into the world is the very voice of Nature which dictates to the mother that she has a duty to nourish her child herself."[72] This manual went on to supply a rational explanation as to why it was so important that she do this personally. It elucidated that the mother's first milk, *colostre* (colostrum, which today we know contains proteins and antibodies that protect the suckling baby from infection) acts as a purgative that rids the newborn's body of *meconium* (the English cognate today for "newborn stool"), a poisonous and potentially lethal substance in its system. In a day the mother's *colostre* turns to genuine milk at the moment when the cleansed infant begins to need nourishment. For this reason, whenever a mother does not nurse her baby, regardless of the reason for this, it is necessary to wait twenty-four hours before giving the infant to a wet-nurse. "Thus, the first wish of Nature, after childbirth, is that the mother give her breast to her child."[73]

Millot was not the only writer who raised comparisons with other cultures. Thomas Duverne de Praile, who described and popularized the theories of the English physician William Buchan, Rousseau, and the French doctor Alphonse Leroy, argued that mothers in civilized nations have a moral duty to nurse their infants in light of the example of maternal devotion furnished by the American savages whose women gave milk to the graves of their dead infants for several weeks. By analogy, so-called civilized women should, at least, breast-feed under ordinary circumstances.[74]

Breast-feeding was supposed to be a universal duty of mothers in more than the geographical sense. It was the duty of rich and poor alike. Mme Gacon-Dufour maintained that wealthy women still should personally care for their children from infancy in order to be able to enjoy their riches in the best of health and to insure that their youngsters receive the finest care. Poor women ought to do likewise because their children also need to grow up healthy and vigorous, but so they will be able to work for a living and even support their parents if need be.[75]

Only one popular manual claimed that there was another enormous advantage to breast-feeding, one that others did not mention either because they had not thought about it, believed it to be false, or even if they thought it were true, possibly it would run counter to their stated purpose of trying to increase population. This was the notion that nursing gave a woman a respite of about eighteen to twenty months to recover from childbirth before she was again susceptible to pregnancy. Women who refused to nurse had two or three babies in rapid succession and died as a direct consequence, was the warning Bret laid on the recalcitrant.[76] But it should be noted that this exceptional 1810 manual was really a reprint of a treatise he had originally written in 1784, when the hiring of wet-nurses by upper-class women was frowned upon less than after the Revolution.

Authors also compiled long lists of the evils that would result from fail-ure to obey the dictates of Nature. Undoubtedly, much harm would befall both the negligent mother and the innocent child. The latter would digest its milk poorly and fail to develop its potential intelligence.[77] It might even have convulsions if its wet-nurse has any "moral shocks."[78] At best, if out of total disregard for her charge's welfare the wet-nurse has long orgasms, she will produce only sour milk, which is the natural consequence of such behavior.[79] Moreover, a mercenary nurse is apt to gorge infants on a pablum of wheat flour, which ferments in little stomachs and weakens them.[80] Both mother and child, of course, would suffer from the severing of the psychological bond of love between them.[81] But the undutiful woman alone would risk immediate and long-term physical consequences, such as breaking out in abscesses, lengthening her recovery period, losing her charm and beauty, shortening her life, and eventually making menopause a terrible time of life for her.[82] The one frightening malady that she was most apt to invite was milk fever, which might cause her to go insane or even die very soon.[83] In order to convince readers thoroughly of the truth and utter significance of all of this, Millot selected for the fron-tispiece of his 1809 manual a picture of a woman nursing a baby with the caption: "If there is under heaven any object that merits the gaze of the Divinity, it is, without dispute, a Mother who breast-feeds her Child."[84]

If all French mothers were expected to nurse their own babies, then facts about diet and duration became crucial. How many teeth must a child have before it is weaned? In order to prevent its demise during dentition, patri-otic mothers must wait until after baby has twenty teeth,[85] which is the full set of milk teeth that is normally complete at about thirty months of age. During this two-and-a-half-year period the mother must get enough but not too much rest and must abstain from eating *crudités*, salted or pickled meats that will pass into the milk to give the baby ulcers, canker sores, and sometimes even scurvy and consumption.[86] Meanwhile, the woman should routinely feed her baby as often as it wants to nurse without feeling any side effects.[87] By making sure her nipple falls into the back of the child's mouth, she can avoid the irritation from dentition and insure adequate supply.[88] At first, milk should be the infant's only food, but later it can take a little soup or biscuit. After several weeks a pap may occasionally be given but only rarely and only when it is made from bread crumbs, never from flour.[89] This should be made from well-baked bread crumbs boiled in water and added to unheated milk, whenever fresh milk is available.[90] While teething, babies should be allowed to chew on breakfast rolls—this is better than a special object, a *hochet*—or even a liquorice root.[91] It is best for the mother to wean sucklings during the summer.[92] To accomplish this, nursing should gradually be limited to twice daily before finally severing the child. The mother should be sure to get plenty of exercise, try not to catch cold, avoid humidity, and so forth. This should be followed by taking a purgative a few days later.[93] The baby needs to eat all the food it wants; however, never give it table food. The latter will not only make it sick but will cause the child to become a *gourmand* and have a sensual personality. The solution is to feed the baby separately from the family. Ripe fruit is especially good for growing children.[94] Green fruit, spices other than salt, pastry, butter, and alcoholic beverages should never be given to toddlers.[95] A vegetable diet is better for them than meat, which is harder to digest, despite the fact that humans are omnivores.[96] Mme Gacon-Dufour said that she knew this to be true because she herself never ate meat until the age of eight and has always been a healthy person.[97]

While breast-feeding was thought to provide infants with the nourishment necessary for survival and the development of good health and character in adulthood, it had additional positive and negative effects. Among the ways it affected the mother's mental health was to extinguish nymphomania and homesickness. While nursing would not cure hysteria entirely, it did weaken its effects.[98] The importance of the nurse's own diet was appreciated. If a nurse was not well nourished, they knew she could not produce good milk. Moreover, since nurses transmit diseases as well as passions to their little ones just as pregnant women do, these maladies have to be treated expeditiously. Of these, the one that was most frequently discussed in popular manuals and was really the most undesired outcome of breast-feeding was the transmission of syphilis from woman to child, and vice versa.

Pregnant women with syphilis were urged to be treated immediately in the hope that they would not infect their offspring. To complete the infants' cure, they were told that they absolutely must breast-feed.[99] But if the mother's breasts became too inflamed and ulcerated to permit nursing, she had to find a wet-nurse willing to take precautions or, barring that, use a docile, lactating goat or ewe. Manuals supplied recipes for medicating the quadrupedal nanny using water of liquorice root, barley flour, and mercuric oxide with honey added to mask the flavor of the metal so that the animal would drink it.[100] Youngsters who were already weaned were supposed to be bathed up to the neck in river water and mercuric oxide for half an hour at a time. They also were made to drink as much cold couch-grass water with liquorice root as they would, regardless of the season.[101] Because it was believed that syphilis also could be transmitted orally through the use of common drinking cups and even by merely sharing the same bed, authors gave the impression that it was a very common disease that was not considered as solely sexually transmitted as it is today, much as if it were like a variety of poison ivy that could be inherited as well as acquired. Certainly, it was discussed openly like any common ailment with natural causes for which there ought to be simple, natural, internal and external remedies.

The Physical Education of Children

In addition to all the ramifications of breast-feeding, mothers were instructed about the importance of bathing children from the moment of birth on as a primary aspect of what was termed "physical education." The principal belief that underlay advice of this kind was that children should not be pampered or else they would grow up to be delicate weaklings. Hence, gradually children were to be accustomed to hunger, cold, and fatigue. A newborn baby was supposed to be washed immediately either with soapsuds and salty, tepid water or with wine, beer, butter, or any alcoholic or other soapy substance in plain water. Afterward, its whole body should be rubbed dry with old cloths at room temperature.[102] Gradually, the morning bath water should be made cooler so that by about the fifth or sixth month, it is cold but not freezing. Hence, rain water and river water is about right, whereas spring water may need to be exposed to the sun for a few hours.[103] Most authors agreed that cold baths were especially good for the feet, and some went so far as to claim that they strengthened the knees and loins.[104] Millot, however, really got carried away with this therapeutic notion: "If the French government would require cold baths all the time, in twenty years the army would have vigorous soldiers—more vigorous than they are today."[105] Although such writers were sometimes insensitive to the child's feelings, they did realize that subjecting a six-month-old child to a cold bath in the early morning would be somewhat of a shock to its system and that inexperienced mothers might be hesitant. Duverne de Praile advised them fearlessly to plunge the baby headfirst into the cold water while singing gay songs to the little tot, thereby causing the child to associate baths with pleasure at an early age.[106] Gradually, too, baby boys and girls should be bathed in larger tubs, even wash tubs, so that they gradually learned to swim, an important skill to acquire regardless of wealth or social position.[107] Besides giving children complete baths, their feet and private parts should be washed two or three times a day. If this was just before going to bed and it was really cold, warmer water could be used.[108] The point writers tried to get across was that "our body, like our face, can endure the cold if we are accustomed to it."[109]

Another equally important facet of the physical education of children, the need for exercise, commenced at birth. Lack of exercise, it was believed, was partly responsible for the high mortality rate among foundlings in hospitals.[110] Mothers were told to give infants daily dry rubdowns until they were old enough for real exercise; and the best time for this was just after they awoke, while their stomachs were still empty.[111] Exercise was believed so important for the development of both body and mind that mothers were warned that their daughters would have convulsions if they did not see that they got enough exercise.[112] Child's play was considered significant and necessary for good health and was supposed to prevent melancholia and hypochondria[113] in addition to providing exercise. The physical activities begun at birth must continue throughout the years of formal schooling. "To correct the weakness of a portion of the French people, children ought to do calisthenics in schools as they do at Fontainebleau," was Millot's opinion, because "today many people are weak and cannot hold up when it is necessary." He also added that "fewer people would be sick and invalids" if physical education were mandatory.[114] Mothers, therefore, were advised that they had a special duty to strengthen their child's physique lest it be permanently retarded: "You will have warped its mind and it could never acquire any of the sciences."[115]

Because of the emphasis on exercise it is not surprising that all popular manuals took a strong stand against the use of *maillots,* swaddling clothes, which kept babies immobile. *L'Ami des Jeunes Femmes* claimed that during the preceding thirty years families had been reverting to the use of this "cruel"[116] device, which causes insomnia, raised shoulders, and misshapen legs and ankles.[117] Instead, they should be dressed loosely in a manner allowing all possible freedom for movement of their limbs. Baby clothes were nongendered. During the first three years they should only wear, in addition to diapers, a little sleeveless flannel vest loosely tied in the back and onto which a little petticoat could be sewn. A dress of the same or another fabric could be worn over this, provided that it was thin, supple, and very light weight. At night, a simple shirt that allowed the baby complete freedom of movement even while asleep was considered sufficient.[118] When babies are ready to walk, they should be allowed to pull themselves up from their play rug. In keeping with this strict advocacy of freedom of body movement, mothers were also told never to put their children on leashes, as nursemaids were sometimes seen doing.[119] Thus, popular writers offered women plenty of advice about child care, for both mental and physical well-being, much of which corresponded with Rousseau's emphasis on freedom and Nature but which also was somewhat altered in accordance with the Spartan psychology of the imperial military regime.

Beauty and Personal Hygiene

Although popular manuals focused a great deal on the child, they also were vehicles of information from which women, whether with families or childless, could learn how to take better care of themselves. The usual subjects found in women's magazines today—hair care, clothing, cosmetics, beauty, and sexuality—were treated so that women living in both urban areas and more remote regions could work at self-improvement and find solutions to the problem of keeping the men in their lives happy.

Beauty was a concept used to describe a woman's interior qualities as well as her exterior appearance[120] and reflected the holistic thinking so typical of the era. Beauty also was viewed as the exterior manifestation of good health, achieved by leading a moderate lifestyle, getting plenty of exercise, and breathing pure air.[121] Women were assured, however, that all men do not share the same ideal of beauty. That explains why, they said, some men are captivated by blondes while others go for brunettes or why some men like their women on the hefty side while others prefer them skinnier. But in any case, a beautiful body was no guarantee of the presence of a beautiful soul within. For this reason, no one should ever marry solely on the basis of looks.[122]

Being at eye level, the face was a focus of male attention, and discussions rival today's Ivory soap commercials. The best guarantee of a pretty face was vaccination against smallpox,[123] and mothers should see that their daughters received this attention. Avoiding venereal disease also promoted good looks. Most cosmetics were considered bad for the skin largely because they contained lead and mercury, which manuals warned are absorbed by it, thereafter causing cramps, spasms, and all sorts of nervous and pulmonary diseases.[124] So a fresh natural look achieved through the use of mild soap and water was considered most conducive to good health and beauty (although manuals were published containing cosmetic recipes).

Proper hair care also was deemed important. The old style of powdering hair was considered just as unhealthful as the use of cosmetics. Moreover, the contemporary unpowdered style saved a significant quantity of flour from being wasted and avoided the danger from breathing bad powder. The old coiffures piled high atop the head gave women migraine headaches, as having too much hair always does to the woman with a sensitive head. The hair itself is also affected by illness and exercise of the passions. Sickness causes it to hang limp and lifeless and to resist curling, while sadness, fear, love, and joy all affect the behavior of every strand of hair, too. Involvement in contention causes hair to fall out and eventually, if it continues, baldness.[125]

Besides natural-looking skin and short hair, the imperial ideal of beauty incorporated the notion of pearly, clean, evenly spaced teeth or dentures. The necessity of beautiful teeth was promoted by dentists who wrote manuals. One example entitled *Le Dentist des Dames* (1812), by Joseph Lemaire, quoted one of Voltaire's lesser-known sayings in order to appear authoritative:

> *Il a tout, il a l'art de plaire;*
> *Mais il n'a rien, s'il ne digère.*[126]

The central message Lemaire tried to convey to parents was that "people fail to attach enough importance to the thirty-two solid instruments, which form what is commonly called the *moulin de la vie*."[127]

Lemaire advised well-to-do mothers who wanted to optimize the dental health of their offspring how to do this.[128] Between the ages of six and twelve, the child's mouth should be inspected four times a year, and if it is too crowded,[129] some teeth should be extracted by an experienced dentist who knows which ones to remove: "A dentist should act like a wise gardener who prunes vegetables to make them better later on."[130] Any mother contemplating sending her daughters to a *pension* ought first to ask the headmistress whether she has a dentist visit the school twice monthly to examine all the girls' mouths.[131] If girls have beautiful teeth when they return to their families at the age of fifteen or sixteen, their appearance will make them more marriageable. "Beautiful teeth will triumph," for as Rousseau said, "There is no such thing as an ugly woman with beautiful teeth."[132] Lemaire claimed that at parties he had often witnessed men avoiding dancing with blue-eyed, rosy-cheeked women with gracious manners and naïve modesty but who, when they opened their mouths, had long, black, crooked teeth covered with tartar.[133] Moreover, women "who neglect their teeth fail to sense the dignity of being human because Man is the only animal that smiles and shows his teeth."[134] It thus became an obligation to brush every morning and to pass a feather toothpick between the teeth after meals. Once a week, young people should brush with a special powder that he prescribed; but eschew tobacco, because that "revolting" stuff permanently discolors the teeth; furthermore, never clean them with corrosive acids.[135]

Halitosis was of as much concern to Lemaire as the condition of the teeth themselves, especially for married women. He pointed out that "the most beautiful words in the world will sound bad coming from a foul-smelling mouth." He warned that uttering sweet nothings in a husband's ear "would fail to arouse voluptuous sensations" under such conditions. "If your husband whose body is pressed against yours does not make love to you," he opined, "the reason could be your halitosis."[136] During pregnancy, women were counseled to take especially good care of their teeth by brushing after each attack of morning sickness,[137] due to the acidic quality it gave their saliva. Given such opinions about beautiful teeth and sweet breath, with the opinions of Voltaire and Rousseau to support them, it is no wonder that some women became self-conscious about their teeth. For official portraits even the notoriously beautiful Empress Josephine, whose cavities precluded the enjoyment of sweets, hid her unsightly teeth behind the pussycat smile of her carefully pursed lips.

The aspect of women's clothing that received most attention in these manuals was not style per se but its healthfulness. It was explained that the psychology of dress was that the more women cover themselves up, the more pleasing they appear to the opposite sex. As one anonymous author phrased it, this fact is based upon the physical law that "all charm is lost in direct proportion to its usage," as the state of matrimony too often proved. By going almost naked, women attract the attention of men whose eyes are quickly worn out by the sight of so much of them. In addition to the risk of displeasing men in the long run, a woman endangers her health by exposing her shoulders and chest to chills. "If her breasts get chilled, she is in great danger because these are intimately connected with her womb and it too will become chilled." "Chilling causes puerperal fever," he noted, "the most terrible malady to which women are susceptible."[138] Such medical reasoning reinforced the religious point of view expressed elsewhere. *De l'Education Chrétienne des Jeunes Gens et des Jeunes Demoiselles* (1811) contained a story about a sixteen-year-old girl from Franche-Comté whose confessor told her to dress modestly and to avoid current fashion because it is evil to make the men who will look at you dressed that way to have dirty thoughts.[139] Thus, it ought to be taken into account by parents and dressmakers that costume influences the morals of society as well as the health of the wearer. Such modesty was compatible with the emperor's stylistic preference late in the empire, when he dictated that higher necklines should veil women's breasts, their symbols of sexual power.

Manuals of Household Management by Female Authors (or Country Living Made Easy)

Just as literate women could learn how to look beautiful, they could also acquire a wide variety of scientific and practical knowledge about running their homes and farms wisely from household management manuals of the day. The enterprising Mme Gacon-Dufour wrote the most important of these handy books while she was in her early fifties. Hers went through numerous editions. A longtime resident of Normandy, as a girl she had been educated in a *pension* operated by the Sisters of the Convent of Montfort-l'Amaury,[140] widowed, and remarried. During the Napoleonic era, she and

Mme Chauveau de la Miltière patented a kind of potato paste or flour, which they manufactured and distributed through fourteen retail shops.[141] Gacon-Dufour, a practical but educated woman, recommended that brides prepare for their future roles and for sharing their husbands' tastes by reading alternately such disparate pairs of books as a philosophical work by Montaigne and *La Maison Rustique,* Parmentier's *Pour la Culture des Pommes-de-terres* and Fénélon, Plutarque and *L'Art de la Manipulation du Pain,* Buffon and *L'Éducation des Bêtes à Laine,* or Newton's philosophy and *La Science d'une Bonne Fermière.* Reading these titles would prepare them to practice the art of housekeeping.[142]

Mme Gacon-Dufour believed that being able to read was of the utmost importance to the country woman. "A woman who does not know how to read," she lamented, "will treat her cow like her mother treated hers and will earn a meager profit from it." On the contrary, the woman who can read about how to care better for her cow will feed it properly, prevent it from becoming sick, and thereby draw more milk from it.[143] Moreover, a broadly educated woman would be equipped to comprehend why the archaic practice of bleeding cows in the springtime was dangerous for the animal's well-being or why, as a precaution against their becoming sick after eating hay all winter, it was prudent to feed cows bunches of chicory in order to stimulate their milk production with the change of season.[144] She also told her readers to milk cows thrice daily during the month of June to produce more milk. When selecting milkmaids, she advised caution. "Milkmaids must treat cows with the greatest gentility" because cows are temperamental and refuse to give their utmost to people whom they fear or detest. The udder should always be washed before milking begins. To ensure that proper milking procedures are being followed, the farm woman should assist at milking sometimes to show the milkmaids proper demeanor.[145] The cows also should be kept away from the grapes because eating them makes their milk sour and less creamy.[146]

The *Recueil Pratique d'Économie Rurale et Domestique* and the *Manuel de la Ménagère* also contained bits of wisdom regarding other livestock. For example, in spite of the saying "dirty as a pig," these are the cleanest animal and the tidy homemaker should be sure to keep her pigs clean. In winter, sows and boars could be fed by mixing boiled white potatoes and milk curds with the leftover dish water. To make piglets tasty after they are butchered, put salt in their diet.[147] Rabbits are considered economical because they cost nothing to feed and "one rabbit, two pounds of mutton, an old chicken and a pound of back-fat make a potluck stew for ten people; actually, the rabbit is no longer good to eat because the flavor boils out of it, but it makes excellent broth."[148] As for deciding which breed of sheep to purchase, she recommended French sheep since they were considerably cheaper and almost as good as Spanish ones.[149] The wise shepherdess would feed her flock more salt in July and August and shear them three times to separate the wool into three qualities.[150] Also, mating of sheep should be planned so that lambs would be born in June when there is more grass during the growing season, instead of January, as was then customary.[151]

With so much livestock, a household, and possibly children to manage, it was so critical for a woman to have the assistance of a good sheepdog that Mme Gacon-Dufour wrote an entire chapter explaining how women should train and care for their working dogs. Personal interest demanded that the animal never be beaten or mistreated in any way. Its doghouse should be cleaned, and if insects bothered the animal, it should be washed in lye water. Any summer ticks, of course, should be picked. Women should remember that "the dog is such a precious animal, so good, so lovable, that it is a kind of duty that one fulfills by tending to its needs. It is not the dog which is obligated, but the master; such good as he does his dog, could never equal the services that this good animal could render him." While caring for the guard dog demanded a good deal of attention from the farm woman, training it was described as a simple task: just take a puppy to the pasture with a full-grown dog and the puppy will follow its example. Soon it will be able to do the work of ten people.[152]

Meanwhile, back in the kitchen, the educated housewife could realize further savings. If resourceful, she fried leftover fricasseed chicken, made croquettes from yesterday's spinach, transformed scraps of beef, veal, leg of lamb, and fowl into hash, and made cauliflower au gratin to vary the menu. Unless women economized by such means, the cost of living would quintuple and they probably would face financial ruin, the manual warned.[153]

Other ways to be thrifty were to manufacture substitutes for products that had been made scarce or expensive by the interruption of France's maritime trade with the colonies, such as sugar, pepper, coffee, and tea. Mme Gacon-Dufour said that for years she had been cultivating and giving her friends seeds from M. de Choiseul-Goufflier's *pois-café* (*lotus tetragonolobus*, Lin; this is sometimes the "coffee bean tree"). Three or four spoonfuls of real coffee beans could be put in a pot of water with six or seven spoonfuls of these peas to produce a real coffee flavor superior to that of wild chicory.[154] She also had been trying to devise a means of solving the sugar shortage, which started when Bailly was mayor of Paris, and she painstakingly described her latest procedure for clarifying honey, a much quicker and easier method than the more involved ones devised by men.[155] Instead of buying ground pepper of questionable purity, she urged readers to use a long pepper or pimento in preparing ragout. Cloves for spicing up stew could be replaced by the use of a bunch of dried carnations or pinks from the garden. A refreshing tea could be prepared by using the leaves of a plant called *petite sauge* (sage), which were most flavorful if grown in full sunlight.[156] All of these were ways to "prevent gastronomical pillage" by being frugal.[157]

Besides these helpful cooking hints, Mme Gacon-Dufour also incorporated physiocratic ideas into her manuals to the extent that she encouraged women to introduce beneficial new crops to enrich the soil and thereby enrich the nation, whose wealth depended upon its farmers.[158] She argued against large farming operations, which ran counter to the general interest, and advised enterprising women not to rent adjacent land. Instead, she advised them to practice intensive cultivation in order to alleviate the poverty that existed in rural areas as well as in big cities.[159] Poor country children who went to town to beg once a week should be hired instead for such simple tasks as cutting wood and picking up sticks, lest they grow up to become lazy vagabonds.[160] As timber is cut, enlightened people reforest the land for the benefit of future generations. Trees planted around a field would stop soil erosion and hold irrigation ditches firmly after heavy rains. Trees could also be planted in boggy areas that otherwise would be wasted.[161] Exactly which type to plant should be decided according to soil conditions and the terrain; however, "the public interest is that oak is preferable to all other woods." Concomitantly, "dark woods ought to be encouraged in areas where there are forges and tile-works, because they produce much charcoal. . . ."[162] Reforestation could be easily achieved without "manpower," literally—by employing a group of about thirty women and children coordinating their efforts—because brute strength is unnecessary for planting seedlings.[163]

Mme Gacon-Dufour rounded out all of these instructions about how to be a good steward of Nature's bounty by supplying monthly schedules of all the chores that women should perform relating to growing crops, raising animals, and cultivating useful and ornamental flowers. She also gave detailed instructions for making soap—something quite logical in light of her great insistence on cleanliness in every aspect of homemaking, from bathing the pig and the dog to child care: "It [cleanliness] is a sacred trust confided to us."[164] Thus, such manuals certainly conveyed the idea that women were supposed to take pride in systematically keeping clean and being industrious year-round. Ignorance of how special tasks should be performed could not be an excuse for idleness when detailed instructions were available from older women who had extensive experience in all phases of home economics and who seemed to be fascinated by the opportunity that professional housekeeping afforded women for the achievement of personal satisfaction.

. . .

Male humanistic authors of manuals of home economics and sex express the belief that female identity was defined by Nature and limited by sexuality. The female breast was considered to be the locus of morality, and emotions strongly affected women's health. Yet much about woman's nature, like that of the universe, remained mysterious and beyond the comprehension of thinking individuals. The bourgeois value of hard work that was inculcated was tempered with emphasis on the need for love, beauty, and both physical and intellectual satisfaction in women's lives. Ethical considerations regarding politically motivated theories of human engineering and racism, ways of improving Nature that had the potential to make women virtually into super "baby-making machines" that turned out clones for the nation went unnoticed. Belief in human improvement and perfectibility was widespread. The belief in progress and behaviorism was extended to include women among the things that could be made better through proper instruction (obedience, on her part). Overall, the view of female nature that is assumed by humanistic writers is that from a rational point of view, women are neither weaklings nor useless creatures but the superior sex. As the women who wrote housekeeping manuals observed, nurturing women contribute more to society than the mere masculine sex with only testicles—the sex that is even unnecessary to the efficient operation of a farm or to achieve reforestation of natural resources. After all, an educated woman plus a well-trained dog could do the work of ten men. So the wealth of the nation did not depend upon brute strength and brains; it depended upon creative, informed, energetic female subjects who were aware of ecology and zealously trained in domesticity, woman's traditional occupation.

That abiding perception that there must be an inescapable controlling relationship between the sex organs of women's bodies over their minds was present less in the humanistic manuals penned by both sexes than it was in those prepared solely by the women who operated boarding schools for girls or in sexist remarks that can be traced back to the emperor personally. In any case, in the medical politics of the age of Napoleon, the discourse of humanistically trained philosophical-anthropological authors marked them as the liberals in the debate regarding women's autonomy and right to self-creation.

If we situate this chapter within the context of feminist history and the quarrels of the literary world, we can see that these authors extended the discourse of the contemporary "war of the sexes," which was being waged via printing presses (especially Parisian ones), to rural areas—the geographical location where three-fourths of French women actually lived.

4

The First National System of
Midwifery Education

I T WAS CLAIMED during the Napoleonic era that midwifery, first mentioned in the Bible in 1725 B.C., when Rachel had been assisted by a midwife,[1] was raised to the level of a science between the years A.D. 1700 and 1800. This notion is supported by the history of obstetrics, which indicates that the establishment of individual midwifery schools was already quite a popular idea in many European states during the Enlightenment.

Among the earliest eighteenth-century rulers to order the establishment of a practical midwifery school was Empress Maria-Theresa of Austria, who reserved a Viennese hospital for indigent pregnant women as a training center. In the early 1760s institutes for training midwives and obstetricians also opened at Copenhagen and Cassel. In 1775 practical schools were established at Moscow, Dresden, and Fulda and two years later at Magdeburg. The year 1779 dated the beginning of childbirth instruction at Jena where four years later Professor Johann Christian Starke performed a cesarean section that was successful from the standpoint of both mother and child. Eventually, the Habsburg Emperor Joseph II, noted for his particular *bienfaisance,* reunited his mother's lying-in hospital at Vienna with the large hospital of that city where, beginning in 1784, midwives, doctors, and surgeons studied childbirth together. To assist the study of obstetrics (as well as other fields), he commissioned in Florence, Italy, the creation of beautifully colored and realistic-looking wax anatomical models for the *Josephinum.*[2] Seventeen eighty-nine was the year that Pope Pius VI founded his midwifery school at Rome. Finally, in 1797, the Russian Empress Maria Federovna established a special hospital at St. Petersburg for pregnant women and lying-in that also trained midwifery pupils. The midwifery school that was incorporated into the University of Heidelberg as an institute under the direction of the Faculty of Medicine in 1805 had previously existed in the locality of Mannheim near Karlsruhe in the late eighteenth century. Thus across the European continent, enlightened governments— of large and small political entities—made midwifery education practical in

one or more major cities of the realm by coupling training with public assistance for needy women and their infants.

But nowhere was there a rational, comprehensive midwifery educational
system whose design was grand enough to meet the actual needs of all
classes of the entire rural and urban population of an entire country.

For various reasons some women needed assistance during natural childbirth; and, if there was no knowledgeable person available to provide it, a
whole host of dreadful scenarios might result, the worst being the death of
both mother and fetus. The belief was widespread on the national level that
such personal tragedy, when compounded thousands of times over, resulted
in diminished population. Humanistic philosophy, as well as the economic,
political, and military self-interest of Enlightened rulers, made it imperative
to take steps to ameliorate the perceived, needless loss of souls. Indeed, an
important group of philosophers—the so-called populationists—challenged the mercantilists' emphasis on trade. These natalists claimed instead
that the wealth of a nation depended on the size and character of its population. Of course, by the time of the First Empire, the population of France
was beginning to expand quite rapidly; the *perception* of diminishing population nevertheless persisted.

Madame du Coudray

In France, the self-proclaimed heroine of late-eighteenth-century populationists was an amazing woman, Angelique Marguerite Le Boursier du
Coudray (1714 or 1715–1794), a charismatic spinster who labored for four
decades (from the 1750s through the 1780s) to fill the midwifery educational
vacuum in the provinces. Because none of her introspective personal papers
seem to exist, little was known about this interesting and very public
woman until the publication in 1998 of Nina Rattner Gelbart's brilliant and
aptly titled biography, *The King's Midwife: A History and Mystery of Madame
du Coudray.*[3] According to Gelbart, initially du Coudray solicited and
obtained the patronage of Louis XV through three royal brevets to finance
her itinerant pedagogical journeys to any locale that would sponsor the
offering of her courses. Intendants or parish priests worked as advance men,
recruiting larger numbers of young, inexperienced women volunteers as
students, as well as representative male surgeons. These courses usually
lasted from six weeks to two months.

Because her outreach was aimed primarily at ignorant women who could
not read, Mme du Coudray supplemented the successive editions of her own
highly (sometimes color) illustrated manuals with demonstrations on cloth
obstetrical manikins of her own design. Her *"femme artificielle"* represented
the female anatomy only from the torso to the knees, which she used along

with an artificial fetus to teach pupils individual maneuvers to turn or to extract breech infants from the womb. Du Coudray was flagrantly entrepreneurial about selling these "machines" to the royal intendants in order to assure the permanence of her training in the art of midwifery for their provinces as well as for raising the cash required for her itinerant practice.

The use of obstetrical manikins was not unique. Because of the shortage of cadavers and the difficulties involved in using them (especially in summertime) in the seventeenth and eighteenth centuries, both male and female French and Italian anatomists began to make amazingly lifelike wax figures, which were used for teaching. In the 1750s an apothecary's daughter, Marie-Catherine Bihéron (born 1719), who learned the art of illustration not by formally attending an academy or university, but by studying with an older woman, Mlle Madeleine Basseporte, created a famous anatomical collection.

As her fame spread, Mlle Bihéron was invited to lecture before the French Royal Academy of Sciences in 1759. The secret to her success was that she obtained cadavers from intermediaries who usually stole them from the military, and she kept them in a glass case in her garden, which enabled her to carefully study every detail of the human body. Mlle Bihéron had begun to innovate by making models from secret but more permanent materials than wax and clay. It was said that her models were so lifelike that they lacked nothing but the smell. She also made fine obstetrical models, which were ideal for teaching midwifery and gynecology, and which she advertised for sale from her Paris apartment. Of Anglo-French extraction, Mlle Bihéron taught anatomy to John Hunter, the Scottish doctor who raised surgery to the level of a branch of science in eighteenth-century London. In 1770 she demonstrated her obstetrical manikin of a pregnant woman, which included a removable coccyx, a dilating cervix, and removable fetuses, to the French Royal Academy of Sciences. In 1771 she had the honor, along with the chemist Lavoisier, of lecturing a third time before the Academy of Sciences when the Crown Prince of Sweden visited. Eventually Mlle Bihéron became famous enough to sell a complete set of anatomical models to Empress Catherine II of Russia. However, despite her superior talent, without a government pension, patronage, or a teaching chair, it was difficult for Mlle Bihéron to earn a living in Paris because she competed for anatomy students with the doctors and surgeons of Paris, who zealously guarded their teaching monopoly. In addition to teaching classes at her home, another way Bihéron earned income was to charge an admission fee to the curiosity-seekers who came to her apartment on Wednesdays to view her collection.[4]

A second Parisian woman, a Mme Lenfant, was also part of the competition Mme du Coudray faced at this time in the Paris market. Instead of the wax or waxlike models Mlle Bihéron manufactured, Lenfant's obstetrical models were crafted from leather.

But Mme du Coudray was not going to be outdone by the competition. She very shrewdly took great pains to make hers the most lifelike obstetrical manikin available through the addition of sponges or sacks filled with clear and red fluids (representing amniotic fluid and blood, respectively). Also, her later models incorporated actual human pelvic skeletal remains as structure for the stuffing, along with covering that represented the various parts of female anatomy involved in parturition. Her intention that one of her most expensive, silk models be kept in the provincial archives of principal cities was forward looking. As successive classes of midwives in training quickly wore out the cheaply made models, the surgeon-demonstrators whom she had trained to carry on her mission could refer to them when they made the necessary repairs to their own.

Du Coudray's talent for teaching, her midwifery textbooks that rivaled those of male authors, and her ultrarealistic manikins, coupled with her tenacity in the face of growing hostility among male accoucheurs, all contributed to her growing popularity, which continued under the reign of Louis XVI. But another aspect of her success was her ability and willingness to accommodate herself to contemporary ideology that indicated the contemporary position of women in rural society. For example, in 1780, when Louis XVI and his ministers requested the then sixty-five-year-old du Coudray to give lessons at the Royal Veterinary School at Alfort near Charenton, she accepted the charge. This meant that she helped male veterinarians transfer and apply their knowledge from the birthing of large animals, such as cows and sheep, to human mothers through her demonstrations on realistic midwifery manikins. After all, it was common knowledge that even ignorant shepherds knew from experience how to extract the legs of quadrupeds from their mothers' wombs. Given the government's mind-set, the slight distinction between female livestock and farmers' wives in labor could easily be bridged by presenting a few lessons to veterinary students who were destined to become trusted individuals in the countryside. And if she had refused, one of her competitors among the male accoucheurs might have taken the job in order to curry the king's favor. The award of a stipend along with a retirement pension by both kings Louis XV and Louis XVI obliged Mme du Coudray to save babies any way she could.

But by the time of the Revolution of 1789, Mme du Coudray's two heirs—her teaching assistant, the young surgeon Jean-Pierre Coutanceau (died 1805) and his wife Marguerite Guillaumanche du Coudray Coutanceau (died 1825), who prior to her marriage had also styled herself

"Mademoiselle de Vannes"[5]—both had realized that while the use of manikins served a purpose, it was no substitute for practicing childbirth on live women in labor. Too many pupils trained the old way simply panicked and fled when they were suddenly faced with the drama of life-threatening situations. Consequently, the Coutanceaux, who were recognized by Louis XVI's brevet, strove to supersede Mme du Coudray's stellar but itinerant approach with the establishment of a permanent lying-in clinic at Bordeaux, where pupils could perfect their skills initially learned on manikins by actually practicing on poor mothers. Mme Coutanceau also published a far less expensive midwifery manual than her aunt's earlier, lavishly illustrated ones so that more people could afford to own a personal copy. It is also noteworthy that the younger woman defended a more feminist position regarding women's natural superiority over male physicians and surgeons in the practice of midwifery by claiming that only by having other women attending her during childbirth could a mother safeguard her modesty, a characteristic of femininity that would be greatly emphasized during the First Empire. Thus the bolder Mme Coutanceau was ready to compete against "midwives-in-trousers" in her own little "war of the sexes." Eventually, the Coutanceaux's son had the good fortune to become the brother-in-law of the era's foremost military surgeon, Baron Dominque Larrey; so through marriage, the Coutanceaux gained an entrée for their ideas about midwifery education to reach the social circle of doctors whom Napoleon relied upon to fill his important positions in the military and civil administration.

As an indication of the government's abiding interest in the increasingly controversial midwifery issue, in 1786, in cooperation with the Royal Society of Medicine, M. de Calonne circulated a questionnaire among the intendants to gather data in their provinces on local practicing midwives, a circular that would later serve as a model for Napoleon's minister of the interior and prefects. Yet the public call for more and better midwifery education that appeared in the *cahiers de doléances* in preparation for the meeting of the Estates General of 1789 suggested that the public expected more social assistance to come from the Old Regime as it was becoming financially deadlocked on the eve of the Revolution.

As an emissary of the monarchy for over a quarter century Mme du Coudray reached possibly four thousand younger peasant women who wanted to become better-trained midwives than the older generation of largely ignorant female practitioners. In the process of building her business, Elizabeth Goldsmith and Dena Goodman have observed, "She used publicity to construct a life outside the bounds of marriage and family, but in so doing, like other women before her, she found herself uneasy in the glare of publicity."[6] Advancing age and politics finally led to du Coudray's retirement in the early days of the Revolution. Ironically, General Lafayette's popularity was at its height circa 1789–1791, an era historians go so far as to call "the Years of Lafayette." However, in the rush of events, Parisian politicians failed to recognize the importance of continuing the work begun by the controversial midwife who had first made herself famous by delivering the future Marquis de Lafayette at Chauvaniac in 1757. Moreover, Mme du Coudray and her niece were unable to collect their salaries and pensions, which were then in arrears. Consequently, du Coudray's own success in the capital as well as in the provinces where she pioneered as a midwifery teacher was ephemeral. Sadly, the dedicated woman's fame quickly vanished along with the monarchy; and, as Gelbart maintains, her origin and much else about Mme du Coudray still remain a mystery.

La Maternité of Paris, an Enduring National Institution

France had a long tradition of maternity care for poor urban women, and La Maternité, the hospital that was to become the national school of midwifery under Napoleon, traced its origins back to the maternity service at the Hôtel Dieu in fourteenth-century Paris. In spite of the fact that the Hôtel Dieu had been made infamous by great puerperal fever ("childbed fever") epidemics in the seventeenth and eighteenth centuries, a midwifery school was established there in 1787. However, while the Hôtel Dieu had formal regulations for training midwifery pupils, its program always remained inadequate because there were never more than eight pupils enrolled at one time and instruction was poor.[7] This hospital-based midwifery school in Paris was merely analogous but inferior to those of other enlightened monarchies.

Napoleon's administrators were aware that among the *cahiers de doléances,* prepared for the Estates General of 1789, there had been complaints about the frightful mortality rate during childbirth and demands for comprehensive instruction for midwives, although no grand design was offered.[8] After the end of the Old Regime and in response to public demand, the National Convention decreed on 25 Messidor, year III (July 13, 1795) the creation of a separate successor maternity hospital at Val-de Grâce, a former Benedictine community in the Saint-Jacques quarter on the southern edge of Paris that was located adjacent to the Baroque chapel, which had been donated in the seventeenth century by Queen Anne of Austria, mother of Louis XIV, as a thank-you gift to God for granting the conception and birth of her much-desired son. (This historic series of buildings currently serves as a military hospital, medical library, and archives.) When the maternity hospital was later moved from Val-de-Grâce nearby to the former Oratory and Port-

The frontispiece of Mme Boivin's volume of notes taken from Mme Lachapelle's repetitions of midwifery lessons at La Maternité shows the newly constructed neoclassical east facade facing the garden. From Marie-Anne Boivin, *Mémorial de l'Art des Accouchemens . . . Dédié à Mme LaChapelle.*

Royal monastic buildings on rue de la Bourbe and (ironically) rue d'Enfer, the pregnant patients and teachers moved there together so that care and instruction could continue without interruption. Still, the hospital was not really a normal school but a refuge for indigent women who were in their last month of pregnancy and for starving foundlings or orphans who needed wet-nursing.

The official credit for transforming the childbirth section of the Port-Royal Hospital into the Ecole de la Maternité is given to Napoleon's minister of the interior from 1800 to 1804, the distinguished chemist and administrative genius, Jean-Antoine Chaptal (1756–1832), who in conjunction with Prefect of the Seine Frochot and the Administrative Council of Hospitals, reorganized the school on 11 Messidor, year X (June 30, 1802). Before the revamping there had been only four apprentices and a midwife-in-chief;[9] but the next year fifty-four pupils were recruited from twenty-one departments.[10] By 1813 that figure had climbed to a total of 194 enrollees[11] with 161 candidates for diplomas.[12] After graduation, most of the women returned to their native localities to practice and to teach local midwifery courses, as the government intended.[13]

For the duration of the empire, in addition to formally preparing a significantly larger number of midwives and serving as a central normal school of midwifery that offered model courses,[14] Napoleon's La Maternité also had three other purposes. Two purposes were highly publicized: to conduct scientific research in order to diminish the number of mothers who died from puerperal fever and to reduce the frightful mortality rate of foundlings.[15] However, a third important, but evidently sensitive, kind of research was kept quiet. Only after the fall of Napoleon were details about the rather abhorrent but necessary empirical and statistical experiments disclosed. Imperial researchers actually dropped fetal corpses and stillborn infants' remains, under controlled conditions, then performed autopsies to examine how their skulls and other bones cracked in each situation. Gradually, patterns emerged according to how high, onto what kind of a surface, and with what amount of force the infant was dropped or thrown. The statistical and empirical evidence gathered from the autopsies of the tiny victims could then be compared with the story of the accused about how an infant had been accidently injured during unassisted or sudden onset of labor. In any case, the research angle was taken most seriously as they tried to transform forensics into a modern science.

In contrast to other enlightened despots, Napoleon clearly envisioned a vast midwifery system with an orderly and centralized administration. The midwifery educational system he devised also was multitiered so that it radiated out from the capital to reach even the most remote areas of the expanding empire. To complement the Parisian teaching hospital a network of midwifery schools was conceived with one situated in the principal city of every department. (Of course, for choosing this approach he would be subject to the criticism that by giving each *département* equal treatment, more populous areas would still face a shortage of midwives via this national system.) Furthermore, an attempt to control and to determine the number and qualifications of practicing midwives was made when all health personnel were legally required to register under the law of 19 Ventôse, year XI (March 10, 1803). Certificates were issued to those (then mostly senior women and widows) who had been registered under the Old Regime, examined by a medical jury, approved by obstetricians or master midwives, or graduated from recognized schools such as La Maternité at Paris, Montpellier, or Turin. This system made it illegal for those presumably unqualified midwives who refused to register properly to practice their art, since they were circumventing the government's quality-control mechanism.[16]

To survey local conditions concerning the difficulty and magnitude of the task ahead, Champagny, as Minister of the Interior, initiated a circular addressed to all prefects, dated 18 Vendémiaire, year XIV (October 10, 1805), which consisted of twelve questions about what hospices or hospitals in the departments were used most frequently for lying-in, whether separate delivery rooms existed therein, how many births occurred annually, whether there was a staff surgeon knowledgeable in obstetrics and a midwife to assist him, and how much all expenses would be for operating a midwifery school in that locale. In response to this request the various prefects returned their questionnaires; and where courses were nonexistent the more zealous prefects devised impressive elaborate and highly detailed proposals. The prefects then received permission to proceed with the procurement of nightgowns, chamber pots of modest quality in keeping with the users' common social position,[17] surgical instruments, and textbooks at prices specified down to the last centime. Once courses were under way, the prefects provided Paris with progress reports and financial statements.[18] In later years, as the empire expanded into non-French areas such as Tuscany, Florence, Geneva, and the Netherlands, either new training schools were established in these regions or preexisting ones were encouraged by the imperial government to continue their traditional work.[19]

With very few exceptions, the prefects strongly advocated the establishment of departmental midwifery schools. Obstacles to their creation were that in the most sparsely populated regions, insufficient numbers of unwed or indigent mothers gave birth with public assistance to provide enough practical training for pupils, that no teachers were available, that no health facility existed where a course could be offered, or that local resources were

Oil portrait of Jean-Antoine Chaptal, Napoleon's Minister of the Interior from November 6, 1800, to August 6, 1804. As a physician and chemist, he advanced technical training, industry, and agriculture. The portrait is by Antoine-Jean Gros, who was J.-L. David's favorite pupil. Antoine-Jean Gros, French, 1771–1835. *Count Jean-Antoine Chaptal,* 1824. Oil on canvas, 136.5 × 114.3 cm. © The Cleveland Museum of Art, Leonard C. Hanna, Jr. Fund, 1964.54.

lacking to finance such a project. Frequently, the prefect's plea for support of a localized training system was stated dramatically: "[A]s many women and babies perish each year as are killed by the most terrible war because of the ignorance and immorality of midwives," thereby resulting in a pattern of "routine murder" through malpractice; hence schools should be opened for the "good of humanity" as a great act of "*bienfaisance* [Christian charity]."[20] That these pleas were sincere and the need for educated midwives real is attested by the fact that some professors, who had been offering instruction before Napoleon's effort to systematize the chaotic public assistance services had gotten under way, had taught successive courses to midwives although government officials had been unable to pay their salaries.[21] There were seven areas where the prefects felt that formal training for rural midwives was so crucial to saving lives that they actually paid agricultural families money for the missing pair of hands for each day the young woman was in school.[22] Additionally, the health-care crisis worsened during wartime when the *officiers de santé* were conscripted, resulting in the loss of their skills to the residents of their native departments.[23]

Reasons the prefects put forth in support of the establishment of departmental midwifery schools emphasized greater economy,[24] as well as the great distance and reluctance of most rural married pupils to travel to Paris for a stay of one or two years away from their families.[25] But the limited linguistic ability of likely candidates seemed to be the most insurmountable obstacle. In some areas, in Corsica for example, midwifery was a poorly rewarded or even unpaid occupation;[26] and while some of these women might be induced to attend a local school, there was certainly no way to make them learn a language that they regarded as foreign to qualify them for admittance to La Maternité.

Besides the obvious linguistic problems with Dutch, German, and Italian midwives,[27] there was difficulty even within the historic borders of modern France where Breton or patois dialects were used entirely by the class of women who were interested in this vocation and by the pregnant women upon whom they would practice at a hospital of charity.[28] Grégoire Sicard, the foremost teacher of deaf-mutes, was especially concerned about the need for regional midwifery instruction in the south of France, expressly in the former provinces of Languedoc, Rousillon, Guyenne, Gascony, and the Basque area where, he believed, thousands of babies needlessly died at birth.[29]

The recruiting posters for midwives that were printed and displayed by the prefects were suitably bilingual.[30] In time this difficulty occasionally manifested itself in the actual courses that were established so that while lectures and demonstrations were presented in French by the professor, the

midwife who served as his teaching assistant led the repetitions of midwifery lessons, which were really recitations of the midwifery catechism, in
the local dialect.[31] Furthermore, if the Minister of the Interior allowed the
teaching of courses in a language other than French, the officially required
textbooks then needed to be translated too.[32] Using such accommodating
tactics, departmental schools were more easily able to recruit the peasant
women who so desperately needed to be recruited to keep France from
becoming underpopulated.

As an indication of the importance the emperor placed on midwifery
education, regulations for the departmental midwifery schools were personally drafted by the Minister of the Interior on 27 Nivose, year XV (January
17, 1807)[33]—the day after Napoleon had dispatched from Warsaw a letter to
the Grand Chancellor of the Légion of Honor concerning the provisional
organization of the training school at Ecouen (directed by Mme Campan)
and similar institutions for educating daughters of veterans.[34] The new regulations that ordered the midwifery schools were sent to the prefects in February 1807.[35] Thus, by 1808, parallel to but outside of the functioning of the
Imperial University, the organization of midwifery education at public hospitals was operative and many problems were being worked out with the
benefit of experience. Recruitment efforts became successful enough that
enrollment at La Maternité, the Parisian normal school of midwifery,
became selective between 1808 and 1813.[36] The younger women graduating
at Paris each year were returning home to serve as the certified teachers of
midwifery in the local hospital/training schools—the purpose for which the
prefects had recruited them and financed their education. Because the new
local teachers had been prepared in the rigorous Paris program and could
recite the textbooks verbatim, the prescribed midwifery curriculum, theoretically at least, could easily be made uniform everywhere. It incorporated
four distinct elements: (1) theory and practice of accouchement, (2) vaccination, (3) phlebotomy, and (4) the study of medicinal plants.

A detailed description of the actual setting at La Maternité in which the
midwifery pupils typically were to learn their art was contained in the
Mémoire Historique et Instructif sur l'Hospice de la Maternité prepared in
1808 by the civil hospital administrators Hucherard, Sausseret, and
Girault[37] and an official report for the Conseil General des Hospices prepared by one of its members, the politician and lawyer Claude-Emmanuel
Pastoret.[38] Interestingly, the *Mémoire* was prepared, in part, to inform foreign sovereigns who wanted to create similar institutions in their realms
about the Napoleonic achievement.[39] As described by these officials, in the
childbirth section of La Maternité, up to about 130 pregnant women at a
time occupied separate, curtained beds in alcoves in clean, ventilated wards

containing from ten to thirty beds each. Beside each bed was a cradle to receive the newborn child. The daily routine began at 7:00 or 8:00 a.m. according to the season. Upon arising, the patients dressed, made their beds on which the sheets were changed every month, and straightened up the room before a bell summoned them to the workshop, where they remained until 11:30 a.m., making clothes for their babies, foundlings, and indigents. From 11:30 until 3:00 in the afternoon they dined on soup, boiled meat, and vegetables and afterward walked or (in winter) warmed themselves in the ward. The 3:00 bell called them back to work again until 6:00 p.m., when it was soup time. The wages the women received for this work were forfeited whenever they violated the strict rules of conduct.[40] The patients observed silence in the refectory and took turns clearing the tables and washing dishes.[41] The matrons watching over this orderly workhouse wore black woolen dresses, ornamented at the throat with a silver medallion of Saint Vincent de Paul, and white linen bonnets over their hair.[42] In the course of an average year, 1,800 to 1,900 births occurred, perhaps five per day, thereby making the practical portion of the curriculum feasible.

The midwifery pupils were instructed by a midwife-in-chief and a male professor. The head midwife gave three lessons daily, each lasting two hours, whereas the professor lectured twice weekly on the theory of childbirth. In addition, the chief midwife developed the professor's lessons in her *conférences*, putting his words into her own in order to make them more meaningful to the less-educated, lower-class trainees. The pupils were divided into attending or service groups and each of these groups, in turn, assisted whatever women were in labor, while the midwife-in-chief supervised. Whenever a difficult delivery occurred, the head midwife called together the most advanced pupils and made a decision as to which one of them would perform the delivery. If the case became extremely difficult, the mistress took over herself while the students observed her procedure. Whenever forceps were advised, and this rarely happened, the professor was called, unless speed was critical; for example, an infant whose umbilical cord was misplaced around the head, or perhaps a patient was convulsing or hemorrhaging. Then to save a life or lives, the head midwife hastily proceeded to apply the forceps herself.[43]

Part of the midwifery pupil's formal training involved more than just observation and memory. She had to write a report on the remarkable details of each delivery she performed, which was given to the professor after the head midwife had corrected it. After delivering a woman in labor, each pupil followed her progress for several days, filing daily reports on her condition. Care of newborns, especially treatment of infants resulting from long and difficult labor, was also taught to every pupil at La Maternité.[44] In this way patients benefitted from continuous and knowledgeable care while hospital personnel routinely kept good medical records on the progress of their charges. (And the statistical part of the records could also be used later for research projects.)

The adoption of three official textbooks and a five-piece instrument kit[45] for use by all national midwifery students further promoted the creation of uniformity between the curriculum of the capital and the departmental schools scattered across the empire. That the required books and instruments for departmental students who studied locally and for those designated to travel to Paris to attend La Maternité were actually purchased by the prefects becomes clear from an examination of their financial records. The three texts, which together cost thirty-one francs and seventy-five centimes, were the two-volume *L'Art des Accouchemens* and the shorter *Principes sur l'Art des Accouchemens, par Demandes et Réponses, en Faveur des Élèves Sages-Femmes,* both by the premier obstetrical surgeon Jean-Louis Baudelocque; and *Mémorial de l'Art des Accouchemens* by Mme Marie Gillain Boivin. These three complementary works are a testament to imperial midwifery teaching. Baudelocque's catechism was abstracted from his longer work to facilitate memorization by his pupils.[46] Boivin composed her *Mémorial* from the notes that she herself made as a student at La Maternité and from her observations of further lessons as she continued to work there as a teacher and administrative surveyor for many years.[47] Essentially, what these official textbooks contained were illustrated lessons on the ways infants presented themselves for delivery, and when labor did not operate naturally, how the midwife was supposed to solve the mechanical problem of passing a body of known dimensions through an opening of known dimensions. This mechanized conceptualization of the process of birth was in keeping with Napoleon's own perception of women as "machines for making babies."[48]

A notable aspect of imperial midwifery teaching methods, in addition to the more obvious ones, was the use of leather-covered manikins with moveable parts. The "abdomen" of the pregnant manikin opened to reveal the position of a replica of a fetus or, as in the case of twins, two fetuses. The various prefects had the Minister of the Interior approve their orders for this kind of amphitheater equipment.[49] Such devices permitted demonstrations and practice without encountering risk to human subjects. The use of manikins obviated or at least supplemented the practice formerly accepted in Paris of demonstrating on the cadavers of pregnant women that sometimes were submerged in water, although infrequent references to continuing use of cadavers do occur in medical books of the period.

No wonder graduates took great pride in their ability to complete this vigorous, modern training program. For example, in 1810, Anne Victoire Gillain proudly added to the signature of a letter she wrote to the editor of the Parisian medical journal, the *Gazette de Santé*, "*Maîtresse sage-femme de Paris, et s'honorante du titre de élève de l'hospice de la Maternité.*" She wrote to take the journal to task for not giving more credit to the late surgeon/accoucheur Professor Baudelocque for his contributions to the success of La Maternité, as well as to protest against the editor's practice of omitting the full official title of midwifery graduates who had received diplomas from La Maternité. Although the editor did not seem to appreciate Gillain's criticism entirely (he put her in her place by calling her a "generous Amazon"),[50] he nonetheless proceeded to defend midwives and bash surgeons in the present three-way rivalry over turf, which he thought was ensuing between physicians, surgeons, and midwives.

The editor also volunteered his opinions at length about why only females ought to be permitted to perform midwifery. His seven reasons for excluding male surgeons from accouchement are an example of overkill. (1) The practice of midwifery by females originated in antiquity among all civilized peoples and we should emulate our great predecessors. (2) The process of delivering babies in the presence of men violated women's modesty and chastity. (3) It posed a health risk as well for the woman when a male stranger had physical contact with her body. (The editor then complained about the chain of events so characteristic of the long-standing rivalry between physicians and surgeons.) (4) Some men became surgeons by default because their intelligence was inadequate for them to succeed as physicians. But once they became surgeons and had assisted a woman's labor, they arrogantly began treating her for gynecological problems that ought to be treated only by a fully qualified physician. (5) Long-suffering women with their superior patience, humanity, and greater religiosity have greater aptitude for mastering the theory and practice of midwifery, coupled with a natural ability to relate intimately with other women in a manner that is impossible for any male to do. Then the editor brought accoucheurs into the controversy. (6) Accoucheurs are not just ignorant about medicine. Initially, they failed to master that field before they went into surgery, but having failed a second time at general surgery, their fallback becomes accouchement and requires still more limited skills. (7) Male surgeons who operated on all sorts of patients risked carrying contagion from their other cases to women lying-in who are highly susceptible to absorbing illnesses from the least contact.

The *Gazette de Santé* went on to elaborate that the changing of clothes or use of lotions are not effective prophylactics. Since the vocation of midwives is childbirth exclusively, they carry no such risk of spreading miasmas and fevers from infected patients they attended previously. While the ideas summarily presented in the *Gazette de Santé* vehemently championed physicians over surgeons, it also argued strongly for the rights of these well-trained women to exercise a monopoly over childbirth when it accused surgeons of killing pregnant women by spreading contagion to maternity wards through their mere appearance in that female domain.[51]

Famous Midwifery Faculty during the First Empire

Although those who practiced obstetrics and midwifery usually were obscure persons whose glory did not match that of imperial generals, the leading teachers in Paris whose pedagogy radiated down through this national system from the capital to the countryside earned sizeable reputations and incomes. The outstanding male professors were Jean-Louis Baudelocque (1746–1810), whose textbook and catechism for midwives have already been mentioned, Antoine Dubois (1756–1837), and François Chaussier (1746–1828).

J.-L Baudelocque, a native of Picardy, was the most famous pupil of Solayres de Renhac of Montpellier (1737–1772). He also studied in Paris under famous midwives at the Hôtel Dieu and the Collège de France. Baudelocque had made his mark as one of the chief surgeons at the Hôtel Dieu and for his manual, *Principes de l'Art par Réponses, en Faveur des Elèves Sages-Femmes,* first published in 1775, of which the government purchased six thousand copies as guidance for midwives. His longer work on the art of accouchement of 1781 was reprinted in 1789, 1796, 1807, 1815, and 1822, which is some indication of his lasting reputation and importance. Although he was a noted surgeon and author, he also seemed to enjoy teaching women. After he was named surgeon-professor-in-chief at La Maternité, he personally quizzed midwifery pupils every day as he made his rounds of the wards in this charity hospital.

Yet Baudelocque's reputation was Europe-wide, and his clientele included such notable women as Mme Fouquier-Tinville under the Terror (her husband was a public prosecutor of that bloody era) and under the expanding empire of Napoleon I, the queens of the satellite kingdoms of Spain, Holland, and Naples. Unfortunately he died just at the height of his career—after being officially commissioned as accoucheur to Napoleon's young and inexperienced second wife, the Empress Marie Louise.[52] As accoucheur of the imperial family, for each delivery Baudelocque was promised a fee of 10,000 francs contained in a diamond-studded gold box of equal value.[53] Ironically, at the same time, some of the most humble, destitute, unwed mothers in France received Baudelocque's services free of charge at La Maternité.

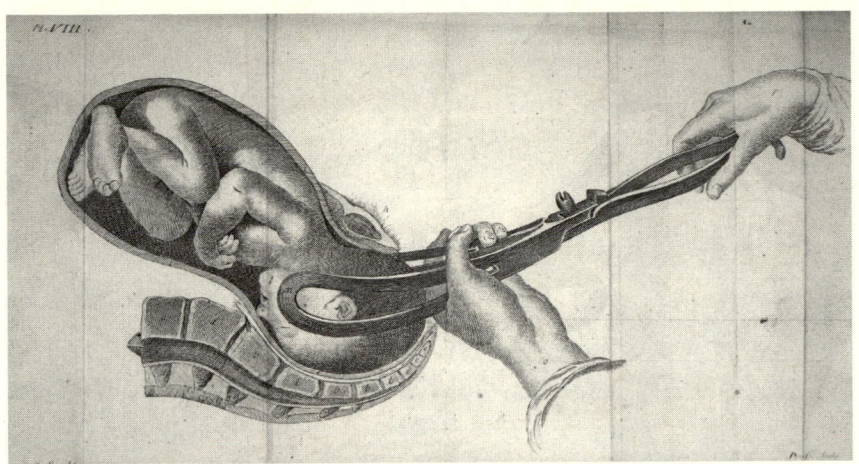

One of the many illustrations from the obstetrical textbook of Docteur Jean-Louis Baudelocque. From Jean-Louis Baudelocque, *L'Art des Accouchemens*. Used with permission of the Dittrick Medical History Center, Case Western Reserve University, Cleveland, Ohio.

Baudelocque shared the mechanical conception of childbirth prevalent in that era. His mentor Solayres de Renhac had "described the six classic positions, which have been taught to generations of medical students."[54] While Medieval authors had imagined impossible fetal positions, Baudelocque used more empirical methods in his hands-on approach: presumably using cadavers submerged in water. He took an actual fetus and experimented, placing it every conceivable way inside a female pelvis. His findings were more than ninety possible fetal positions, seventy of which he described in his midwifery catechism of 1775. However, even seventy really was too many fetal positions to memorize, especially considering the little formal education of many of these women.

Baudelocque showed better sense about other problems, though. He shrewdly sensed that the contagion of childbed fever might be carried from patient to patient by the kid leather covers on forceps (the leather covers had originated with the British obstetrician William Smellie to smooth the surface of wooden forceps), so he removed the covers and simply inserted these metal instruments more carefully. Baudelocque was also considered very skillful at performing cesarean sections, and many of his patients survived despite the lack of antiseptics, anesthesia, and antibiotics.

Baudelocque's most important contribution to modern obstetrics was the use of the large callipers, which still bear his name, to estimate the inside capacity of the female pelvis from outside measurements alone to within one-twelfth of an inch precision. Consequently, the external conjugate has since been known as Baudelocque's diameter.[55] It was used until modern radiology could be employed to replace it. This improved pelvimetry helped to determine whether surgery, which was so risky in those days, was really necessary in order to save mother and child.

Antoine Dubois, who was ten years younger than Baudelocque, came from an impoverished background. He attended the Collège de Cahors (Lot) as a scholarship student before leaving for Paris at the age of twenty to live with an aunt near the Louvre. He became a seminarian at the Collège Mazarin, but after a year he decided on medicine instead. (It was unusual for surgeons of the day to have completed college education.) Dubois worked his way through surgical training by giving (French) reading, Latin, and math lessons and doing secretarial work while his uncle provided meals. He studied with the great surgeon Desault who likewise had humble origins. At age twenty-five, Dubois finally began to teach anatomy, as well as operating medicine and accouchement. Interestingly, Louis XVI's last official nomination was to make Antoine Dubois Professor of Anatomy in 1791.

After its reorganization of medical education, the Convention gave Dubois the Chair of Anatomy, which made him Baudelocque's successor. As a sign of his scientific importance, Dubois went with Bonaparte to Egypt as a member of the Institute of Cairo. After Napoleon fled Egypt, General Jean-Baptiste Kléber (1753–1800) was left in command, and it was Dubois who attended his wounds. So when he grew homesick, Dubois was permitted to return to France (on a ship with Louis Bonaparte also aboard), although for this he fell into disrepute with Napoleon who considered him disloyal because he fled from Egypt without his direct authorization. Regardless of this fall from grace, Dubois's clientele kept him too busy to see much of Napoleon Bonaparte socially at Malmaison or the Tuileries, but he developed an important friendship with Jean-Nicholas Corvisart, the court physician and leading clinician. It was the latter who eventually persuaded Bonaparte to overcome his old grudge against Dubois and, because he was the best qualified, appoint him *accoucheur en chef* at La Maternité and as Marie Louise's accoucheur when Baudelocque, who had held both positions, died (at age sixty-four) a few days after the royal wedding.

Consequently, it was Dubois's good fortune indeed to deliver the King of Rome and to be the doctor who revived Napoleon's heir apparent by means of mouth-to-mouth resuscitation. In a day when the average physician could not expect to earn over 2,000 francs per year, Dubois was rewarded with 100,000 francs in addition to an annual salary of 25,000 francs and the distinguished title "Baron of the Empire." Despite such great recognition and social prominence, like his distinguished predecessor Baudelocque, Dubois really spent most of his working hours not on well-to-do private patients, but at La Maternité teaching midwifery pupils who were recruited from the lower classes and demonstrating on pregnant women who were their social peers.

In 1822 Dubois's liberalism cost him his appointment. However, after the Revolution of 1830 reversed the conservative trend, he became Dean of the Faculté de Médecine, where he attracted great numbers of students. His calm, friendly disposition allowed him to invent the method of modern clinical teaching wherein the patient, professor, and medical students all interact in discussing cases. His great contribution to surgery was simplification of procedures and more use of the hand and fewer tools. He is credited with inventing female lithotomy (removal of stones from the bladder by cutting), and a kind of forceps bears his name. Unfortunately for our purposes, he wrote little because, as he said unpretentiously, "I know too much and too little." So he published nothing and left only his skills and the memory of his placid, blue-eyed gaze and intelligent forehead in the minds of numerous disciples who were practicing at midcentury.[56]

Far less is known about François Chaussier, who was the same age as Baudelocque but had a far less dramatic career. His background was obscure since he started teaching at the Dijon Academy and, at the same time, practicing medicine as a physician instead of a surgeon. He gradually developed a fine reputation there for teaching in three fields: anatomy, chemistry, and materia medica. While in Dijon, he had some interaction with Guyton de Morveau, who experimented with theories of fumigation to stop the spread of disease and fevers in hospitals.

In 1794 Chaussier attracted the attention of the national Convention, which called him to Paris to work with Antoine-François Fourcroy on a plan to create a comprehensive école de santé, which would teach all fields of medicine. His proposal envisioned one professor and one adjunct for each course. After some passage of time he expected teaching to become uniform so that the faculty could be split into two schools; however, the Convention adjusted his proposal to commence with the establishment of three écoles de santé: Paris, Montpellier, and Strasbourg, with a professor and an adjunct professor for each of the courses at all three locations.

After turning the project over to Fourcroy, Chaussier returned to Dijon in order to continue his usual work of teaching and healing. He was called to Paris a second time after the École de Santé got under way to become its professor of anatomy. He also taught a physiology course at the École de Médecine de Paris. Subsequently, he became professor of the course in chemistry and medicine at the École polytechnique, a position he held until 1815.

Chaussier published some short essays, but he never published a major work. He drafted a manuscript on legal medicine and had it printed, we are told, but never put it into circulation. The research on episiotomy (incision of the perineum to facilitate labor), teratology (study of monstrosities), and legal medicine that he conducted at La Maternité helped the teaching hospital to achieve its further purpose of advancing medical knowledge and facilitating social justice. The three *Discours* that he gave to the midwifery students at La Maternité in 1805, 1806, and 1807 were published. Chaussier earned part of his reputation from writing reports and giving consultations on legal medicine.[57] Unlike their colleague Baudelocque, Dubois and Chaussier lived to become octogenarians.

Preeminent Female Teachers: Mme Lachapelle and Mme Boivin

The two most outstanding female midwifery teachers, the role models whose methods were emulated throughout the empire, were Marie-Louise Dugès Lachapelle (1769–1822) and Marie-Anne Victoire Gillain Boivin (1773–1841), author of the famous textbook.

Veuve (widow) Lachapelle, as she was known by many contemporaries, was the granddaughter and daughter of midwives. For her work as midwife-in-chief at the Hôtel Dieu, the largest public hospital in Paris, her mother, Marie Jouet Dugès (1730–1797), had earned as great a reputation in her own day as her flashier contemporary Mme du Coudray. Mme Dugès had learned the art of midwifery from her mother, with additional training at the maternity ward/school at the Hôtel Dieu, which she herself eventually came to head. After Jouet married Dugès, who was a health officer, he shared his medical knowledge with her. This enabled her to qualify for appointment as the legal-medical midwife to the Châtelet law courts and prison. In later years, when she resided at the Hôtel Dieu, her extraordinary administrative ability became apparent as she reorganized the service for pregnant women, wrote textbooks for the midwifery pupils who assisted her, and generally improved patients' care. Consequently, she left a sterling legacy for her daughter whose life and career were patterned after her own.

As a youngster, Marie-Louise Dugès accompanied her mother on her rounds at the Hôtel Dieu de Paris, thereby "absorbing" the art of midwifery at an early age. It is said that by the age of twelve she was performing complicated deliveries and at fifteen was able to perform single-handedly a version that was potentially fatal if handled incorrectly. She married a man like her father when in 1792 she married Lachapelle, a surgeon at the Hospital Saint-Louis; but, unfortunately, her husband died within three years. Like her mother, she had one daughter who, however, broke away from family tradition and became instead a nun. When her mother died in 1797, young

Mme Lachapelle, midwife-in-chief of La Maternité, was awarded a doctor of medicine degree from a German university. She went on to publish a book on gynecological surgery. From A. Delacoux, *Biographie des Sages-Femmes Célèbres* . . .

Widow Lachapelle was appointed to fill her vacated position at the Hôtel Dieu, teaching beside the great Professor Baudelocque.

Because of her medical experience and reputation as a good administrator at the Hôtel Dieu, Mme Lachapelle was asked by Minister of the Interior Chaptal to direct the new normal school of midwifery and children's hospital that the Napoleonic government established at Port Royal, La Maternité. In fact, some sources claim that it was she who planned the organization of the institution for Chaptal, who subsequently made the formal regulations for its operation on June 30, 1802.[58] There, with her manual skill and keen mind, Lachapelle earned a reputation as the preeminent midwife of the First Empire. Moreover, she kept such good records of forty thousand cases that the statistics she compiled advanced scientific knowledge of childbirth beyond what had been known during the Enlightenment regarding length of pregnancy and duration of labor.

We are fortunate to have contemporaries' descriptions of Mme Lachapelle's bedside manner as well as her public persona. La Maternité owed much, if not most, of its success to her selfless devotion to her duties. Midwifery was grueling work, sometimes requiring the performance of horrific procedures. Death and blood were everywhere, but she treated her students like members of her own family, supporting them physically and spiritually. No wonder she commanded so much respect that no one questioned her authority, yet she was loved by those around her. She moved through the wards, going wherever she was most needed, encouraging patients here and patiently teaching staff members there, thus earning for her displays of goodness and kindness the aphorism, *la bonne Madame Lachapelle.* Military historians like to talk about how much difference the presence of Napoleon himself on a battlefield made to his men and how his presence sometimes overcame very unfavorable odds against winning. Similarly, an analogy could be made about the importance of the presence of the "good Madame Lachapelle" when a poor, suffering, indigent woman was almost scared to death during a hard labor. At ease and fully in command in her own secluded space—a publicly operated yet private "world of women" that she had largely fashioned—the midwife-in-chief could look into a patient's face and immediately discern exactly the right thing to say to console her and assuage her suffering.

In public Mme Lachapelle's demeanor changed. A. Delacoux, writing in 1834, said that she displayed such a degree of modesty, even humility, that strangers mistook it for an affectation. She also was a good conversationalist, but unlike (in his opinion) so many self-important women, she did not show off her superior knowledge or abilities unless she was in a situation that required their application. By the time of the birth of the King of Rome, Lachapelle's reputation also was Europe-wide, so she was interviewed several times by the most influential persons at court regarding the production of an heir to the throne. Nevertheless, Delacoux continued, she agreeably acceded to the custom of the times for monarchs to employ male accoucheurs instead of midwives when she quietly assisted Antoine Dubois from behind the scenes during the near-tragic breech birth of young Empress Marie Louise.[59]

Several sources vaguely claim that "Lachapelle studied with Naegele in Heidelberg," but this is problematical. If so, it had to have been informally because women were not permitted to study at the faculty of medicine of the University of Heidelberg before 1900; nor is Lachapelle's name listed among the pupils of the Heidelberg Midwifery Institute, which moved there from Mannheim in 1805 and existed until 1823.[60] Moreover, Franz Carl Naegele (1778–1851) only succeeded in joining the Heidelberg faculty in 1807 and after becoming "Professor Ordinarius" only began to direct the midwifery institute in 1810. Nevertheless, it is an interesting avenue worth pursuing that Lachapelle, who was then close to forty years of age, would leave Paris to somehow study medicine and surgery in Heidelberg, under the great German medical professor Naegele.

Naegele was the son of a Bavarian military surgeon and teacher who lectured on physiology and legal medicine. After studying with his father, Naegele furthered his medical studies at Strasbourg, Freiburg, and Bamberg, where he obtained his medical degree in 1802.[61] After marrying the second daughter of Professor Franz Anton Mai, who held the obstetrical chair at Heidelberg until his death in 1810, Naegele was finally hired by that old (established 1386) and distinguished university.[62] It is interesting to think that a French woman who would not be admitted to the Paris medical faculty might instead go to Germany to study medicine and surgery. Moreover, to succeed as a German student Mme Lachapelle, who had had no opportunity to attend distinguished secondary schools or colleges as men did, would have needed an excellent command of German and Latin in order to follow the courses or learn from Naegele.

The personable Dr. Naegele (who, we are told, became popular with medical students because he told jokes in his lectures) was nine years younger than Lachapelle. Yet, in time Naegele would become the acknowledged leading German researcher whose powers of observation were so remarkable in the history of parturition. For example, it was he who discovered the principle that was known for years in medical studies as "Naegele's oblique," which is the fact that regardless of its exact position, an emerging fetus turns its head on an angle in order to accommodate the shape of its skull optimally with the oval configuration of the mother's pelvic bones. Through experience, Naegele also discovered significant errors in previous authorities' writings on midwifery.[63] "Furthermore," according to Walter Radcliffe, "he would appear to be the first to realize that the frank breech is a better dilater of the maternal passages than a footling presentation."[64] Their interaction in Heidelberg surely would be mutually rewarding for the brilliant young Professor Naegele and the more experienced French midwifery teacher.

Mme Lachapelle was a fine example of the courageous manner in which Imperial and Restoration women lived as well as the way they were expected to deal with their own mortality. As her days were numbered, Mme Lachapelle courageously hid her own suffering and continued to give her midwifery lessons and practice her obstetrical skills until a stomach ailment, possibly cancer, took her in 1821 at about age fifty-two.

But Mme Lachapelle's teaching lived on in the book that she wrote entitled *Pratique des Accouchemens, ou Mémoires, et Observations Choisies, sur les Points les Plus Importants de l'Art; Sage-Femme en Chef de la Maison d'Accouchemens de Paris* in three volumes whose publication commenced in 1821—the year of her death—and continued until 1825. This book shows that while her male colleagues respected her, she was an independent thinker. Like all practitioners of the day, she conceived of childbirth as a mechanistic process; however, while Dr. Baudelocque had classified childbirth into a mind-numbing ninety-some fetal positions, Mme Lachapelle simplified the matter, just as Naegele did in his famous, short, 1819 article in the German *Archives of Physiology* and later republished in his book *Mechanismus des Geburt* (1822), by reducing the number of possibilities to twenty-two—still enough positions to challenge the mind of the midwives who had to memorize these flawlessly.

Furthermore, Lachapelle believed that midwives should rarely interfere with Nature. Her records show how seldom forceps, version, and surgical interventions were used: in her 40,000 cases, she used forceps only 93 times, version 125 times, symphisiotomy twice, and cesarean section once. Symphisiotomy was a relatively new operation; as if sensing the potential this surgical procedure held for future use in the nineteenth century (after Joseph Lister invented antiseptic surgery), Lachapelle devoted the entire third volume to this topic.

Mme Lachapelle also wrote many articles recording her observations for the periodical *Annuaire Médico-Chirurgical* and furnished statistics for the members of the Conseil d'administration des hospices. As stated previously, she worked closely with Baudelocque until his death in 1810. He seems to have admired her, although he thought her greater reluctance to use forceps and to eschew employing them merely to shorten labor made her seem (to him) "old-fashioned." Others might see Baudelocque's male bias as a reflection of his own shortcomings. Regardless of these opinions, Lachapelle should be equally credited with making La Maternité the premier institution of its kind in the world at that time. For a quarter century the compassionate, selfless, extremely slender, and obviously overworked woman, who (unlike her predecessor Mme du Coudray) always dressed in a manner considered appropriate for her calling in modest black high-necked gowns with

Mme Boivin, pupil of Mme Lachapelle. Mme Boivin also became a skilled surgeon and was awarded a doctor of medicine degree from a German university. From A. Delacoux, *Biographie des Sages-Femmes Célèbres . . .*

white collars, was regarded as the foremost midwife in the capital. Her name still remains prominent today in the history of French obstetrics for such innovations in patient care as emergency surgical repair of a torn perineum and saving both mother and child by means of dilation plus version in cases of placenta previa, which occurs in about one out of every two hundred pregnancies.[65]

Marie-Anne Victoire Gillain was born in 1733 at Versailles, but she was educated by an order of nursing nuns at a hospital at Etampes, which is to the south of Paris near Orléans. In 1797, she married Louis Boivin, who worked as an assistant for the Bureau of National Domains. When she soon was left widowed with a young daughter to support, she decided to continue the medical studies that had been interrupted by her marriage. Mme Boivin went to Paris to study midwifery at the maternity section of the Hôtel Dieu, where Mme Lachapelle, who was only four years her senior and also a widow with one daughter, became her teacher and friend. After receiving her diploma in 1800, Boivin established herself at Versailles to practice, but not for long. When her daughter was killed, Boivin returned to Paris to assist Mme Lachapelle, as chief *surveillant* of La Maternité for the next eleven years. At that time, Boivin developed close ties to Dr. Chausssier. It has been alleged that professional jealousy of her colleague Mme Lachapelle led Mme Boivin to resign her position at La Maternité in 1811 and to accept instead a position for servants' wages at a Paris hospital for fallen women.[66]

Nevertheless, in 1812 the Hospice de la Maternité published the first edition of her famous *Mémorial de l'Art des Accouchemens,* which contained the notes she had taken there as she followed Mme Lachapelle's teaching and practice. The manual for midwives contained a folding table and 133 full-page, simple wood engravings from drawings made by the author, notably showing the application of forceps and the various positions of the fetus in the womb. Although it contained nothing new, its methods have been called "up to date" and its instructions "clear and precise." According to Walter Radcliffe, "She had a very full account, for example of breech delivery, with instructions how to bring down extended arms, how to carry out Giffard's manoeuver, and how to apply forceps to the after-coming head. She was in favor of Levret's curved forceps, and always applied them to the sides of the head, namely the cephalic application."[67] *Mémorial* also included the classic aphorisms of Mauriceau as well as an annotated bibliography of contemporary literature.

Although she led a life of poverty and deprivation, Mme Boivin refused the offer of Mme Lachapelle's position when the latter died in 1822, as well as an offer of employment from the Empress of Russia. Several sources say that Mme Boivin regretted never receiving a medical degree from a French university or being admitted to the Academy of Medicine; however, the German University of Marburg sent her a diploma of Doctor of Medicine in 1827, as a testimony to her ability amidst the prevailing Romantic, sexist social milieu to develop skills equal to those of her male counterparts who practiced obstetrics.[68]

Between 1818 and 1823, Mme Boivin published several articles about her own cases and her uterine speculum in the *Bulletins de la Faculté de Médecine* and in the bulletin of the Académie royale de médecine de Paris. Boivin's more advanced writings on gynecology included *Nouveau Traité des Hemorragies de l'Uterus* (1818), and *Traité de Maladies de l'Uterus et des*

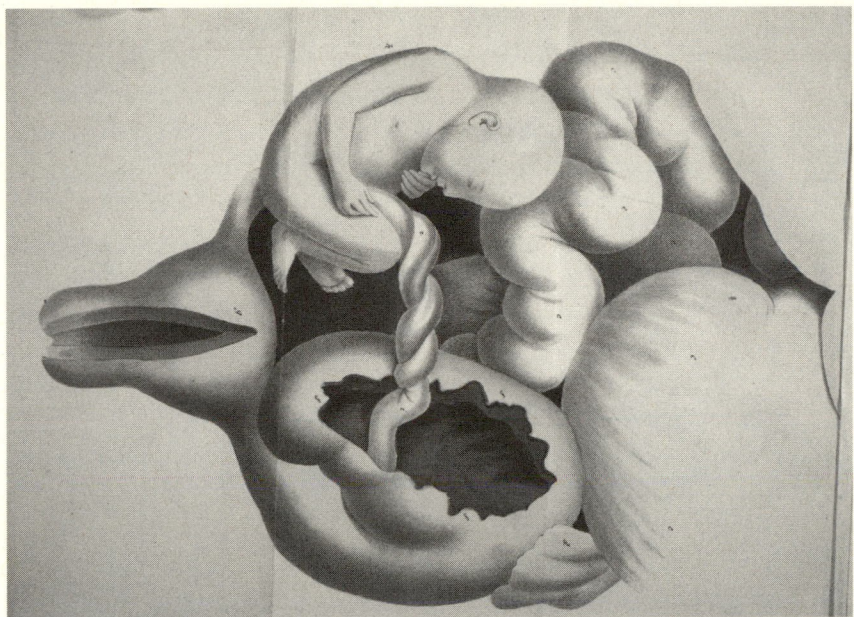

Tubular pregnancy observed at La Maternité in 1816. The fetus was developed in the left Fallopian tube. After the spontaneous rupture of that canal, which served as an organ of incubation, the patient soon died. The fetus was found situated on the left iliac fossa. From Marie-Anne Gillain Boivin, *Chirurgie Utérine*.

Annexes (1833), with 41 hand-colored plates and 116 figures. Since Mme Lachapelle's nephew helped her publish these works, it seems questionable whether Boivin's decision to leave La Maternité was really due to professional jealousy between the two midwifery teachers, as many sources claim. Moreover Boivin was known as a person "of great strength of character and noble intellect," who "had at the same time a very lovable nature."[69]

In her gynecology manuals, Mme Boivin showed why she became one of the leading gynecologists in Paris. Radcliffe also points out that "she used the vaginal speculum, which had been reintroduced by Joseph Claude Récamier (1774–1852), after years of neglect, not for obstetrics but for the inspection of the cervix uteri." She also "was undertaking surgical treatments which in other countries were the prerogative of the men. She was one of the first surgeons to amputate the cervix uteri for a cancerous growth." Hence, small-minded, chauvinistic professors of the medical faculty had good reason to become jealous of her successes, as they reportedly did.[70]

Obviously, Mme Boivin was the same "Gillain," the so-called generous Amazon, who had gone public by sending the infamous letter to the editor of the *Gazette de Santé* in 1810 that evoked his ranting out against surgeons but made midwifery the sole province of women. Possibly her plain outspokenness had much to do with her mysterious departure from her position at La Maternité and her inability to find another in Paris that paid a decent salary. It is noteworthy too that she published not under her maiden name, but under her married name (as we saw earlier with "Madame" du Coudray, a spinster); probably, the title "Madame" made books on such an intimate subject as the female body sell better, especially to surgeons and physicians. Furthermore, despite the setbacks early in her career, Boivin continued to labor on in her chosen field for many years. She advanced to become recognized as an innovative and skillful gynecological surgeon renowned for her exemplary dedication and determination to lay claim to a place for women in French medicine. Finally, following the careers of both Lachapelle and Boivin suggests that there was interaction between French and German obstetricians during this era, since the former was associated with Heidelberg's Naegele and the latter received an M.D. from Marburg. German universities seemed to be more welcoming to the idea of women becoming skilled in gynecological surgery.

Special Treatments in the Curriculum

All personnel at the midwifery schools, regardless of status or wealth, participated in the desperate effort to overcome puerperal fever. When the epidemic of September and October 1811 first broke out at La Maternité, cadavers of the victims were studied to determine the cause of death so that the sick could be properly treated.[71] Initially, blood-letting was tried, but the doctors soon realized that most women whose treatment was blood-letting died from the fever anyway.[72] The medicines commonly administered were potassium sulfate and antimony.[73] To check contagion at La Maternité Chaussier introduced the use of the fumigation process devised by the chemist Guyton de Morveau to disinfect the air; however, Chaussier used equal parts of sulphur and saltpeter.[74] Beyond the general fumigation effort, Chaussier also helped to devise an apparatus to administer aromatic vapor to the stricken women in their beds.[75] These efforts seem to have been largely ineffective, although the mortality rate from puerperal fever worsened after the Restoration of the Bourbon Monarchy.

After the Napoleonic era, the real cause of puerperal fever finally was understood correctly and methods for dealing with it became successful through the discoveries of the Hungarian physician Ignaz Semmelweis (1818–1865), the English surgeon Joseph Lister (1827–1912), and the French chemist Louis Pasteur (1822–1895).[76] However, the explanation for the degree of success achieved "accidentally" during the First Empire may simply be greater cleanliness. For instance, even the sidewalks outside of La Maternité were washed by the hospital staff.[77] These fumigation and sanitary efforts were likewise adopted at some departmental midwifery schools.[78]

So that imperial midwives would be better skilled in the correct use of pharmaceutical plants, a course was incorporated into the curriculum by the 1807 regulations to familiarize midwives with 150 to 200 varieties in both fresh and dry form, what these were good for curing, and how to prepare infusions. Although some information about medicinal plants was included in the textbooks used nationwide, Chaussier, whose reputation partially rested on a plant nomenclature that he had devised, conceived a project to establish at La Maternité a garden where the carefully cultivated plants were arranged in rows according to natural families. This living illustration aided the learning of the lessons given to the pupils by the pharmacist under the doctor's direction.[79] Moreover, it is a further example of the very practical and applied scientific pedagogical approach institutionalized in this era.

Finally, measures aimed directly at preventing abortion and infanticide (see Chapter 9) and at reducing the mortality rate of foundlings were built into the midwifery training schools by operating a nursery for feeding and care at each location. The Imperial Decree of January 19, 1811, legally mandated usage of the *tour,* that is, a revolving cylinder of wood where unwanted children could be deposited anonymously in lieu of their being murdered or exposed to the elements (a sort of "baby drop," as the concept is now termed in twenty-first-century Germany and the United States where it is in vogue again as an alternative to abortion).[80] As a result of the adoption of the policy of allowing mothers to stay on for two years as nurses of two babies—one of their own plus a foundling or orphan—the lives of even more infants were preserved.[81]

Treatment of Syphilis

Syphilis, which is both a sexually transmitted disease and a congenital one, was another disease prevalent among people of all classes. Its treatment posed particular difficulties for the public midwifery schools and lying-in hospitals. Contemporaries already knew that the disease could be transmitted to the fetus through the placenta and thought that it also might be transmitted during labor if the infant touched open lesions as it passed through the birth canal. If left untreated in pregnant women syphilis causes miscarriage, stillbirths, or birth defects in newborns such as blindness, deafness, or "saddle nose" (the falling in of the bridge of the nose due to its destruction by an ulcer).[82] Moreover, syphilis can be exchanged: nursing mothers transmit the disease through their breast milk while syphilitic infants can also pass the disease back to clean wet-nurses by touching their nipples with their infected saliva. So treatment of pregnant women with syphilis seemed urgent.

Several methods were used for treating syphilitic women, but the three that were most important during the years from 1789 to 1839 were fumigation, friction, and internal digestion.[83] Mercurial fumigations were achieved by funneling smoke toward the patient's body from cinnibar burning on coals, and was appropriate for local treatment. Frictions customarily involved first bathing, then taking a purgative, after which the surface to be treated was prepped with a razor. Then mercurial ointments (use of hog's lard for the grease was avoided because it might go rancid) or lotions were rubbed on the patient's skin for about a half hour so that the metal was absorbed through the pores. Finally, the area was bandaged, and the whole process was repeated every day or so. But the most direct treatment was internal digestion of mercuric compounds, which they knew were highly toxic. While differences of opinion existed as to whether pregnant women really ought to be treated at all, those who felt it was more harmful to wait until after they came to full term than to proceed immediately did think pregnant women should receive higher dosages than nonpregnant women; but, the timing of this was deemed crucial. Midterm seemed best so as not to cause miscarriage early or late in the pregnancy. To optimize the effectiveness of taking mercury, some doctors suggested that pregnant syphilitic patients also drink good wine, exercise in fresh air, and take a tonic, which should be followed by a mild laxative to purge the metal.

The feeding of syphilitic infants posed special problems, especially regarding the foundlings, many of whom probably were abandoned because signs of the disease were recognizable at birth or their mothers had died during childbirth, possibly because they had the most acute stage of the three-stage disease or were too weak to survive the toxic treatments. When motherless children were infected, they were usually assigned to a syphilitic wet-nurse who underwent treatment to heal herself and the child simultaneously through the mercury that concentrated in her breast milk.

When a suitable wet-nurse was unavailable, officials might substitute a nanny goat to which mercuric compounds were administered. This treatment was done by means of two methods. Jacques André Millot's 1809 work, *Médecine Perfective,* offered a recipe for syphilitic medicine to feed a goat containing a liter of liquorice root water, a half-liter of finely sifted barley flour, a small measure (a *cuidre à bouche*) of oxygenated muriate of mercury (a solution made of twelve grains per French pint of distilled water). If the goat refused to drink this, Millot said to add honey to disguise the metallic flavor.[84] P. A. O. Mahon suggested an alternate way to get the mercury into the goat's bloodstream, which was to make a simple wound on the goat's thigh that was dressed daily with a mercurial ointment.[85] The surrogate mother was led indoors, right into the nursery where the rows of wicker cradles were suspended from the rafters, and made to stand astride the baby's cradle so that the infant could reach up and nurse on the goat's teats. Thus, the medication passed from the nanny goat's wound into its bloodstream, thence into its milk, which in turn the nursing child sucked directly from the udder. This process mercifully bypassed the high risk of contamination from the use of baby bottles (typically a wine bottle with a dirty piece of sea sponge as a stopper, which was unsterilized before the time of Louis Pasteur's discoveries about the bacteria in milk). We know from one of François Fodéré's treatises that nanny goats were still employed at the foundling hospitals in Metz and Arras in 1825.[86]

As proof of how toxic the mercuric medicines were, eventually the nanny goats used to feed the syphilitic babies died prematurely. Today we know just how toxic mercury is and the dangers of imbibing or adsorbing it: acute exposure causes excessive salivation, nausea, vomiting, chills, fever, coughing, tightness in the chest, and a metallic taste. Nevertheless, French Revolution–era physicians were astute in thinking that a pregnant woman and her fetus could be treated together, since some forms of mercury can cross the placental barrier. Additionally, lactating women would accumulate a concentration of mercury in their breast milk. The clever use of nanny goats as surrogate wet-nurses solved the problem of a shortage of wet-nurses nor did the goats have to be paid a fee for their important services, while the process also protected clean women from becoming infected. This practice undoubtedly saved the lives of many foundlings who otherwise would have starved to death or died of bacterial infections from crude attempts at artificial feeding. The treatment of syphilis during pregnancy and after birth aimed at increasing the infants' viability, and mortality tables suggest that this treatment, for whatever reason, may have been somewhat effective. This humanitarian effort shows us the softer side of the official social policy of the First Empire.

Despite its reflection of the medical thinking of the times, the formal organization, teaching methods, goals, and daily concerns of the national system created by the First Imperial government resulted in an ordered, rational, humanistic achievement. In Paris alone, between the years 1804 and 1814 about eighteen thousand to nineteen thousand babies were born at La Maternité, who might otherwise have perished, not to speak of the foundlings who also wet-nursed there. By establishing training schools in every department of metropolitan France and throughout the empire as it expanded through conquest and annexation, unfortunate women and their infants were paid the sacred debt of social security that had been promised by the *Declaration of the Rights of Man and of the Citizen*. That Napoleon truly venerated the role of motherhood in deed as well as word is evidenced by his encouragement of more and better midwifery schools to improve obstetrical care. His patronage also contributed to the myth of Napoleon as the infants delivered in these safe places grew to adulthood and the women thus educated traveled back home, or all over the French empire, as graduates to deliver the future generations of men and women.

Contemporary Observers: John Cross and Edwin Lee

Contemporary eyewitnesses confirmed the very positive assessment of the Napoleonic approach to midwifery education that involved women as medical subjects, students, and teachers. Among those eyewitnesses was the English surgeon who was familiar with medical education in several European countries. John Cross, who visited La Maternité in 1815, admitted that he "was not a little surprised at . . . first entering the hospital with Monsieur Chaussier, the Physician-in-Chief, to find the wards crowded with female students."[87] Nevertheless, in reflecting upon his visit he wrote:

> I do not think it is of so much importance whether the practice of midwifery be in the hands of males or females, as that those who exercise it should be well informed. The latter purpose seems to be as fully answered as possible by the school I am considering, and this constitutes its greatest advantages. *Les elèves sages-femmes,* who reside for twelve months at l'Hospice de la Maternité, and about whose instruction so much pains are taken and so much attention bestowed by the medical men attached to it, are, there can be little doubt, quite as good practitioners at the completion of their education, as the male students in midwifery in any country. In England midwifery is unfortunately held in so little consideration, that the making of any regulations regarding the practice of it, is either forgotten or neglected by those public bodies, which have been constituted for the purpose of improving all branches of medical and surgical science, and diffusing the benefits of them over society; and therefore the majority of midwifery-practice is (and there seems to be reason to fear that it will continue to be) carried on by men of slight education, or by old women who have no education at all.[88]

Thus, immediately after the fall of Napoleon the French midwifery education system created by Napoleon I was still recognized as being avant-garde because it provided quality specialized training for nonaristocratic women far in advance of what was available in contemporary England.

During the Restoration, when the prosperity of the wartime economy turned into a recession, enrollment at La Maternité dropped significantly. Nevertheless, the very positive evaluation of the French national normal school for midwifery made by John Cross was later inadvertently reinforced by another foreign visitor who espoused far more sexist and classist attitudes about poor women's unworthiness to practice midwifery. Edwin Lee, an American physician from Philadelphia who visited comparable European medical institutions in 1837, offered his opinion that the low tuition at Paris's La Maternité provided too much opportunity for poor women to become properly trained midwives; whereas, he preferred the contrasting English policy of excluding lower-class women by keeping such training relatively expensive.[89]

In light of such opinions coming from abroad, it would be patently absurd to suggest that it was the policy of the Napoleonic government to drive women out of the practice of midwifery so that men could take over or that lower-class French women were denied entry into this profession because they could not afford the education. On the contrary, the imperial redesign of the midwifery educational delivery system aimed at exactly the opposite; it already had begun annually to graduate classes of new midwives in Paris and the provinces in far greater numbers than previous regimes. Since childbirth was perceived as a healthy process rather than an illness, the prevailing mentality was that women were naturally better suited to practice midwifery and to safeguard the woman's femininity. While the masculization of childbirth technology had already begun in the eighteenth century, Napoleon and his administrators believed that producing more, better-educated women as midwives was the best solution to rectifying the horrible, neglected situation that they had inherited, especially in rural areas where infant mortality rates were dreadful. Because the empire was abbreviated and ended so abruptly, the imperial policy failed to provide all the large numbers that were needed. But if Napoleon had won at Waterloo, he could have continued his national program, which, if successfully carried out, would have resulted in making midwifery a governmentally sponsored and subsidized scientific profession for women, thereby stemming and reversing the earlier trend of masculinization and medicalization of childbirth once and for all.

The problem with Napoleonic centralization of midwifery education was that although its higher standards raised the quality of its Paris graduates and hopefully the quality of their provincial students in turn, as long as the costly Napoleonic military campaigns drained finances as quickly as they killed conscripts, the government could not provide enough federal support to the most heavily populated *départements*. Moreover, simply the passage of regulations regarding certification of midwives' qualifications did not automatically assure the obedience of some of these women, many of whom defied threats of fines and punishments by refusing to register properly. Finding solutions to these challenging problems was left up to the ingenuity of the local prefects.

Napoleon and Chaptal tried to give the midwifery profession more prestige. But as long as after they received their diplomas midwives had no guaranteed salary and had to depend upon payment from people too poor to pay for their services, this could not become an attractive career for intelligent and energetic younger women. Nor, without income, could the newly trained midwives repay their debt to the nation for the free training they had received by performing several decades of service. Naturally the midwife's situation did not improve in times of economic recession in a society with no safety net for the poor or when population became a far less important issue to the government, as it did after the end of the Napoleonic wars.

The extra wet-nursing services that clients of the midwifery training schools provided to foundlings and orphans for two years were an important social benefit. Infant mortality was a complex and troubling issue. Throughout the eighteenth century there was a superabundance of advice, really a discourse, on breast-feeding for a reason—because infant mortality rates were aggravated by maternal indifference. Upper-class women were side-stepping their roles as mothers, which had defined their identity previously. To many, including the naturalist George Louis Leclerc, the Comte de Buffon (1707–1788), breast-feeding was considered repugnant for making a woman seem like a milk cow. Some husbands did not like the way nursing wives smelled; and the fact that doctors said having sexual relations with a nursing woman would spoil her milk interfered with sexual pleasures. Society women were bored by childcare, and tending to one's own children was not considered chic. So women of the court who set the tone for others to emulate continued to send babies, soon after birth, to wet-nurses in the country, with whom they often had no further contact until they returned the little corpse. Elizabeth Badinter saw this maternal indifference as tantamount to infanticide.[90]

The midwifery profession was one area of science in which women were welcomed. In the eighteenth century the way women learned midwifery was through apprenticeship with a female relative, like Mme du Coudray who apprenticed her "niece" or Mme Lachapelle who was taught by her mother. But as public hospital settings were created as places of teaching and learning medicine, opportunities increased for other women who had no connections to acquire formal training in public institutions and even had the expenses of their education paid by the government. It would not be too great a leap from the opening of this public space to women to forcing open the doors of other kinds of medical education. German university faculties already appreciated the knowledge and skill of a few exceptional women who used Reason to know their own and their sisters' physical bodies intimately. This may have contributed to some male anxiety.

5

The Biomedical Foundation of Domesticity

Discourses of Surgeons

THE POSITIVE OPINION of women's abilities that humanistic authors of manuals on home economics and sex transmitted to their readership stood in stark contrast to that of Napoleon's elite medical scientists. The latter had the benefit of more hands-on experience dissecting cadavers as well as the opportunity to surgically remove tissue from women patients for actual comparison with men's. Moreover, their use of such empirical methodology and better histological techniques should have led them to discard the errors of folk medicine and centuries-old prejudices that killed patients or hindered the process of healing. In fact, some of these scientific doctors' philosophical beliefs in animism and vitalism represented a direct challenge to the mechanists and their mechanism. Historians of medicine even gave them credit for laying the foundations of modern anatomy and physiology. Consequently, when they turned their attention to questions about woman's nature, we would expect them to be the foremost progressive thinkers of the age of Napoleon. Their failure is a complicated story.

The interests of Napoleon's scientists were unlike those of innovators of prior centuries who would have been more interested in the state of women's souls. These modern men belonged to the more secularized post-Revolutionary generation when doctors first became the high priest–like guardians of morality concerning the body. Their findings and the metaphysical conclusions they drew from clinical practice are included in the lessons they presented at medical schools, in treatises written for professional colleagues, and in the journal[1] articles they published in order to advance the medical knowledge of the Western world. They revealed much about the relationship of scientific knowledge with ideology and power in that cultural setting. Napoleonic surgical discourse about women's correct social role was both a justification for the political relationship of the two sexes in the imperial patriarchy and a response to noteworthy contemporary arguments by feminist educators that women were men's equal if given the same educational opportunities and a positive environment for growth.

Although, as we have seen in Chapter 1, the emperor insisted that women be kept submissive and that they should properly function as the naturally organized machines they are for making babies, the strength of women like his mother was also a constant theme of his discourse. "Women have made war like soldiers," he said, and they have committed "unparalleled atrocities. . . . The women of the marketplace are as robust as the majority of young men."[2] Another of his remarks should be recalled: "The mother in a poor household is the person in charge of the house."[3] These statements may be interpreted to suggest that he saw this strength only in urban, lower-class women. Nevertheless, his actions imply his confidence that all mothers of France and her satellite kingdoms were capable of keeping the rural economy going while their menfolk fought his wars of conquest. Although Napoleon's omission of women's education from the Imperial University has gotten considerable attention, rarely is it acknowledged that he created the first national system of midwifery education in Europe, for which he had the Minister of the Interior personally draft regulations in January 1807.[4] After his Austrian marriage the emperor added a second institution designed to save women's lives—the Société Maternelle—a charity that distributed assistance to needy mothers and made quite an impression on the medical profession, as we shall see later.[5] So while the emperor spoke of female strength (albeit coupled sometimes, in his opinion, with feeble-mindedness), some feminist male educators, as well as some physicians who were old-fashioned men of art, wrote about women's potentially brilliant minds. Even the doctors who were dedicated to the life sciences contributed to the dialogue.

"Scientific" Discourse about Differences

In ancient Greece, Hypocrites, the father of medicine, had initiated the discussion of the differences between men and women, and Napoleon himself talked about gender differences when he was on Saint Helena. So it is not surprising to find that imperial doctors likewise continued to show interest in *la différence*. Initially two sexes exist, they believed, due to a mysteriously different kind of movement, of excitation, inside the mother at the moment of conception. From then on development diverges, with the females developing into fragile "machines" who are likely to be sick all their lives.[6] Already while the fetus was still in the womb, some doctors claimed they could smell the difference in the developing fetus, an inference based upon the assumption that animals carry a male or female odor throughout their lifetimes if they are not hermaphrodites.[7] From infancy, woman's being is due to the uterus, which predominates over the three other principal centers of bodily functioning: the heart, the brain, and the gastrointestinal system. This is what gives women uterine temperaments. Having too weak or too strong a uterus relative to the other vital organs has unfortunate results; however, only the latter—clitorimania or nymphomania—is of great concern to doctors.[8] Such thinking emphasizing uterine or physical primacy over mental control of health was reminiscent of the physiopsychology of La Mettrie, something vitalists would have pointed out as objectionable.

Although they generally believed that the uterus maintains primacy over the other organs of the female body, they were willing to concede that the basic uterine health of individual women can be affected by environmental factors such as education, lifestyle, and climate as well as by the patient's state of mind, and these factors might often be related to social class. Women who attend balls and engage in riotous living would have the most difficulty with puberty and menstruation, more so than women who remain cloistered at home. Surely, climate, education, and lifestyle either cause precocious puberty or retard a young girl's maturation, which ordinarily occurs between the age of twelve and fourteen, they thought.[9]

In his *Traité des Maladies Physiques et Morales des Femmes* (4th ed. 1812), Boyveau-Laffecteur commented on the danger of stale air in closed carriages, boudoirs, and theaters. He thought big cities, especially the European capitals, were unhealthful places for women with asthmatic or hysterical conditions.[10] Rarely are sterile women found in the countryside. The winter season is worst for urban women's illnesses because fireplaces do not provide uniform heat. His remedy for patients with drafty apartments was to install a Desarnod or a Franklin stove.[11] The concerned doctor urged them to safeguard their health by dressing appropriately for their age and not according to fashion trends. He further revealed his conservative nature by commenting didactically on the immorality of women's fashions and specifically warned them against wearing flimsy ball gowns, which would expose their flesh to night air, or against wearing high-heeled shoes and "mules" (scuffs) on their feet like Chinese women. Instead, he prescribed the wearing of Greek-style footwear: flats with ankle straps or ribbons, which he called "the footwear of a free being."[12] As for what kind of water is best for women to drink, he thought river water best, and that the Seine's surpassed all others.[13] As to diet, he urged women always to leave the table hungry.[14] All of these are measures of his solicitude for female patients.

While most of his advice was aimed at well-to-do women, Boyveau-Laffecteur was not insensitive to the plight of poor city girls, possibly born also of poor parents or as a result of prostitution and illicit sex, and whose organs and general health had been ruined during their adolescent years spent as prostitutes. He pleaded in his book for wealthier women to adopt these girls instead of hiring male servants. If only women would take them into their households to help with chores, they could be saved from prostitution and maintain good health; and because the guardianship of caring adoptive mothers would protect them from sexual exploitation, bachelors would be forced to pay their debt to society by marrying in order to obtain sex.[15] Thus, the metropolis was perceived as providing a harsh environment that was fraught with dangers to women's health, where the problems of rich and poor were inherent within their respective elite culture or counterculture. The bonding of upper- and lower-class women was one doctor's solution to pressing social and moral problems. But the primacy of the uterus and, concomitantly, women's powerlessness against the social hazards of the modern urban environment did not wholly account for their need for help from specialists in gynecology, for so many other differences were perceived as well.

When surgeons took a closer look at women's other tissues and bones, they found striking differences from men's. In the writings of Joseph Capuron, we find out not only, for example, female bones were whiter, smaller, and oilier, but the short bones were spongier.[16] Continuing on, he described the different cartilages, muscle fibers, and other tissues. Women's entire vascular system differed in character, and the vessels that supplied the generative organs were of larger caliber and more expandable. Women's nerves, of course, were more delicate, so they could be overwhelmed with agitation in response to stressful situations. The heart and stomach were smaller, the intestines narrower. When he proceeded to examine brain tissue he found that in women "the cerebral pulp is less dense," so it is no surprise when he later informed us that women's minds were "naturally light," hence easily "bored by the serious and profound."[17] He also noted that women's lungs were firmer and paler in color. Women's skin differed in texture as well as color—the lily white and rosy pink shades of their flesh were signs of great beauty to him. Furthermore, their longer, fuller heads of hair tended to remain on their heads to a very advanced age whereas men were bald at thirty or forty. After considering all of this information, he concluded that women were not inferior versions of men, after all, but different beings altogether who were here to fulfill an entirely different role.[18] Clearly, a doctrinal purpose informed Capuron's observations of women's internal organs as well as outward appearance.

Likewise, Joseph Vigarous, who had taught gynecology at Montpellier for several years, saw men and women as distinct beings who have their own illnesses. While he, too, catalogued the many differences he perceived between the sexes, he stated that the question of sexual equality is a vain dispute. He saw men and women as being equal in what they hold in common but that everything that is derived from sexuality is different. He agreed, he said, with the distinction noted by Rousseau but added that the problem is figuring out exactly what parts of women's bodies are derived from sexuality and what parts are not.[19]

Stress on the primacy of the uterus logically led some surgeons to relate all of the numerous female illnesses to uterine lesions.[20] While there used to be only six hundred female diseases, now there are twelve hundred female diseases,[21] one claimed. Dr. Vigarous believed that all of these develop from four categories of uterine problems: menstrual irregularities, other vital organs sympathizing with a uterus that was out of sorts, displaced uterine lesions, or pregnancy.[22] Dr. Boyveau-Laffecteur, for his part, believed that syphilis was responsible for doubling the number of women's diseases.[23] In addition to the increasing number of gynecological ailments, they thought women were harder to treat because they are reticent as a result of religious prejudices and social institutions so that when they finally complain of unwellness, they are already incurable.[24]

Fear of Nymphomania

Among the many nervous diseases from which women suffer, of great concern was nymphomania, a mental and physical disorder that the biomedical community believed caused women constantly to long for sexual intercourse. But far more of a woman's constitution was involved than just irrepressible sexual desire. This sexual fury was thought to normally be accompanied by respiratory difficulty, indigestion, back pain, sunken eye sockets, convulsions, and finally, heart failure.[25] Hence, it was explained as being a potentially fatal disease due to the fact that "the order of nature is inverted when females attack males."[26]

Nymphomaniacs verbally and physically provoked and threatened men who ignored their advances, a situation that only enraged these poor creatures who had old or cold husbands or who were actresses, recent widows, or young girls who could not attract sex partners. This condition flared when women read lascivious books, looked at pornography, sang, and drank coffee or alcohol. Nymphomania was located in the uterus and all the internal and external genital organs (tubes, ovaries, vagina, clitoris, etc.). But Dr. Vigarous (who had such a way with words) exclaimed: "It is ridiculous to say it is only located in the clitoris. You may as well say that hunger is located in the mouth!"[27] Starting in the uterus then, this dominant organ caused the brain to sympathize, whereby delirium set in. Besides, if it were located in the clitoris, the victim could hide it as so many women do manage to do with less serious diseases.[28] Even Dr. Pierre-Jean-Georges Cabanis, who was not actually a surgeon but was instrumental in the "science of man" movement (see Chapter 6), opined that this degrading illness had such a simple cause—slow inflammation of the ovaries and uterus—yet it turned the most docile, proper girl into a violent maniac who went after men far worse than any prostitute ever would.[29]

Another expert on nymphomania, the romantic Dr. August Schweighauser of Strasbourg said that he believed the ovum had such avid desire to be fertilized that it overwhelmed the sperm, which could not keep from doing what the ovum ordered. Besides dismissing the traditional notion that the sperm made an existential decision to penetrate an ovum in order to create new life,[30] he also provided histological proof of how nymphomania spreads to the ovaries. He noted that in "the cadavers of women who died from nymphomania, the ovum are much more voluminous than ordinarily."[31]

Etienne Esquirol, a disciple of Phillipe Pinel and a leading alienist of the era, was more specific. In his 1805 medical thesis on the role of the passions as causes, symptoms, and ways of curing mental illness, he left us a more realistic portrait of imperial women whom he had actually diagnosed and treated for nymphomania.[32] "Who," he asked rhetorically, "is this female maniac: her sunken and haggard eyes, her short and precipitous breathing . . . ?" He continued to tell how she hallucinated, seeing her lover in every male, on the walls or all around her. By contrast, she perceived all females as "monsters who want to tear the object of her delirious passion from her." She gained no respite from sleep and was "devoured by a hot thirst." As the illness prolonged itself, she grew "thin and dehydrated," the psychiatrist observed.[33] Furthermore, he supported this with numerous case studies. But he said that many people of both sexes could recover from the various kinds of "alienation" if people talked to them nicely, treated them lovingly, and persevered at coaxing them to eat.

The patient in one of Esquirol's case studies was a thirty-year-old woman who had courageously survived the French Revolution, but who later became a nymphomaniac, leaving her husband and children in order to pursue lusty pleasures. When she was brought to him, in July 1803, her condition was so serious that they had been wetting her down with cold water and kept both her hands and feet tied. Esquirol tried to treat her kindly and prescribed walking (with a servant) as therapy for her, as he did for most of his patients. He considered walking better than drugs for inducing healthful sleep and also, as it did in this woman's case, it could restore menstruation.[34] So, despite all the surgical and scientific discourse about inflammation of the ovaries and uterus, there actually was hope for some women who were diagnosed with nymphomania—provided they were taken to an enlightened psychiatrist like Esquirol.

In extreme cases, the surgeons had a method of treatment that sharply contrasted to the humane approach of Esquirol. In fact, they were amazingly silent most of the time about their own surgical cure for nymphomania, although they did attempt to justify drastic interventive measures by painting a bleak picture of the disease. For what that was, we must go to imperial legal medicine textbooks[35] where we find that the irreversible, surgical form of intervention was clitoridectomy[36] (excision of the clitoris), which is analogous to amputation of the penis in a male.[37] It is appropriate to point out here that most surgeons were still using bandages rather than stitching on gynecology patients,[38] so prescribing clitoridectomy was a dangerous cure indeed, because of the greater possibility of infection from urine on the bandages used to hold the wound together to allow healing. In any case, surgeons seemed somewhat reluctant to talk about this solution in their texts, thereby relegating it among indecent or unmentionable subjects and possibly avoiding trouble with the imperial censors.

The Milk Deposits Controversy

By the Napoleonic era, scientists had already denounced many folk superstitions.[39] Yet, they still engaged in lively debate over the question of whether breast milk circulated throughout the body to cause many diseases, most notably puerperal fever. In fact, a competitive examination for the position of chief of surgery at the charity hospital of Lyons was held, in 1806, on the subject of milk deposits in general and principally those situated in the ovaries and ligaments of the womb.[40] Pre-Revolution medical books that were reprinted during the empire, such as Louis Vitet's was in 1804, contained long sections on milk deposits existing in disparate locations, including the breasts, the uterus, the extremities, and even the eye and elsewhere in the head. Goiter was cited as an additional example of a disease caused by milk deposits.[41]

But other authors rejected the theory of milk deposits. For example, F. Pelissot, who rejected this notion in 1807, reviewed the literature in the field to discover that the ancients had never believed in the spread of milk deposits causing diseases because Nicholas Puzos (1686–1753) had been the first to publish this notion (posthumously) in 1759.[42] Another person who strongly rejected this idea was Dr. Claudius Montain, who criticized proponents as "lacking in imagination, study, and judgment,"[43] before he revealed the limitations of his own scientific attitudes by informing his imperial readers, in 1808 no less, that some women have six breasts (although two is normal) and the color of breast nipples correlates with hair color.[44]

Ethical Issues

Another raging medical controversy regarding women's health during the Napoleonic era was between the cesareans and the anti-cesareans. This debate was taken up in medical journals as well as in books. Dr. Sacombe of Carcassonne, who had studied at Montpellier and subsequently at the *collège* of Navarre, led the opponents. Sacombe used his talent to write and to compose rhyme in the new periodical *Lucine Française*,[45] which started publication in year XI. Sacombe's calumnious magazine contained such literary forms as poems on childbirth and in one issue (year XIII), an anti-cesarean play entitled "Henry VIII et Jeanne Seymour" to publicize the fact that Seymour had died having a cesarean section. Moreover, this play was performed by the medical students of his anti-cesarean medical school at a ceremony to celebrate the erection of a bust of the emperor,[46] whom Sacombe hoped to influence.

While he sought the emperor's notice, Sacombe vociferously libeled the greatest surgeon-accoucheurs of the era, including Jean-Louis Baudelocque and Antoine Dubois, in the years prior to Napoleon's marriage to Marie Louise. In one of his poems, entitled "Descent into Hell," the first victims the reader discovers in the inferno are those killed by two accoucheurs. One infant recites the cruel fate that took him below:

> Crédule j'attendais de l'art un prompt secours,
> Quand Dubois . . . j'en frémis . . . après un long discours,
> Aux yeux des spectateurs, sans pudeur me découvre,
> Et me perce le sein, qu'en sa rage il entr'ouvre.[47]

Furthermore, while Sacombe labeled Fourcroy "the continuator of Robespierre" and said that Pelletan "organized crime" at the Hospice of Humanity of Paris, he called Baudelocque and Dubois "assassins." In fact, Sacombe went beyond hurling insults: he harassed Baudelocque until the latter took him to court—and won—for slandering his actions in the Tardieu Case, involving a patient whom Baudelocque had lost in a cesarean operation. Some sources even claim that Sacombe's hounding accelerated Baudelocque's death. Sacombe likewise pursued Dubois over the Vasseur Case, in which the mother died but Dubois saved the baby girl, whose name became Césarine. Dubois patronized the unfortunate girl, but Sacombe tracked down the father and urged him to go after Dubois for damages and justice for the alleged murder of the Vasseur woman at the hands of Dubois. Eventually, it was said, "honest people" persuaded Césarine's father to drop the charges, lest he appear ungrateful for the help Dubois had extended to the orphaned girl whom he had delivered from certain death.[48] Undoubtedly, Sacombe's dogged unprofessionalism made life miserable for his arch enemies, the pro-cesarean advocates.

Despite such theatrics, slander, and litigation, most imperial surgeons became proponents of this procedure, and Napoleon did not outlaw its practice—a policy decision that, in some people's minds, put him in the company of such public favorites as Catherine de Medici and Robespierre![49] Something else that set Sacombe apart from the majority of his contemporaries was his opinion that childbirth is not an illness and thus ought to be entirely natural, without any surgical intervention whatsoever, unless the mother already was dead and the child could be salvaged through such intervention.[50] Obviously, such extreme anti-cesareanism would have put the surgeons out of the business of delivering babies, if it had become law. Emotions ran so high on this economic as well as philosophical issue that advocates of cesarean procedures engaged in name-calling too. They labeled men like Sacombe, whom they accused of being too cowardly to operate, as *sages-femmes en culottes*[51] (midwives in trousers), which being consistent with the contemporary sexism cast a low blow to their rivals' good intentions. Moreover, those whom Sacombe vilified received a great deal of sympathy and support from their male colleagues in the Academy of Medicine.

In any case, Doctors Baudelocque, Dubois, H. Ansiaux fils, and Alphonse Leroy were among those men who performed cesareans and episiotomies successfully.[52] The reason the debate ensued was the fact that imperial law was mute on the issue of whether to try to save mother or fetus whenever a choice was deemed necessary.[53] Over and over again, doctors advocated opting for the woman because if she lived, she could have several more children, and she could rear her living children. She should not be sacrificed needlessly on the altar of motherhood if they could intervene to save her.[54] This was, of course, what the emperor himself instructed Antoine Dubois to do when Marie Louise's labor became difficult. But the greater volume of writing favorable to C-sections did not keep the surgeons who performed them from complaining that some of their colleagues abused the technique by resorting to it more often than was necessary.[55] So here, the woman's right to life normally took precedence over the child's.

Assuming that surgical ethics favored the mother's life, it followed logically that it was sometimes ethical to kill a malformed fetus. Surgeons viewed such predicaments gravely because they found it hard to know for certain whether a fetus was dead or alive inside the womb, unless putrefaction had set in.[56] To avoid unnecessary infanticide, Capuron urged surgeons

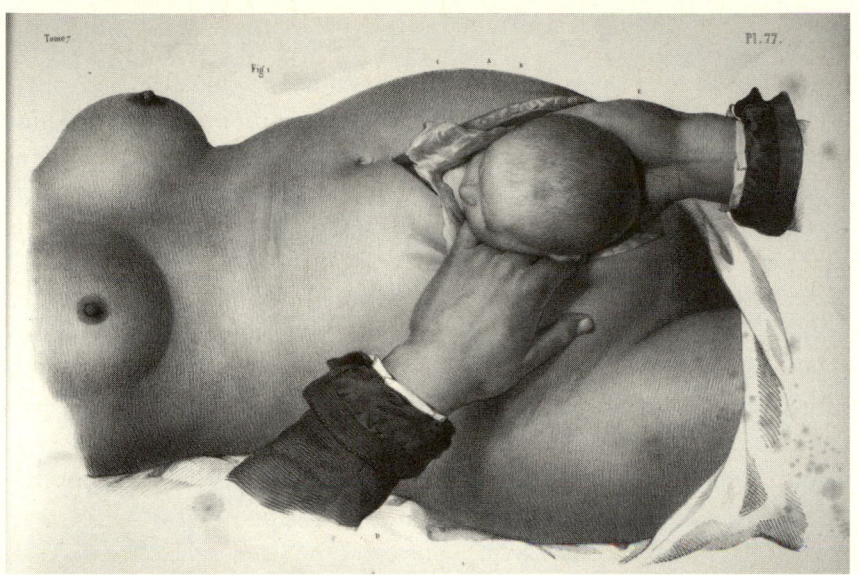

Opération Césarienne Médiane (cesarean section down the middle). Surgeons learned how to perform operations with the help of books like this one, which consisted of one folio volume of written instructions describing how to perform standard operations and a second folio volume entitled "Atlas," made up of colored plates (each containing one to three figures) on the right-hand page with a brief description of the operation on the left. From Bourgery and Jacob, *Traité Complet de l'Anatomie de l'Homme Comprenant la Médecine* . . . Digital photo taken by Laura Travis. Used with permission of the Dittrick Medical History Center, Case Western Reserve University, Cleveland, Ohio.

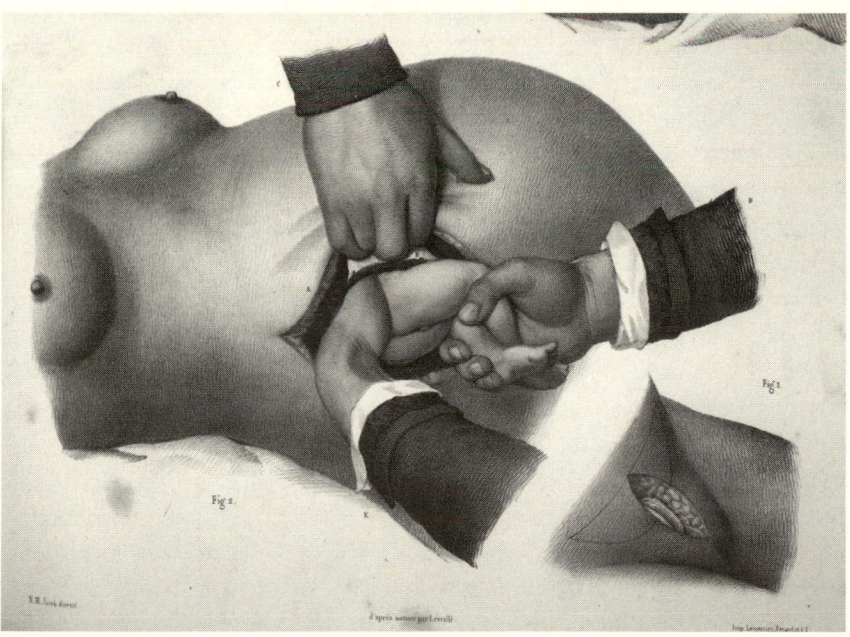

Opération Césarienne Latérale (cesarean section down the side). From Bourgery and Jacob, *Traité Complet de l'Anatomie de l'Homme Comprenant la Médecine* . . . Digital photo taken by Laura Travis. Used with permission of the Dittrick Medical History Center, Case Western Reserve University, Cleveland, Ohio.

first to consult their colleagues if time allowed, then to proceed as if the fetus were alive so that possible error would favor the unborn. He warned against recourse to cutting instruments until manual rescue and the use of forceps or other flexible tools had failed. Recourse to cesarean-section was supposed to be saved for the most serious cases, where embryectomy (mutilating the dead fetus by piercing the skull and crushing the head to make it small enough to extract through the birth canal) would still be a futile process, due to the adult size of a hydrocephalus head, for example. Ultimately, incising the mother sometimes was the surgeon's final recourse and when this happened, the malformed child might have to be sacrificed. As Capuron stated, the examples of hydrocephaloids living to adulthood were so rare that "it would therefore be an injustice, even against humanity, to sacrifice a mother to conserve such a child, when they cannot make her bear it by ordinary means, and with the aid of nature." Then he proceeded to describe in detail the procedure for a surgeon to follow to crush and extract the fetus of a child "that one kills when it is impossible to save it. . . ." This he found less deplorable than submitting a woman to a cesarean operation just to extract a malformed fetus that is going to die anyway.[57]

Nevertheless, there were cases regarding other kinds of deformities for which imperial surgeons arrived less easily at ethical opinions, namely, what to do about Siamese, or conjoined, twins whose births threatened their mother's life. What ought to be done when the fetus is a "monster," if it has two heads or bodies joined? To kill conjoined twins after birth was morally and legally considered the same as the murder of normal persons. Capuron reasoned that the surgeon could argue that conjoined twins were less worthy to live than their mother; however, the example of two Hungarian girls who were joined at the kidneys yet survived to age twenty-one countered that response.[58] On the other hand, he was keenly aware of other arguments favoring the mother. Performing a risky cesarean might be unjust to her. "How can we weigh her life against that of Siamese twins leading a vegetable existence?" he asked. "What consolation can we give her for her suffering or sacrifice for the sake of some deformed creature who is more likely to horrify her than to stimulate a feeling of love, whom she will be ashamed of having conceived, and whom she would rather see dead than saved?" If the conjoined twins were dead, the answer was simple: break them up and extract them. Where they were viable, it was permissible to kill one twin joined at the head or trunk in order to assure the survival of the second one. Nevertheless, sometimes it was impossible to know what to do, he concluded.[59]

In any case, Capuron advised recourse to section of the vulva (*la section du pubis*), as perfected by Jean-Louis Baudelocque on cadavers at the Hôtel Dieu de Paris, as the least hazardous form of surgical intervention at such times. Even so, Baudelocque himself had claimed that of the forty-one pregnant women on whom he had operated, only twenty-seven mothers lived along with thirteen of their babies. The C-section was even more dangerous, with only slightly more than one in three (47 or 48 out of 111 were Baudelocque's precise figures) women likely to survive.[60] "It is the nicest way for a baby to be born," he said, "but the results for the woman are redoubtable,"[61] although he did believe that a few surgeons recently had improved their success rates. For this reason, he never would proscribe the use of the cesarean operation entirely. Certainly when the woman is dead, operate and take the baby. Once the parents have made the choice, accede to their wishes; take a syringe and baptize "this unfortunate victim of maternal egoism" before sacrificing it, thereby avoiding the worse of two evils—which would be to lose both lives instead of just the child's. Since the law was mute on this controversial issue, the surgeon could thus uphold the cardinal principle: do all possible good and avoid all possible harm.[62]

The Society of Maternal Charity Inspires a Plan for Training Female Gynecologists

Among the cesarean proponents just referred to was the doctor for whom a medal was struck for developing the symphysiotomy operation—Dr. Alphonse Leroy.[63] Of this group, Leroy engaged most actively in creating social policy. In 1811 he produced a treatise entitled *De la Conservation des Femmes, Ouvrage Utile à la Population*.[64] In this political work, Leroy commenced by praising Napoleon and Fourcroy for creating the Imperial University, which of course was presently restricted to male students. Then he went on to say that when the public noticed that "women seem to have been almost forgotten by the piercing eye of the immortal Napoleon," his "imperial *bienfaisance*" compensated (for leaving women entirely out of the government monopoly over) higher education by creating a partnership between women's private charitable organizations and the imperial government whose sole purpose was to provide instruction in motherhood—the Imperial Society of Maternal Charity.

Leroy's strategy was to make it seem that Napoleon had created this organization when he knew very well that Napoleon had only revived it. According to Christine Adams, who has published two recent articles on these women's groups,[65] the original Paris branch had been created in 1788 by Anne-Françoise d'Outremont, Mme de Fougeret. As the daughter of an executive at the Hôpital des Enfants-Trouvés, this woman was familiar with the frightful mortality statistics among the growing number of foundlings, which corresponded to the unavailability of wet-nurses to feed them. Under these circumstances the best remedy seemed to be to recruit noble women to contribute money and to volunteer as visiting ladies to deal one-on-one with poor but moral mothers who needed assistance to feed their starving infants. The honorary president of this charitable society was Queen Marie-Antoinette; consequently, by 1793 or 1794, the society became a casualty of the times.

Private charity was once again encouraged by the consular government as it strove to restore order to civil society, and the Paris Society of Maternal Charity was revived in 1801. At that time the government gave it a subsidy of 1,000 francs per month. First Lyons, then other provincial cities began to establish or reestablish branches over the next few years until, in 1810, during the pregnancy of Empress Marie Louise, the emperor's mind focused on making her the patroness of poor mothers who were struggling against poverty to nurture rather than abandon their infants. From Anvers, Napoleon decreed on May 5, 1810, the creation of the Imperial Society of Maternal Charity with an initial endowment of 500,000 francs, a considerable sum. The umbrella organization, which was nominally headed by the empress, was placed under the direction of the Minister of the Interior, with all the new chapters created in every major city placed under the oversight of a council composed of one hundred women at Paris. Napoleon hoped to raise another 500,000 francs from the elite women members who, in addition to monetary donations, also had to volunteer their time and service to visiting the indigent mothers. As recompense for advising and encouraging the needy clients along with providing surveillance to assure that they were spending the money they received frugally enough, these society matrons were given the opportunity to socialize with the empress, which elevated their prestige in the community. However, Adams says that Napoleon had an unspoken, dual purpose in mind—these societies were planned with the view of improving the morals of the rich female patrons as much as those of the poor recipients of the charity, since the message they were supposed to deliver was that all women must breast-feed their own babies. It was Napoleon's way of fighting the perplexing problem of maternal indifference among elite and poor women. Despite some resistance on the part of elite and provincial elite women to donate so much money to help the poor, Cardinal Fesch (Napoleon's uncle), who served as the secretary general of the society, did recruit a roster of five hundred women members within a few months. Eventually, when the regulations for the societies were finalized, allowance was made for some women to volunteer services only in lieu of money because the labor-intensive work of careful oversight of families was tough and depressing, requiring as it did that the visiting *dames* had to venture into the worst neighborhoods where their clients naturally lived. Sometimes the maternal societies delivered more than a layette for the baby and money for food for the mother; for example, in 1811, the Parisian society paid for apprenticeships for twenty-eight orphaned girls whose families had been on assistance. Other instances were the establishment of a crèche for working mothers in Limoges' porcelain industry and others provided vaccination or medical services. The fact that many branches outlasted the many regime changes that followed during the course of the nineteenth century attests to their success as private charity before the welfare state.

Dr. Alphonse Leroy took the emperor's renewed interest in funding and centralizing the Société Maternelle in 1810 as a signal that Napoleon was ready to look kindly upon other ideas for improving womanhood and women's health in order "to assure the happiness of the French Empire."[66] So Leroy obliged with his futuristic proposal. He stressed the need for more trained doctors and midwives than the late Baudelocque had been able to train at La Maternité, and said that their education should be joined to the Imperial University.[67] He also proposed to create two ranks of midwives as additional, female *officiers de santé* (a category of medical doctors who were usually expert in matters of hygiene, public health, epidemiology, and legal medicine). The country women with less education would hold the rank of Second Class, but the better-educated midwives would form the First Class. The latter would be assimilated with the doctors and permitted to deliver babies in urban hospitals.[68] He even proposed that thirty women be selected to become gynecologists,[69] and that these women should study this specialty along with male medical students, since women are capable of so much. He phrased his opinions this way:

> They say women are not suited for medicine. I believe the opposite. Women have tact, sensitivity. . . . The Congregation des Dames Hospitalières has always done good work. If women have excelled in the arts, in poetry, in painting, in literature; if they have understood, explained, developed Newton, how can we believe them incapable of studying, of knowing what happens within their bodies, which affects their sex, themselves as individuals, their children and all humanity?[70]

Moreover, in antiquity, a midwife had been called a *sage-femme,* that is, a "wise woman"; and she was ranked in the social order as highly as a philosopher in Egypt, Judah, Greece, and other parts of Africa and Asia. Once again, after receiving a first-rate medical education, which incorporated theoretical as well as clinical training, only women should be allowed to be licensed to teach midwifery, in order to restore the stature of their profession back to its prior level of excellence.[71]

Not only did Leroy urge upgrading the quality of gynecology and midwifery education available to women, but he urged expanding the production of licensed students throughout the empire sixfold.[72] If this were done, he foresaw great results:

> Provincial cities will have medical training centers comparable to those of Paris, rural midwives will be instructed, male accoucheurs will be as progressive and knowledgeable as women, many babies who now perish will live, . . . the status of midwives will be honorable and honored and lead all women toward being more useful. Many midwives will earn great fame.[73]

Leroy concluded his call for more and better medical education for imperial women with a suitable appeal to the emperor:

> Napoléon Ier has won, by his supernatural exploits, the surname of *Très-Grand;* now he wishes to add to that the title of *Père du peuple,* of whom his august spouse will become the *mère;* this is what he has indicated by his creation of the Société Maternelle.[74]

This brief sketch of the discourse of surgeons touching upon a few of the vital medical issues of the period raised some interesting points. First of all, a real difference appeared between the way Napoleon perceived women as being strong while the majority of these "scientific" doctors saw the exact opposite: weaklings who seem to have been getting twice as sick as men, at the outbreak of the Revolution. This disparity can partly be explained, after all, by the fact that the doctors' only legitimate reason for seeing patients was illness. It should also be remembered that a drastic change was occurring in medical knowledge and licensing, as well as the fact that in aristocratic circles obstetrics and gynecology were shifting away from being women's fields to men's. In any case, scientists transformed childbirth and lactation from natural processes into illnesses. When they examined females' tissues, bones, and body fluids, they were not looking for relatively equal strength pound for pound but for selective evidence to support their personal prejudices. Surgeons based their biological models on contemporary social norms. In other words, imperial surgeons were having trouble making the leap from being philosophers to empiricists when they effortlessly pirouetted back to sexist gender ideology in spite of their best efforts not to do so. They were at odds with Napoleon who held fast to his perception of women being as strong as his own mother. The emperor tried to spread that more physically powerful image via his propaganda while surgeons willingly provided new physiological grounds for more political inequality.

Another point was the stress they placed on the importance of the uterus, which made women walking wombs. To these authors, biology was destiny. Because they believed that the brain and the heart reigned over the male body and the uterus over the female, their next idea following that logic was to believe that women were different, not equal. This again showed a failure to grasp the empirical method. But then common sense led a doctor like Leroy to realize that women could understand such things as physics and astronomy, probably because he knew women who did. In sum, changing scientific theories about sexuality coming on the heels of the Revolution, with all its accompanying sexual nuances, seemed to have created confusion in the world of surgery as well.

The discourse on the causes and character of nymphomania now seems curious in our age of sexual liberation and promiscuity. Perhaps their own sexual anxiety caused these early forerunners of modern psychiatry to be so afraid of these sick women whose psychological problems caused them to reverse the contemporary power relationship between men and women. Understandably, surgeons were secretive about the sexual mutilations they performed in an effort to "cure" nymphomaniacs, but which certainly caused horrible suffering and posed terrible risks of infection before the invention of modern anesthesia, antiseptics, and antibiotics.

Progressive surgeons were unable to develop a consensus yet on some issues, such as whether breast milk traveled through the body to cause fevers and other illnesses. Nor could they decide definitively about the value of cesarean sections or when it was appropriate to use them, although support for employing C-sections seemed to be increasing as they became more successful. Although they could not agree on therapeutics and surgical intervention, they more easily defended female subordination instead of leaving that open to debate as well.

Finally, Leroy's response to Napoleon's exclusion of women's education from the Imperial University indicated that some members of the intelligentsia were quite aware of the omission. Leroy chose this point in time to come forward because of Baudelocque's death. He respectfully waited until then to criticize the highly admired midwifery professor at La Maternité whose opinions were frequently cited by surgeons as authoritative. Once Baudelocque was gone, Leroy eagerly offered his expertise to draft a revised, more simplified, official midwifery textbook than Baudelocque's in order to make the curriculum easier for the barely literate pupils to master. Although theoretical disagreement with his colleague Baudelocque over the number of presentations of the fetus (see Chapter 4), personal ambition, and

Napoleon's recent initiative with the creation of the Société Maternelle motivated him, Leroy did grasp the essential fact that the first national normal school of midwifery needed to produce graduates in larger numbers in order to meet the needs of France's larger departments. Remarkable too, is his plea for female gynecologists—long before mid-century. His modern confidence in women's mental abilities echoes that of the feminist educators and authors of housekeeping manuals.

In conclusion, this overview of the body history of the First Empire showed the political side of medical culture. Contrary to what we would imagine, the more surgeons examined tissue, the more sexually biased they became in comparison to the liberal, humanistically trained physicians—even more sexually biased than Napoleon himself. As an occupational group, the surgeons' conservative outlook was matched only by that of the mistresses of schools for young ladies. Leroy, who was far in advance of his time, was the one notable exception to the blatant sexism among the surgical community. In fact, Leroy's radical plans to make women specialists who could compete with males in the medical profession constituted an effort to blur the sexes and contribute to the ongoing "war between the sexes." The social significance of the surgeons' mind-set is that either consciously or subconsciously, they collaborated in the political policy of restricting women to the home and thereby, to public silence. Such preoccupation diverted them from achieving genuine progress in medicine, which, like all sciences, requires objectivity in order to discover truth about the natural mysteries of how the body functions and to learn how to intervene successfully in remediable cases. But by trying to make society in general, as well as their affluent clients in particular, believe that women were weaker and sicker than they really were, the surgeons secured their own and their colleagues' financial futures and places in society, just as the school mistresses did by teaching young ladies to be more "feminine" and dependent. As surgeons did this, they also took midwifery and women's medicine out of the hands of the experienced but formally uneducated women and men who had practiced "popular" medicine for thousands of years. The surgeons' inability to adapt quickly to empiricism helps largely to explain why it would be several decades before women would necessarily be any better off for having consulted them. Improving quality of life for women through biochemistry was still an aspiration.

Napoleon seems to have known instinctively that these medical scientists did not know how to think clearly, despite the fact that they did their share of manipulating women into submission and thereby helped fulfill his desire that women's lives be kept private and domestic. What's more, surgeons (including his favorite, Dominique Larrey) had a reputation for being overly anxious to use the scalpel—something that Napoleon personally feared.[75] The emperor, who did not share the surgeons' opinion of women as weaklings, was correct in being skeptical about the superiority of male midwives and continued, agreeing with Leroy's basic idea, to think that official policy for the masses ought to be to entrust more well-trained women with the care of their helpless sisters.

6

The Glandular Theory of Difference

Dr. Cabanis and the "Science of Man"

THIS MANUSCRIPT OPENED with a survey of Napoleon's mechanistic ideas about women's nature in which he mentioned their soul and limited reason as well as the destiny of the female body as a "baby-making machine." We then surveyed the literary quarrels over women's capacity to use reason. Men, like Ponce Denis Ecouchard Lebrun and Sylvain Maréchal, argued that the reasoning ability of the female mind was limited to production of mediocre creative works. Therefore, women should refrain from reading and writing careers that lead them into public space or make them celebrities; instead, they should devote their lives to generation and domesticity and inspiring men to create great works. We also sampled manuals and textbooks for self-improvement and the home-schooling of children and found a range of opinions regarding the woman question. But the debate was not restricted to the emperor and his immediate circle of friends, the literary elite who published their opinions in books and journals, or male and female educators.

However they were labeled, the nucleus of meaning behind all of these simultaneous discourses was the burning question of "the physical and the moral." This was, however, the central discourse in the contemporary medical movement known as "the science of man." The leading figure in this was the eminent physician Dr. Pierre-Jean-Georges Cabanis (1757–1808), whose reputation survived the nineteenth century and who is remembered as a founder of psychophysiology. French medicine is notorious for its alliances with politics, and this was no less true for the Napoleonic era. Cabanis's personal involvement started with his election (representing the Seine) in 1798 to the Council of Five Hundred as a republican moderate. He supported Bonaparte's coup d'état of 18 Brumaire (November 9–10, 1799) by writing an address to the nation on 19 Brumaire. Weeks later, Cabanis issued another address upholding the new constitution, which he said was written for them and not by "their ill-considered dictation."[1] While Cabanis opposed some of Bonaparte's actions, mainly on anticlerical and liberal grounds, he exercised care in never actually becoming a leader of the public opposition. He enjoyed significant benefits from imperial patronage by accepting several prestigious positions including that of senator, professor at the École de Médecine de Paris, member (after the reorganization of 1803) of the Institute's Class of French Language and Literature, and commander of the Légion of Honor.

The Idéologues

On the private level, Cabanis attached himself to a prominent group of contemporary thinkers who styled themselves as *Idéologues*,[2] or advocates of a new science of ideas. According to Emmet Kennedy, his biographer, A. L. C. Destutt de Tracy coined the term in 1796 as a descriptive label for medical theorists who believed in a sensationalist "science of ideas," regardless of whether their methodology was philosophical, physiological, or geographical-anthropological. However, Napoleon first used the term in a disparaging way to criticize "republican intellectuals who turned against his regime, some of whom—Emmanuel Sieyès, C. F. Volney, and Georges Cabanis—had earlier supported Napoleon's coup assuming that he would preserve basic liberties."[3] Historiography on the *Idéologues* has attempted to make long or short lists of members by either defining them narrowly and insisting that they must have frequented the salons of Mme Helvetius and Mme Condorcet and published their opinions in the group's journal, the *Décade Philosophique,* or using the term broadly and simply including anyone in three generations of medicine who shared their theories about ideas. In any case, Elizabeth Williams compiled a list of sixteen members, including Georges Cabanis, François Chaussier, J.-L. Moreau de la Sarthe, A.-B. Richerand, Pierre Roussel, and Pierre Sue. All of these *Idéologues* were linked to the "science of man."[4]

Dr. Cabanis, whom contemporaries described as being a rather tall, slender man with delicate health,[5] came from Conac in the department of the Corrèze. When he arrived in Paris at the age of fourteen in 1771, he already was a highly opinionated young man, yet his passion was moderated by his sense of justice and appetite for learning all kinds of things.[6] In 1773 he traveled to Poland as secretary for two years to the bishop of Vilna, Prince Massalsky. After he returned to Paris, he was introduced to the economist Turgot and through the latter to Mme Anne Catherine de Ligniville d'Auricourt Helvétius (1719–1800), widow of the late encyclopedist Claude Adrien Helvétius who had died in 1771. Mme Helvétius treated Cabanis, who was still a teenager, like an adopted son.[7]

Mme Helvétius gave Cabanis social connections by introducing him to the illustrious people in her circle. While he came to know Mirabeau and Voltaire, Cabanis's ideas conformed with those of other acquaintances and masonic lodge members, such as d'Holbach, Diderot, and d'Alembert, as well as with the American sages Benjamin Franklin and Thomas Jefferson.[8] But he developed such a strong relationship with Condorcet that when the author of *On Progress of the Human Mind* (who favored women's education) passed away, Cabanis became the guardian of Condorcet's son and his widow, Sophie.[9] His ties to the Condorcets became family ties when Cabanis married Condorcet's sister-in-law, Charlotte Grouchy, the sister of Sophie and of the *chausseur* General Grouchy, whom Napoleon ultimately designated as his twenty-sixth marshal in 1815. These were splendid connections given the revolutionary tidal wave that would soon sweep old ideas from their moorings and open future careers to a new generation of talented people.

During his teens and while he actively participated in the salons, Cabanis wanted to become a poet, which led him to undertake the translation of Homer's *Iliad*. But when his father made him choose a career, he was inspired by Greek medicine.[10] He thus came under the guidance of Dr. Dubreuil, whose lessons in medicine he followed for six years[11] with the same relish as he had letters. Cabanis was received as a degree candidate in medicine in 1784 and, until the Revolution of 1789, practiced and lived in Auteuil, where Mme Helvétius also resided. There, he earned a fine reputation as a humanitarian physician for doctoring all kinds of people, including the indigent.[12]

When Cabanis entered the medical profession, the leading medical philosophy was "the science of man." This movement was characterized by materialism coupled with optimism that medical therapeutics and hygiene could contribute to the social transformation of French society. "The science of man" originated in the medical philosophy of the Montpellier vitalists around 1750 and lasted until around 1850 when it disintegrated into its composite disciplines—physiology, anthropology, and philosophical medicine. So for roughly a century its adherents engaged in a discourse on the urgent problem of understanding the relations between the physical and the moral, the body and the mind. The discourse spread from Montpellier Faculty of Medicine to Paris, and one of the places where doctors from the capital came into contact with its principles was in Mme Helvétius's salon at Auteuil. The Montpellier vitalists' therapeutic methods consisted of observation (of healthy and ill patients), analysis, and classification, to which they added a portion of sensationalism in order to explain how the mind communicated with the body. Sensationalism was especially important for doctors like Cabanis whose interests were in learning how ideas originate and how they tell parts of the body to respond. Cabanis believed that *sensibilité* encompassed all the mental faculties of reason, imagination, feeling, and judgment—the broad range of human experience. Since he believed that medicine had to be grounded in physiology, then tied to sensationalism, for Cabanis, feeling was the crux of life: "from the moment we feel, we exist." Thus, Cabanis anticipated the specialty of psychophysiology. Another aspect of "the science of man" that impinged on the woman question was its proclivity to classify human types according to race, sex, age, climate, and geography, which these optimistic medical revolutionaries supposed would assist politicians in finding solutions for social problems. This overview of the origin of "the science of man" in Montpellier vitalism and sensationalism helps to situate Dr. Cabanis within French medicine of the Revolutionary era.[13]

Not merely did Cabanis survive the Revolutionary period, the altruistic young doctor also advanced professionally. He became administrator of the hospitals of Paris and then was active in the reorganization of the Schools of Medicine. Being a liberal rather than a radical Jacobin, his moderate ideology enabled him to uphold the Directory for a time, to display anti-Jacobin sentiment in 1797, and to serve in the Council of Five Hundred. Nevertheless, Cabanis participated in Napoleon Bonaparte's coup d'état of 18 Brumaire (November 9–10, 1799). The physician and fellow member of the Institut Balthasar Richerand said in his funeral oration for Cabanis that the deceased had taken an active role in that event because "he believed that the vessel of the Republic battered by so many tempests, had need for new pilots."[14] Subsequently, Cabanis backed charismatic young General Bonaparte during the consulate by publishing a work defending the lawfulness of the new government; it was phrased in such a way as to win the approval of those who distrusted the masses or "the people" to speak for themselves and rule themselves.

In time Cabanis took his place in the Senate among France's most distinguished men. From then on, as a recipient of Napoleon's patronage for men of sciences and letters, he was free to devote himself to writing highly imaginative works on medical philosophy, which could be based upon his broad interests and interaction with the great minds of the time, as well as on his own medical experience. However, before he died in his early fifties in 1808, which was only four years after Napoleon's coronation, Cabanis's enthusiasm for the emperor had dissipated.

Dr. Cabanis became ill in the spring of 1807 when he suffered the first of three serial strokes. He had spent his final years quietly in the country. To his many friends, admirers, and visitors he liked to recite Hoffmann's dictum that "Nervous apoplexy is Nature's recompense for long works of the mind." After he died on May 5, 1808, his body was subjected to surgical scrutiny. His remains were ceremoniously pantheonized in Eglise Sainte-Geneviève as a sign of the great esteem in which he was held by the Napoleonic government. When his eulogy was read at the November 24 meeting of the Paris medical faculty, as was customary, noteworthy details of his autopsy were shared and later published for posterity:

> The opening of the cadaver showed the left ventricle of the heart had a volume and strength at least three times the ordinary volume and strength. The wall of this muscular cavity was more than an inch thick so that at first glance, anyone could observe the evident disproportion between the power of this central agent of impulsion and the rest of his machine.[15]

Ironically, Cabanis's own autopsy report attested to the popularity of mechanistic discourse circa 1808, at the Faculty of Medicine itself.

The Science of Man[16]

While the writings Cabanis left behind shared many of the preoccupations of the friends he had made during his youth prior to the Revolution, clearly he was a beneficiary of and contributor to the scientific progress made by his own generation. His creative writings, which help to explain why he was officially revered, became part of the imperial legacy to the future of French medicine. For this reason, Cabanis has been the subject of several biographies. Martin Staum's expert opinion argued in the most recent one, *Cabanis—Enlightenment and Medical Philosophy in the French Revolution* (Princeton University Press, 1979), is that, placed in context, Dr. Cabanis was a moderate yet liberal thinker. Staum wrote:

> Both in society and in the individual . . . Cabanis hoped to achieve a dynamic equilibrium between the "natural" and the free and the "artificial and the regulated."
> Cabanis's goal was to establish a "science of man" that would unite physiology, "analysis of ideas," and ethics. He thus sought to modify physical temperament in such a way as to insure the mental health of the individual while promoting moral values and social harmony.[17]

Cabanis disseminated his special ideas about the new "science of man" and the connection between the physical and mental health of both sexes in the two parts of his treatise entitled *Rapports du Physique et du Moral de l'Homme,* which he published in 1798 and 1802, respectively, with a second edition coming forth in 1805. More than two decades after the second half of *Rapports* first appeared, it was also included in the publication of his *Oeuvre Complètes* (1824), so that not only had imperial readers been exposed to his thinking, but the scientifically literate could purchase new copies during the later years of the Bourbon Restoration. The moral philosophy of medicine elaborated in Cabanis's *Rapports* was based upon his understanding of human physiology and body chemistry in which he paid special attention to the inherent differences between men and women.

Basically, Cabanis's opinion of woman's nature placed great emphasis upon the importance of sexuality. Like Old Testament writers, the ancient Chinese sages, and William Shakespeare, among others, Cabanis saw human life as a progression through stages. Each age has its maladies and each age meets death differently.[18] For him, the stages of woman, which were more pronounced than for man, were the fetal stage, infancy and childhood, adolescence, womanhood—the prime of life—and finally, old age.

According to Cabanis, the embryo or fetus in the womb, while not yet really "alive" because its lungs do not yet breathe to sustain its own life independently, does receive sensations from its external environment.[19] It hears sound, for instance, because sound travels through the fluid in which it is freely suspended. The fetus may also see light.[20] Besides these external stimuli, the mother and fetus engage in sympathetic behavior—they transmit illnesses to each other.[21] Then too, external stimuli and natural laws influence the unborn during "prelife."[22] While the human fetus is receiving both kinds of stimuli in utero, it lives from humors nurtured by the mother's vessels. Notably, throughout the discussion of the fetal stage, Cabanis avoided the contemporary controversy over the determination of the sex of a child by simply saying that we probably will never unveil this mystery.[23]

The Stages of Life

Childhood, said Cabanis, was the first stage of real life. In infancy the child was nurtured by the mother's milk produced by the specialized organs she has for this purpose.[24] Quite marvelously, without any training the newborn was able to nurse,[25] which is a complex physical activity. Throughout childhood, odor did not affect humans.[26] Moreover, during this time, relatively small distinctions characterized the sexes. All their muscles, bones, and glands were similar and their shoulders and pelvises had about the same volume. Even mentally, they behaved the same, sharing the same petulance, mobility, appetites, ideas, and passions. This explained why babies were traditionally dressed in unisex clothing. Yet, unlike animals, it took humans years before they actually gained the ability to reproduce.[27]

Gradually, slight differences did appear, however. Girls had a natural instinct to adore babies and seize every available opportunity to practice mothering and babysitting. Girls who were isolated from the company of younger children played instead with dolls and pretended to wash, dress, feed, put them down to rest, and so on, just as they would if they were mothers themselves.[28] Boys began to move less gracefully and paid attention to little details, whereas girls started to become vain and developed the art of conversation long before boys had any notion of how to use this ability to get what they wanted.[29]

Then came pubescence, the single most important time in a woman's life. What happened then to transform the previously sexually dormant girl into a woman? Cabanis went to the core of this question. The sudden transformation was caused by secretions of the sex organs. Cabanis thought that these surely were real glands;[30] and like all glands, the sex glands were sympathetic.[31] The chemical product of the glands was injected into the bloodstream and carried throughout the body. It thereby traveled to the chest and to the brain so that these parts of the body underwent a natural metamorphosis. The action of the ovaries made women's eyes twinkle while their facial aspect became more timid and reserved.[32] The emerging nubile woman became ready to reproduce the species with the onset of ovulation and menstruation. More specifically, the ovaries themselves produced chemicals that went into embryos and which were reabsorbed into the blood.[33] But not merely the body is changed in this biochemical process, the mind underwent an equally dramatic change in the way it thought, felt, sympathized, and so forth. Males underwent puberty too; as they entered manhood they were for the first time dramatically different from females. Glandular "liquor" caused male voices to deepen, their physiques to change, and their faces to break out, a sign of new vigor.[34]

Cabanis's epistemology for glandular secretions being the root cause of sexual differences came from his observation of humans as well as poultry. Cabanis reasoned that mutilated males acted feminine, and women who never menstruated acted masculine.[35] In an earlier footnote, he had also called attention to the fact that chicken farmers induced capons (castrated roosters) to set hen's eggs by rubbing vinegar on the skin exposed after their under-feathers have been plucked.[36] Although he claimed not to comprehend the causes of these behavioral changes toward the female nesting instinct, he did say that it was absurd to search for mechanistic explanations and that it might be more worthwhile to consider physiological ones if we were ever going to surpass the knowledge of the ancients.[37] Furthermore, he warned, girls and boys whose sex organs failed to mature normally would become ill and sometimes only fully recover after marriage—through successful practice with using their sex organs.[38]

In any case, the stage of full-fledged womanhood was characterized by a new physiological and mental state because the uterus and ovaries caused fibers and cells to become more abundant.[39] Concomitantly, women's cerebral pulp was as feeble as the rest of their tissues that were more mucous or mushy than men's. This difference in brain cells of females was responsible for their ability to be more quick-witted and sensitive.[40] Because women's muscles were relatively feeble, their dislike for violent exercise led to a preference for a sedentary lifestyle. In fact, leading a nonsedentary lifestyle aged more active women prematurely.

Socially, a woman's life was predetermined by her anatomy. Being weak, women sought protection because they knew they could not survive alone. Mentally, women were predisposed to delicate work and lacked the ability to think profoundly. Hence, the weaker sex became coquettes. Men, of course, were exactly the opposite—repose was bad for them and their stronger minds.[41] Philosophers who claimed women were held down by education and by society were wrong, Cabanis said, because they simply did not know female physiology. Female savants were doomed to failure beforehand, and they could not avoid losing their charm because being a scientist, he believed, was totally alien to women's faculties. However much a man loved his wife, he could never take pleasure in seeing her carry a musket or making an infantry charge, running a factory, or ruling a nation. Her true place was in the home, as Rousseau and Dr. Roussel argued. Those few women who were somewhat successful at intellectual pursuits really did not fit into either sex: they were mistakes of nature.[42] The only path to happiness possible for women was to stay at home and please their husbands, and only thus could they gain respectability, leaving public affairs to men (the strong and intelligent sex).[43] Women really lacked enough capacity for the strong level of reasoning that was necessary for meaningful participation in public affairs, he concluded.

Women in the prime of life had a great need for intercourse, according to Cabanis, in order to maintain good health. Nor were the effects of abstinence the same for both sexes. Generally, women could tolerate excess of "the pleasure of love" (his term for intercourse throughout the entire work) better and withstand deprivation worse. For an idle woman who lived alone deprivation was far worse to suffer than for a man in like circumstances.[44] A sexually starved, bilious, and melancholic lady would develop inflammatory illnesses or convulsions, accompanied by a nasty personality change. Only women whose fibers were exceptionally spongy ought to practice therapeutic chastity.[45] Furthermore, Cabanis sadly acknowledged that very sensitive patients needed to refrain from "the pleasures of love"; yet, restraint was most difficult for this personality type that not only craved love the most but was most apt to become easily impregnated. Indeed, midlife was a woman's prime time because she could enjoy the pleasures of breast-feeding and incubation. Cabanis noted that several wet-nurses and other women had confided to him that the former produced pleasurable feelings in their genitals and the latter "orgasms of the uterus," which he thought must off-set the routine discomfort of gestation.[46]

Cabanis believed that women's lives alternated between periods of well-ness and suffering and too often suffering dominated.[47] Certainly, the final stage—the menopausal stage—was filled with suffering. As the uterus stopped functioning, women lost their sensitivity, their voices changed, and hair grew on their faces. They even lost their desire to care for children. This was especially true of old maids, although some grandmothers did go against nature and continued to want to be around their grandchildren.[48] Surprisingly, Cabanis showed far less interest in this unattractive stage than in any of the others.

Finally, lest readers think that Cabanis meant for women or anyone else to use their physical weakness as an excuse for idleness, he included a pas-sage on the personal and social value of work. He issued his prescriptive on working because he believed it was good for morality. He knew that since antiquity, wise men had considered work as essential for the good life: it conserved the individual's strength and health and produced personal and public wealth besides leading to the development of good sense and good manners. We could therefore surmise that hard work would make Cabanis's ideal woman a naturally moral person.[49]

Now what can we make of Cabanis's views on woman's nature? This was not an easy question to answer because on the one hand, many important French doctors of that era were uninterested in publishing their philosoph-ical views while many of those who did, did not speak to the same issues. For example, most surgeons were more interested in disseminating surgical techniques than in philosophy and ethics. So we must try to make an assess-ment on the basis of the partial evidence.

Compared to our surveys in Chapters 3 and 5 of both types of medical literature of the Napoleonic era, Cabanis's theory about the glandular secre-tions at puberty being largely responsible for physical differences between the sexes as well as for female domesticity was unique. Others followed the direction of Roman Catholic theology and explored the details about what actually happened at the moment of conception and whether the ovaries or the testicles determined the sex of offspring. Possibly, Cabanis's materialism and atheism helped to explain why he had no trouble ignoring the Church's dogmatic assertions about conception, and (unlike Napoleon, who did it in jest) he never spoke of the soul either in the mind-body nexus. Instead, he shifted focus to puberty as being the event in time of dramatic sexual change. Logically, of course, this kind of emphasis enhanced the significance of menopause as a subsequent change of life as well, but Cabanis failed to give equal time to that because, as he explained, male and female sexuality had already become fixed with the onset of puberty so neither sex reverted thereafter to its previously ungendered design. Puberty was simply the center of his focus.

Cabanis's views differed in many ways from Napoleon's opinion, although both men lacked genuine religious faith and emphasized work as important for society's prosperity and happiness. First of all, Napoleon's education led him to be a mechanist. His thinking seemed to have been strongly influenced by Descartes and La Mettrie. For example (as we saw in Chapter 1), he loved to tease the ladies about being merely "baby-making machines." But the single most important person who influenced Napoleon's personality was his mother, Madame Mère, as she was called during the empire. If tiny Letizia Ramolino Bonaparte was anything, she was a strong person. Besides bearing numerous children beginning in her early teenage years, she fought in the Paoli-led Corsican struggle for liberation beside her young husband, who predeceased her by more than five decades. And ever dubious of the enduring quality of her children's enormous and rapid successes, she failed in her duty as the emperor's mother to show up for his coronation (which may have been partly due to her disapproval of Josephine, who was being crowned as empress), whether he liked it or not.[50] Nevertheless, although Napoleon never said he loved his mother, publicly he seemed to admire and respect her, and (even though he exaggerated—in a good way) he talked proudly and lovingly about the obstacles she had surmounted in order to give her children a better life. Consequently, Cabanis's view of women as natural weaklings ran directly counter to Napoleon's early experience. Napoleon also perceived women vendors in marketplaces and poor women as being strong and recognized that they often had to play the stabilizing role in families when males failed to do so or could not because they became mentally and/or physically handicapped, a condition to which his wars contributed mightily. The emperor probably would have laughed at Cabanis's remarks about the musket-wielding female being unlovable since his teenage pregnant mother had fought bravely, riding horseback, handling weapons, and lugging supplies over Corsica's mountainous terrain in the struggle against French conquest of their homeland. Napoleon had more understanding of real-life situations and the dangers women faced in lawless areas. While Napoleon admired female courage and thought women could be ferocious fighters in defense of the *patrie,* he did share Cabanis's low opinion of female savants. For example, Napoleon's annoyance with Mme de Staël's involvement in politics made him run her out of Paris. But then the emperor likewise exiled her colleague Châteaubriand; so it was not their gender that got them into trouble with the emperor's gendarmes. While Cabanis's scientific instincts about the importance of glands was monumental and marked him as modern, his view of women as weaklings made him appear even more socially reactionary than Napoleon.

But what effect did such theoretical ideas have on women's actual lives? Cabanis may have been only a moderate Jacobin; nonetheless, he used "the science of man" to justify the totally unenlightened, Jacobin-led political program of silencing women's voices in the public sphere. In other words, he earned a distinguished place among the members of the literate medical community that played a role in the domestication of French women during the Directory, consulate, and empire. This pressure on women to devote their lives entirely to homemaking and reproduction may have contributed to the population explosion that occurred during the Napoleonic era. As the norms of domesticity became progressively stricter, some women probably experienced psychological problems adjusting, leading to depression or other mental and physical dysfunctions. During his rise to fame, Cabanis assumed an administrative leadership role in medical institutions that treated women patients. Doubtless, his cold opinions would have chilled the climate of opinion inside their walls regarding the display of sympathy for sensitive, intelligent, or creative women trapped in this cultural and legalized bondage.

As we have seen, as the power of the clergy diminished following the Revolution, the vacuum was filled by the elite, scientifically trained doctors and surgeons who became the new high priests who reigned over the female body. Their idea of Nature's intentions left women virtually no voice, choice, or self-determination. Unfortunately for women's sake, medical progress such as the discovery of sex glands, or what later would be termed "hormones," did not naturally lead to such achievements as the empowerment of women, the freedom to be real "adults" when they married, or political and economic equality with men. Cabanis's medical philosophy was unique, and he was heading toward the modern understanding of sexual development; but, instead of using his new theory to advance women, his philosophical bias was a throwback to an earlier time. As Elizabeth Williams phrased it, in "the science of man" "there was a profound reluctance to leave the past behind."[51] Consequently, Cabanis was just another, perhaps louder voice, heard from the long line of outstanding French scientists on the government payroll and recipient of imperial patronage who used physiology and sensationalism to reenforce the pervasive sexist ideology reintroduced into that era whereby biology was destiny.

Unfortunately from the perspective of women's liberation, the influence of Cabanis's ideas lasted far into the nineteenth century. The tendency of "the science of man" to type humans' physiology according to race, sex, and age (in addition to climate and geography) distorted woman's nature doubly and the nature of women of color a third time. Medicine privileged men and labeled women "childlike" in order to justify their unequal status. Furthermore, imperial women were additionally caught in double jeopardy in the sense that after Napoleon made peace with the Church in 1801, by means of the Concordat, the Gallican Church, which was antifeminist, was strengthened by Napoleon in order to stabilize order; and, "the science of man," which had evolved from Montpellier vitalism valorized domesticity. Thus, atheistic materialist medicine worked hand in glove with politics and the Church. Imperial womanhood paid the bill for historical events in the Revolution that nobody seemed willing to forget—or forgive. Radical women behaving like men had risen up in a violent manner, intruded into public space, joined the crowd, participated in the journées, demanded a voice at the podium, marched here and there with male heads on the ends of pikes, participated in and observed public festivals, organized patriotic societies, and scared many doctors of medicine (a profession that tends to dislike conflict) to death for more than a decade afterward! Not only did stressed out men fear the return of ordinary civil war, but actual "war between the sexes," which Napoleon quite seriously had said women would win if such a war ever got started.

In addition to working closely with politics and the Church, "the science of man" associated with and assisted the judiciary in the solution of social problems, as we shall see in Chapter 7.

7

Women's Issues in Napoleonic-Era Textbooks of Legal Medicine

THE TERM *médicine légale* ("legal medicine") requires some introduction since it is not a familiar term to most people.[1] It should be pointed out that "medico-law" and legal medicine were not interchangeable terms since the former pertained to the field of law regarding things medical while the latter was a medical field that is associated with and assists the judiciary. Again, professionals working in the former were trained lawyers, the latter were licensed doctors. Usually the professionals active in the field of legal medicine had received the sort of education that was typical of medical practitioners, either as humanistic physicians, surgeons, or military surgeons. But some were accoucheurs who had earned the title of "doctor of medicine." Others, such as the *officiers de santé*[2] who served as one of the special public health officials or "hygienists," had a shorter or more limited education, training, or apprenticeship, were licensed to practice outside of Paris in a single department by its special *jury médical,* and could not perform surgery unless a licensed surgeon was present. Sometimes an *officier de santé* earned so little money from legal medicine that he had to practice a trade on the side (which suggests something about social class). In some instances, a trained midwife might also be used by a court for gathering evidence about a woman's physical and/or mental condition or in court as an expert witness.

As one would expect in late-eighteenth- and early-nineteenth-century France when medicine was heavily influenced by Montpellier vitalism and "the science of man" but had not yet disintegrated into the composite disciplines, the concept of legal medicine was a broad one with vague boundaries that overlapped other areas of medicine. It, of course, included morbid anatomy: issues relating to finding the cause of suspicious deaths, murder whether from poisoning, drowning, strangulation, starvation, violence, physical abuse, or the like. But legal medicine also embraced all forms of jurisprudential medicine involving living persons, including regular medical examinations, ethical determinations, and medical detective work as well. Manuals of legal medicine also spoke to matters such as quarantines, sequestration (of lepers, for instance), vaccination, puerperal and other fevers, fumigations, dietary deficiencies such as scurvy, and so many other kinds of issues related to public health.

In courts of law physicians and public health officials testified as expert witnesses in cases regarding living persons' bodies. The delicate cases coming to authorities frequently resulted from sexual transgressions, someone's or a couple's failure either to control or to exercise their bodies in appropriate ways. For the aristocracy, male lineage was extremely important. As a result, for accused males, impotence (such failure to perform could lead to annulment of a marriage) and paternity (the result of performance) might be examples of accusations that needed investigation. Cases regarding women's bodies were more likely to involve questions about rape, incest, virginity, or conception. A decision might be needed to clarify whether a handicapped person of either sex was legally eligible to marry; and, if already married, an opinion might be sought about whether the marriage could be ended by annulment rather than divorce due to the discovery of physical impediments. Puberty, determining the legal sex of children born with ambiguous genitalia, the removal of infants born to lepers during sequestration, venereal diseases, wet-nursing and artificial feeding, lunacy, abortion, and infanticide were some other legal-medical issues. So there was a wide, wide range of subject matter to this challenging, interdisciplinary field that pertained to parenting, social problems, and civil contracts, in addition to criminal prosecutions. Because the subject was so broad, comprehensive treatises on legal medicine usually had to be multivolume works to cover such a wide range of issues encompassing various climatic conditions and geographical terrains, variables that affected health as much as race, sex, and age—all the human types in which "the science of man" was interested in refining.

Modern Legal Medicine

During the Napoleonic era authors drew the line between the ancient and modern eras of legal medicine at 1600. Prior to that date, they believed there had been four distinct periods in the history of legal medicine: the ancient period of the Hebrew priest-judges and the Egyptians; the Roman period; the medieval period of Salic and Germanic law; and the period of canon law from 1200 to 1600. Although the modern period began early in the seventeenth century, it was really only in the French Revolutionary/Napoleonic era that modern legal medicine was established definitively.[3] The medical profession was then engaged in the process, which had begun during the Enlightenment, of supplanting the Church as the arbiter of women's bodies and feminine sexuality.[4] Since legal medicine was not, strictly speaking, an art of healing like the other branches of medicine, the name might have been a misnomer,[5] which was used for lack of a better term. Rather, it dealt with the application of medical opinions and knowledge to judicial proceedings. Moreover, legal medicine represented a convergence of the ideas of the medical and legal professions, both of which were male dominated, in the actual administration of justice. The Napoleonic courts were, therefore, a "crossroads" of interaction between two systems that collaborated in determining woman's place and role in imperial society.

The three subdivisions within French legal medicine were called (1) determination of death, (2) generation, and (3) rights and duties.[6] It was primarily in the latter two areas that so many "privacy" issues occurred. Manuals of legal medicine provided uniform guidance for all criminal and civil law courts when they became engaged in discourses pertaining to the female body, the fetus, and the child.

Authors of Legal Medicine Manuals

The surgeon Jean-Jacques Belloc (1730–1807) of the Department of Lot et Garonne is honored by reference works as the modern founder of French legal medicine. He and his students disinterred cadavers so as to have bodies for dissection. The principles Belloc taught his pupils were published in the year IX (1800–1801) as *Cours de Médecine Légale Judiciare, Théorique et Pratique,* and reedited in 1811 and 1819.[7]

The anatomist-obstetrician Antoine Dubois (1756–1837) also was an important founder of legal medicine but unfortunately he never published. However, after 1793 Dubois worked as the assistant of the Ideologue François Chaussier (1746–1828), who probably was the first teacher of legal medicine, while both men's official positions also included the inspection of military hospitals. After accompanying General Bonaparte to Egypt, in 1801 Dubois created a *maison de santé* himself and eventually would rise in professional stature officially to become the accoucheur of Empress Marie Louise when she delivered the King of Rome in 1811.[8] As an experienced professor, his colleague Chaussier prepared the legislative project for the organization of the schools of public health at Paris, and later became a physician at La Maternité, the new national normal school of midwifery, as well as professor of chemistry at the Ecole Polytechnique; but his publications on legal medicine did not come until the 1820s.[9]

A fourth medico-legist, syphilis expert Paul Augustin Olivier Mahon (1752–1801), was professor of legal medicine at the Ecole de Médecine de

Paris. His three-volume *Médecine Légale, et Police Médicale* (1802) was published posthumously,[10] as was his work on syphilis in pregnant women, newborn babies, and youngsters.[11]

Finally, François-Emmanuel Fodéré[12] (1764–1835), who assumed the professorship in legal medicine at the Faculté de Strasbourg early in 1814, earned the title "Nestor of legal medicine."[13] Between 1796 and his death in 1835 Fodéré produced more than twenty treatises on diseases, social welfare, and nursing handbooks, including two treatises on legal medicine and public health that were accepted as classics for half a century:[14] *Les Lois Élairées par les Sciences Physiques* (1798) in three volumes and the six-volume work, *Traité de Médecine Légale* (1813).

The works of Belloc, Chaussier, Mahon, and Fodéré as well as the doctors' opinions whom they cited exemplify the state of the art of imperial legal medicine. That their multivolumed, prescriptive manuals doubled in length in about a decade suggests the vastness, activity, and advances made in this field.

The basic women's issues selected from these authors' works for discussion here are (1) prohibition of marriage, (2) rape, (3) conception, and (4) abortion. (A fifth—infanticide—will be treated separately in Chapter 9.) While the authors themselves felt that the issues were important in their own right, often going on at length about how they ought to be handled, all of these related in some way to the current misperception that a population problem existed. However, exactly the reverse was happening—a population explosion. Moreover, by means of the signing of the Concordat of 1801 Napoleon restored the Gallican Catholic religion as the dominant religion of the French people, thereby acquiescing to Catholic moral teachings. Thus, the notion of life beginning at conception became the basis for French medical and legal interpretations—a notion that would have great importance as a challenge to women's privacy.

The Right to Marry

In considering whether a person had the right to marry, Napoleonic experts in legal medicine took three things into consideration: the physical needs of the subject(s), the children who might issue from the marriage, and the rights and duties that the State/society attached to marriage as an institution.[15] Recognized limitations curtailing this right included physical deformity, hereditary problems, and certain diseases. Mahon, who had only positive things to say about marriage, claimed that "sexual desire is almost irresistible" and that single people were societal parasites since they contributed nothing to society.[16] Moreover, he suggested, the genitals of pious churchmen who observed their vows of celibacy shriveled.[17] Likewise, he claimed that celibate women could be driven crazy by lust, developing *l'heure du berger* (a sort of unbridled passion at the auspicious time for lovers, the gloaming or twilight time) or *fureur uterine* (a form of madness caused by the celibate woman's unfulfilled uterus). However, intercourse or wet dreams could restore such crazed women to normalcy.[18] He added that in England suicide was most frequent among celibates and that suicide was increasing in France as more people were avoiding marriage.[19]

Nevertheless, in the rush to increase population, society should not permit people to transmit hereditary or communicable diseases such as epilepsy, consumption, hypochondria, and leprosy to offspring.[20] Although Fodéré agreed with Mahon that lepers ought not be allowed to marry, he admitted that some of the lepers' children he had seen appeared "very beautiful and healthy."[21] Belloc was emphatic about forbidding girls with deformed pelvic areas to marry because pregnancy would necessitate surgery that risked killing them.[22] He referred doctors to Jean-Louis Baudelocque's obstetrical textbooks as an aid in determining whether a particular woman had too serious a deformity to deliver safely.[23] Mahon felt that limiting the rights of handicapped people was necessary for the good of society, although he did think that they should retain inheritance and property rights and that to end their lives under any circumstances was criminal.[24] Furthermore, while people with venereal diseases could then legally marry, Mahon opined that such marriages ought to be invalidated with a monetary award going to the deceived or injured party.[25]

Age was further reason for prohibiting marriage. The Code Napoleon, Section 482, no longer recognized a designated age when "impuberty" suddenly became puberty or made someone eligible to marry, so everyone was regarded as a minor until age twenty-one, unless emancipated by marriage. Nevertheless, Fodéré set the age of puberty at fourteen for boys and twelve for girls, the ages established by Roman law; but, to marry that young in France required a dispensation from the State. While the Napoleonic government did allow girls to marry at fourteen and boys at eighteen, girls under twenty-one and boys under twenty-five still needed parental consent.[26] Mahon thought that boys should not marry before age twenty-five and girls before eighteen because, in his opinion, early marriage produced sterility.[27] Another authority, Belloc, advised eighteen and twenty as the ages at which girls and boys should marry in order to preserve optimum health.[28] Imperial experts in legal medicine viewed the customs of both celibacy and early marriage as detrimental to public health.

Determining the age of puberty was important to other issues besides marriage law—rape, for instance.

Rape

"Rape" *(viol,* also the root of the French and English words for *violence)* occurred by definition whenever a woman resisted a sexual attack made upon her against her will. Hence, attacking a drugged woman or a female imbecile was also considered as rape because it involved a sexual act committed either against her will or without her will being developed enough ever to give consent. Even a prostitute could be raped if violence was used. Rape was thought so atrocious a crime that severe punishment was considered appropriate to pay for the injury suffered by the woman.

But the French experts instructed attending physicians to keep one point in mind—the almost complete impossibility of rape, except for gang rape committed by armed men, and then the results were so obvious that a medical opinion would hardly be necessary. The Strasbourger Dr. Fodéré suggested that for a virtuous woman, only the fear of death is greater than her fear of loss of honor—a fact that gives her the advantage over her attacker. Although a girl of twelve could be raped by a man of twenty-five to thirty, a woman of eighteen to twenty could only be raped if her life were threatened. He also cautioned physicians to remember that a physically developed eleven- or twelve-year-old female might welcome sexual advances and *want* to make love. Furthermore, he warned that the complaint of a young healthy woman against an elderly man or an invalid should be regarded as malicious.[29]

In ordinary cases, permissible evidence of rape included a doctor's testimony about physical signs on the victim's body, the written report of the local *officier de santé* who investigated the case, testimony from the victim's neighbors[30] about her character, and any witnesses to the crime. Proof of rape, as Fodéré outlined it, generally required four conditions: (1) constant resistance on the part of the victim; (2) unequal strength between the rapist and the victim; (3) the woman cried out for help;[31] and (4) traces of violence remained on the victim's body. Significantly, the experts did not consider the presence or absence of the hymen as sufficient proof of virginity, intercourse, rape, or even the possibility of pregnancy because so many obstetricians cited examples of cases about exceptions to general beliefs in this regard. Instead, in legal medicine this information had to be joined with other salient facts in arriving at a decision.[32] The notion that the feeling of female sexual satisfaction was necessary for conception to occur, which heretofore had been accepted by medical lawyers, also was discarded.

Imperial experts agreed that rape might indeed result in pregnancy.[33] For this crime the Code of 1791 had modified the centuries-old rape laws that prescribed the death penalty with a six-years-in-irons sentence for ordinary rape (of an adult woman) and twelve years in irons when it was committed against a girl under fourteen or for gang rape. In the harsher Code of 1810, however, there were a number of gradations ranging from solitary confinement at hard labor for a short period to forced labor for life, according to the circumstances.[34] Thus, rape was never a capital crime in Napoleonic France, and it was difficult to prove; but it could result in a life sentence at hard labor, which was a lighter penalty than under the Old Regime but a heavier penalty than in effect during the 1790s to 1800s. In reality, convictions did occur, as when in April 1806 the Cour de Cassation reversed an acquittal of an attempted rapist of a girl under fourteen who had been willing to have sex because the man, Sicard, had corrupted a minor.[35]

Conception

Conception was another concern in imperial medico-law. The authorities agreed upon only three circumstances when a woman could be completely ignorant of the fact that she had conceived: (1) if she had the mental capacity of an idiot; (2) if she had been taken advantage of while asleep with the proviso that she was not a virgin—a virgin would be awakened; and (3) if she had been drunk, drugged, comatose, or asphyxiated.[36] Fodéré, too, believed the above, but unlike other experts, he had abandoned the prevailing belief that women knew when conception occurred because conception produced such perfectly wonderful yet distinctively recognizable feeling like none other. Most writers then, who believed that the woman always knew, thought that an excitation or movement of the woman's entire body was required to assist the male's seminal fluid in traversing the uterus to reach the fallopian tubes.[37] The way Dr. Mahon idealized conception was in keeping with vitalist sensibility, the reciprocity between the body and the mind acted under the pressure of passion. This event was accompanied by

> Quelqu'effet différent de l'effet ordinaire, par des frissons, ou de legers spasms involontaires, par un vif chatouillement rapporté vers les organes de la génération, par la durée de la sensation du plaisir, par son étendue et sa perfection.[38]

That being the case, a woman could never plead ignorance of pregnancy in the event she did something to jeopardize the life of the fetus. If so, she had in fact intentionally murdered her child, which was tantamount to infanticide. French legal authorities were familiar with the Roman and canon law regarding the question, "when does life begin," but rejected their distinctions about a child not being formed or being formed at certain times during the period of gestation.[39] Mahon, actually writing just prior to

Napoleon's signing of the Concordat reestablishing the Catholic religion, stated that experience and modern knowledge of anatomy proves that human development progresses so smoothly from conception through birth and on to adulthood that no one can draw a line and say that the soul joins the body at a specific time if not at conception. Besides, he asserted his considered opinion that such philosophical disputes are fruitless.[40] For contemporaries, the Concordat was meant to close off debate, making the safest guess—the "pro-life" position—the official dogma, regardless of how it affected woman's sanity.

Abortion

The logical implication of the Napoleonic State's legal doctrine that life begins at conception was that abortion had to be considered a serious crime. It was in fact also a common crime. Thus the authors of legal-medical textbooks devoted a good deal of space to reviewing the known history of abortion laws in a manner that itself exhibited the transition from theological to secular concerns as the foundation of justice. Fodéré pointed right to the ancient Stoics. (Remember the importance of Stoicism in the body history of the years 1792–1794 when the Cult of Antiquity made men live and die in public space like Stoic heros.) He said that the Stoics considered abortion as neither parricide nor homicide. Since the fetus had not yet breathed, in their view it lacked a soul and, therefore, was simply not a human person. While the Holy Bible (Old and New Testaments) did not explicitly proscribe against abortion, Christianity after Constantine unequivocally condemned it without even taking into consideration the abortionist's intentions. The French Code of 1791 specified a mere twenty years in irons as punishment for committing abortion. The Penal Code of 1810 punished both the abortionist and the women who had the abortion with life imprisonment.[41] As Fodéré explained, the law was made more stringent because legislators believed that the incidence of "embryoticide" had increased due to the invention abroad (he did not say where) of new surgical instruments for this purpose, which were being imported to France.[42] Discussions of the French Codes omitted theological intricacies.

Both Mahon and Fodéré (who wrote at the beginning and the end of this era, respectively), agreed that there was one case, however, when abortion should be legal—to save the mother's life.[43] In such situations when the right to life of both mother and child conflicted, midwives and obstetricians were supposed to "do the most good" or "avoid the greatest harm." Because mortality tables showed that so many children died before the age of five, Fodéré stated that it was morally wrong to risk the woman's life for the uncertain life of the child.[44] These authors were aware of the unpopularity of their opinions among conservative Catholics who believed the mother should sacrifice herself to procure the baptism of her infant. But still, these public health officials opted for the mother, as Napoleon himself did when Dubois consulted the emperor's wishes about Marie Louise's complications during the breech birth of the King of Rome.[45]

Protecting the rights of the child once conceived and once outside the womb was another important concern. From 1556 until 1810, all expectant women who hid their pregnancies became suspected criminals. The laws of the *ancien régime,* Revolution, and First Empire required unwed pregnant women to register their condition with the *officiers de santé* in order to prevent secret abortions. Of course, an unregistered unwed mother found with a dead newborn was highly suspect. Mahon was skeptical about whether a woman could deliver so quickly that her baby could drop fatally on its head or that she could be so senseless after labor that she could not give her baby the necessary life-sustaining care it needed. Maternal love was so strong, he believed, that being in a state of convulsions (which could result from kidney failure in an eclamptic pregnancy) during and after labor was the only instance wherein he could imagine a woman not behaving dutifully; but anyone claiming to have taken convulsions as a defense had to be able to prove it.[46] According to Mahon, the most common cause of infant death was criminally negligent ligature of the umbilical cord, which would result in the child bleeding to death. He conceded, however, that this might happen accidentally, even inside the mother's uterus, in which case the accused was innocent and the fetus stillborn.[47]

Regardless of his personal feelings and the emotional impact of some of these tragic criminal investigations and the public outrage they aroused, the expert in legal medicine was counseled to consider himself as more of an official defender of the innocent than as a prosecutor.[48]

Thus the Napoleonic medical and legal professions worked closely together in the discovery process in administering justice. The legal medicine manuals and textbooks revealed how physicians grappled with an endless number of human problems in their day. All the while, however, the members of these professions consciously or unconsciously participated in the process of forcing women to exchange one master for another—formerly canon law and the Roman Catholic Church, now the Napoleonic Codes and the Imperial State. As they merged politics and morality, these male professionals relied upon their interpretation of history, experience, reason, and cultural values, as well as contemporary medical knowledge and medical theory including "the science of man." In their effort to be objective they consulted statistics and dismissed fruitless, outdated arguments about moral issues that were beyond their ken. (Doctors had a tendency to espouse atheist materialism anyway.) Conception, even for these laymen, still remained largely a mystery as Mahon's sensationalist description of what a woman must feel when she conceives. In the case of rape the new law gave women more protection than the legal system had afforded them during the French Revolutionary era, but less than they had enjoyed during the Old Regime. Often the rights of the fetus conflicted with women's rights and privacy.

In conclusion, through the contributions of these legal-medical professors, the regime's policy concerning female domesticity, the desirability of marriage for both sexes and encouragement of reproduction, and the child's right to life from conception onward, if strictly adhered to, would have resulted in increasing the population of France. Nobody was yet concerned about the individual freedom or civil rights of the politically unempowered sex—after all, they had representation and the right to participate vicariously. Yet, the professors of legal medicine generally felt compassion for poor women and teenage mothers who were unmarried, hence unprotected from poverty and public humiliation. In cases where they might easily have, the authorities seemed reluctant to condemn women for engaging in premarital sex. Sexuality and a strong sex drive were considered good things that Nature had provided women because without them, women would not be able to produce abundantly, which is precisely what the regime hoped to achieve in order to guarantee the future of the nation.

In the following chapter we will try to put a human face on legal medicine by looking at specific case studies of desperate women who were tried for crimes of infanticide. Through these highly publicized cases we get a glimpse of how the medical experts actually interfaced with the judges and juries in the historical setting. In this way, the medical theory of "the science of man" infused imperial jurisprudence whose mission it was to establish the boundaries between the sexes and to maintain the division of space into the public and the private.

8

Medical Discourse about Criminal Cases

Infanticide and Woman's Nature

THE INCIDENCE OF INFANTICIDE was of serious concern to government administrators and the medical and legal professions during the First Empire. Broadly defined, the term *infanticide* then meant the violent and premeditated death of a viable fetus or a child born alive and capable of receiving baptism. Since the Church asserted that life began at conception, abortion of a viable fetus in any trimester of age was as serious as the murder of a child of any age whatsoever. Furthermore, when used without qualification, *infanticide* was interchangeable with the contemporary term *neo-naticide* since it presumed first that the murder had been committed on an infant rather than on an older child and second that the perpetrator was its own mother.

The subject obviously preoccupied various contemporary authorities because they sometimes devoted many pages to it in their publications. These sources were largely medical treatises, textbooks for future or practicing physicians, and manuals of legal medicine. The manuals were designed for use by public health practitioners, such as the *officiers de santé,* and the medical police who investigated crimes and provided medical testimony to the courts in civil and criminal human rights–type cases. But other primary sources, such as annotated collections of legal cases and appeals, the earliest French medical journals, and even articles in ladies' magazines, offered insights into the public mentality regarding infanticide crimes. And because government censorship was in place, we can assume that whatever appeared in print was an opinion tolerated by the regime if not outright official propaganda. This literature enabled us to analyze how the law and the medical establishment collaborated on behalf of the unfortunate victim, a presumably outraged society, and the Napoleonic State in administering justice to the female suspect—the "murdering mother."[1]

Once again we alert the reader that the misperception about French population comes into play here: that population actually increased during the French Revolutionary/Napoleonic era although contemporaries often believed that due to the high number of war-related deaths, the reverse was true—that France was losing population due to all the casualties. Consequently, a strong popular sentiment existed in favor of safeguarding as many young lives as possible in the private as well as in the public spheres. Infant mortality rates of roughly 20 percent or more were already deemed excessive even without intentionally killing more babies.

The origins of French infanticide laws, nevertheless, dated back to the sixteenth century and had remained unchanged for a long period. The Edict of Henry II of 1556[2] remained in effect until 1791 and considered infanticide a capital offense. It prescribed the death penalty for hiding a pregnancy and then killing the child, which amounted to premeditated infanticide. After 1791 the laws became more complicated, evolving too rapidly given the speed in which they could be institutionalized in pre-industrial society so that sometimes even lawyers became confused about what the law actually was. During the Revolution, the Constituent Assembly attempted to ease the punishment, but following upon the Concordat with the papacy, the Napoleonic Criminal Code restored the death penalty for this crime.[3] Infanticide became a unique form of murder that was considered far worse than ordinary murder. It therefore became punishable not just by life imprisonment at hard labor, as were regular instances of murder, but by execution.[4] Moreover, imperial courts distinguished between voluntary and involuntary infanticide. In October 1811 the appellate Cour de Cassation ruled that even if a jury decided that a woman was innocent of voluntary infanticide, if the evidence suggested that she had indeed killed her child (albeit involuntarily), without giving her the benefit of a retrial the judge could assign correctional punishment[5] instead of allowing her to go free, as she would have as an innocent person against whom charges had been dismissed. Thus, a chronological overview of the rewriting of French infanticide law suggested that the right to life of children expanded, or at least, children's potential value to society as future breeders or soldiers appeared to have increased throughout the era while the murdering woman's right to life diminished in inverse proportion to the perceived heinousness of this criminal act. Moreover, the return to religion seemed to tip the imperial scales of justice in favor of more vengeance and less mercy for the female perpetrators than the enlightened, liberal Revolution had briefly shown.

Authors insisted that the methods women used to kill babies were already well known, although some hesitated to enumerate them for fear that such publicity might inspire or tempt women who might be premeditating this crime to copy one of these violent means. Other physicians, surgeons, and medico-lawyers simply indicated them.[6] Such cold-blooded methods fell into three general categories: (1) voluntary crime, (2) involuntary crime, and (3) legal infanticide, which we shall survey in turn.

Intentional methods included neglecting the physical requirements of newborns at home as well as public exposure or abandonment, especially in frigid weather; strangulation; drowning in rivers or by casting unwanted infants into latrines, cisterns, or the like; dropping infants on their heads during or after childbirth; and criminal ligature of the umbilical cord.[7] According to P. A. O. Mahon, one of the most prominent authorities on legal medicine, the last was the most prevalent cause of death either through failure to tie the cord properly or by severing it completely so that the newborn or fetus bled to death.[8] A frequent allegation was that sometimes the cord was used by mothers to strangle the baby so that its death appeared accidental. Midwives, it also was claimed, often used strangulation as a convenient way to get rid of unwanted babies.

Unintentional methods, of course, included accidental strangulation by the umbilical cord inside the womb. Other involuntary means were a woman being too ill to properly tend to the cord—suffering convulsions during labor, for example;[9] abandoning a child in an unheated *tour,* a revolving wooden receptacle built into the outside wall of a courtyard in order to permit anonymous abandonment (see Chapter 9 for a detailed history of the *tour*), at a foundling hospital coupled with failure of the attendant to respond promptly to the ringing of the bell;[10] failure by a husband to call a midwife to attend his wife's confinement before difficulties developed that required assistance during labor;[11] and the hiding of a pregnancy by unwed, often teenage parents who were totally ignorant about what to do when labor suddenly occurred while they were alone in hiding to conceal their shameful secret. Moreover, the plain ignorance of untrained midwives, notably ones in remote rural areas, was widely held responsible for the lamentable infant mortality rate.[12]

Legal infanticide occurred when after due consideration of circumstances, surgeons who had to choose between saving the life of the mother or the fetus, opted for the mother.[13] In such instances forceps or various cutting instruments were used to extract all or dismembered parts of fetuses that were malformed (perhaps hydrocephalic ones), conjoined twins joined at the head or trunk, or even well-formed but presumably dead fetuses. Fetal skull crunching, mutilation, and so on[14] were necessary in an era when episiotomy (an incision made in the perineum between the vagina and the anus when there is a need to relieve pressure on the baby's head, to allow more space when forceps are used, or in case of a breech birth), cesarean section, and induced labor[15] at an early stage of pregnancy were still in experimental stages (before the closure of wounds with stitching had replaced the wrapping of bandages, and silk—not linen—thread for surgical stitches came into use), thus making use of more modern but less gruesome methods of extraction too hazardous to preserve the mother's life. However, before embarking on such a course of action, the surgeon baptized the hopeless infant in the womb by means of a syringe,[16] thereby obviating the necessity of jeopardizing the life of the mother in order for her to give birth to a live, intact fetus only so that it could be baptized by a priest before it died of natural causes anyhow. Napoleonic-era medical authorities saw this kind of infanticide as a gray area of the law[17] wherein members of their profession were called upon unwillingly to play God.

Certain investigative procedures for suspected infanticide cases developed in Napoleonic legal practice. In all instances specific points had to be determined:

1. whether the child was viable;
2. whether it was alive or dead after delivery;
3. if dead, whether it was born dead or died subsequently;
4. what the cause of death was;
5. how old it was.[18]

Obviously, to answer the above questions, the victim's body had to exist and be recovered. Moreover, a public health official or court physician had to examine the mother in order to prove that she had actually given birth at a time corresponding to the time of death of the victim.[19] Because the prosecution had to prove that the infant had breathed, experts devised ways to show scientifically that lung tissue had indeed functioned and, in the case of a suspected drowning, filled with water.[20] To assist the courts in establishing viability, tables of average weights and lengths of fetuses at each month after conception were compiled by government agencies and incorporated into manuals of legal medicine for ready reference.[21] Examples of model reports from the First Empire were published then,[22] and continued to be published during the Bourbon Restoration,[23] to educate experts about the best investigative procedures to follow and even to show them the necessary facts that ought to be included in filing a good report in order to facilitate the administration of justice.

Actual Cases

A search for examples of well-documented Napoleonic-era infanticide cases has yielded a few outstanding examples found in various types of sources. In 1803 *Le Petit Magasin des Dames*[24] described the case of a nineteen-year-old accused who previously had been a sweet and virtuous person. But after being seduced and finding herself pregnant, she hid her pregnancy for the first six or seven months. To accomplish this, she had to work day and night in order to earn enough money to secure the services of one Pelletier, a "cruel accoucheur," who demanded a fee of 300 francs for a secret delivery. Finally, when she was seven months pregnant and overcome with fatigue from overwork, her story reached a crisis: following an accidental fall, she went into labor. She gave birth alone at about 10:00 a.m. Four hours later, her thirteen-year-old sister, who thought she was simply ill, came to her room to check on her. The younger girl found her older sister in a frightful condition, bathed in blood and psychologically disturbed at being dishonored. Beside the bed, a live baby was resting in an armchair. Not realizing what she was doing, the younger sister decided to help by proposing to throw the baby into the latrine. This thought so horrified the older sister who had recently given birth that she fainted.

Meanwhile, the younger girl proceeded to help her by disposing of the baby. Fortunately, the new mother revived shortly and regained her senses. She tried unsuccessfully to retrieve the child—it had fallen too far to be reached. "Providence was attentive," however, and some neighbors, upon hearing the young mother's cries of distress, came to the rescue of the infant in the abyss, who was still alive. When the rescuers eventually brought the infant to its mother, she recognized it as hers.

The magazine article concluded that in such situations it is hard to know what really happened. Several people, we are finally informed, were willing to attest to the mother's good character before her pregnancy. Thus we can assume that neither she nor her younger sister, who actually threw the unwanted baby into the latrine, were prosecuted. The medical description of the mother right after childbirth was from the perspective of holism, noting her physical as well as obvious mental distress, but attributed the latter to peer pressure rather than postpartum depression. Furthermore, the magazine mentioned the roles of the two adult males involved: the wicked seducer as well as the greedy accoucheur. In the end, the shamed young mother redeemed herself by accepting the child. This is the type of values-laden story about an attempted infanticide that was presented by a popular magazine to its intended audience of literate women early in the Napoleonic era.

The records of the Cour de Cassation were another source of information about a few specific infanticide cases. In 1806 these records showed that the conviction of Rosalie Boucan was overturned. Although the details of the case were not supplied, it is apparent from the facts that the jury, which had tried and convicted Boucan, had failed to consider whether she had committed infanticide either through negligence or imprudence. The appellate judge pointed out that articles 373, 374, and 380 of the Code of 3 Brumaire, year IV (October 25, 1795) stipulated that whenever the verbal inquiry report attached to the act of accusation stated that infanticide could have been caused by thoughtlessness rather than willful negligence, this fact had to be submitted to the jury when it determined guilt.[25] Hence, we see that judicial reports of this high court focused on judicial procedural errors, rather than on sentimentality or religious beliefs. But as in the case previously discussed from three years earlier, the mother was not relentlessly pursued in the name of justice. Moreover, in this case the higher court was not as harsh on the mother as the lower court's procedure had been. This, however, was still before the Napoleonic penal code and criminal procedures went into effect.

Another type of legal source, which was certainly much more detailed, was an official *Rapport sur un cas d'infanticide* made by physicians engaged in the practice of medico-law. An 1809 report[26] prepared by professors from the Faculty of Medicine at Paris at the request of the Luxembourg neighborhood police commissioner provided the facts for the case of Nanette Tillard, who presumably gave birth on Thursday, November 9, of that year. The policeman escorted the doctors to a first-floor room in a dwelling near the Saint Germain *foire* (fairgrounds) where the accused lived with her mother, we are told. There they found her in bed, where they conducted a thorough physical examination. They noted first the appearance of her face, skin color, and eyes. Then they felt her pulse and touched her skin for texture and temperature. A breast exam came next. They observed the shape of her breasts and examined her nightgown to check for milk stains before actually touching her breasts to see whether she was lactating. The examiners then proceeded to check her abdomen, abdominal muscles, and belly button where they noticed stretch marks and evidence that her womb had been extended. When they were through pressing her abdomen, they examined her genitals, even the color and odor of her bodily discharge as well as looking at her soiled linen. A precise description of the state of the birth canal and womb along with the extent of dilation was noted. The last step in the doctors' physical exam was an internal pelvic exam (via touching) to determine whether the structure of Tillard's womb was normal enough to have an easy labor. Their conclusions were:

1. that she had given birth three or four days previously, which was confirmed by the condition of her breasts, their secretions, her odor, her genitals, her womb, and her abdomen;
2. that no illness other than childbirth could produce this combination of symptoms;

3. that with the shape of her pelvis and uterus, she could deliver easily and quickly.

The physicians also examined the infant's cadaver carefully. They reported its sex—female—and that it was large, fat, well formed, and showed no sign yet of putrefaction. It weighed six pounds one ounce (2,978 grams),[27] which was the ordinary weight of a strong and healthy full-term baby, as they noted in their report. It was 494 millimeters (about 19 inches) long, also ordinary. Then its umbilical cord was measured (196 millimeters) and also examined for irregularities, before the rest of the baby's remains received attention. When they saw a bruise on the baby's leg, they dissected the part to discover how deep the injury went below the skin. After all this, they got to the face and the head where they spotted trouble. Extensive details about the fractures to the skull and internal bleeding were supplied, including the location and length of the broken bones. The doctors observed that no other parts of the body except the head showed any outward sign of violence before they performed an autopsy on the interior of the trunk and body. From all the above they found that:

1. the dead child was full-term, born alive and healthy as proven by the solidity of the bones;
2. it had presented itself headfirst;
3. it had breathed completely (as indicated by the lungs), but it had died shortly after birth (as indicated by the fact that the intestines were filled with meconium), and it had been dead for three or four days;
4. its death could not be attributed to a hemorrhage of the umbilical cord, suffocation, or natural and ordinary cause;
5. the cause of death could not be attributed to falling on its head during delivery because there were too many fractures of the skull;
6. its death ought to be attributed entirely to skull fractures, internal bleeding, and brain damage caused by beating shortly after birth on the right side of the head and face.

From the foregoing report we saw how seriously these forensic scientists took their work, supplying us with more details, perhaps, than we find comfortable, but with a scientific approach that was most convincing. Undoubtedly, these reports were a significant part of the discovery process of typical investigations of the day.[28] The only omission, of course, was the accused's motives for murdering the child and whether there were any extenuating circumstances. But it would be wrong to jump to the conclusion that such careful and formulated reporting, so customary with Napoleonic administrative style, left the murdering mother no chance to arouse the sympathy of jurors or to arouse reasonable doubt in their minds, for there is more.

J. P. Maygrier, editor of the *Annuaire Médical* (1810),[29] provided his readers with his own narrative version of the same case so that we can learn the whole truth as well as the final disposition of the case. According to this early medical journal, it was Anne Tilliard [sic], a twenty-five-year-old native of Jussy in Haute-Saône, a day-laborer, who lived near the Saint Germain *foire* who gave birth on the ninth of the previous November. He said that she had committed premeditated infanticide on her newborn child, which was found two days later between the straw pallet and mattress of her bed. Tilliard, an unmarried woman, already had a four-year-old child; nevertheless, her aunt thought she was a moral person, and consequently took her in. When she refused to eat and complained of headaches, the aunt summoned a physician. Anne Tilliard denied that she was pregnant to both her aunt and the doctor but claimed that since she had not had her period for ten months, this explained why she felt ill. At 8:00 p.m. on November 9, Dame Tilliard went downstairs to her shop where she discovered her niece having violent convulsions. She helped Anne upstairs and into bed. An hour later, the older woman went up to check on her and found her niece in the middle of the room, amidst blood. Anne claimed that she had been flooding from the resumption of her menstrual period, and the aunt believed her but nonetheless called for Dr. Decelles. Again Dame Tilliard and the physician tried to get Anne to admit that she was pregnant, but she still stuck to her story, insisting that she just had cramps and a swollen abdomen.

Two days later (November 11), when Dame Tilliard was going through an armoire, she discovered an afterbirth wrapped in an old cloth. She showed this to Dr. Decelles, who identified it as the placenta of someone who recently gave birth. At this point, they were able to get Anne to admit that she had delivered a stillborn baby. She insisted that she had not killed it, and said that she had hidden it under the mattress of the bed in which she and her aunt slept together. They then pulled out the body of a baby girl, which the doctor said had been dead for several days and which had died of violent means. Dame Tilliard and the surgeon gave statements to the police and brought the police commissar to question her right away. At that point, Anne admitted that she had been two months pregnant when she came to Paris; that the father in Jussy was Carteret, a married man; that she had lied to her aunt about her condition; and that she had the baby on November 9; but that it had been born dead. Afterward, she said, she wrapped it up in a cloth and hid the body in the bed and the placenta in the closet.[30] Dame Tilliard positively identified the cadaver as the one found in her bed.

According to Maygrier, two professors from the faculty at La Maternité came together to examine the accused in Dame Tilliard's bedroom: the accoucheur, Dr. Jean-Louis Baudelocque, and the midwifery teacher (and also one of the Ideologues belonging to the Auteuil salon frequented by Cabanis and influenced by his formulation of "the science of man") François Chaussier. Maygrier repeated the findings of their official report, as already detailed above, before going into her defense.

Anne's first line of defense was that she had hidden her pregnancy from her aunt for fear that her aunt would throw her out and she would have no place else to go. On the morning of November 9 she said she went down to open the shop but fell over backward just before her aunt came downstairs. After Dame Tilliard helped her back upstairs to bed, she went into labor. She delivered while standing up; however, she insisted that she had fallen down as she expelled the child. Because the child appeared stillborn, she slapped only one of its legs a little, then applied salt to its head and rubbed it some more, but it still failed to cry. It was possible, she allowed, that she had taken it by the neck—she could not be sure—but regardless of what she did to stimulate it by slapping it a little with her hand, it never cried. Dame Tilliard corroborated this by saying that she never heard the crying of the baby either, although she could have stepped out of the shop below to a neighbor's at the precise moment when the baby came. Such was Anne's explanation of what had transpired.

Maygrier's account focused next on the medical examiners' response to Anne's defense. Their report had stated the cause of death as fractures rather than suffocation from insertion under the mattress. Maygrier said that Baudelocque and Chaussier later were called to testify before the jury. Initially they said that because Anne claimed her innocence, they had re-examined the child's body; nevertheless, they persisted in asserting their original opinion that it had been a live birth. They admitted, however, the possibility that the baby girl had fallen at birth and thereby inflicted the fractures on itself. Then they went on to introduce something quite interesting—that sometimes women experience temporary insanity, and that this may have been her condition when she killed the baby. They left it up to the jury to decide whether Anne Tilliard was only guilty of involuntary murder.

After these legal-medical expert witnesses testified, Anne's aunt and Dr. Decelles repeated their initial accusation exactly, Maygrier continued. Then the First President of the court questioned Anne himself. Finally, the court proceeding was adjourned until the following day, Saturday, the twenty-third of December. At that time the *procurer-général* gave a résumé to the jury, pointing out the problem of determining premeditation and volition. Furthermore, he pointed out the interest of society in such a case. This summation was followed by the oration of Maugeret, Anne's attorney. He said that since she had already been a mother for four years, she had no reason to fear the loss of her reputation or honor. He asked, "How could a good mother like her suddenly turn completely into a monster?" (Maygrier noted that Maugeret had posed this question as a ploy to arouse the jurors' emotions.) With this, Anne having nothing else to add in her own defense, the jury retired to deliberate. Two hours later they returned with their verdict: that Anne Tilliard had killed the baby, but that it was uncertain that she had killed it voluntarily. So the court acquitted her of the charges.

The combined sources of information for the Tillard Case of 1809 illustrated how the medical profession and the legal system cooperated at this time. The behavior of the doctors was especially enlightening because while their official report about the autopsy on the child left little doubt about the cause of death, they later maintained that the murdering mother might have suffered from temporary insanity—certainly an extenuating circumstance, and one that was a popular defense in many criminal cases in the following century. In any case, by suggesting the possibility of temporary insanity, Baudelocque and Chaussier as well as the defense lawyer were able to raise enough doubt in the jury's mind to save this unmarried but twice pregnant, penniless, working-class woman who had sought refuge in Paris with her bourgeois aunt. Moreover, the decision in the Tillard Case held and was never appealed.

In 1811, however, the records of the Cour de Cassation[31] note very briefly and without providing any details of the circumstances of the case, that an error was found in the trial of one Anne Tychenne on October 24. A jury had decided that this "girl" accused of infanticide was not guilty of intentionally committing this crime. The high court decided that this ruling did not let her off completely: since she was guilty of involuntary murder, the courts should punish her for *"homicide commis par imprudence sur la personne de son enfant."* A footnote to the Cour de Cassation records[32] said that the relevant observations had been made in previous rulings of the Cassation on 11 Brumaire, year VII (November 1, 1798) and May 29, 1806. Evidently, not all mothers guilty of involuntary infanticide got off as easily as Tillard did; depending on the circumstances a distinction was made between prudent and imprudent behavior coupled with good intentions. Possibly the great reputation of the compassionate Doctors Baudelocque and Chaussier had tipped the scales favorably in Tillard's temporary insanity decision.

At the end of the First Empire, in 1814, two other infanticide cases added to the pattern emerging from this review of cases based on available types of documentation. Prunelle mentioned in his history of legal medicine[33] that sometimes these experts helped to establish the innocence of the accused. He cited as proof an example of a young girl accused of infanticide because she had been seen near the scene of the crime. However, when the legal doctors examined her, they found that she had never had a baby. Prunelle pointed out the complexity of his profession that had to draw its findings from many fields: physics, chemistry, natural history, human anatomy, comparative anatomy, pathology, therapeutics, and surgery, as well as psychology.[34] But during that same year, the Cour de Cassation ruled that the court that had sentenced Marie Patain to life at hard labor for throwing her newborn son into a well should have instead executed her according to articles 400 and 473 of the Code of Criminal Instruction and articles 295, 300, 302, and 304 of the Penal Code.[35] This suggested that by 1814 the various professions and jurists at the different levels of the system were endeavoring to balance the scales of justice between excessive leniency and excessive harshness, but the medical doctors as well as the citizens who served on juries may have believed less in capital punishment for women than did the highest court of the land, the Cour de Cassation. In reasserting the execution requirement, the high court was reverting to the situation that had existed prior to the amelioration of punishment that was introduced during the Constituent Assembly era early in the Revolution. In other words, the high court reverted back to the policy of the Ancien Regime.

Women as Victims

These infanticide cases show us doctors of legal medicine and the legal system cooperated during the Napoleonic era in the administration of justice on behalf of the victim—the child—with the mother being the accused. Over the years, as the legal system became stricter and tried to correct ambiguities resulting from the redrafting of the codes, the murdering mother could expect justice to be dealt out to her in a more uniform fashion. However, the doctors involved in the legal system as expert witnesses added a scientific element coupled with an element of compassion injected with insight from the new psychophysiological theory of the relations of the physical and the moral, "the science of man."

But did anyone's compassion go so far as to consider the murdering mother herself as a victim? The answer is yes. For one, Costard commented that men corrupt women and make the world evil, and since judges in courts of law are male, it is no wonder women are often found guilty of crimes.[36] Other doctors and legal medicine professors wrote this notion into their textbooks in the context of infanticide. A. Lecieux, for example, advocated free burial for infants who died within nine days of birth since poor families hid the corpses of newborns because they had no money to bury them.[37] Charles Gardien counseled doctors to favor the accused: *"le médecin légiste, . . . doit plutôt se considerer comme défenseur officieux que comme juge. . . ."* Furthermore, Gardien stated that he agreed with the late-eighteenth-century Scottish obstetrician William Hunter's notion that women accused of the crime of infanticide were less criminal than people imagined, that they were more worthy of compassion than of the rigor of the law because they would never commit such a repugnant crime against Nature if they had their senses. He concluded:

> Je crois, avec l'auteur [Hunter], que les circonstances qui accompagnent ce crime atroce, en changent l'espèce, et en modifient considérablement l'atrocité. La mère, dominée par un sentiment de honte insurmontable, et par le plus violent désir de conserver sa réputation, ne peut prendre sur elle d'avouer sa foiblesse et d'encourir l'infamie; le désespoir s'empare de son âme à proportion qu'elle sent le danger augmenter . . . la tête se perde.[38]

Hence, the medical profession ameliorated the harshness of the law when applied to rich and poor murdering mothers whom they perceived to be societal victims who had to be driven crazy before they acted contrary to Nature. The two sexes were not alike as human beings sharing a single nature: women were different from men, and being a good mother was an innate part of a woman's true nature.

It is also interesting to note that while the use of the temporary insanity plea shows the influence of the latest psychophysiological theory, the kindly doctors of legal medicine cited for their involvement were not mean-spirited regarding the women in these dreadful cases, an attitude that at times seemed to run through the discourse of Dr. Cabanis when he justified unequal treatment of women by pronouncing them too weak and feeble-minded to enjoy a life in public space, and so he could relegate their whole being to domestic space. The psychophysiology doctrine of the First Empire eventually would feed into modern neuroscience.

9

The Nineteenth-Century Discourse of Napoleon's Program to End Infanticide

IN THE PREVIOUS CHAPTER, we considered from the contemporary perspective several highly publicized infanticide cases in which the testimony of medical experts and the decisions of the courts were sympathetic to mothers. In addition, many articles, pamphlets, and treatises were published during the course of the lengthy jurisprudential and political debate over the *tours* that lasted from the First Empire of Napoleon I until late in the Second Empire of Napoleon III, a period of roughly six decades. These published sources made it possible to look at the broader history of the infanticide issue with the view in mind of evaluating the effectiveness of the Napoleonic *tours* along with Napoleon's motives for building them.

The Tours

Originally, the *tours* were cylindrical, revolving, wooden devices that were built into the courtyard wall of a hospice. They were perhaps a meter high with a little bed of straw on the floor, and were intended to be a receptacle for abandoning unwanted infants safely as well as anonymously. Probably the earliest one in France had been constructed at Montpellier, a city that would become a center of Protestantism in the Reformation Age and be known for a tradition of excellence in medical science, especially for the vitalist-sensationalist doctrine and the "science of man" in the eighteenth century. The Montpellier *tour* reputedly was copied in Rome[1] by the activist Pope Innocent III (1198–1216), a learned theologian and jurist. So, even a pope considered it an ethical and moral idea.

Technically, there were two kinds of *tours* in different places over time. The *tours libres* were secret places to leave children while *tours surveillés* were watched by a guard so the person doing the deed was known. (Hereafter, use of the word *tour* implies a *tour libre*.) A third category of place where children could be abandoned legally was a registry where parents signed a book so they could reclaim the child if they ever changed their minds. However, these distinctions became blurred because some Sisters of Charity accepted children at the door without asking questions.[2]

However, in 1811, Emperor Napoleon I ordered the installation of *tours* at foundling hospitals in the major city of every *département* of the expanded French Empire.[3] At face value this seems like a very Christian and humanitarian deed, but this move was extremely controversial then and throughout the first half of the nineteenth century. Politicians of all stripes questioned Napoleon's motives. Bonapartists, of course, claimed that this measure was a necessary step aimed at eradicating the horrifying crime of infanticide. The Napoleonic administration suggested that the emperor's decision made him a modern-day Saint Vincent de Paul (1581–1660, a priest who was canonized in 1737 and renowned for his assistance to foundlings in Paris). The official uniform for midwives who attended government midwifery schools even included a brooch with an image of Saint Vincent de Paul to be worn at the throat of their modest dress. On the other hand, the emperor's harshest critics accused him of only wanting to make soldiers and sailors of the boys whose lives were thus saved. His charity was likewise diminished by the fact that the little ones' chances for ultimate survival were so slim. Once inside foundling homes, unhygienic public institutions with high mortality rates, exposure to contagious diseases and artificial feeding (remember, this was before the pasteurization of milk) endangered their bodies. Their minds were also affected since the fact that the foundlings could not bond with their mothers was believed to affect their personalities adversely.[4] Extremists uttered wide-ranging praise or railed with criticism of Napoleon in this regard. A fair assessment hung somewhere in the balance.

Infanticide and the Law

The crime of infanticide was common in France during the nineteenth century. Not a handful or a couple of dozen, but actually hundreds of cases were tried under successive regimes. For example, in 1868, Ambroise Tardieu, a professor of legal medicine who had practiced for twenty-five years, wrote that "everything written on infanticide would fill a library and many Germans defended theses [on infanticide] at their universities for the last half century." Tardieu claimed that he had personally seen eight hundred cases. Moreover, he stated in the Preface to *Etude Medico-Légale sur l'Infanticide* his opinion that infanticide, what he thought was the most frequent crime in the countryside, was the toughest and most complicated subject in all of legal medicine to prove scientifically.[5] Given the state of hygiene, the medical technology, and the lack of adequate numbers of trained midwives, many babies aborted or died at birth or soon afterward simply due to natural causes. Venereal diseases were a scourge that complicated the feeding of infants whose mothers died during childbirth.[6] There were epidemics of infectious puerperal (or childbed) fever[7] and numerous other fevers that took the lives of mothers and infants. In addition, doctors were encouraged to opt for the mother in dangerous cases, which is proven by the existence of manuals that tell which cutting instruments to use to legally terminate pregnancies of malformed fetuses and how to extract them.[8]

At that time, doctors also accepted the existence of puerperal insanity as a distinct, temporary type of depression following childbirth (today we attribute this to sudden, dramatic changes in hormone levels and can treat it);[9] there also were psychiatric specialists who observed other types of nervous breakdowns following childbirth, which must have contributed to the ratio of mentally ill patients among the lower classes being seven women per five men.[10] Furthermore, people could be prosecuted for "omissions," such as holding an infant incorrectly (so that it gagged on its own mucus) or failure to keep it warm or to nourish it, or for not cutting and tying the umbilical cord properly. And doctors or midwives, too, sometimes behaved negligently, as when ghastly dismemberment of the infant resulted from incorrect techniques being employed in cases of breech birth.[11]

The history of French law seems to acknowledge the complexity of determining whether an intentional, premeditated act of violence had really occurred from two points of view: first, for most of French history, legal language had kept infanticide statutes separately from ordinary murder and assassination (premeditated murder) in order to provide protection for such helpless beings as newborn babies; second, in the later nineteenth and twentieth centuries, the mother was given special consideration and awarded more lenient punishment than other perpetrators or accomplices to the same crime. So infanticide was not quite as simplistic as saying it was the willful murder of a live, newborn child.

The historical development of infanticide laws was not smooth. In the classical world long before the development of any notion of children's rights, moral parents could kill their own children. Hence, the Greek tragedian Sophocles was credible when he told the story of Oedipus Rex, an infant maimed in the foot and "exposed" in a solitary place by his royal parents who foresaw him committing parricide if they nurtured him. Originally, a Roman child had no right to life until its father, the *pater familias,* made it a member of the family cult. Before Christianity influenced Roman law, if an infant had physical handicaps, it could be left for exposure in the wasteland to starve or be devoured by animals, all quite legally. However, the Hebrews punished infanticide by death, and their unusual humanity toward infants and children, which the teachings of Jesus of Nazareth promoted further, fed into the medieval and early modern stream of Judeo-Christian tradition. In Western Europe, Salic law (best known for forbidding females and those descended from the female line from inheriting titles or crowns) required only a fine or forfeiture for killing a child under twelve years of age. And under Saint Louis (born 1214, reigned 1226–1270, canonized 1297), a French mother's first murder went unpunished unless she killed a second child.[12]

Eventually, Henri II's Edict of 1556, in effect until 1791, laid the foundation for modern French laws by considering infanticide a capital offense for which two circumstances were necessary to achieve a conviction: the accused woman must have concealed her pregnancy and labor as well as deprived the infant of baptism and Christian burial. Nevertheless, in 1660, Guy-Patin claimed that six hundred women had confessed to this crime in a single year.[13] Henri II's stiff penalty was reconfirmed by Henri III in 1586, and again by Louis XIV in 1708. To make the death sentence more effective, in March 1731, a new regulation was added, providing for the exhumation of the cadavers of infants resulting from concealed pregnancies in order to determine whether they had been full-term and born alive.[14]

The changes in the penal codes during the French Revolution caused confusion among judges, juries, and lawyers about the prosecution of infanticide. This confusion lasted far into the next century, judging from the cases reversed in appeals courts[15] and statements to this effect in manuals of legal medicine. The Penal Code of 1791 did not implicitly abrogate the death penalty as many contemporaries thought when the language assimilated infanticide into the category of ordinary murder, which was then punishable as involuntary or premeditated, with the latter form still being a capital offense.

But the Edict of 1556 did get changed significantly by the Code of Brumaire, year IV (October–November 1795). Under the Directory, declarations of pregnancy were no longer obligatory under pain of death; while concealment suggested guilt, it was no longer proof of a crime. Mitigating circumstances also had to be considered since infanticide was subjected to the rules of common law for homicides and punished like any other murder or assassination until the Penal Code of 1810.[16]

From the National Convention until 1810, preventive measures devised to deal with the social problems of unwed mothers supplemented the foregoing changes in the laws. Destitute "girls" were paid a public assistance stipend while nursing their babies so that they had a third choice besides killing them. But a few more *tours* were also constructed in urban hospitals so that anyone—mothers, fathers, midwives, or relatives, who were the commonest perpetrators—could abandon unwanted children. However, over time and as the incidence of infanticide continued to rise, the public complained that welfare payments encouraged some women to take advan-

tage of public generosity. They claimed that immoral women got themselves pregnant just to get on the dole, then put their infants in the *tours* so
they could hire themselves out as wet-nurses. They would then get pregnant
again and continue the vicious circle. The young age of some of the girls
advertising for wet-nursing jobs was thought particularly vexing to
morals.[17] The Police Bulletin of February 10, 1808, prepared by the Minister of Police for the emperor, reported sixty-one convictions and thirty-
seven arrests for infanticide in the sixty departments of the Midi and eastern
France (the 2° Arrondissement) during 1807.[18] This was the climate of
opinion and incidence when Napoleon undertook to revise the criminal
code.

It is noteworthy that the timing of this revision of the criminal code of
1810 was concurrent with the need to step up conscription to replace the
armies being decimated by Napoleon's overextension of the front in the
Peninsular Campaign.

Step 1: Reforming Infanticide Law, 1810

In 1810 the infanticide question was debated in the Conseil d'Etat. Their
drafting committee's original language punished everyone guilty of committing infanticide, or of being an accomplice to the crime, to deportation.
However, several members, including Arch-Chancellor Cambacérès, who
was considered the best legal mind in the empire, thought this was too
lenient and argued for the death penalty because infanticide was a more
horrible crime than murdering an adult; moreover, he rejected the notion
that the fear of being dishonored was the mother's usual motive. But Treil-
hard (1742–1810), who was in charge of drafting the Penal Code of 1810, and
Berlier (1761–1844), who often opposed Napoleon's views in the Council of
State, argued for deportation for two reasons: because (1) they sympathized
with the women's suffering that must have led her to try to hide her shame
by killing her "fruit"; and (2) they predicted that by making the penalty too
strong, juries would continue to be so predisposed toward acquittal that
there would be no convictions; thus, no deterrence.[19]

In the end, the Conseil d'Etat decided to adopt the death penalty urged
by Cambacérès. Persons found guilty by a jury were supposed to be sent to
the scaffold, period. No mitigating circumstances were permitted to be considered. Even a person who committed infanticide involuntarily, and therefore had no "intent," could be punished.

The severity of the Napoleonic Code resulted in the problem foreseen by
those who favored a maximum penalty of deportation. When a jury had to
choose between sending a mother to the guillotine and acquittal, they often
let a guilty woman off because the penalty seemed too harsh—or so it

The frontispiece to Frédéric Masson's *Napoleon: Lover and Husband* is this engraving of Bonaparte looking handsome in the uniform of a general and wearing his famous hat over a short haircut. From Frédéric Masson, *Napoleon: Lover and Husband.*

seemed to the judges in the 1820s.[20] In addition to public opinion working against the Penal Code of 1810, the medical profession made convincing use of the puerperal insanity plea. Furthermore, evidence of confusion about the changes in criminal law is found in the records of the Cour de Cassation (the highest appeals court), which increased lesser sentences that had been rendered previously by lower courts in 1811 and 1814.[21]

Step 2: The *Tours* Were Universalized, 1811

Another step in Napoleon's multifaceted approach to infanticide prevention took effect on January 19, 1811, when he instituted universal usage of *tours* in foundling hospitals in every *département* of the expanded French Empire from A (Aisne) to Z (Zeidersée). His new policy was to allow the indigent women who came to these lying-in hospitals to remain for two years as nurses of two babies: their own and a foundling that had been deposited in a *tour* or an orphan whose mother had died in childbirth. After that time, the mothers were sent away with their clothing and a small sum to start a new life for themselves and the child. Perhaps 256 or 269 *tours*[22] were actually constructed to prevent infanticide, an indication of the widespread faith administrators had in their efficacy as a humane solution to a significant social problem.

Napoleon also considered the future of the children whose lives were saved by the *tours*. In the mid-eighteenth century, Victor Riquetti, Marquis de Mirabeau, and François Quesnay had authored an anonymous work entitled *L'Ami des Hommes, ou Traité de la Population*,[23] in which they urged the creation of Royal foundling homes. These Physiocrats proposed that when the male foundlings reached ten years of age, they start training with a peasant family for agricultural work, commencing with the herding of livestock, or volunteer for the army. The girls should stay on and apprentice for careers at the children's homes or other hospitals. Subsequently, the *cahiers de doléances* emphasized the need for more of these institutions. The ideas in the Physiocrats' populationist treatise were repeated in another anonymous book published in 1802, entitled *Essai sur un Point Important de la Législation Pénale à l'Occasion d'une Cause d'Infanticide Jugée à Dijon le 29 Pluviôse An 10*.[24] Napoleon, of course, thought the boys would make good cabin boys for the navy or soldiers, but he extended their education, and consequently their childhood, to age twelve (compare this to the situation in England, where five- to six-year-old boys were handed over to factories and coal mines as workers) after which time they had to earn their own living and get off the "welfare rolls."

Government-Funded Research in Legal Medicine

A final aspect of Napoleon's infanticide prevention policy should be recalled—namely the scientific research programs conducted at his midwifery/foundling hospitals. Not only did doctors keep detailed records of the manner of presentation of all babies born there, along with birth weight and size (statistics that they published annually in imperial medical journals)[25] and the weight of lung tissue (for determining whether the child had breathed after birth), but they actually conducted forensic experiments with dead fetuses and the corpses of infants.

Understandably, the details of these early experiments on human remains, which were performed by the Ideologue midwifery professor

François Chaussier and his successor, A. Licieux, were not publicized while Napoleon still governed but were divulged during the Restoration. For example, in order to help determine whether deaths of infants whose skulls had been fractured were accidental or deliberate, they performed a controlled experiment in which fifteen corpses of newborns were held up by their feet and dropped on their heads a half meter from the ground onto typical surfaces found at crime scenes, in order to discover the patterns of the cracks in the bones if force was not used. Then this was repeated from one meter. The idea was to accumulate statistical evidence to corroborate suspects' stories.[26] So Napoleon's infanticide prevention program was complex and modern, incorporating actual research on dead bodies and applying forensic science to the legal process of discovery. This kind of anthropological anatomy was included within the medical science of man.

Infanticide Law after the Empire

During the Bourbon Restoration, public sympathy continued to favor the "murdering mother" being given special consideration. Article 5 of the Law of 25 June 1824 kept the death penalty while easing her situation: the judge (and not the jury) was empowered to reduce the sentence rendered by a jury for a convicted mother from "death" to "life at forced labor." But the death penalty remained in force for anyone else connected with the crime. As was the case under the Penal Code of 1810, the jury still was not supposed to consider attenuating circumstances.[27] Consequently, some women who had undoubtedly killed their babies got off because juries felt the law was unfair.

Finally, the revisions in the Penal Code of 1832 did take attenuating circumstances into account for the mother. It added this to the jury's instructions, so if these were admitted, the court had to back away from using the guillotine.[28] After that, in the minds of contemporaries, the only remaining controversial language was whether the law should say that the murdered child had to have been "born alive" in order for a murder to have been committed, as all the laws had said until then, or whether it should be changed to prove that the child was "born viable."[29] The 1832 law on infanticide endured for the remainder of the nineteenth century, and since 1824, the murdering mother has consistently received some form of favorable treatment.[30]

Under the successive regimes starting with the Bourbon Restoration, claims continued to be made that the *tours* did not prevent infanticide as much as they encouraged abandonments (see Table I), which in turn required the government to spend additional money unnecessarily to raise these children. The public's feeling was that the existence of the *tours* as a safety net for the most desperate poor women was abused.

Table I[31]

Year	Number of Abandonments
1819	99,346
1825	117,305
1830	118,073
1833	129,699

Consequently, some hospitals gradually removed their *tours*. When that happened, some people who shied away from killing took unwanted babies to neighboring *départements,* actions that skewed statistics on the correlations between the incidence of infanticide[32] and the effectiveness of the *tours* as a deterrent. Finally, an 1855 book explained that from 1835 to 1843 infanticide really was 20 percent higher in *départements* that had suppressed the *tours* than in *départements* that kept operating them.[33] Moreover, 1859 statistics (see Table II) demonstrate the correspondence between the number of accusations of infanticide and the number of *tours* closed that same year.

Table II[34]

Year	Number of Infanticide Accusations	Number of Tours Closed
1826	117	1
1835	119	20
1840	137	2
1845	130	9
1850	164	5
1853	196	2
		Total: 39 closed

What we see in Table II is that as the government continued to destroy the *tours* between 1826 and 1853, the number of infanticide accusations rose. (There is no way of telling whether the crime of infanticide increased or whether it just was reported more.) An additional fact is that from 1836 on, the crime of infanticide increased more than other kinds of crime.[35]

A profile prepared in 1868 of the usual perpetrator of infanticide was also insightful for evaluating Napoleonic attitudes. The suspect was female about 92 percent of the time. Three-fourths of those accused were unmarried. Rarely did two married people commit it together. Most perpetrators were servants, either rural or urban. From 1826 to 1850, 83 percent of infanticide perpetrators were illiterate; whereas, from 1850 to 1868 79 percent were illiterate. Of 2,776 accusations between 1851 and 1865, the most occurred in the month of March: 313. (March arrivals had been conceived in June, assuming they went full term.) Overall, the profile had stayed more or less the same since the Napoleonic era.

A table of autopsies performed at the Morgue de Paris over the thirty years from 1837 to 1866 resulted in 726 accusations of infanticide. Yet, these trials resulted in more acquittals than other crimes: 374/1,000. Between 1844 and 1864, the most frequent methods used to kill 555 infants were:

1. Suffocation, 281/50.6%
2. Throwing into a cesspool, 72/13.0%
3. Fractures of the skull, 70/12.6%
4. Strangulation, 60/10.8%
5. Submersion, 31/5.6%
6. Lack of care, 14/2.5%
7. Miscellaneous (wounds, starvation, combustion, hemorrhage), 27/4.9%

They believed that the skull fractures resulted from throwing the child over a wall or dropping it from a high place or down into a construction site; however, many times its death seemed to result from being kicked or stomped by a *sabot* (wooden shoes peasants wore—not just in the Netherlands) of the father or even the girl's father who wanted to hide his daughter's pregnancy.[36] Obviously, infanticide methods could be exceedingly brutal. Since the child was the victim, the public's interest in expressing outrage against it through the venue of prosecution outweighed any woman's right to personal or physical privacy.

One opportunity that later nineteenth-century legal and medical experts saw Napoleon I missing was the tightening of the system against the men responsible for these unwanted pregnancies. Authors such as Abbé Gaillard admonished the emperor for failing to zero in on paternity and make the responsible culprits, sometimes adulterous older men or the "dead-beat dads" of that era, pay for their lust.[37] An economy that could provide full employment to both sexes was also beyond the capacity of preindustrial France, and single parents really needed permanent jobs to preserve family values.

Infanticide and child abandonment were pressing family issues from the eighteenth through the nineteenth centuries. As Buffon and others stated, these crimes were frequently committed even before the French Revolution of 1789 weakened the hold of the Church over moral values and caused many charitable religious institutions to shut down and disperse their experienced personnel. By the 1800s the French people were looking to the State to assume responsibility for child welfare and to abate these crimes by enforcing and rewriting infanticide law. It seemed to make good sense to contemporaries to address the perceived urgency of increasing the birthrate during the French Revolutionary Wars to offset the immense losses of manpower. To this end, Napoleon created the national system of midwifery education in order to remedy the ignorance of the untrained midwives, a condition that the Old Regime's chaotic efforts had failed to change. He thereby saved more mothers' lives during childbirth as well as the infants of unwed (often teenage) mothers and poor women who formerly had lacked prenatal care.

Once they were born alive, babies had to be nourished. As we saw in Chapter 5, Napoleon also decided that the most efficient and efficacious way to encourage the breast-feeding movement was for the imperial government to support private efforts. He assisted indigent families whose mothers agreed to breast-feed their babies and tried to reform the morals of upper-class mothers at the same time. The latter became the volunteers who contributed money and/or their personal service to the Society of Maternal Charity. The emperor bank-rolled them with an endowment of 500,000 francs, which he expected to be matched in donations or service in kind from the "visiting ladies"—mothers helping mothers—who joined branches of the society, which were scattered around France in the major cities.

Furthermore, Napoleon tried to save the lives of as many unwanted infants as possible by instituting the construction of the *tours* in every department of France. Yet the emperor was not in as much of a hurry to get foundlings into the military as he might have seemed, since he extended the childhood of foundlings to twelve years of age—twice as long as that of comparable English poor children and only two years short of the accepted marriageable age for upper-class French women. Napoleon's apparent generosity, which allowed the youngsters to grow up more before being sent to military service, may perhaps be explained by the fact that he was framing a professional military. Consequently, boys had to be mature physically in order to shoulder rifles and heavy backpacks in forced marches. (However, this explanation was not found in contemporary literature.) During the economic downturn of the Restoration, it was argued that the Napoleonic *tours* ought to be abolished—not because they were ineffective but because the saving of so many children required the State to spend too much money on feeding and clothing them; and budgets for this purpose were cut.[38] This implied that the *tours* had been too successful. Thus the basis of the political quarrel over the "baby-drops" shifted as they slowly began to disappear.

The persistence of Napoleon's humanistic conviction that as many infants as possible ought to be preserved—for the good of the nation—stood in stark contrast to the writing of an American author whose works circulated in France. Dr. Theodore Romega Beck, M.D., stated in his two-volume treatise published at Albany, New York, in 1823, *Elements of Medical Jurisprudence,* that he approved of infanticide because the principles of Thomas Malthus supported this.[39] Such Malthusian Darwinism was the antithesis of eighteenth-century natalist theory. In contrast then to Dr. Beck's philosophy, Napoleon's natalism could be considered anti-Malthusian.

From the foregoing we can see that the extremists at either end of the political spectrum were wrong about Napoleon's motivation for creating a national system of *tours*—the issue was multifaceted and far more nuanced.

10

Women's Medicine and Surgery from the Patient's Point of View

Adrienne Noailles Lafayette and Frances Burney d'Arblay

S O FAR OUR INVESTIGATION of woman's nature and the Napoleonic educational, medical, and jurisprudential system has treated women, in general, as objects of study. In their discourses enlightened thinkers sometimes elevated women's femininity, at other times writers denigrated it. Many of the surgeons and scientifically trained doctors believed that sexually determined differences dictated what women's social role should be. Even some female educators called for putting the "other sex" in their prescribed place, for domesticating them in the private space inside the home. In real life, however, daughters, wives, mothers, female patients, and working women were individual subjects who had to navigate the social structure and institutions to survive, moving carefully between the public and private spaces. Fortunately, we are privy to fine collections of letters and documents left by two important families of the era—the Noailles-Lafayettes and the Burney-d'Arblays. These papers encapsulated how women coped with disease and sought and received help from their physicians and surgeons. Their biographies offer a glimpse into the heart of real Napoleonic family life.

The d'Arblays and the Lafayettes Meet

The Peace of Amiens (1802) between Great Britain and France, which suspended the French Revolutionary Wars, made it possible to resume travel between England and the continent. One traveler who took advantage of this ceasefire was the already-famous English novelist and diarist Frances "Fanny"[1] Burney d'Arblay (1752–1840), who went abroad with her eight-year-old son to rejoin her French-born husband. General Alexandre d'Arblay had already returned to his homeland soon after the preliminary peace was made in order to see his French relations and to find employment. Shortly after Fanny Burney's arrival, in May 1802 the d'Arblays accepted the invitation of General Gilbert Motier de Lafayette and his wife, Adrienne Noailles (1759–1807), to visit them. The Lafayettes then resided in

Château de La Grange. From William Cutler, *The Life of Lafayette.*

The signature of Adrienne Noailles Lafayette on her last will and testament, dated April 5, 1804. She was always conscious of the importance of her arranged marriage, which joined two important noble families in France. Like many modern women, she never gave up using her maiden name with her married name on business letters, and she handled financial affairs herself. From the Marquis de Lafayette Microfilm Collection, Reel 4, Folder 45, Cleveland State University Library Archives. Used with permission from the Fondation Josée et René de Chambrun.

Brie, about thirty miles from Paris, at "La Grange-Bléneau," a fifteenth-century château with woodlands and farms, which Adrienne had inherited from her grandmother.[2] The two women had just met for the first time the previous week. Mme Lafayette, despite her infirmities, had climbed three flights of stairs to the d'Arblays' Paris apartment to extend the family of three a personal invitation to spend a weekend with them in the country.[3]

The two women's husbands were old friends with much in common. General d'Arblay had once been Lafayette's aide-de-camp in the French Army, serving with him in the Army of the North and in the National Guard. Later each had fled from the excesses of the Revolution—Lafayette over the northern border to Austrian territory and d'Arblay to England. Both had returned from exile to their beloved country of France under the magnanimity of Napoleon's amnesty. Furthermore, Lafayette and d'Arblay had produced a stream of letters lobbying to have their respective military pensions restored. Curiously, their financial situations also were similar in that both husbands were supported by very devoted yet strong-willed, more level-headed wives who had their own incomes. When Gilbert Lafayette first returned to France from being imprisoned by the Austrians at Olmütz, he did so without Bonaparte's permission. Consequently, he dared not set foot in Paris because his name was still on the list of proscribed *émigrés*. "Noailles-Lafayette"[4] (the signature his wife, Adrienne, used to sign business letters) was determined to recover whatever portion remained unsold of her noble family's ancestral properties, which had been confiscated during the course of the French Revolution. In order to do this she *walked* all over the country. She walked because the Lafayettes could then afford neither to own equipage nor to hire someone to take them anywhere. Thereafter (we can tell from the La Grange archives), Adrienne managed the household herself, balanced the account books, and paid all the bills. From the household accounts we learned, for example, that she even provided her idealistic husband with a monthly allowance of 48 francs of "pocket money."[5]

Mme Lafayette's older friend Fanny Burney d'Arblay also supported her husband and young son, but with the proceeds and investments from her series of Gothic novels. The first one, which catapulted her to fame, was *Evelina or a Young Lady's Entrance into the World* (1778), a novel told in letters about a woman's search for a father and husband, which has been called the first popular novel in English literature about a woman that was written by a woman.[6] The more sentimental and melodramatic *Cecilia or Memoirs of an Heiress* (1782) came next. *Camilla or a Picture of Youth* (1796), which she wrote shortly after she married d'Arblay, was a courtesy book for a young girl that taught the lessons of propriety, prudence, and fortitude. Obviously the two generals had married exceptional women, although the

Lafayettes' marriage had been arranged for them by relatives when they were almost children, and the d'Arblays' was a companionate marriage made after they first met in midlife.

General Lafayette at forty-five years of age was no longer the tall, impressive, soldierly figure he had once been. He had broken his femur in February 1802, and demonstrated his faith in scientific medicine by optimistically and stoically submitting to an excruciatingly painful and ill-conceived experimental therapy. The plan for his recovery was to apply traction to his leg in an effort to keep it from shortening, but the traction was so tight that it caused the skin on his hip to turn gangrenous. He was forced to use a wheelchair to attend the wedding of his daughter Virginie. Eventually, he was rehabilitated to the point of using a cane for the rest of his life to compensate for his lameness. Such limited activity contributed eventually to his becoming too overweight to mount a horse: hence, Lafayette was precluded from actually becoming a "man on a white horse," as Napoleon seemed to fear, except in a figurative sense.

Now in her early forties, his partner Adrienne showed signs of aging too. Her once-dark hair was already streaked with gray. Fanny Burney, who was known for her keen powers of observation, recorded her impression of Lafayette's "virtuous & heroick Wife": she "is by no means handsome, but has Eyes so expressive, so large, & so speaking, that it is not easy to criticize her other features, for it is almost impossible to look at them."[7] Burney also explained how Adrienne's mobility had become limited: "by some Cold, or mismanagement, & total want of exercise, in the Prison of Olmütz, some humour has fallen into one of her ancles [sic], that, though it does not make her absolutely lame, causes walking to be so painful & difficult to her, that she moves as little as possible, & is always obliged to have a stool for her feet."[8] Burney was right; Adrienne's youthfulness had been extinguished by everything that she had endured.

Adrienne had married at the age of fourteen (when Gilbert was sixteen). By age sixteen, she had given birth in 1775 to her first daughter, Henriette, a delicate child who perished in 1777, while Lafayette was in America. A second daughter, Anastasie, arrived that year. Her third child and only son, George Washington, was born after an especially painful pregnancy two years later—on Christmas Eve in 1779. Her fourth and youngest child, Virginie, was born two months prematurely in 1782, the year Lafayette reached his legal majority at the age of twenty-five. By age twenty-three and still technically a minor, Adrienne had completed childbearing.

Besides early physical trials that contributed to premature aging, Adrienne had been subjected to extraordinary emotional turmoil. Even as a teenager, she had always fainted whenever she became overexcited. Her

General Gilbert Motier de Lafayette with the short hair-style worn during the Napoleonic era and Restoration. From Bayard Tuckerman, *Life of General Lafayette*, frontispiece.

fragile health, which had been shaken by the anxieties of Lafayette's adventures in America coupled with the difficult series of pregnancies, was further tested during the Terror by the traumatic losses of her devout mother and sister to the guillotine. This was compounded when they received no Christian burial; instead their remains were tossed into a common grave at Picpus on the eastern edge of Paris. Following Lafayette's defection or flight across the French border and subsequent capture by the Austrians, his delicate wife, who always was susceptible to chills, was imprisoned in Paris during the cold winter of 1794–1795.

Once released after three years of separation from her husband, Adrienne and her two daughters Anastasie and Virginie voluntarily joined Lafayette who himself was ailing in the prison of Olmütz. With Adrienne as care-giver, Gilbert soon recovered. However, apparently, the inactivity and stress of extended incarceration in two small rooms, a nutritionally poor diet, and uncomfortable living conditions led to a medical crisis for Adrienne. She became feverish, headachy, and her arms and leg swelled so that she could neither walk nor write without soon experiencing great pain. According to her daughter's account, her fever started in October 1796 and persisted for eleven months.[9] Abscesses formed on her swollen limbs. Adrienne's request for permission to leave the prison to seek special medical attention in Vienna was denied unless she agreed not to return to the prison—a precondition she found unacceptable after overcoming so much to end her prior separation from her husband. Yet there was not so much as an armchair to provide comfort in their austere living quarters. A German-speaking military doctor named Dr. Kreutschke[10] (with whom Lafayette could only communicate in Latin) saw Adrienne at the prison, but he found himself baffled by her condition. He suspected a hematological disease, which he termed "a dissolution of the blood," but he could prescribe no effective treatment, although he visited her regularly (when he delivered the Lafayettes' mail). By the time the family was released into the hands of the United States of America Consul in Hamburg, in September 1797, Adrienne was terribly ill and thereafter was never completely well for extended periods.

Adrienne's peripheral edema seemed for a time to improve and the fever went into remission; however, she had to be carried in an armchair to witness Anastasie's wedding on May 9, 1798. But once more the family's economic situation seemed to overrule her suffering. Her painfully swollen legs recovered enough for her to walk with the help of a cane to Paris and around the city to rearrange the family's finances.

The stoic Lafayettes would not allow Adrienne's poor health to limit their hospitality. According to Burney, they lived "with the utmost simplicity and economy . . . , kept no sort of equipage, dress in the plainest and cheapest style. . . ." While she acknowledged that in his public appearances some people thought Lafayette behaved pompously, at home he was "all that is reputable & amiable, fond, attentive, & instructive to his children, . . . & displaying, upon every occasion the tenderest gratitude to the wife, who followed him into captivity, & to whom, from that period, he became, by universal account, far more warmly & exclusively attached than he had ever been formerly: though her virtues & conduct had always been objects to him of respect & esteem."[11]

Lafayette took great pride in showing La Grange to visitors. He was especially proud of its collection of American artifacts; innovations in agricultural engineering; the fine livestock and animals (dairy cows, sheep, swine whose pen was sanitized by running springwater to wash away any odor, and a menagerie of exotic fowl imported from many lands), and the lovely landscape itself so remarkable for its fields of genetically improved higher-yielding crops.[12] Thus, during the springtime of 1802, Lafayette found himself untroubled by any thought that his soul mate of almost three decades might ever predecease him.

The friendship of the two couples, who in France moved within the same social circle,[13] endured. But neither of them could foresee even in May 1805, the last time all four of them were together at George Washington Lafayette's wedding to Emilie de Tracy (daughter of Comte A. L. C. Destutt de Tracy who wrote *Eléments d'Idéologie*),[14] the horrific medical crises that both wives would undergo: Adrienne's only two years in the offing; Fanny's breast surgery in 1811.

Adrienne's Illness and Death

After a decade of chronic suffering, Adrienne's terminal illness began on August 22, 1807, when she was stricken with violent pains in the stomach, accompanied by high fever. The details of her care are a bit sketchy. Although the Lafayettes kept Dr. Sautereau[15] at La Grange for many years and occasionally a "M. Prévost"[16] (who may have been "the surgeon of Alay"[17] mentioned in the account books), Dr. Lobinhes was also on call from Paris. Because her mother had not recovered after three weeks, a concerned Anastasie consulted Dr. Lobinhes to whom she dashed off a letter on September 11. He immediately sent his opinion from Paris: "I do not think the fever that your mother had yesterday after eating was brought on by what she ate; it is more probable that it is a little relapse [*une petite rochute*], and in this case it is necessary to administer wine of quinquina [cinchona or Peruvian tree bark from which quinine is derived] right away in a dosage of two spoonfuls every three hours." He felt this would settle her stomach if the dosage were mild enough not to irritate it. He dismissed the need for an evacuation, which he thought would further irritate her stomach.

On September 20, Lobinhes wrote to Adrienne: "I have the pleasure to learn from you yourself that you are improving and in the same proportion as your stomach pain diminishes. This proves that you must continue to convalesce and continue to follow with scrupulous exactitude everything that you are doing." He went on to mention that he thought that the open blister on her leg, which he thought might abscess since it was weeping, was not an entirely bad occurrence since it alleviated some of the swelling. Nevertheless, he ordered some cautery to close this wound. To the news that the antiscorbutic (normally a remedy for scurvy) wine gave her headaches and heart discomfort, he expressed astonishment. If this continued, he thought she should take a bottle of bouillon first thing in the morning. Moreover, he urged that she be transported from La Grange to Aulnay, as soon as possible, so that he could come from Paris (bringing along his wife and children!) to attend her in person there.

On October 7, Dr. Lobinhes apologized for being unable to provide help after receiving an intervening letter about a "crisis of Saturday" too vaguely explained to enable him to give a diagnosis. However, the current letter in hand to which he was responding, was more precise. "I see that neither the fever nor the vomiting has returned, but the stomach weakness is worse." This called for lighter food and less of it, "only bouillon thickened with cream of rice or potato flour." He suggested that a couple of hours before dinner, they give her "a spoonful of elixir of *garus* in coffee, and if this is not enough, several times in the morning and twice in the evening some spoonfuls of senna [dried leaflets of cassia plant, a mild laxative] in a cold infusion," containing some dried centuary (a bitter herb to settle the stomach by strengthening stomach secretions) and orange leaves sweetened with orange blossom syrup. Finally, he now *begged* them to bring Adrienne to Aulnay.

A few days later as he was about to set forth, Dr. Lobinhes penned another letter to Anastasie: "I have seen with satisfaction that Madame your mother after having taken the emetic and three medicines has suffered at first diminution of feeling, and afterwards the disappearance of the fever entirely." But he was not wholly pleased. "These evacuations however necessary have the effect of weakening her and irritating very much her nerves and stomach," which made it difficult for her to keep down any food. Consequently, this time, he prescribed a mixture of Rata or Madeira wine, ordinary water, and herbs, before eating a few spoonfuls of thin porridge, which was all she could keep down. If the fever returned, he said, the feverfuse quinquina would have to be ground into a powder. Finally, he prescribed the ultimate remedy in the tradition of the "cooking physicians": "I would like you to make a *pot-au-feu,* especially for your mother, and that it be made only of chicken and veal. Such broth is gentle and ought to congeal when it cools." In any case, he would await the patient at the residence of her Aunt Tessé.

At last Adrienne was brought on October 11 to Aulnay, which was about three leagues (approximately nine English miles) from Paris. Leaving her in the personal care of Dr. Lobinhes, her apparently unconcerned husband and young son, George W., set out to visit Lafayette's elderly aunt in Chauvaniac. Yet Adrienne did not stabilize as she had done so many times before. This time the family decided to transport her to Paris proper, so that she could benefit from what was then perceived to be the best medical care in the world. Unfortunately, proximity to Paris did not help.

Lafayette and his son were unexpectedly summoned to Adrienne's side from Chauvaniac, only to find her condition had worsened. Gilbert later wrote[18] that for some unknown reason he had never really believed what the doctors had said about a defective pylorus (the opening of the stomach into the intestine), so he was completely unprepared for her deterioration. Nevertheless, Lafayette's calming presence appeared to help Adrienne to rally somewhat the following day. She confidently explained to the family friend Mme Simiane that she had a "*maligne* [malignant] fever," and after undergoing a course of treatment prescribed by her doctor, she would recover as usual.

As her fever continued, at times Adrienne's mind lapsed into hallucinations and delirium. In the former state, she imagined she was living in biblical times in Egypt or Syria with Attalie and the family of Jacob. In her delirium, she focused on stressful or joyful events in her life such as the journey to Olmütz to share Lafayette's imprisonment or the birth of her son. Meanwhile, Lafayette kept his daily vigil at her bedside engaging in a sweet repartee with his "angel," the wife he would refer to in his letters as "this incomparable woman." Always Adrienne was a perfect patient, always taking her medicine when asked and thanking everyone for their attention. Lafayette held her stone-cold hands for days. Her body was covered with blisters and peeling skin, which she tried to make light of by saying that she looked like a flayed animal. When she felt a seizure coming on, she motioned Gilbert away to spare him; but he refused to leave her side. Lobinhes, who continued to see her, sent off messages to the emperor's physician, the leading clinician of the era Dr. Jean-Nicolas Corvisart,[19] both seeking advice and summoning him to come immediately. All in vain. Lobinhes could only prolong Adrienne's life; he could not save it. At last only the heated blankets, with which her daughters and nurses covered her, insulated the last bit of life inside. She expired with her family seated in a semicircle around her bed on Christmas Eve at 11:45 p.m., the twenty-eighth anniversary of the birth of her only son, George Washington.[20]

Taking their cue from Lafayette's letters of bereavement[21] and Anastasie's biography of her mother,[22] historians have interpreted Adrienne's death as the culmination of a love story. After all, Adrienne's last words to Lafayette (whose extramarital affairs in his youth, including the one with Mme de Simiane, whom his wife had forgiven, had been known to her) had been quite touching: *"Je suis toute à vous."* He carried this message around his neck in a locket for the rest of his life.

The Cause of Adrienne's Death

Setting sentiment aside, however, from what did Adrienne die? Among the household accounts documents in the more recently microfilmed La Grange Collection were several pages of itemized bills for medicines for Adrienne from the pharmacist Leloup, which cover the period from April 20, 1806, to May 1, 1807. A meticulous study of these suggested that tuberculosis, peripheral vascular disease, congestive heart failure, or possibly kidney failure was probably not the *immediate* cause of her death.

Adrienne's prescriptions included numerous sets of leeches; stones for cautery; emetics and botanical remedies that included poppyheads and laudanum (a narcotic cordial containing opium that acted as a sedative), marshmallow (althea) root to soothe her mucous membrane (similar to modern cough drops), blackberry jelly, saffron, and dozens of citrons (the largest member of the citrus family—often ten inches long—whose pulp is unusable but the peel is candied). Most important among these receipts were also nine prescriptions for various forms of lead—either "lead cerate" (a cerate is a smearing mixture containing beeswax), "lead," or "concentrated lead." Because there are also receipts for plasters, we can theorize that the lead cerate was to smear on the plasters (strips of gauze). These in turn were placed on her legs, which were so swollen that they blistered and the skin was broken wide-open enough to require cautery, hopefully to act as an astringent. The plasters were then wrapped with gummed bandages (also supplied by the apothecary) to promote the absorption of the chemicals as well as to increase the circulation. Someone's thinking must have been: if some external application of lead cerate was therapeutic, why not facilitate healing from the inside out? So over about a three-month period, somebody ordered eight bottles of liquid lead compounds for the forty-eight-year-old patient.

From this sample,[23] it appears that Adrienne died from lead poisoning. The symptoms of her last illness—intense stomach pain, headaches, hallucinations, vomiting, delirium, and convulsions—are all consistent with this. If more of Adrienne's prescriptions are ever catalogued, we might know how much more she imbibed before her death. Interestingly, Lafayette, who knew his wife best, doubted the physician's diagnosis of a defect in the pylorus, but he also blamed her death on being "at the critical age."[24] This last statement suggested that some of the herbs purchased from the local drugstore that were intended to stop bleeding may also have been aimed at decreasing vaginal hemorrhaging, something that might occur at the onset of menopause. In any case, Lafayette's faith in science overruled any suspicion that iatropic disease (illness caused by a doctor's treatment) had accelerated Adrienne's death. Moreover, according to Robert's *Dictionnaire Alphabétique et Analogique de la Langue Française* (1973), it was not until the late nineteenth century that *Saturnisme* entered the French language as the term for lead cholic[25]—as its dangerous toxicity especially when applied to open wounds and ingested became fully appreciated.

Adrienne and Gilbert Lafayette dealt heroically with her medical condition, both during her lifetime as well as after her death. In their prolific correspondence the Lafayettes never talked about Adrienne's terrible astringent and anti-inflammatory treatments, applications of leeches, and so forth.

Pharmacy bills for Adrienne's medications from the pharmacist Leloup at Rosay for April to July 1806. Notice that "Extrait de Saturne" (extract of lead) appears twice, along with lead cerate on January 4 and 5. From the Marquis de Lafayette Microfilm Collection, Reel 4, Folder 45, Cleveland State University Library Archives. Used with permission from the Fondation Josée et René de Chambrun.

The details of her medical treatments were entirely too unspeakable for them to voice.

How did people in those days manage to cope with such treatments that led to the untimely death of a loved one? They focused on the arrangements and drew comfort from each other and from the listening and recitation of liturgy. Upon her death, the Lafayette family immediately drafted a death notice for the newspapers and arranged for her burial mass and interment among her relatives at what had by then become a hallowed burial place—Picpus Cemetery—on the eastern edge of Paris near Bercy. (Adrienne herself had much earlier taken a leading role in the inscription for its purchase.) Her husband was also comforted by the thought that one day he in turn would be laid to rest beside her. Although he had never pretended to share Adrienne's pious Roman Catholic faith, Lafayette ordered memorial masses said annually on the anniversary of her death, as Adrienne had wished.

As a widower, Lafayette lived on until May 20, 1834, when he was seventy-seven, but he remained inconsolable over the loss of his angelic wife. It is not too difficult to understand his unhappiness. He had married Adrienne at sixteen. Although he almost certainly experimented with other women at the court of Versailles during the early years of their marriage, the shared experience of the incarceration at Olmütz had drawn them together permanently. In her mind her early sacrifice—being separated from him when he went to America to become a general in the American Revolution and diplomatic liaison between the colonists and the court at Versailles while she stayed at home bearing their children—did pay off. Moreover, throughout her life she was comforted by a deep religious faith drawn from the religious instruction her mother injected into her homeschooling.

Fanny Burney's Childhood

If the stoically heroic Lafayettes never talked about Adrienne's terrible astringent and anti-inflammatory treatments, leechings, and other treatments, Fanny Burney d'Arblay's ailment was even more unspeakable. Yet she faced it in an equally heroic manner. Born in 1752, seven years before noblewoman Adrienne Noailles, and as a commoner in Georgian England, her early life contrasted sharply with Adrienne's.

As a youngster, Fanny Burney[26] was a tiny child with a weak frame; in fact, she appeared that way all her life. While she was extremely shy and meek in public, she behaved just the opposite within the circle of her family and friends. (Her father was the famous musicologist Dr. Charles Burney.) However, Burney's most notable physical problem during her childhood years seems to have been with her vision: both eyes were extremely nearsighted. Fanny may also have been dyslexic, a disorder that was little understood at the time. Partly because of her vision problems, her father totally neglected her education so that she had to teach herself her letters and how to read, which she did when she was eight to ten years of age. Her natural mother died about this time while giving birth for the ninth time. These events coincided with the beginning of Fanny's compulsion to write social commentary.

The first sign of stress affecting Burney's health occurred in 1781 when she succumbed to nervous exhaustion in the rush to meet her deadline for publication of the novel *Cecilia*.[27] However, the first enduring health problems she encountered occurred between the years 1787 and 1791 when she was Second Keeper of the Robes to England's Queen Charlotte—a post she accepted, in part, because at age thirty-four, being the last unmarried child in the family, having no dowry, and never having gotten on well with her stepmother,[28] she was a homeless spinster who needed security in her old age. At her father's insistence, she accepted the post that promised her a pension for her retirement. But she soon became physically exhausted at court by serving really as a personal maid to the demanding monarch and being made to stand absolutely motionless beside the queen for long hours; moreover, she missed the contact with the literary world, which she had enjoyed since the publication of her first novel. And the perceived "insanity" (actually the hereditary disease porphyria) of George III contributed to the turmoil of courtly life, which seemed to fly from one crisis to another. Because of his daughter's poor health, Dr. Burney managed to negotiate her release from Royal service with a pension of 100 pounds a year for life.

In 1793, while visiting her sister Susanna, Fanny Burney met General Alexandre d'Arblay,[29] two years her junior, who was then a penniless former French Army general who had joined the colony of French *emigrés* residing at Juniper Hall near Norbury Park, an estate belonging to the Locke family. Her courtship with the gay, amusing, affectionate, and affable officer took off immediately. Because d'Arblay was a Roman Catholic, impoverished, and a constitutionalist in French politics, her father disapproved of the match. Regardless, Fanny leaped into marriage on July 31, 1793, when she was forty-one years old.

The d'Arblays' only child, a son named Alexander,[30] arrived the next year, 1794. But Fanny had to stop his breast-feedings when she developed an ulcer on one breast. She attributed this to something transmitted to her from the infant through nursing, possibly from Alex's thrush (also known as the fungal infection candidiasis, which can spread from a child's mouth to a site under the mother's breast), a common occurrence in conjunction with diaper rash and of little concern. Mixing motherhood and work, she continued her writing and published *Camilla* when she was forty-four.

Although subscriptions were purchased by such famous people as the novelist Jane Austen and the politician Edmund Burke, it was somewhat of a literary failure. Nevertheless, it provided her with enough money to build a small cottage on the Locke's estate in Surrey, which she dubbed "Camilla Cottage" and where the family lived until 1797, with Fanny as the breadwinner.

Finally, the preliminary signing of the Peace of Amiens (October 1801) meant that the homesick General d'Arblay could return to France with the goals of visiting his French family and securing his military pension, as well as finding gainful employment. So desperate was he for this that he even offered to join the French expedition to the swamps of Saint Domingo—but with the qualification that he would never be asked to fight against his wife's countrymen. However, due to his reluctance to fight the British, d'Arblay missed out on a mission that turned into a medical catastrophe with the outbreak of yellow fever. Napoleon as first consul excused the general's feelings, even expressed sympathetic understanding of his predicament, since d'Arblay was after all, he said, "*Camilla's* husband."

A Decade in Paris

Fanny could not stand being separated from her husband for long, and she and her son joined General d'Arblay in Paris in 1802—for what she expected would be a year's duration but which turned into a decade due to the resumption of the French Revolutionary Wars. Because she was such a well-known novelist, she was immediately introduced to the fabulous Parisian social scene and met all the worthies. Besides attending a *masque,* the theaters, operas, and art exhibitions, she attended a review of Napoleon's troops where she found the fashionable ladies outrageously dressed in the newest French style—their clothing had drapery that clung to and revealed their bodies. She took notice of Bonaparte's sallow complexion and serious, brooding manner, too. She also witnessed an examination at Mme Campan's school (see Chapter 2) where the ladies present included the first consul's sister Caroline Murat and step-daughter/sister-in-law Hortense, as well as the famous painter Elizabeth Vigée-le-Brun. In 1803 she was initially charmed upon meeting the distinguished Dr. Pierre-Jean Georges Cabanis (see Chapter 6), who presented her a copy of his philosophical medical works; but she was quite taken back when she read it and learned that he was a materialist! Needless to say, she also found her English wardrobe quite out of keeping with the current mode of Paris fashion when she exclaimed: "Three petticoats! No one wears more than one! Stays? Everybody has left off even corsets! Shift-sleeves? Not a soul now wears even a chemise."[31] But her prudishness, the proportions of her figure, and near poverty precluded her from becoming trendy. Fortunately, the d'Arblays' visit to La Grange had been followed by the recovery of the general's military pension and the landing of a minor civil-service post as a *rédacteur* (one who drafts documents) in the administration of buildings in the Ministry of the Interior.[32] Thereafter, they no longer had to rely solely on Fanny's income.

But life was not almost perfect for long. In 1805 Burney developed a lump in her right breast, which she felt came from the ulcer she had developed years before when she had nursed her son; however, the lump, to use her own words, "yielded to strict fasting & asses milk"[33] and resolved. Symptoms recurred in August 1810, when an annoying small pain in her breast gradually increased, but she did not seek immediate medical treatment. She hoped that by being careful and keeping warm, it would likewise vanish in a few months. Finally, her husband and a close female friend, Mme de Maisonneuve, the author of housekeeping manuals, persuaded her to consult a physician for examination. She did, but Dr. Jouet's prescribed treatment only seemed to increase the pain. So she sought a second opinion from Dr. Antoine Dubois,[34] a busy professor of anatomy, surgery, and obstetrics, and since the death of the great Dr. Baudelocque, the official accoucheur to Empress Marie Louise, whose pregnancy was under way. Dubois greatly reassured Fanny that nothing was serious and gave her a prescription to try for a month, before speaking at length, privately with her husband. From the dreadful looks on their faces after their consultation, she guessed that "a small operation," a partial removal of her diseased breast, was necessary to preserve her life.

Mastectomy was not a new operation; in fact, the basic procedures for it had already been well established by the late seventeenth century and perfected by Pierre Dionis (1643–1718), the surgical demonstrator at the Jardin du Roi for eight years who taught surgical pupils how to become masters of twenty-five required operations, including mastectomies. Dionis's work, *Cours d'Opérations de Chirurgie Démontrés au Jardin Royal* (1707), was so popular that it went into its eighth posthumous edition in 1777, edited by his pupil George de la Faye who himself had risen from the military to become the royal demonstrator in surgery. For his fifth demonstration, the plates in Dionis's surgical manual showed all the necessary mastectomy instruments to assemble beforehand. The preface to his techniques revealed the contemporary mentality vis-à-vis cancer: "Cancer is by unanimous consent the most horrible of all the evils that attack humankind. While rabies and the plague kill in less time, they do not seem as cruel as cancer, which leads as surely, but more slowly to the grave, while causing suffering that make us wish every day for death." Dionis also observed that breast cancer usually struck women aged forty-five to fifty, about the time they reached menopause. While Dionis was fully prepared to operate to stop this killer, he also agreed with Hippocrates's notion that sometimes it was better to leave some cancers alone. Dionis's reasoning was that intervention could irritate the lymph and cause the sugars to ferment to form salts, thereby worsening the cancer. Therefore, the surgeon ought to find palliatives to make the pain supportable and give the patient a good death.[35]

In the Napoleonic era, the nature of cancer and how its wildly growing epithelial cells invaded surrounding tissue was better understood. The anatomist and physiologist Marie François Bichat (1771–1802), whose study of tissues laid the basis for modern histology, had finally arrived at the modern understanding that cancerous tissue is pathologically different from normal tissue and that breast cancer has nothing to do with women's salts and sugars fermenting, "humours" swelling, greater capacity to feel emotions, or other theories of the Enlightenment. However, this new knowledge was of little comfort to a woman who had just been diagnosed by perhaps the most highly respected specialist in women's diseases and childbirth in France (which meant in the world since French medicine was preeminent) who had declared that the hard mass she felt in her right breast undoubtedly was cancer. Despite the advance in pathology, the prognosis for mastectomy was still so bad that leading authorities in legal medicine such as François Fodéré cautioned against it, claiming that it was an operation that only surgeons who were money hungry or trying to enhance their own reputations at all costs performed in order to inflict useless suffering upon the unfortunate victims, sometimes hastening their death.[36] Still, the public knew that a few lucky women had survived a mastectomy, the most notable example being the surgeon Gendron's successful operation on Queen Anne of Austria, mother of Louis XIV.

Nonetheless, the prospect of submitting to a mastectomy, even a partial one, came as shocking news to the d'Arblays. But neither the approach of doom nor the pain in her chest, arm, and shoulder served to paralyze this spunky fifty-nine-year-old wife and mother into passivity. Obviously, she needed to write her will without delay, so she did. As days passed, Mme d'Arblay also knew that while the disease was progressing, she was getting no action from her doctor, which heightened her distress.

When it seemed that Dubois had apparently become too preoccupied with the Royal confinement to find time to perform her operation immediately, Fanny took matters into her own hands. She personally wrote to Dr. Dominique Larrey. As a young doctor, Larrey had started the Société Médicale d'Émulation along with Xavier Bichat and J.-L. Alibert, a medical society that contributed greatly to the development of the medical science of man.[37] He gained enormous surgical experience performing amputations on the battlefields (as many as two hundred amputations in twenty-four hours). Now Larrey received Burney's letter begging him to take over her case. (Fortunately for her, Larrey was currently in Paris and not on campaign with the Grand Armée, which would have taken precedence.) Larrey responded to Mme d'Arblay's urgent request by choosing the quickest and most professional route. Instead of meeting initially with her himself, he arranged a general consultation with a full surgical team, consisting of Dubois, himself, and two other military surgeons, François Ribe[38] and the *Idéologue* Jacques-Louis Moreau de la Sarthe.[39] Dubois really thought Mme d'Arblay's condition was entirely hopeless, so evidently he had only *seemed* disinterested in order to spare her feelings. But since Larrey was nevertheless willing to try, the surgeons told her that they wanted to perform the operation.[40] Certainly, the surgical team would be laboring under far better conditions than they normally had when they operated on campaign.[41]

The Mastectomy

The mastectomy was scheduled for three weeks later, September 30, 1811, at Mme d'Arblay's home, in her salon. She was told in advance only that she should prepare a chair and piles of towels and folded bandages—and that she would suffer. She arranged for her husband and son to be out of the house to spare them the sound of her screams—for this was still the era of preanesthetic as well as preantiseptic surgery and except for fainting twice,[42] she would be awake throughout. While following her request, Larrey only sent her a note at 11:00 a.m. that the surgery would be at 1:00; however, Dubois subsequently had an emergency that delayed everything for two more hours. She was further startled by learning that she should make ready a bed instead of a chair, which suggested that she would be supine instead of seated throughout her ordeal, a less dignified position for public nakedness. She also was ordered to keep only one serving woman in the house in place of the three she had previously planned to have attending her during the surgery. Consequently, the patient who lost the moral support of those women's familiar presence anxiously awaited the men's arrival for at least four hours—from 11:00 a.m. until 3:00 p.m. When the clock struck that hour, Burney quickly penned "last" notes to her son and husband, in case she did not make it through the operation.

After her ordeal, Fanny remembered Dr. Moreau preparing her by entering the salon–turned–operating theater with a drink of laudanum, a wine cordial whose opium content was supposed to send her into a relaxed dreamlike state. As it turned out, the mere sight of four doctors and three assistants—no women, just seven men all tolled—dressed in black suits, marching in, completely terrified her. She was an exceedingly shy person in public; what's more, her novels revealed her special sensitivity to males inflicting social and physical violence on females. She felt engulfed now being surrounded by more men than she had expected who would observe and carry out the surgical mutilation of her breast. Julia Epstein argued that it was "the framework of dominance and submission that she found as oppressive as the physical pain."[43]

Yet facing the danger squarely, Burney defiantly mounted the bed unaided before Dubois positioned her suitably on the mattress. While he discretely draped her face with a handkerchief to shield her from the spectacle, the cambric was so thin that she was still able to see the men's silhouettes and the hand signals they used to communicate directions.

At the outset, she thought the surgeons seemed at odds over how large an incision to make, a decision that corresponded to how much breast they believed ought to be removed. Then she detected Dubois's hand and forefinger signaling three procedures: first, to make a vertical incision followed by a second one horizontally—much like making the sign of the cross, it seemed to her; finally, his finger drew in the air the third procedure—a complete circle. A complete mastectomy! Either naïvely or through wishful thinking, she had missed the other clues to the fact that the surgical team had assembled with no intention of removing just a small portion of her breast, which might be considered a lumpectomy of sorts. They had planned all along on a complete mastectomy in a three-stage procedure that would take Larrey, who was famous for the speed of his amputations, perhaps twenty minutes of effort.

At one point, Larrey asked who would hold the breast for him while he made the circular incision? At this juncture, Mme d'Arblay bravely but unsuccessfully tried to volunteer herself in order to keep as much of her breast as possible from being amputated. But patient participation was totally out of the question in the surgery they had planned for her. Her role was to be submissive.[44]

In an effort to help her endure the pain, Dubois asked whether she had screamed during childbirth; he seemed pleased to learn that she had, instructing her to scream as soon as she felt the need. When the cutting began, Burney did succumb to the pain and later remembered maintaining one long, continuous, agonizing scream that seemed to go on forever, one that she would remember for the rest of her days.

Overcome with the sensations of the cutting and sawing, and then the feeling of this cutting continuing against the grain, Burney finally ceased being a spectator, shut her eyes tightly, and listened to their voices. When Larrey (whose face had become streaked with her blood) seemed to be done, she heard him ask the others whether anything more needed to come off.

Dr. Moreau pointed out where he thought more flesh needed to be scraped down to the bone, and Dubois detected something more after that. Ultimately, all the surgeons were satisfied that they had excised all the cancerous portion including all vestiges of the crab-leg-like roots, so they proceeded to finish up, close the wound, and bind her breast with heavy bandages to soak up the normally profuse bleeding.[45]

The patient's female attendant and Dr. Larrey's senior assistant kept an all-night vigil at her bedside. This young man wrote a succinct medical history of the postoperative period that provided details about the recovery.[46] He informed us that at 3:45 p.m. the surgeons had removed a cancerous, hardened tumor about the size of a fist adjacent to the *pectoralis major* muscle along with all its roots. She then experienced the expected and prolonged muscle spasm for which he administered an antispasmodic to calm the muscle. She finally had moments of agitated sleep toward 2:00 or 3:00 a.m. At 4:00 a.m., she became nauseated and the vomiting weakened her. This was followed by a period of calm and two hours of peaceful sleep. On the day after the surgery, Larrey came at 10:00 a.m. to find her feeling better than he had expected she would this soon, without fever, feeling little pain in the wound, and the blood had not soaked through the bandages as sometimes occurred. The chief surgeon prescribed a light diet consisting of cream of wheat and meat gelatin, along with alternate servings of chicken broth and a gummed barley with lemon beverage. That evening, medication would help her sleep—a mixture of linseed (seed of the flax plant, containing a fatty oil) and the narcotic, poppyhead.[47]

After the operation, Burney determined not to tell her relations in England, especially her father, about her mastectomy, but somehow her sister learned of it. Consequently, after many months of recovery, she penned a detailed description not only of the operation but also of her feelings at each juncture, which she sent to dispel the family's concerns about the state of her health. She sent this letter with a copy of the aforementioned report of Larrey's assistant attached through the naval blockade to England, with instructions to Esther about who should be allowed to share her letter as well as who should be kept in the dark. This document became the first patient's account of a preanesthetic mastectomy.[48] There is a certain tragic irony here in that a sensitive female novelist whose plots had always been about the ways contemporary society's manners violated women had to undergo such an act of medical violence performed by an all-male cast to one of her most symbolic female body parts in order to save her life. Afterward, writing "the unspeakable" was Burney's logotherapy that facilitated her recovery, although using her hand to write pained her terribly for the rest of her life.

An illustration from Dr. Bougery's surgical textbook showing how to remove a cancerous breast by cutting through all the layers of tissue. The technique did not change from the early 1800s through the 1840s. From Bourgery and Jacob, *Traité Complet de l'Anatomie de l'Homme Comprenant la Médecine* . . . Digital photo taken by Laura Travis. Used with permission of the Dittrick Medical History Center, Case Western Reserve University, Cleveland, Ohio.

Burney was famous as a social observer, and her feeling about the surgeons was right on the mark. Whether she knew it or not, some of these men were leaders in the medical science of man movement of vitalism-sensationalism. We have already seen how many of these scientists felt as Cabanis did about the relations between the physical and the moral in women's bodies and how this determined their place in society. Larrey also had a reputation for being a strict disciplinarian and autocrat in dealings with his associates, his medical students—and his wife. No wonder they repelled Burney's willful attempt to participate in the surgery. Her home became transformed into public space the moment the surgical team entered, and Burney had always been afraid of being in the public eye. To their way of thinking, there could be no role for her there even if she was a famous author—she was still just a woman on the cutting edge of life and death. Burney had been appalled when she first learned of Cabanis's materialism, and we know that at least two of these surgeons were closely associated with his philosophy; but in choosing a surgeon she did not let that bother her anymore than d'Arblay's Catholicism.

Burney Resumes the Role of Caregiver

Despite a long and painful recovery from the surgery, in 1812 (while Napoleon was occupied with the Russian Campaign) Fanny finally obtained an official passport to England and returned alone across the channel with her draft-age son. Once again on her native soil, she turned her attention to the nursing needs of her aged father, who was then ill. She oversaw his caregiving until his death in April 1814.

Although he was a Roman Catholic, General d'Arblay acquiesced when Fanny made the decision to properly educate their son in preparation for ordination into the priesthood of the Church of England, since it would secure his future against all forms of adversity.

After Napoleon's first abdication in 1814, General d'Arblay returned to the French Army and was appointed to the King's Bodyguards. Once more the declaration of peace made her free to travel so Fanny joined her husband in Paris but fled to Belgium along with many others after Napoleon returned from Elba in March 1815. Consequently, she was in Brussels during the Battle of Waterloo in June. (Thackeray used her diary of this event in *Vanity Fair*.) D'Arblay had gone to the Trèves area in an effort to raise an army in support of Louis XVIII when he was badly kicked by a horse and further injured by unskillful surgery on his right leg. Upon receiving this news, Fanny left Brussels and went by carriage around the lines to fetch her beloved husband and take him back home with her to England to recover. Again she consulted her friend and savior Dr. Larrey, who had now become Baron Larrey, with whom she had continued to correspond. She heeded his professional recommendation by taking General d'Arblay to Bath for "dry pumping," a newer form of water therapy that directed a stream of water under pressure against an area in lieu of immersion of the whole body. Nevertheless, General d'Arblay remained an invalid on half-pay (which was slow in coming) until he died on May 3, 1818, ending their marriage of nearly twenty-five years. Fanny Burney remained as inconsolable for the remainder of her life as Gilbert Lafayette became after the loss of Adrienne.

We have a portrait of her from Sir Walter Scott, who described the novelist's appearance at age seventy-four, when he met her in 1826 (when Scott was forty-four): "An elderly lady with no remains of personal beauty, but with a simple and gentle manner, a pleasing expression of countenance, and apparently quick feelings. . . ."[49]

Not only did Burney outlive her husband, her only son also predeceased her in 1837. She died peacefully on January 6, 1840, on the anniversary of her sister Susanna's death. Thus, the former surgical patient outlived Adrienne Noailles by more than three decades and Lafayette, the legendary "Hero of Two Worlds," by six years.

Any commentary on the medical history of these two women seems anticlimactic, since their stories were so powerful and pathetic. Certainly, in keeping up appearances these incomparable, heroic women—Adrienne Noailles Lafayette and Frances Burney d'Arblay—demonstrated the strength of imperial wives "in sickness and in health." As patients they endured great, medically inflicted suffering. But they were as strong physically as their marriages. Moreover, despite their different ages when they married and that Adrienne's was arranged while Fanny's was a love match, neither woman's actual role as devoted wife made her the lesser marriage partner of a famous husband. Both couples' marriages endured through politically dangerous, revolutionary times. All four of them had a great compulsion to write letters and journals, which helped them endure the harshness of life in that time. Both women did not allow the fact that their husbands did not share the same religious convictions as they did become a problem in their marriages. Above all, these women should be hailed as survivors.

From a broader perspective, these two medical biographies also well illustrate the accuracy of Napoleon's instincts vis-à-vis physicians and his preference for surgeons. He warned friends, such as Arch-Chancellor Câmbacérès, against the dangers of taking too much medicine,[50] and greeted Dr. Corvisart, whom he appointed to run the medical service of his court precisely because he did not prescribe too much medication, perhaps not too tongue-in-cheek with: "Grand Charlatan, whom have you killed today?"[51] The fallen emperor in final exile on Saint Helena repeated his previous statement that through ignorance or error, physicians killed as many people as generals.[52] Nevertheless, he said he respected the masterful surgeon, Jean-Dominique Larrey, possibly more than any other man he had ever known.[53]

11

Reflections

THESE DISCOURSES, mostly but not all by men, are proof that the debates of the seventeenth and eighteenth centuries about all the ideas in the loaded term *the woman question* were ongoing; and they certainly did not cease before the French Revolution of 1789 or after 1799 either. As we have seen, there were unfinished discourses involving women's body-mind nexus during the years 1799 to 1815, and even retrospective ones after the Bourbon Dynasty was reinstated. These were found in a wide variety of places such as books, journals, textbooks, advice manuals, records of the Cour de Casssation, records of the Prefects, and elsewhere. (Their titles may be found listed under Primary Sources in the Bibliography and arranged in chronological order separately so that they may be studied comparatively by year of publication.)

Regardless of whether these discourses were in the fields of education, medicine, or legal medicine their nucleus of meaning involved the relations between the physical and the moral in feminine bodies and minds. The rubric of "mind" covered all or some of the following depending upon the author's theoretical bent: the mental faculties of sensibility, emotion, passion, capacity to use reason and to store knowledge as memory, and ability to read and write prose and poetry.

The discourses were focused on the characteristics of women in general rather than exceptional women who were explained away as if Nature had colored outside the lines, so to speak, or freaks of Nature who should not be emulated. Authors attempted to peel away the effects of civilization, environment, race, climate, and/or age—just leaving sex and reason in order to judge women's natural characteristics, which in turn determined women's designated social function in society. Finding answers to the woman question had become more urgent than in the eighteenth century because the Revolutionaries who initiated political democracy wished only to give women representation and not direct participation in politics or any other activity that was of a public nature; however, they needed to find a rationale to justify doing this. As Geneviève Fraisse argued, sexual division was inherent in the birth of democracy. Admittedly, these discourses were sometimes ongoing, incomplete, fragmented, unbalanced, and visible when we look at them from the perspective of certain disciplines, but they did occur in a historical setting—the consulate and the French Empire—so they are legitimate objects of study that bring deeper meaning to the study of historical events.

Geneviève Fraisse dated the moment in the democratic revolution when things started to get better for women not at 1789 but at 1800, which is within the time frame of the Napoleonic era. She also argued that the male Revolutionaries' insistence on sexual difference was fueled by their anxiety about the confusing or blurring of sexual identities. As I quoted Fraisse saying in my Preface, "the historical period, the Empire, did not seem to assure them." What did Napoleon or his administrators do that gave them the idea that he was blurring sexual difference? What did conservative Revolutionaries think he did that was so contrary to their own opinions that it could be blamed for their sexual anxiety? We need to review Napoleon's achievements and look for clues:

1. Endowment, reorganization, and regulation of the urban Societies of Maternal Charity in Paris and forty cities
2. Creation of the Légion of Honor Girls School at Ecouen
3. Creation of the Légion of Honor Girls School at Saint-Denis
4. Creation of the House of Orphan Girls at Paris, in the *marais*
5. Creation of the House of Orphan Girls at Barbeaux, forest of Fontainebleau
6. Creation of the House of Orphan Girls at Loges, forest of Saint-Germain
7. Authorization of an official journal of education, *Annales de l'Éducation*
8. Creation of the First National System of Midwifery Education:
   (1) La Maternité—national normal school for midwifery teaching, wet-nursery for infant orphans and foundlings, and hospice for *fille-mères*
   (2) Local midwifery training courses at departmental lying-in hospitals
9. Construction of the departmental *tours* in major cities

It would take quite a stretch of the imagination to suspect that the creation of the Légion of Honor girls schools and orphanages for girls from military families were the cause of this distrust of the Napoleonic government—the beneficiaries were sisters and daughters of France's greatest heros. Perhaps there were a few men who objected to the *Annales de l'Éducation* being edited by a woman, Pauline Guizot. There were ongoing discourses about the frivolity of women learning to read, since they lacked reasoning ability, or writing poetry, since their minds were mediocre at tasks requiring creativity, a masculine attribute. Journals were springing up in many fields, and they circulated in public to coffee houses and cafés where they were shared. They also were brought into the home. Being a woman journalist was, indeed, going public with one's ideas. Moreover, espousing an official educational philosophy as it did, this journal really was political—some might think, a field better left to men whose stronger bodies and minds capable of more profound thinking were naturally better suited.

However, given the climate of opinion, the Society of Maternal Charity and the national system of midwifery education along with the rest of the program to stop infanticide are far more likely to have been the causes of antifeminist opposition.

The first institution, the reorganized Society of Maternal Charity of Paris with all its associated branches in major cities, such as Lyons and Bordeaux, was part of the public/private campaign and partnership to persuade mothers of all social classes to breast-feed their own babies—hardly a subversive activity at first glance. The society's goal was to improve the dreadful infant mortality rates by saving the lives of infants and foundlings who formerly had been sent to wet-nurses in the country, a dangerous practice. But it also was a political plan to improve the morals of upper-class women by overcoming the maternal indifference that motivated women to send their babies away because rearing children bored them or ruined their social life. At the same time, the "visiting ladies" were supposed to persuade poor women of good character to breast-feed their infants and love them enough not to leave them on the steps of the church, or some such place, thereby turning them into foundlings with a 50 percent chance of survival.

But from another perspective, the Society for Maternal Charity could be misinterpreted as being a sort of political club that trained upper-class women to leave their homes to do social work in the public sphere. This experience taught upper-class women how to forge alliances with the working poor, strategies that could be used in the future if women ever decided to become "politically active" in the traditional sense. Napoleon's uncle, Cardinal Fesch, who ran the organization, had trouble finding as many women to donate large sums of matching money to double the government's endowment as Napoleon had hoped for, although others volunteered their services instead. It would not be too great a leap from there to sending upper-class women out to work as salaried employees. If they get used to leaving their homes to go into the public sphere on an errand for the government—spreading its propaganda—what will they think of doing next? The effect of this plan in the long range is a bit ambiguous.

Finally, we come to the new national system of midwifery education. This one must have set off all sorts of bells and whistles among anxious males for two reasons: (1) it involved the teaching of science to women, and (2) it attempted to reverse the eighteenth-century trend of the medicalization of childbirth by male accoucheurs who had been trying to take over this profession from uneducated women. Not only were the women being paid by the national government and the prefectures to train for this profession by studying at Paris for two years, but they also were supposed to return to their native departments to teach their own courses to local women as career health professionals. And many of these women learning a paid profession were married women with families! Here again we have the Napoleonic government politicizing institutions in the most private areas of public life and reaching out to intrude upon the domestic sphere. It must have appeared to some men that a squad of well-trained midwifery teachers were reclaiming turf lost in a previous battle of the sexes. Dr. Leroy even went so far as to propose that the Napoleonic government should train its own female gynecologists by sending women to attend the medical schools beside the men.

The final thought that comes to mind about how Napoleon made men feel anxious because he seemed to be blurring the sexes is that he always insisted to whomever was listening that women were strong like his mother. Letizia Bonaparte was a traditional Corsican wife and woman; but in many ways, as a widow, a category that was privileged in imperial society, she emerged from the complementarity of her marriage with Carlo as very much a modern woman whose frail little body had a mind of its own. Although he designed some innovative programs to benefit women and female orphans, her son was not really a feminist, but he did respect the influence of women on the family, a lesson he had learned at home at his mother's knee.

In her theories about the body history of the French Revolution, Dorinda Outram tried to explain why it was that middle-class male Revolutionaries did not run away in fear from the guillotine and why they condemned women for behaving (as they saw it) just like women—when what they meant was that they let go of their human emotions and sympathized and empathized with their neighbors and friends. She maintained that the men's reaction to the crisis was to role-play Stoic heros of classical antiquity, even to the point of electing to commit heroic suicide or to accept being guillotined before the lower-class public. Of course, in the eighteenth century and the Revolutionary era before the advent of Napoleon, education was classical and Latin was the language, so students were taught about classical heros, like the Stoics, as part of their training in morals and values. It was only in the Napoleonic lycées that the history curriculum changed to the use of newly written textbooks, which Napoleon commissioned or encouraged, that modern French history in the French language began to edge out Latin and the classics. So what Outram says makes sense. She goes on to say that Napoleon established such a stable government with a bearable level of crisis that men no longer needed to role-play to discipline their bodies. The question she raises, though, that begs for an answer is what became of this stoicism during the Napoleonic era?

As historians of Napoleonic iconography have made obvious, Napoleon himself modeled his public persona after antique heros and rulers (including the medieval Holy Roman emperor Charlemagne), and Jacques-Louis David played a big part in his image-building campaign. But we have also seen in Chapter 10 how Adrienne Noailles and General Lafayette staged her death with a semicircle of chairs, in which members of her family were seated, surrounding her. Enthroned in her deathbed, she played the leading role. Mme Lafayette's bedroom became a public space where she passed in and out of consciousness, and when she went out she imagined herself in the Bible with Old Testament heros—whom she had learned about in her childhood from her mother. This theatrical grandstanding was her response to the crisis of her impending death.

Likewise, there was some role-playing involved when Frances Burney d'Arblay had her mastectomy. She mounted the bed; she volunteered to help hold her breast; she heroically envisioned the operation from a point outside of herself and looked down upon the scene so that she became both subject and object. Mme d'Arblay also arranged beforehand for the male members of her family to be absent so that she would perform this scene of martyrdom alone except for one female servant, enough of a witness to protect her virtue and modesty. Medical crises, like the Terror of the French Revolution, also become theater for these women when a room in their home was turned into a public space.

To pick up on another point that Outram made, she said that the French Revolution did not create a state, it created a new public space where none of the many discourses ever won decisively. We have seen how the medical science of man cooperated with politics and the law during the years 1799 to 1815 in intruding into private space in order to carry out its mission of social reform. This was very obvious in the celebrated cases of infanticide. The medical discourse going on throughout the Napoleonic era was unitary, and through cooperation with law and politics it helped to integrate opinion. Unfortunately for women, however, the new medical theorists still wanted to allot weak, feeble-minded women the diminishing domestic space and save the public arenas for themselves.

The answer to the question of why men were so afraid of women occasionally becomes apparent. The participation of women in the Revolution in active ways rather than merely feeling sensibility and passion, was what really scared them and made them cringe at the mention of feminism. The memory was of women acting like "rapacious monsters" or "rapacious beasts." Such men, and Dr. Cabanis and Napoleon were among them, feared that if a battle of the sexes would occur, feminist women would win. It may well be that the individualist feminism–turned–violent of the Revolutionary women's movement was seen ten to fifteen years later as a "one step forward, two steps backward" situation. In other words, instead of advancing all women away from total male dominance, as the eighteenth-century feminist women had done, it generated a powerful backlash, causing a tsunami that wiped out any gains and eroded the shoreline of the women's sphere as well. The women's sphere was shrinking at the same time as women were being herded into it; so, when it filled, women would break out. In the Napoleonic era we see politics intruding, sending out vectors or tentacles, if you will, into more of middle- and lower-class women's private lives in the name of social reform.

Finally, there is Karen Offen's definition and typology of European feminisms to engage. Offen theorized the existence of two modes of feminism in the French experience: the relational and the individualist. This bifurcation is particularly helpful in understanding the kind of feminism evident in so many of the humanistic manuals of domestic science, home economics, sex, and hygiene during the First Empire written by male and female authors. Women wanted to oppose male dominance without being forced to deny their femininity and desire to have children. In the age of romance, imperial women seemed to be reconciled to political inequality stemming from gender difference if they could have complementarity and companionate marriage as well as have religion restored for comfort. Women's contributions to civilization could be valorized without denying their civil rights. Marriage was still a strong and important institution in post-Revolutionary France, despite the weakening of the Church's hold on morals and the popularity of atheistic materialism, especially among members of the medical profession. Legalization of divorce did not destroy marriage or the family, as some feared. Understandably, relational feminism treated the companionate masculine and feminine couple conjoined in a state of complementarity as the basic unit of society because it improved chances for increasing population, which contemporaries believed would improve the economy and everyone would benefit. Individualist feminism was scarce in this literature, especially after 1804, and writers who espoused it were the exception rather than the rule—and they were more likely to be writing this way from the refuge of Great Britain or Switzerland. In the long run, relational feminism became the French way of reconciling the characteristic of female sexuality with the possession of political rights. Like Napoleon, relational feminism respected the influence of women on family life.

Notes

Foreword

1. Joan Landes, *Women and the Public Sphere in the Age of the French Revolution* (Ithaca, N.Y.: Cornell University Press, 1988), 13.

2. Quoted in Londa Schiebinger, *The Mind Has No Sex?: Women in the Origins of Modern Science* (Cambridge, MA: Harvard University Press, 1989), 1.

Preface

1. Karen Offen, *European Feminisms, 1700–1950: A Political History* (Stanford University Press, 2000) 19–20; "Defining Feminism: A Comparative Historical Approach," *Signs* 14, no. 1 (Autumn 1988): 126–28. Offen is discussed more fully below: p. xxvii.

2. For an analysis focusing on the intricacies of the professionalization of the French medical community and social theory, see: Matthew Ramsey, *Professionalization and Popular Medicine in France, 1770–1830: The Social World of Medical Practice* (Cambridge: Cambridge University Press, 1988).

3. June K. Burton, *Napoleon and Clio: Historical Writing, Teaching and Thinking during the First Empire* (Durham, N.C.: Carolina Academic Press, 1979), 89–90.

4. Joshua Cole, *The Power of Large Numbers: Population, Politics, and Gender in Nineteenth-Century France* (Ithaca, N.Y.: Cornell University Press, 2000), 215.

5. Geneviève Fraisse, *Muse de la Raison: La Démocracie Exclusive et la Différence des Sexes* (Aix-en-Provence: Éditions Alinéa, 1989), 197.

6. Ibid., 195.

Chapter 1

1. Both quotations are from the lead article in the first issue of the official journal of education: François Guizot, "De l'éducation en général et des difficultés qu'elle présente aujourd'hui," *Annales de l'Éducation* (1811)1: 6 and 9.

2. Anne-Louise-Germaine Necker, Baronne de Staël-Holstein (1766–1817), was the daughter of Louis XVI's Swiss Protestant minister of finance Jacques Necker and his wife, Suzanne, who held her own salon attended by such celebrities as the encyclopedists Diderot, d'Alembert, Grimm, and Buffon. Exposed to this stimulating home environment, Staël became a precocious author of extensive works of fiction and nonfiction that included almost every genre of literature. However, she is known today less for her own writing than for those she influenced, the generation that included Victor Hugo and Jules Michelet, and for ushering in, along with Châteaubriand, the age of Romanticism. She struggled to have women's talents recognized. Despite her ties to the Bour-

bon monarchy and to her lovers, the Count of Narbonne-Lara, the Minister of War, and Benjamin Constant, she survived the Revolution, although Madelyn Gutwirth says that unlike Mme Roland, she had no real strategy to do that. Staël tried unsuccessfully to save the king and queen, but did manage to save a few friends through her husband's diplomatic status—in 1786, she had married Eric de Staël-Holstein, who was the Swedish attaché to Paris. After the Terror, she became involved in politics and helped liberal politicians who came to her salon on the rue du Bac rehearse their speeches for the Assembly. Staël left Paris for Switzerland in 1795, and there in 1796 she wrote her first great work, *De l'Influence des Passions sur le Bonheur de Individus et des Nations.* She returned to Paris the following year and fell in with Benjamin Constant, who was politically important during the Directory. But after the 18 Brumaire, which she and Constant welcomed, she gradually became disillusioned with Bonaparte and he with her "boudoir politics," political activism, feminism, and literary success, until their mutual antipathy transformed into open warfare. In 1802 Bonaparte knew of her association with the alleged conspirator Jean Moreau. Her novel *Delphine* (1803), which contains a plea for women's rights, was a further irritation, expressing pro-British and feminist sentiment as it did. From that point on, she was harassed or chased by the secret police. As a result of her visit to Schiller and Goethe's Weimar in 1803–1804, she wrote *De l'Allemagne,* which interested the French in German Romanticism; however, Napoleon took it for an anti-French work and had the manuscript of the first—1810—edition seized and destroyed, so that the 1813 London edition became the first published edition. Coppet in Switzerland became her home base after her father's death in 1804 and a center of international intellectual resistance to Napoleon. Due to her involvement in opposition politics, her life became a series of exiles (described in her *Dix ans d'Exile* [1821]) and pursuits of her lovers, since she was banished from coming within twelve leagues of Paris. Madelyn Gutwirth, *The Twilight of the Goddesses.* (New Brunswick, N.J.: Rutgers University Press, 1992), 246. Martin Staum, "Staël-Holstein, Anne-Louise-Germaine Necker, Baronne de," in *Historical Dictionary of Napoleonic France,* general ed., Owen Connelly (Westport, Conn.: Greenwood Press, 1985), 454. David Bryant, "Staël, Anne Louise Germaine (Madame de)," in *Makers of the Nineteenth Century 1800–1914,* ed. Justin White (London: Routledge & Kegan Paul, 1982).

3. Preceding paragraph based on Henri Vedette, *L'Art de Vaincre les Allemands,* 36–38.

4. Adrien Dansette, ed., *Napoléon: Pensées Politiques et Sociales,* 123.

5. Ibid.

6. Ibid.

7. Ibid.

8. E. Littré, ed. *Dictionnaire de la Langue française* (1878), s.v. *"machine,"* 3: 368–69.

9. Richard B. Carter, *Descartes' Medical Philosophy: The Organic Solution to the Mind-Body Problem,* 4–8; Martin Staum, *Cabanis—Enlightenment and Medical Philosophy in the French Revolution,* 56–71. He relates Descartes, Boerhave, Gaut, Le Camus, Haller, and La Mettrie, all to Pierre Cabanis, the imperial surgeon.

10. Littré, *Dictionnaire,* s.v. *"machine,"* 3: 369.

11. Julien Offray de La Mettrie (1709–1751), son of a textile merchant of Saint-Malo, was a contemporary of the second generation of philosophers, but spent his life practicing elite medicine and writing materialist philosophical tracts. He attended educational

institutions in Normandy and Paris and studied medicine for five years at the Faculty of Paris, briefly at Rome, and for two more years at Leyden with Herman Boerhave. He practiced medicine at Saint-Malo, then served as personal physician to the Duke of Grammont and as physician to a battalion. But when he published his medical satires and scandalous philosophy, he was exiled to Holland. Finally, after *The Man-Machine* appeared, he found refuge at the court of Frederick the Great until his untimely death from food poisoning. Other than these few basic facts, little is really known about his life because he left no correspondence, only his extensive published writings. Because he spent so many years abroad, he could see the shortcomings of the French medical profession of his day. His works display a profound interest in the physiological foundations of human nature, in contempt for metaphysics, and in social reform, all of which were crucial Enlightenment issues. Controversy has surrounded La Mettrie since his death, although he is now enjoying an improved reputation.

12. Aram Vartanian, ed., *La Mettrie's L'Homme Machine,* 13–16, 31–33. Vartanian's comments about the link between Cabanis and La Mettrie's mechanism is cited by Kathleen Wellman, *La Mettrie,* 284. I am indebted to Susan P. Conner for pointing out the importance of La Mettrie in her oral comments at the 1989 Consortium on Revolutionary Europe, 1750–1850, and for sending me the information in the following two notes as well.

13. Work cited, 5.

14. Ibid., 284–85.

15. Nina Rattner Gelbart, "Madame du Coudray's Manual for Midwives: The Politics of Enlightenment Obstetrics," a paper delivered at the annual meeting of the Western Society for French History, University of California at Los Angeles, November 1988.

16. *Dictionnaire de l'Académie Française,* 6th ed. (1835), s.v. *"machine,"* 2: 140.

17. Work cited. (Paris: Lettrage, 2001), 64.

18. Ibid., 69.

19. Steven Englund incorporates Dorothy Carrington's revisionist research on Carlo Bonaparte: *Napoleon: A Political Life* (New York: Schribner, 2004), 10–11.

20. "The Formation of Napoleon's Personality: An Exploratory Essay," *French Historical Studies* (Spring 1971) 7: 6–26.

21. "La premier ascension sociale des Bonaparte," *Revue de l'Institut Napoléon,* 1990–II, no. 155: 23. See also Carrington's monograph, *Napoleon and His Parents: On the Threshold of History* (London: Viking Press, 1988; New York: Dutton, 1990). Her autobiographical essay printed in the September 1997 issue of *Napoleon* magazine (pp. 36–50) gave us a foretaste of her new thesis regarding the literary and intellectual abilities of Charles Bonaparte, which can be read in her last book: *Portrait de Charles Bonaparte d'Après ses Écrits de sa Jeunesse et ses Mémoires.* (Ajaccio: Alain Piazzola, 2002).

22. Work cited, 5–7, 14–15.

23. Ibid., 12–13.

24. Ibid., 42–43 and 81.

25. Ibid., 134.

26. Ibid.

27. Ibid, 232 and 287. Corvisart (1755–1821) had already held chairs at the École de Médecine and the Collège de France before he began his close association with Napoleon in the year X. The emperor frequently took him on campaigns and entrusted

the health of both Josephine and Marie Louise to him. In 1814 Corvisart accompanied
the latter to Blois and later to Vienna. He was admitted to the Academy of Sciences in
1811 and to the Academy of Medicine in 1820. His specialty was diseases of the heart;
regarding his drug therapy, he was an extreme skeptic who bled and purged his patients
but refrained from administering digitalis. The fall of Napoleon affected his life dramatically because he became partially paralyzed in 1815. He wrote books and contributed to
the *Journal de Médecine*. Corvisart's aphorism was: "Medicine is not the art to cure diseases; it is the art to treat them with the goal of cure, or to give the patient at least a feeling of well-being and to calm him." Quoted by Erwin Ackerknecht, *Therapeutics from
the Primitive to the 20th Century,* 103.

28. Ibid., 302–03. For more on Dubois, see Chapter 4.

29. Masson, *Napoleon: Lover and Husband,* 319.

30. All of the above except time of birth is from *Las Cases, le Mémorialiste de
Napoléon,* 136–37. The time is reported in the official newspaper, *Le Moniteur,* March
20, 1811.

31. Marie Madeleine Sophie Armant (1778–1819), the young dare-devil widow of
Jean-Pierre Blanchard, continued her husband's profession doing solo flights for cele-
brations. She made her sixteenth ascension on June 24, 1810, to celebrate the marriage of
Napoleon and Marie Louise. On March 20, 1811, she was engaged by the government to
start spreading the news rapidly so that the whole country could celebrate the birth of
the King of Rome. Later, as part of the emperor's private celebration at the Château de
St. Cloud, she made a nighttime ascension in a balloon from which a star of fireworks
was suspended. Her penchant for jazzing up her act with evermore delightful fireworks
displays contributed to her death during an ascension on July 6, 1819—contemporary
prints show her lifeless body entangled in the rigging of her collapsed balloon that had
been punctured by a steeple. Her popularity as "official aeronaut" transcended the
imperial regime. Mme Blanchard was buried in Père Lachaise Cemetery in Paris under
a monument that was purchased with public donations. Rachel R. Schneider, "Jean-
Pierre and Marie Madeleine Blanchard: Foremost Pioneers in Ballooning" (Master's
thesis, University of Akron, 1977), 105–10, 113–19, passim.

32. The O'Meara version, including the quotation and the important analysis, is
from a fascinating article by the conservator of the Casemate Museum at Fort Monroe,
Virginia: Chester Bardley, "Les Opinions de Napoléon sur les Complications de l'Accouchement," *Realités* (December, 1969), 21–25.

33. The following description of the birth of the King of Rome is based on the
eulogy of Antoine Dubois published in E.-Fréd. Dubois [d'Amiens], *Eloges lus Dans les
Séances Publiques de l'Académie de Médecine (1845–1863),* 136–42.

34. Our source points out the importance of this—the famous British accoucheur
of the royal family, Smellie, had made an error of giving out the sex of a fetus before it
was known whether it would survive or not, thereby arousing false hopes for a male
heir. Ibid., 140.

35. Geneviève Fraisse, *Reason's Muse: Sexual Difference and the Birth of Democracy*
(Chicago: University of Chicago Press, 1994), 1–3.

36. Ibid., 38.

37. For the original texts by these feminists see: Geneviève Fraisse, *Opinions de
Femmes* (Paris: Côté-femmes, 1989).

Chapter 2

1. Work cited, v-vi.

2. *Les Femmes Célèbres de la Révolution* (1802), v–vi, xi, and xiv.

3. *Le Plutarch des Jeunes Demoiselles . . .* (1806), 1: v.

4. Work cited, 194.

5. Ibid., 201.

6. Ibid., 310.

7. Gabrielle Reval, *Madame Campan, Assistante de Napoléon,* 288 and 291.

8. Editor C. Cattois in *Antoinette Le Groing La Maisonneuve, Essai sur l'Instruction des Femmes* (3rd. ed., 1844), xiv.

9. *Essai sur le Genre d'Instruction Qui Paraît le Plus Analogue à la Destination des Femmes* (Year VII), 15.

10. Ibid., 13–14.

11. *Le Retour des Vendages Contes Variés à la Portée des Enfans de Différens Âges.* 3 vols. (Paris: Genet, 1813).

12. Ibid., 2: 83.

13. *La Mère Gouvernante,* 83.

14. *Le Retour des Vendages,* 1: 1–16.

15. *La Mère Gouvernante,* 18.

16. Ibid., 97.

17. Ibid., 98. Renneville also taught disregard for wealth in another work published at the end of this era, *La Fée Bienfaisante ou la Mère Ingénieuse* (1814), 17.

18. Ibid., 175.

19. Work cited, 30.

20. Ibid., 50–51.

21. Hubert Wandelcourt, *L'École de la Vertu et de la Politesse, Ouvrage Destiné aux Petites Ecoles des Villes et des Campagnes* (1808), x.

22. To Louis-Mathieu Molé, March 1806, in Adrien Dansette, ed., *Napoléon: Pensées Politiques et Sociales,* 239.

23. Cattois in Legroing La Maisonneuve, *Essai sur l'Instruction des Femmes,* xxxiv–xxxv.

24. Quoted by Nada Tomiche, *Napoléon Écrivain,* 228.

25. Legroing La Maissonneuve, *Essai sur le Genre d'Instruction Qui Paraît le Plus Analogue à la Destination des Femmes,* 295.

26. Reval, *Madame Campan, Assistante de Napoléon,* 295.

27. Lagroing La Maisonneuve, *Essai sur le Genre d'Instruction Qui Paraît le Plus Analogue à la Destination des Femmes,* 12.

28. *Plan d'Éducation et d'Instruction Publique* (1801), 86.

29. "Projet de Pensions de Filles aux Frais de l'Etat," *Archives Nationales* 29 AP 75, 474.

30. *Essai sur la Mégalanthropogénésie ou Art de Faire des Enfans d'Esprit, Qui Deviennent des Grands Hommes . . .* (1801), 294. The idea of a woman's athenium did briefly become a reality when, in 1808, several women of letters, including Constance Pipelet de Salm, founded a periodical, *L'Athénée des Dames.* For the duration of two issues, these women were claiming the right to debate issues publicly. Despite making some bold statements in announcing their woman's journal, they still said the content was

intended only for recreation and instruction; from a feminist standpoint, the few articles it carried were subdued. Geneviève Fraisse, *Reason's Muse: Sexual Difference and the
Birth of Democracy* (Chicago: University of Chicago Press, 1994), 56–59.

31. *Discours sur l'Éducation des Femmes . . .* (1810), 14, 21 and 59.

32. *Traité des Maladies Physiques et Morales des Femmes* (4th ed., 1812), 261–64.

33. *Contre le Projet de Loi de S*** M***, Portant Defense d'Apprendre Lire aux Femmes*
(1801), 10. Geneviève Fraisse devoted the first chapter of *Reason's Muse: Sexual Difference
and the Birth of Democracy* to this literary quarrel. (Pp. 1–16.) The third person to join
the quarrel was Mme Clément-Hémery, a typographer and journalist by trade, whose
more extremely feminist views demanded equal rights for women. See also: Françoise
Aubert, "Les femmes doivent-elles apprendre à lire? Une polémique en 1801," *Studi Sull'
Uguaglianza Contributi alla Storia*, 2 vols., ed. Corrado Rosso (Pise: Golliardica, 1973) I:
76–97. Also by Aubert, *Sylvain Maréchal: Passion et Faillité d'un Égalitaire* (Pise: Golliar-
dia, 1975). Aubert interprets the responses of these women to Maréchal's antifeminist
polemic as being rather weak; whereas, Fraisse brings her knowledge of philosophy and
logic into her historical analysis to demonstrate how none of this was only a "joke."
Fraisse shows how this case study, with its three points of view (Maréchal and Clément-
Hémery at opposite extremes and Gacon-Dufour in the middle), contained all the elements that framed the debate over women's reason during the rest of the nineteenth
century and into the twentieth. Consequently, Fraisse used this quarrel as her starting
point, and then she moved backward in time before going forward in her brilliant essay.

34. Jacques Godechot, *Les Institutions de la France sous la Révolution et l'Empire*, 637.

35. *Essai sur le Genre d'Instruction Qui Paraît le Plus Analogue à la Destination des
Femmes*, 39.

36. *Plan d'Éducation et d'Instruction Publique*, 87.

37. The following section on Fanny Burney's visit to Mme Campan's school is
found printed in various editions of Burney's diaries and journal; for example, see:
Brimley Johnson, *Fanny Burney and the Burneys* (London: Stanley Paul & Co., 1926),
70–82.

38. Rebecca Rogers, *Les Demoiselles de la Légion d'Honneur* (Paris: Plon, 1992), 25.

39. Ibid., 19–20, 23.

40. Ibid., 22.

41. Letter to Cambacérès, *7 Oct. 1804. Correspondance de Napoléon Iᵉʳ, Publiée par
Ordre de l'Empereur Napoléon III*, 32 vols. (Paris: Henry Plon, 1858–1870), 10: 12.

42. Rogers, *Les Demoiselles de la Légion d'Honneur*, 22.

43. Ibid., 22–23.

44. 5 March 1806, *Correspondance de Napoléon Iᵉʳ*, 12: 151. The actual decree creating
the schools for daughters of Légion of Honor members was signed by Napoleon at
Schönbrunn on 15 December 1805, after the battle of Austerlitz. These schools had been
suggested to him by Roederer in 1802.

45. Letter to M. de Lacépède, Grand Chancellor of the Légion of Honor, 16 January
1807, ibid., 14: 202.

46. Ibid.

47. "Note on the Establishment of Ecouen," 15 May 1807, ibid., 15: 225–29. See also:
June K. Burton, entry: "Ecouen," in *Historical Dictionary of Napoleonic France*, ed.

Owen Connelly (Westport, CT: Greenwood Press, 1985), 163–65.

48. Rogers, *Les Demoiselles de la Légion d'Honneur,* 28–29.

49. Barbara Scott, "Madame Campan," *History Today* 23, no. 10 (Oct. 1973): 689.

50. Rogers, *Les Demoiselles de la Légion d'Honneur,* 25.

51. Barbara Scott, "Madame Campan," 689.

52. *Correspondance de Napoléon Ier,* 690. His first visit was in 1809, almost two years after it opened.

53. M. S. Ratier, *De la Condition et de l'Influence des Femmes sous l'Empire, et Depuis la Restoration* (1822), 141–46.

54. Ibid., 288.

55. Ibid., 289.

56. Rogers, *Les Demoiselles de la Légion d'Honneur,* 35–36.

57. Ibid., 37.

58. Ibid., 39.

59. Preceding paragraph based on ibid., 43–46.

60. See: Michelle Paucton-Grasset, "La Pédagogie Familiale de l'Epoque Napoléon-ienne," *Revue de l'Institut Napoléon,* 104 (July 1967): 117–29.

61. Geneviève Fraisse points to Pauline de Meulan Guizot (1773–1827) as proof of the fact that since the Revolution had leveled society; regardless of men's former privi-leged status, men and women writers had to compete against each other in the job mar-ket. Meulan needed a job to support not only herself, but her sisters and mother as well. After publishing her first novel in 1799, Meulan was on the staff of *The Publiciste* as a critic. Fraisse says that after she married Guizot, she gave up her literary career, but that is inexact because she edited this education journal until the fall of Napoleon. *Reason's Muse: Sexual Difference and the Birth of Democracy,* 68.

62. Work cited, "Des Modifications que doît apporter dans l'éducation la variété des caractères," 1 (1811): 65.

63. Notably on the co-education of poor children in Germany; ibid., 1: 383–84.

64. "Du Sevrage, des Différens Alimens et de Leur Influence Relative sur les Diverses Dispositions et sur le Développement des Enfans," ibid., 2 (1812): 32. This arti-cle also stated that children should not drink wine, coffee, or chocolate, 26.

65. "Journal Adressé par une Femme à son Mari, sur l'Éducation de ses Deux Filles," ibid., 3 (1812): 15–27.

66. Ibid., 342–45.

67. "Le Chapeau," ibid., 4 (1812): 369–84.

68. "Des Moyens d'Emulation," ibid., 2 (1812): 70.

69. "La Robe de Toile," ibid., 1 (1811): 243–54.

70. "De l'Autorité des Parents," ibid., 4 (1812): 257–63.

71. "Journal Adressé par une Femme à son Mari, sur l'Éducation de ses Deux Filles," ibid., 2 (1811): 273–76.

72. Ibid., 3 (1812): 90.

73. Ibid., 2 (1812): 75–85 and "L'Imprévoyance," 1 (1812): 308–20.

74. "Des Moyens d'Émulation," ibid., 2 (1811): 9–10.

75. "De l'Autorité des Parents," ibid., 4 (1812): 257.

76. "Journal Adressé par une Femme à son Mari, sur l'Éducation de ses Deux Filles," ibid., 2 (1811): 209.

77. Ibid., 3 (1812): 85–90.

78. C. Cattois in Antoinette Legroing La Maisonneuve, *Essai sur l'Instruction des Femmes* (3rd ed.; 1844), xiv.

79. Legroing La Maisonneuve, *Essai sur le Genre d'Instruction Qui Paraît le Plus Analogue à la Destination des Femmes,* 42–45.

80. Abbé Blanchard, *Précepts pour l'Éducation des Deux Sexes à l'Usage des Familles Chrétiennes . . . Redigés et Mis en Ordre, d'Après son Manuscrit, par Bruyset aîné, de l'Académie de Lyon, de la Société d'Agriculture et des Arts de la Même Ville* 2 (1803): 300–01.

81. Ibid., 11 and 236–37.

82. Work cited, (1802).

83. Work cited, (1810).

84. Work cited (1806), 1: iv–v. Some of the women he included in the book were Cleopatra, Frédégonde, Héloise, Joan of Arc, Mme de Maintenon, Catherine de Medici, Queen Christine of Sweden, and the seventeenth-century Mme de Staël.

85. Ibid., viii. For a complete description of boys' history lessons and textbooks see June K. Burton, *Napoleon and Clio* (Carolina Academic Press: Durham, N.C., 1979), 33–48.

86. Girard de Propriac, *Le Plutarque des Jeunes Demoiselles,* ix.

87. *L'Historien des Jeunes Demoiselles,* 261–64.

88. For example, see: Mme Sophie de Renneville, *Élémens de la Lecture à l'Usage des enfans* (1812).

89. Renneville, *Correspondance de Deux Petites Filles* (1811).

90. Stephanie de Warchouf, *Velocifère Grammatical ou la Langue Français et l'Orthographe Apprises en Chantant. . . .* (1806).

91. One work that included all of these was J. B. La Perrière, *L'Arithmétique des Demoiselles Appliquée au Nouveau Système Métrique* (1811).

92. J. A. Millot, *Le Nestor Français, ou Guide Moral et Physiologique* (1807), 1: 221–22.

93. Renneville, *Amusements de l'Adolescence, ou Lectures Agréables et Instructions à l'Usage des Deux Sexes,* 1: 28.

94. Jérôme de Lalande, *Astronomie des Dames* (4th ed.; 1817), 5–6.

95. See: Chapter 4. Geneviève Fraisse, *Reason's Muse,* 131 n. 80.

96. Abbé Henri-Baptiste Grégoire (1750–1831) was already renowned as an egalitarian, liberal politician, educator, and author of textbooks, but most notable to members of the Institut de France for his advocacy of Jewish emancipation and abolition of black slavery. He also proposed the ending of discrimination against lepers. Born near Lunéville, Lorraine, his father was a tailor. Although he received a Jesuit education, Grégoire became an adherent of Gallicanism. First a teacher, then village curé of Embermenil, he emerged as leader of the provincial lower clergy while serving as the deputy of La Meurthe at the Estates General in 1789. He took the Tennis Court Oath and became President of the National Assembly. He also served on the Committee of Public Instruction. As a juring priest, adhering to the Civil Constitution of the Clergy, he supported the Constitutional Church. Later, he became bishop of Blois and also represented the Department of Loir-et-Cher in the Convention. He got into difficulty in 1794 over a reflection on liberty trees, but nevertheless survived the Terror. In 1795 he was elected to the Council of Five Hundred. He organized the Société des Amies des Noirs. His election to the Senate under the Consulate was controversial because he opposed the Con-

cordat along with other policies of Napoleon. He belonged to the Institut and after Napoleon reorganized it, he was reelected to the Class of History and Ancient Literature in January, 1803 (until his elimination again in 1816). As further indication of his lack of subservience to Napoleon, Grégoire voted against the emperor's divorce from Josephine. The first edition of his *Histoire des Sectes* (1810) was seized by the Imperial Police after about only fifty copies had been circulated. As a liberal, independent thinker and ecumenicist, Grégoire's political ideas kept him on the outs with Louis XVIII's government too. He spent his last years writing on numerous humanitarian topics pertaining to all forms of discrimination, whether black, female, Jewish, lepers, or servants' inequality. In 1822 he made a political statement by resigning his appointment as commander of the Légion of Honor and again when he published a second edition of his abdication statement in 1828. An edition of his works published in 1977 contains 143 texts published between 1788 and 1831. Although Grégoire spent his final years out of public office, he remained so popular that when he died at the age of eighty-one (in 1831), an estimated 20,000 workers and students attended his funeral, detached the horses, and drew his coffin to the cemetery of Montparnasse. Most of his work was translated into several European languages. Joseph-Marie Quérard, *La France Littéraire* (Paris: F. Didot père et fils, 1827–39), 3: 462.

97. Abbé Grégoire, *De la Domesticité chez les Peuples Anciens et Modernes* (Paris: A. Egron, 1814), 129 and 171.

98. Ligne had become famous for his military experience and for being an inspired, prolific author who mastered various philosophical literary genres, including military history, all of which he wrote in the French language. Born in Brussels into a premier family of the Low Countries, after serving brilliantly in the Seven Years War he rose to a trusted position as military adviser to the enlightened emperor of the Holy Roman Empire, Joseph II. In this capacity, he was sent on two missions to Russia, where he fought for Catherine the Great in the Russo-Turkish War of 1787–92.

As a man of letters, Ligne corresponded with Rousseau and Voltaire. His active salon life in Belgium was interrupted by his exile following the rebellion of 1789. He produced a vast series of *Mélanges Militaires, Littérares et Sentimentaires (1795–1811)*, which comprised 34 volumes. The final volume of the preceding contains a textbook, *Petit Plutarque de Toutes des Nations*. Ligne also published *Oeuvres* in 1807, in thirty volumes. Mme de Staël published *Pensées du Prince de Ligne*, which went through five editions in 1809 and 1810. For the various editions and contents of his works see Quérard, *La France Littéraire*, 5: 305–07.

99. Grégoire says to see *Oeuvres et Pensées de Prince de Ligne* (2 vols.) (Geneva: J. J. Paschoud, 1809), 2: 48–49. Grégoire, *De la Domesticité chez les Peuples*, 192.

100. Ibid., 193.

101. Ibid., 194–95.

102. Ibid., 197–201.

103. Ibid., 201–03.

104. Ibid., 204. Grégoire also proposed creating retirement homes for servants. He cited a German example for female domestics that was underwritten in 1811 by 200 to 300 families. Grégoire cited his source of information: *Le Moniteur*, 13 March 1811. Ibid., 215–16.

105. *Essai sur la Médecine du Coeur; Auquel on a Joint les Principaux Discours Pronon-*

cés à l'Ouverture des Cours d'Anatomie, d'Opérations et de Chirurgie-Clinique de l'Hôtel-Dieu de Lyon, Savoir: 1° sur l'Influence de la Révolution sur la Santé Publique; 2° sur la Manière d'Exercer la Bienfaisance dans les Hôpitaux; 3° sur la Douleur; 4° sur les Maladies Observées dans l'Hôtel-Dieu de Lyon Pendant Neuf Années; 5° l'Éloge de Desaut. (Lyons: Garnier, 1806), 7.

A second edition of Petit's *Essai* appeared in 1823, 1826, and 1828.

106. Preceding paragraph based on Grégoire, *Des Gardes-Malades, et la Nécessité d'Establir pour Elles des Cours d'Instruction* (Paris: Baudoin fils, 1819), 5–8.

107. Ibid., 9. See: Chapter 7 for Fodéré's biography and a fuller discussion of his ideas on imperial women's human rights issues.

Chapter 3

1. Quoted by Mme Gacon-Dufour in her moderately feminist tract, *Contre le Projet de Loi de S*** M***, Portant Défense d'Apprendre à Lire aux Femmes, par une Femme Qui ne se Pique d'Être Femme de Lettres* (1801), 33. She was responding seriously to Sylvain Maréchal's polemical brochure. Among other strong remarks, she opined indignantly that he ought to be committed to an asylum for writing it. See: Geneviève Fraisse, *Reason's Muse* (Chicago: University of Chicago Press, 1994), 26–32. Mme Albertine Clément-Hémery wrote a radical feminist response: ibid., 32–36.

2. P. Roussel, *Système Physique et Moral de la Femme, ou Tableau Philosophique de la Constitution, de l'État Organique du Tempérament, des Moeurs de des Fonctions Propres au Sexe*, ed. Nouvelle (1803), 59–60, 63.

Pierre Roussel (1742–1802), a geometrician, physician, journalist, and political scientist, was born in Aix in the Arriège. He followed the lessons of Doctors Barthez, Lamure, and Venel at Toulouse before going to Paris, where he became closely associated with Bordeu. As his book shows, Roussel was fascinated by women and the female body. He studied the writings of Stahl, which he considered publishing, but apparently never did. He was a skillful writer and enjoyed editing as well. He refuted the work of Bernardine de Sainte-Pierre on the melting of the polar ice caps. Although he was thought to be a good medical practitioner, he was so supersensitive to human suffering that he had to give it up, occupying himself instead with the study of politics and thereby becoming active in the Revolutionary primary assemblies. His *Système Physique et Morale de Femme* was still esteemed as a stylistic model for medical literature in the 1820s. But since Roussel only lived to age sixty, the editions of his work (and there were many) that circulated during the First Empire were all posthumous. The fifth edition (1808) was edited by Dr. Alibert of the Paris Faculty; another edition appeared in 1813; and a seventh edition in 1820. So while Roussel's *Système* had literary merit and a long period of readership, it really disseminated cosmopolitan eighteenth-century ideas among Imperial and Restoration medical enthusiasts. *Séance Publique de la Faculté de Médecine de Paris*, 4 (1807–10): 20; *Dictionnaire des Sciences Médicales Biographie Médicale*, s.v. "Roussel (Pierre)" (Paris: C.-L.-F. Panckouche, 1825), 7: 61–62.

We can prove that Roussel was still taken seriously in the 1820s because, for example, the distinguished humanitarian thinker Abbé Grégoire cited Roussel's statement to the effect that feebleness and sensibility are two constants in female nature. However, Grégoire said that Roussel should have gone further and added these qualifiers to complete his statement: "la religion soutient l'une et dirige l'autre." Grégoire, *De l'Influence du Christianisme sur la Condition des Femmes* (Paris: Baudouin frères, 1821), 38.

3. Ibid., 12.

4. Ibid., 19–48.

5. Ibid., 19.

6. Ibid., 20.

7. Ibid., 31.

8. Ibid., 36–37.

9. Costard, *L'État Conjugal Considéré Sous Tous ses Rapports avec le Bonheur de l'Homme et de la Femme; Ouvrage Utile à Tout le Monde, et Principalement Aux Jeunes Gens des Deux Sexes . . . .* (1809), x.

10. *Histoire naturelle de la femme* (1803), 3: 267.

11. Jacques-André Millot, *Médecine Perfective, ou Code des Bonnes Mères* (Paris, 1809), 1: 144.

12. Ibid., 274.

13. *Le Nestor Français, ou Guide Moral et Physiologique* (1807), 3: 290.

14. Costard, *L'Etat Conjugal*, 194–96. He reminded readers of the adage: "Telle mère, telle fille."

15. Ibid., 199–200.

16. Ibid., 205.

17. *Journal de Médecine* (1812), 25: 411. The medical establishment did not want women to know too much about how their own bodies functioned. Doctors tried to maintain control of these secrets, thereby asserting their power over women.

18. Work cited, 1: 128–29.

19. Ibid., 2: 13.

20. Anonymous. However, *L'Ami des Femmes* is now attributed to P. J. Marie de Saint Urban.

21. *Système Physique et Moral de la Femme*, 147–48.

22. *L'Ami des Jeunes Femmes*, 24.

23. Ibid., 26.

24. Ibid., 27–28.

25. Ibid., 31, n.1.

26. Ibid., 36.

27. Ibid., 39.

28. Ibid., 60–63.

29. Ibid., 58–59.

30. Ibid., 67.

31. Ibid., 42–44.

32. Ibid., 71–72.

33. Jacques Moreau, *Histoire Naturelle de la Femme*, 3: 305; and Millot, *Médecine Perfective*, 1: 57.

34. *L'Ami des Jeunes Femmes*, 68–69.

35. Dubuisson, *Tableau de l'Amour Conjugal* (1812), 2: 38–39. This was, however, published as an anonymous work in 1812 due to its controversial, i.e., arguably pornographic content (from the point of view of contemporaries).

36. For example, Moreau, *Histoire Naturelle de la Femme,* 178.

37. Review of *Essai sur la Mégalanthropogénésis . . . ; par le cit. Robert le Jeune* in *Journal Général de la Littérature de France* (1801), 294.

38. Millot, *L'Art de Procréer les Sexes à Volonté,* (3rd ed., 1802), 424.

39. Ibid., 356.

40. Work cited, 1: 1.

41. Millot, *Médecine Perfective* (1809), 1: 28.

42. Ibid., 1: 30.

43. Dubuisson, *Tableau de l'Amour Conjugal,* 2: 74.

44. Ibid., 31–32.

45. Dubuisson, *Tableau de l'Amour Conjugal,* 2: 77–80.

46. Ibid., 1: 82.

47. Ibid., 1: 86.

48. Ibid., 1: 94–95.

49. Ibid., 1: 96, 39–40.

50. *Gazette de Santé* (1 August 1810), no. XXII: 173. According to Martin Staum, "The Hippocratic Corpus became the most pervasive medical influence." *Cabanis: Enlightenment and Medical Philosophy in the French Revolution,* 50–54. Hippocrates replaced Galen at this time.

51. Millot, *L'Art de Procréer les Sexes à Volonté* (3rd ed., 1802), 422.

52. Ibid., 343.

53. *Tableau de l'Amour Conjugal,* 2: 94–95.

54. *L'Art de Procréer les Sexes à Volonté* (3rd. ed., 1802), xv-xvi.

55. Ibid., 420.

56. Ibid.

57. Ibid., 45–46.

58. *Journal Général de la Littérature de France* (1802), 135.

59. *Tableau de l'Amour Conjugal,* 2: 93–98.

60. Ibid., 95.

61. Review of *Essai sur la Mégalanthropogénésie* in *Journal Général de la Littérature de France* (1801), 294.

62. By the early seventeenth century Hippocrates had again overtaken Galen as a source of authority in medical opinion. For the controversy about this in the context of the origin of the anatomy of difference, which provides extensive bibliography, see Michael Stolberg, "A Woman Down to Her Bones," *Isis* 94 (2003): 274–99. Stolberg claims that Thomas Laqueur and Londa Schiebinger are wrong when they say the change occurred in the mid-eighteenth century; and Stolberg tries to argue that it had already occurred in the late sixteenth century and not for the reasons they gave, but more for professional reasons such as increasing their income. He also illustrates his article with drawings of skeletons from the earlier period to show that anatomists already knew more about the female skeleton at an earlier date and how they interpreted it.

63. *Des Erreurs Populaires Relatives à la Médecine* (2nd ed., 1812), 10, 14.

64. Millot, *Médecine Perfective,* 1: 114.

65. Roussel, *Système Physique et Moral de la Femme,* Nouvelle ed., 253–54.

66. Ibid., 257.

67. Ibid., 252–53.

68. *Médecine Perfective*, 1: 142–43.

69. Ibid., 1: 149.

70. Ibid., 1: 281.

71. *Journal Général de la Littérature de France* (1809), 36–38.

72. Work cited, 77.

73. Ibid., 85–67.

74. William Buchan, *La Conservateur de la Santé des Mères et des Enfans* (1804), 85. Translated by Thomas Duverne de Praile.

75. *Manuel de la Ménagère, à la Ville et à la Campagne, et de la Femme de Basse-Cour, Ouvrage dans Lequel on Trouve des Remèdes Éprouvés pour la Guérison des Bestiaux* (1805), 2: 462.

76. *Mémoire sur l'Éducation Physique des Enfans Couronné en 1784 par la Société Royale de Médecine de Paris* (1810), 58.

77. Millot, *Médecine Perfective*, 1: 242.

78. Ibid., 1: 247.

79. Dubuisson, *Tableau de l'Amour Conjugal*, 2: 39–40.

80. Millot, *Médecine Perfective*, 2: 243.

81. Ibid., 2: 258.

82. Ibid., 2: 261–77 passim.

83. Bret, *Mémoire sur l'Éducation Physique*, 57.

84. *Médecine Perfective*, n.p.

85. *L'Ami des Jeunes Femmes*, 102–03.

86. Mme Gacon-Dufour, *Manuel de la Ménagère*, 2: 469–70, 478. She was perfectly clear about what she thought an infant's constitution could tolerate: "Je conseillerai toujours de donner aux enfans, pour toute nourriture, jusqu'à l'âge de trois ans, du lait . . . ." (By the age of three, they had teeth to bite the nurse!)

87. *L'Ami des Jeunes Femmes*, 90.

88. Ibid., 92.

89. Ibid., 95.

90. Bret, *Mémoire sur l'Éducation Physique*, 116–17.

91. *L'Ami des Jeunes Femmes*, 101.

92. In contrast, mothers in the southern United States avoided weaning during hot weather. For this and other comparisons and contrasts see the excellent article, Sally McMillan, "Mothers' Sacred Duty: Breast-Feeding Patterns among Middle- and Upper-Class Women in the Antebellum South," *The Journal of Southern History* (August 1985) 51 (no. 3): 334–56.

93. *L'Ami des Jeunes Femmes*, 132–33.

94. Ibid., 137–39.

95. Duverne de Praile, *Le Conservateur de la Santé des Mères et des Enfans*, 196.

96. Ibid., ix.

97. *Manuel de la Ménagère*, 2: 478.

98. Millot, *Médecine Perfective*, 1: 309, 342.

99. Ibid., 2: 154.

100. Ibid., 2: 159.

101. Ibid., 2: 164.

102. *L'Ami des Jeunes Femmes*, 114.

103. Duverne de Praile, *Le Conservateur de la Santé des Mères et des Enfans*, 115.

104. *L'Ami des Jeunes Femmes*, 116.

105. *Médecine Perfective*, 1: 135.

106. *Le Conservateur de la Santé des Mères et des Enfans*, 116.

107. Mme Gacon-Dufour, *Manuel de la Ménagère*, 2: 488.

108. Duverne de Praile, *Le Conservateur de la Santé des Mères et des Enfans*, 117.

109. Mme Gacon-Dufour, *Manuel de la Ménagère*, 2: 461.

110. Bret, *Mémoire sur l'Éducation Physique*, 81.

111. *L'Ami des Jeunes Femmes*, 118.

112. Duverne de Praile, *Le Conservateur de la Santé des Mères et des Enfans*, 240.

113. Mme Gacon-Dufour, *Manuel de la Ménagère*, 2: 491–92.

114. *Médecine Perfective*, 1: 138–39.

115. Mme Gacon-Dufour, *Manuel de la Ménagère*, 2: 468.

116. *L'Ami des Jeunes Femmes*, 121.

117. Bret, *Mémoire sur l'Éducation Physique*, 23.

118. *L'Ami des Jeunes Femmes*, 130–31.

119. Ibid., 126.

120. Costard, *L'Etat Conjugal Considéré Sous Tous ses Rapports avec le Bonheur de l'Homme et de la Femme*, 181–84.

121. Duverne de Praile, *Le Conservateur de la Santé des Mères et des Enfans*, 6.

122. Costard, *L'Etat Conjugal Considéré Sous Tous ses Rapports avec le Bonheur de l'Homme et de la Femme*, 185–86.

123. Duverne de Praile, *Le Conservateur de la Santé des Mères et des Enfans*, xvi.

124. Ibid., 7. This is interesting because Mme Adrienne Lafayette used lead astringents. See: Chapter 10.

125. *Médecine Portative, ou Guide de Santé à l'Usage de Toute le Monde*, 108–11.

126. Work cited., 5.

127. Ibid., 3.

128. Ibid., 2.

129. Ibid., 19–21.

130. Ibid., 22–23.

131. Ibid., 43–45.

132. Ibid., 57–58.

133. Ibid., 58–61.

134. Ibid., 67–68.

135. Ibid., 78–82 passim.

136. Ibid., 123–25.

137. Ibid., 128.

138. Ibid., 118–20.

139. Work cited, 338–43.

140. Mme Gacon-Dufour, *Recueil Pratique d'Économie Rurale et Domestique* (1804), 2.

141. Dames Ve Chaveau and Dufour, *Brevet d'Invention Pâtes de Pommes-de-terre, Riz, Sagou, Semoule;* and Mme Chaveau de la Miltière, *Rapport Fait à l'Athenénée des Arts sur les Farines de Pommes-de-terres, 1 July 1810.*

142. Mme Gacon-Dufour, *De la Necessité de l'Instruction pour les Femmes*, vii.

143. Ibid., *Contre le Projet de loi de S*** M***, Pourtant Defense d'Apprendre à Lire aux Femmes*, 48.

144. *Recueil Pratique d'Économie Rurale et Domestique* (1804), 16–17.

145. *Manuel de la Ménagère*, 1: 234–36.

146. Ibid., 1: 109.

147. *Recueil Pratique d'Économie Rurale et Domestique*, 31–33.

148. Ibid., 35.

149. *Manuel de la Ménagère*, 1: 75.

150. Ibid., 1: 90, 93–95.

151. Ibid., 2: 78–79.

152. Ibid., 2: 451–58 passim.

153. Ibid., 2: 400–02.

154. *Recueil Pratique d'Économie Rurale et Domestique*, 91–93.

155. Ibid., 94–98.

156. Ibid., 98–99.

157. *Manuel de la Ménagère*, 2: 400–01.

158. Ibid., 1: 156–57.

159. Ibid., 1: 41; 2: 448.

160. Ibid., 449.

161. Ibid., 2: 440–41.

162. Ibid., 2: 443–44.

163. Ibid., 2: 446–47.

164. Ibid., 2: 399, 442–44.

Chapter 4

1. The preceding sentence is based on Jacques-Frédéric Schweighhaeuser, *Tablettes Chronologiques de l'Histoire de la Médecine Puerpérale* (Strasbourg, 1806), 1, 67, 80, 84, 86, 89, 92, 94, and 97–98.

2. These are still well-preserved and among the most beautiful collections of this kind in the world. Illustrated lecture presented by Dr. Manfried Skopec, director of the Institute for the History of Medicine of the University of Vienna, "Treasures of the *Josephinum*, Vienna's Premier Medical Museum." March 8, 2001, Dittrick Medical History Center, Case Western Reserve University, Cleveland, Ohio.

3. Work cited, (Berkeley: University of California Press). The following treatment of Mme du Coudray and her family is based on my impression of Gelbart's book and facts drawn from it.

4. Kate Campbell Hurd-Mead, M.D., *A History of Women in Medicine from the Earliest Times to the Beginning of the Nineteenth Century* (Haddam, Conn.: The Haddam Press, 1938), 492. Londa Schiebinger, *The Mind Has No Sex?: Women in the Origins of Modern Science* (Cambridge, Mass.: Harvard University Press, 1989), 27–29.

5. Their son became a medical doctor and married Baron Larrey's sister. Larrey created the flying ambulances, which he used to speed up battlefield amputations. But Larrey also performed civil surgeries on women in France and Egypt during the campaign in 1799.

6. *Going Public: Women and Publishing in Early Modern France* (Ithaca, NY: Cornell University Press, 1995), 4.

7. Notably 1662–64 and 1746. Henrietta Carrier, *Origines de la Maternité–Les Maîtresses Sages-Femmes et l'Office des Accouchées de l'Ancien Hôtel-Dieu (1378–1796).* (Paris, 1888), 3–5.

8. Alphonse Leroy, *De la conservation des Femmes, Ouvrage Utile à la Population* (Paris, 1811), 53. Unfortunately, Leroy never said exactly how many of the *cahiers* addressed this problem. The Archives Nationals was still in the process of collecting all the lost *cahiers* when Beatrice Hyslop produced *A Guide to the General Cahiers of 1789* in 1937 (New York: Octagon, reprinted 1968), which was an analysis of nationalism and democracy in about 25,000 *cahiers.* When Gilbert Shapiro and John Markoff wrote *Revolutionary Demands: a Content Analysis of the Cahiers de Doléances of 1789* (Stanford, Calif.: Stanford University Press, 1998), the number of *cahiers* they were able to analyze regarding conditions of social life, political behavior in the revolutionary era, and publicly expressed grievances was 40,000. With the use of computer programs today, it is theoretically possible to ask how many times the words "midwifery" and "midwifery, population and infant mortality" appear.

9. AN F^{15} 1863 plaquet A, nonpaginated document dated 14 Thermidor, year X.

10. AN F^{17} 2468 (Seine). The goal seems to have been eighty pupils that year.

11. Ibid.

12. During the Napoleonic era the number of candidates at La Maternité was: 1801, 121; 1810, 129; 1811, 130; 1812, 143; 1813, 161; 1814, 130. The end of the First Empire marked a decline in enrollment figures. During the Restoration the average number was 60–80. Paul Delaunay, *La Maternité de Paris* (Paris, 1901), 287.

13. Carrier, *Origines de la Maternité,* 41.

14. That the curriculum at La Maternité was to be used as the model for local schools is implicit in the correspondence of the Minister of the Interior to the various prefects. For example, see: AN F^{17} 2472 (Taro) and F^{17} 2473 (Zuiderzée).

15. *La Maternité: École d'Accouchement en 1862* (Paris, 1862), 2–5.

16. However, many failed to register with both the sous-prefecture and the tribunal as required while others neglected to register with either despite the threat of fines of 100 and 200 francs and imprisonment for up to six months for the recalcitrant. AN BB^{1} 207–09 and F^{17} 247 (Sesia).

17. At Besançon the prefect paid 7 francs for the head midwife's chamber pot but only allowed 74 centimes for those serving indigent women in labor. AN F^{17} 2459 (Doubs).

18. See AN F^{17} 2456–73 (Ain to Zuiderzée) passim.

19. AN F^{17} 2457 (Arno), BB^{1} 209, and F^{17} 2462 (Léman).

20. AN F^{17} 2456 (Allier), 2457 (Ardennes), 2459 (Drôme and Ems occidental), 2460 (Frise, Finistère, and Gand), and 2462 (Landes).

21. AN F^{17} 2459 (Ems oriental).

22. The prefect of Gers paid women 75 centimes or 15 sols per day. AN F17 2461 (Gers).

23. The prefect was complaining in Floréal, year X. AN F^{17} 2458 (Corrèze).

24. AN F^{17} 2456 (Ain), 2458 (Charente inférieur), 2462 (Indre), and 2456 (Pyrenées basses); F^{15} 2470 (Orne).

25. AN F^{15} 2740 (Ardèche); F^{17} 2456 (Ain), 2457 (Ariège and Bouches de la Meusel), 2458 (Charente inferière and Cher), 2460 (Finistère and Garonne), 2465 (Pô), and 2467 (Sarre).

26. AN F^{17} 2458 (Corse).

27. AN F^{17} 2460 (Forêts), 2466 (Haut-Rhin and Sambre et Meuse), and 2467 (Sarre).

28. AN F^{17} 2457 (Aveyron), 2460 (Finistère), 2461 (Gers and Gironde), 2465 (Pyrénées basses), and 2467 (Saône).

29. Sicard sent a *mémoire* on this subject to the Minister of the Interior in the year X, AN F^{17} 2468.

30. For example, see: AN F^{17} 2466 (Bas-Rhin).

31. Ibid.

32. In 1812, the prefect of Pô requested that Baudelocque's work be translated into Italian. AN F^{17} 2465 (Pô).

33. Jean Imbert, *Le Droit Hospitalier de la Révolution et l'Empire* (Paris, 1954), 167, n.51.

34. Napoléon to Lacépède, 16 January 1807, *Correspondance de Napoléon Ier Publiée par Ordre de l'Empereur Napoléon III* (Paris, 1858–69), 14: 251. On Mme Campan see: Barbara Scott, "Madame Campan," *History Today,* 23, no. 10 (October 1973): 689.

35. Imbert, *Le Droit Hospitalier,* p. 167, n.51.

36. *La Maternité: École d'Accouchement en 1862,* 5.

37. Work cited, (Paris: Imprimerie des hospices civiles), v–vi.

38. *Rapport Fait au Conseil Général des Hospices . . . Depuis Ier Janvier 1804 Jusqu'a Ier Janvier 1814* (Paris, 1816). Pastoret (1756–1840) emigrated during the Revolution. He returned to France in 1800. Subsequent to becoming a member of the hospital council in 1801, he became a professor of law at the Collège de France (1804) and professor of philosophy at the Sorbonne (1809). During the Restoration he continued his career as a politician and ultimately became Chancellor of France in 1829.

39. Hucherard, Sausseret, and Girault, *Mémoire Historique,* v–vi.

40. Pastoret, *Rapport,* 95–96.

41. Hucherard, Sausseret, and Girault, *Mémoire Historique,* 46–47.

42. Ibid., 7.

43. Preceding paragraph based on a letter from Mme Marie-Anne Victoire Gillain Boivin, a pupil at La Maternité, to the editor of the *Gazette de Santé,* no. 33 (November 21, 1810), 260–61. In her letter, which she expected to be published, she also stressed the linguistic ability of the midwives from the various parts of the empire and the fact that one woman knew Greek and Latin and another translated obstetrical books from English at the surgeon's request.

44. Ibid., 261.

45. The initial regulation on books was dated 8 November 1810; see: article 3. AN F^{17} 2456 (Ain). For an example of a prefect's purchase of the works by Baudelocque and the required book added in 1812, see: AN F^{17} 2457 (Aude). The three textbooks cited below are: Jean-Louis Baudelocque, *L'Art des Accouchemens* (4th ed.; Paris, 1807) and *Principes sur l'Art des Accouchemens, par Demandes et Réponses, en Faveur des Élèves Sages-femmes* (4th ed.; Paris, 1812); Marie-Anne Victoire Gillain Boivin, *Mémorial de l'Art des Accouchemens . . . Dedié a Mme La Chapelle* (Paris, 1812). The instrument kits priced at 24 francs and 90 centimes consisted of one of each of the following items: (1) a female probe—*sounde de femme,* (2) scissors, (3) laryngeal tube, (4) a syringe, and (5) a nozzle for injection—*canule à injection.*

46. Book review in *Journal de Médecine, Chirurgie, Pharmacie, etc.,* 27 (May 1813): 193–97.

47. The dedication page (nonpaginated) said this manual summarized what she learned from Mme Lachapelle and Professors Baudelocque, Dubois, and Chaussier. A long review of the *Mémorial* was carried in the *Gazette de Santé,* no. 22 (1 August 1813): 174–76.

48. Note to Lacépède, Grand Chancellor of the Légion of Honor, May 1807, in *Napoleon Pensées Politiques et Sociales,* ed. Adrien Dansette (Paris, 1969), 240.

49. Examples of references to manikins are found in AN F^{17} 2457 (Aude), 2458 (Charente inférieur and Corse), 2460 (Finistère), 2464 (Vannes), 2471 (Seine inférieur), and 2472 (Taro).

50. Carla Hesse cited two instances where Revolutionary women writers also were called "Amazons" because they voiced political ideas. *The* Other *Enlightenment: How French Women Became Modern* (Princeton: Princeton University Press, 2001), 99 and 139.

51. Volume 33 (21 November 1810): 259–62.

52. Huard, *Sciences, Médecine, Pharmacie,* 221.

53. Ibid., 285.

54. Walter Radcliffe, *Milestones in Midwifery* (Bristol: John Wright & Sons, 1967), 73.

55. Ibid., 64.

56. Ibid., 223. E.-Fréd. Dubois [d'Amiens], *Éloges lus dans les Séances Publiques de l'Académie de Médecine (1845–1863) Tableau du Mouvement de la Science et des Progrès de l'Art (1864),* 1: 111–57 passim.

57. Ibid., 220; *Dictionnaire des Sciences Médicales Biographie médical,* vol. 3 (1821): 232–36.

58. A. Delacoux, *Biographie des Sages-Femmes Célèbres, etc.* (Paris, 1834), 367.

59. Ibid., 372–74.

60. Correspondence of the author with Archivamfrau Hunerlach, 29 June 2001, *Ruprecht-Karls-Universität Heidelberg, Universitätsarchiv.* Frau Hunerlach graciously searched in vain for the name of Marie-Louise Dugès Lachapelle in Signatur: A-557/1–6. On the history of the Mannheim-Heidelberg midwifery school/institute see: Eberhard Stübler, *Geschichte der medizinischen Fakultät der Universität Heidelberg 1386–1925,* Heidelberg: Carl Winters Universitätsbuchhandlung, 1926, 203–07.

61. "Naegele," *Allgemeine Deutsche Biographie,* 218–19.

62. Walter Radcliffe, *Milestones in Midwifery,* 74. Correspondance of the author with Dr. Rainer Brüning, 31 July 2001, *Generallandesarchiv Karlsruhe,* Bestand 205 Universität Heidelberg, Nr. 404. (He also checked Bestand 213 and Bestand 205 but like Frau Hunerlach found no mention of Mme Lachapelle.)

63. "Naegele," *Allgemeine Deutsche Biographie,* 218–19.

64. *Milestones in Midwifery,* 74.

65. "Marie-Louise Dugès, dame Lachapelle," *Nouvelle Biographie Générale* (Paris, 1958), 27: 510–11. Her records were still cited as being useful in twentieth-century American medical histories. For example, see: Albert H. Buck, *The Dawn of Modern Medicine* (New Haven, 1920), 257.

66. Hurd-Mead, *A History of Women in Medicine,* 500.

67. *Milestones in Midwifery,* 75–76.

68. Hurd-Mead, *A History of Women in Medicine,* 500.

69. "Marie-Anne Victoire Gillain, femme Boivin," Michaud, *Biographie Universelle, Ancienne et Moderne* (Paris, 1843), 4: 612–13.

70. Radcliffe, *Milestones in Midwifery,* 75–76.

71. René-Georges Gastellier, *Des Maladies Aiguës des Femmes en Couche* (Paris, 1812), 113–18.

72. Ibid., 231.

73. George Wilhelm Stein, *L'Art d'Accoucher* (Paris, 1804), lvii–lx.

74. See: Louis-B. Guyton de Morveau, *Traité des Moyens de Désinfecter l'Air, de Prévenir la Contagion, en d'En Arrêter les Progrès* (3rd ed.; Paris, 1805).

75. Paul Delaunay, *La Maternité de Paris* (Paris, 1909), 145.

76. Ibid., 142.

77. "La Maternité: Pièces Administratives," *Bibliothèque Historique de la Ville de Paris*, 1803–21. Manuscrit Nouvelles acq. 479, gol. 310.

78. Chaussier's program was ordered by the medical jury of the Department of the Nièvre. *Annales de Chimie*, 2: 18.

79. Hucherard, Sausseret, and Girault, *Mémoire Historique*, 60.

80. See the catalogue of the exposition at La Salpêtrière, October 1960, prepared by Bernard Mahieu, Marcel Candille, and Jacqueline Sonolet, *Saint Vincent de Paul et l'Hôpital*, 48. The *tours* will be discussed more fully in Chapter 9.

81. Claude-François Etienne Dupin, *Histoire de l'Administration des Secours publics* (Paris, 1821), 341.

82. Theodore Roseburg, *Microbes and Morals: The Strange Story of Venereal Disease* (New York, 1971), 78–79.

83. The following paragraph is based on an unpublished seminar paper by Nancy L. Shehata, "The Management and Knowledge of Syphilis in Paris 1789–1839," University of Akron History Department, Spring 1989. Shehata did her research in the special Syphilology Collection at the Allen Memorial Medical History Library, Case Western Reserve University, Cleveland, Ohio.

84. Jacques-André Millot, *Médicine Perfective, ou Code des Bonnes Mères* (Paris, 1809), 2: 159. Note: a French *pinte* is nearly an English quart.

85. P. A. O. Mahon, *Histoire de la Médecine Clinique, Depuis son Origine Jusqu'à nos Jours . . .* (Paris, 1804), 377–78.

86. *Essai Historique et Moral sur la Pauvreté des Nations, le Population, la Mendicité, les Hôpitaux et les Enfans Trouvés* (Paris: chez Madame Huzard, 1825), 575–76.

87. John Cross, *Sketches of the Medical Schools of Paris* (London, 1815), 184.

88. Ibid., 188–89.

89. Edwin Lee, *Observations on the Principal Medical Institutions and Practices of France, Italy and Germany* (Philadelphia, 1837), 19.

90. "Maternal Indifference," in *French Feminist Thought: A Reader*, ed. Toril Moi (New York and Oxford: Basil Blackwell, 1987), 152–61.

Chapter 5

1. The number of medical journals published increased unevenly from eight in the years 1799 and 1800 to thirteen in 1803 and 1806; to seventeen in 1809, 1811, and 1813; and nineteen in 1815. For a complete list of titles see: Ernest Wickersheimer, *Index Chronologique des Périodiques Médicaux de la France (1679–1856) [extrait du Bibliographie Moderne, 1908, nos. 1–3]* (Paris: A. Moline, 1910).

2. Adrien Dansette, ed., *Napoléon: Pensées Politiques et Sociales* (Paris: Flammarion, 1969), 123.

3. Quoted by Nada Tomiche, *Napoléon Écrivain* (Paris: Librairie Armand Collin, 1952), 228.

4. Jean Imbert, *Le Droit Hospitalier de la Révolution et de L'Empire* (Paris: Recueil Sirey, 1954), 167, n. 51.

5. Alphonse Leroy, *De la Conservation des Femmes, Ouvrage Utile à la Population* (Paris: Méquignon l'aîné, 1811), 7.

6. Ibid., 8 and 21–22.

7. Guillou, Letter of 20 April 1810 to editor of the *Gazette de Santé*, no. 15 (21 May 1810): 115 and 117.

8. Charles M. Gardien, *Traité d'Accouchemens, de Maladies des Femmes, de l'Éducation Médicinale des Enfans, et des Maladies Propres à Cette Âge* (Paris: Crouchard, 1807), 1: 2.

9. Preceding paragraph based on J. Capuron, *Traité des Maladies des Femmes* (Paris: Croullebois, 1812), 5–9, 11, 13, and 15. It should be pointed out that the anatomist Marie-François-Xavier Bichat (1771–1802) had only decentralized anatomy down to the level of tissues, not down to cells. So surgeons really focused on tissues as the elementary units of brain matter in this case. See: Charles Coulston Gillespie, ed., *Dictionary of Scientific Biography*, s.v. "Bichat" (New York: Charles Schribner's Sons, 1970), 2: 122–23.

10. Work cited, 4th ed. (Paris: chez l'auteur, 1812), 67.

11. Ibid., 69.

12. Ibid., 83.

13. Ibid., 96.

14. Ibid., 106.

15. Preceding paragraph based on ibid., 261–64.

16. Capuron, *Traité des Maladies des Femmes*, 4. Joseph Capuron (1767–1850), who was born in Gers department and spent his early life in the Toulouse region, intended to become a priest before the Revolution of 1789 occurred. Instead, he became a mathematics and philosophy professor in a *collège* before he went to Bordeaux and then Paris, in 1797, to study medicine. He continued to support himself by teaching and followed courses at the Ecole de Santé for five years, which enabled him to teach anatomy. He decided to specialize in accouchement because of its affinity with math and is remembered as a teacher in this field rather than as a more elite medical practitioner. For years he followed the lessons of Dupuytren at the Hôtel Dieu and later Bouillard at La Charité. He was received as a doctor in 1802, according to some sources, while others say he never graduated from anywhere until 1823, when he was agregated. Capuron spent the imperial era amidst his students, dressed in the robe of an agrégé, sometimes teaching, other times sitting in the audience with the mostly younger aspiring students of medicine.

Capuron was possibly the least ostentatious professor among the faculty of his day. He purposely lived a deprived, monkish life, living inconspicuously in modest, dusty, sparsely furnished lodging in the Latin Quarter where his personal library consisted of worn old books. He always wore the same old redingote, regardless of the season, and ran to the clinics on foot, never riding in a carriage. He earned a reputation during his career for helping the poor and after his death surprised people by the size of his fortune and the fact that he left in excess of 350,000 FF plus 5,000 in rentes to various benevolences and scholarship funds for the urban and rural poor, foreign missionaries, young priests needing education, intelligent farmers who could enrich the countryside, and medical students. Thus, the way he disposed of his goods showed his broad humanitarianism for the unfortunate, as well as his religious faith, both of which need to be kept in mind in analyzing the meaning of his attitudes toward women.

In 1823, this frank, loyal, honorable scientist received his first accolade when he was named to the Academy of Medicine. At age sixty-five he was awarded the ribbon of the Légion of Honor. Blessed with remarkably good health, ultimately he suffered some sort of spell at a session of the academy and died about three weeks later at the age of eighty-three.

Despite the fact that his career advanced so slowly and his interest lay with the poorer classes, he had a remarkably although largely unappreciated influence on contemporary accouchement, for a couple of reasons. First of all, so many medical students were exposed to his increasingly popular lessons over the years. He published his lectures as *Cours Théorique et Practique des Accouchemens, Traité des Maladies des Femmes,* and *Traité des Maladies des Enfans,* which meant that these became textbooks for aspiring physicians and surgeons to memorize in order to graduate. More highly regarded by members of the erudite elite medical community, the Academy of Medicine, was his *Lexique ou Nouveau Dictionnaire des Termes de Médecine, de Chirurgie et des Sciences Accessoires* (1806). A second edition, published in collaboration with Nysten, appeared in 1810; a third in 1814 bearing only Nysten's name as author; in 1824, under authorship of Nysten and Bricheteau; from 1824 to 1855, five new editions as Nysten; and in 1855, a tenth edition by Littré and Robin appeared. In a eulogy read to the academy, E.-Fréd. Dubois (d'Amiens) maintained that various editions of this medical dictionary that were then called "Nysten's," could just as correctly have been labeled "Capuron's." *Éloges lus dans les Séances Publique de l'Académie de Médecine (1845–1863) Tableau du Mouvement de la Science et des Progrès de l'Art* (Paris: Didier et Cie, 1864), 403–05, 418–21, 425–26, 429–34, 462, passim.

Consequently, when we cite Capuron as having said something about woman's nature, we know that he had a wide, captive audience who were required to memorize his lectures verbatim for the exams. The next generation also inherited his ideas as they filtered down through the years into the works of later editors of medical lexicons.

17. Ibid., 5 and 11.

18. Ibid., 9.

19. This text contains lessons Vigarous presented at Montpellier. Preceding paragraph based on Vigarous, *Cours Élémentaire des Maladies des Femmes, ou Essai sur une Méthode pour Étudier et pour Classer les Maladies de Ce Sexe* (Paris: Deterville, 1801), 1: 5–6.

20. Ibid., 1: xii.

21. For example, Boyeau-Laffecteur, *Traité des Maladies Physiques et Morales des Femmes,* 1 and 14.

22. Vigarous, *Cours Élémentaire des Maladies des Femmes,* 1: xiii-xiv.

23. Vigarous, *Traité des Maladies Physiques et Morales des Femmes,* 14.

24. Vigarous, *Cours Élémentaire des Maladies des Femmes,* 1: 3.

25. Louis Vitet, *Le Médecine du Peuple ou Traité Complet des Maladies Dont le Peuple est Communement Affectés–Ouvrage Composé avant le Révolution Française. Tome XI Maladies des Femmes–Accouchemens* (Lyon: chez les Frères Peressi, 1804), 470.

26. Vigarous, *Cours Élémentaire des Maladies des Femmes,* 1: 509.

27. Ibid., 1: 515.

28. Ibid., 1: 516.

29. Cabanis, *Rapports de Physique et du Moral des l'Homme,* in *Oeuvres de Cabanis* (Paris: Bossange Frères and Firmin Didot, 1824), 3: 445.

30. In the late 1980s the imperial notion of the ovum overpowering the weaker sperm made a comeback among feminist medical proponents.

31. Schweighauser, *Sur Quelques Points de Physiologie Rélatifs à la Conception et l'Économie Organique du Foetus* (Strasbourg: chez Louis Eck, 1812), 5.

32. Esquirol, *Des Passions, Considerée Comme Causes, Symptômes et Moyens Curatifs de l'Aliénation Mentale; Thèse* (Paris: Didot jeune, 1805). Jean-Etienne Dominique Esquirol (1772–1840) was the son of a hospital administrator at Toulouse. Alexis Larrey, uncle of Napoleon's most famous battlefield surgeon, Dominique Larrey, worked at the same hospital (La Grave) as chief of surgery, as Dominique did as an aide-major, during the 1789 Revolution. After serving as an *officier de santé* for the Army of the Pyrenées orientales, Esquirol studied medicine at Montpellier and Paris, eventually becoming Pinel's favorite pupil who transcribed and wrote the latter's *Médecine Clinique.* By age twenty-seven (in 1799), Esquirol had his own mental hospital for wealthy patients, although he did not complete the doctorate until 1805. But his thesis made him internationally famous because it was translated first into English, and from that into German and Italian. When Pinel died, Esquirol assumed his mentor's medical role. In 1817, he too started teaching, and in 1823, he became Inspector-General of the University. That same year, Esquirol was also named head physician at the Maison royale de Charenton, which became a model mental facility for other countries to emulate. In addition to his thesis, his 1828 two-volume study, *Des Maladies mentales,* became a guide to this field. It is frequently noted that Esquirol said he could tell the political history of his era simply by looking at the case histories of his alienated patients at the Salpêtrière and Chareton: many thought they were Napoleon's satellite kings and queens or whoever were the reigning crowned heads of Europe at any given time! Esquirol also was a founder of the *Annales d'Hygiène Publique et de Médecine Légale. Biographie Universelle, (Michaud) Ancienne et Modernes.* Nouvelle ed., s.v. "Esquirol, Jean-Etienne-Dominique" (Paris: Chez Madame C. Desplaces, 1855), 13: 68–76.

33. Ibid., 23–24.

34. Ibid., 65–67.

35. See my article, "Human Rights Issues Affecting Women in Napoleonic Legal Medicine Textbooks," *History of European Idea* 8 no. 4/5 (1987): 427–34; see also: infra, Chapter 7.

36. Today, this is sometimes euphemistically called "female circumcision" (more often "female genital mutilation"). Clitoridectomy is one of the four forms of FMG addressed as early as 1980 by a World Health Organization meeting in Geneva, Switzerland, considering it an international health issue for over 80 million Third World women. Apparently, the knowledge that French surgeons used clitoridectomy as a treatment for nymphomania became widely disseminated. George Gregory reported use of it in France in his 1829 textbook, *Elements of the Theory and Practice of Physic,* which became popular on both sides of the Atlantic.

However, from the 1830s to the 1870s, nymphomania was erroneously believed to be related to the cerebellum rather than to the uterus (as imperial surgeons had imagined), due to the phrenological work of the Viennese neurologist Franz Joseph Gall; the French experimental physiologist François Magendie (1783–1855), author of *Mémoire Physiologique sur le Cerveau, lu dans la Séance Publique de l'Académie Royale des Sciences, le 16 Juin 1828* (Paris: Imprimerie de Firmin-Didot) and editor of volumes 2–12 of the *Journal de Physiologie Expériementale et Pathologique, 1822–1831*; and J. Flourens, editor of *La Phrénologie, Journal des Applications de la Physiologie Animale à la Physiologie Sociale par l'Observation Exacte* (Paris, 1837–38).

37. Well-established medical procedures then existed for amputation of the penis, which had been done since at least the seventeenth century for certain diseases—leprosy and possibly elephantitis, for example—that might cause the male organ to become gangrenous or wither from thrombosis. See: Pierre Campet, *Traité Pratique des Maladies Graves . . .* (Paris: Bossange/Croullebois, 1802), 233.

38. For example, see: H. Ansiaux Fils, *Dissertation sur l'Opération Césarienne et la Section de la Symphyse des Pubis* (Paris: Gabon, 1811), 28.

39. Notably the notion that the uterus was a grand canal into which diseases flowed and washed away during menstruation. See: F. Pelissot, *Observations sur les Laits Répandus (Paris: l'auteur, 1807)*, 6–7.

40. G. Alphonse Claudius Montain, *Du Lait Considéré Comme Cause des Maladies des Femmes en Couche* (Paris: Brunot-Labbe, 1808), Avertissement, n.p.

41. Ibid., 48; Vitet, *Maladies des Femmes–Accouchemens,* 510–12.

42. Pelissot, *Observations,* 6.

43. Montain, *Du Lait,* 63.

44. Ibid., 15–17.

45. E.-Fréd. Dubois, *Éloges lus dans les Séances Publiques de l'Académie de Médecine (1845–1863),* 1: 129.

46. *Lucine Française, ou Récueil Périodique d'Observations Médicales, Chirurgicales, Pharmaceutiques, Historiques, Critiques et Littéraires, Rélatives à la Science des Accouchemens* (Paris: chez Lefebvre, an XIII), 3, no. VII: 243 et seq.

47. E.-Fréd. Dubois, *Eloges,* 1: 131 footnote.

48. Ibid., 129–32.

49. Ibid., 2 (of avertissement).

50. Ibid., 315.

51. Antoine Planchon, *Traité Complet de l'Opération Césarienne* (Paris: l'auteur, 1801), 3.

52. The first episiotomy in France was done in 1777 by J. L. Sigault and Alphonse Leroy; the Faculty of Medicine sanctioned it by striking a medal. Schweighauser, *Tablettes Chronologiques de l'Histoire de la Médecine Puerpérale* (Strasbourg: Imprimérie de Levrault, 1806), 90; Leroy, *De la Conservation,* 50.

Leroy taught accouchement at the more prestigious Ecoles de Médecine, while Baudelocque taught the course to the midwifery pupils at La Maternité. Nevertheless, the latter was "uncontestably the premier accoucheur of his century." J. J. Leroux, *Séance Publique de la Faculté de Médecine de Paris 14 Novembre 1810* (Paris: Didot jeune, 1819), 12. A rivalry appears to have existed between the two, at least on the part of Leroy. See: infra, Chapter 4.

53. J. Capuron, *Cours Théorique et Pratique d'Accouchemens* (Paris: Croullebois, 1811), 678.

54. Ibid., 617.

55. Ibid., 620 and 645.

56. Ibid., 593.

57. Preceding paragraph based on ibid., 602–08.

58. Ibid., 617.

59. Ibid., 618.

60. Ibid., 642–45 and 655.

61. Ibid., 654.

62. Ibid., 678.

63. H. Ansiaux fils recounted how Leroy had demonstrated the operation *(symphyse section)* in 1801 on the woman Rogeau, a petite person with small bones. He first made an incision as far as the clitoris, timing this exactly to coincide with the moment when labor should have ended. This incision allowed birth to occur naturally. Subsequently, he brought the flesh together by *bandaging* (not by stitching her), but left a drain for the urine to be eliminated from the incised area. Ansiaux saw considerable risk for the patient because walking might prevent the healing of the rejoined parts. Hence, the woman had to repose for several days. *Dissertation sur l'Opération Césarienne et la Section de la Symphyse des Pubis* (Paris: Gabon, 1811), 28–34 and 37.

64. That the work cited has ninety pages makes it appear to be a serious effort to help women and the nation. Leroy, *De la Conservation des Femmes.*

65. The following account of the societies of maternal charity are based on Christine Adams's two articles: "Constructing Mothers and Families: the Society for Maternal Charity of Bordeaux 1805–1860," *French Historical Studies,* 22, no. 1 (Winter 1999): 65–86; and "Maternal Societies in France Private Charity Before the Welfare State," *Journal of Women's History* 17, no. 1 (Spring 2005): 87–111.

66. Leroy, *De la Conservation des Femmes,* 7.

67. Ibid., 55 and 61.

68. Ibid., 71.

69. Ibid., 86.

70. Ibid., 76.

71. Ibid., 27.

72. Ibid., 72.

73. Ibid., 89.

74. Ibid., 90.

75. Robert G. Richardson, *Larrey: Surgeon to Napoleon's Imperial Guard* (London: John Murray, 1974), 215. Richardson also tells us that Larrey was an autocrat at home who treated his spouse and children the same way as he did his medical students. Ibid., 229.

Chapter 6

1. Cabanis quoted in: Martin Staum, "Cabanis," *Historical Dictionary of Napoleonic France,* ed. by Owen Connelly et al., (Westport, Conn.: Greenwood Press, 1985), 91.

2. In his preface to the third volume, Cabanis wrote that the only really complete work on Idéologue philosophy was Tracy's *Élémens d'Idéologie,* although his colleagues De Gérando, Lancelin, Jacquemont, and Maine-Birau had contributed lesser works. *Rapports du Physique et du Moral de l'Homme* in *Oeuvres Complètes de Cabanis* (Paris:

Bossange Frères and Firmin Didot, 1824), 3: 12. All page numbers for the *Rapports* hereafter refer to this edition.

3. Emmet Kennedy, "Ideologues," *Historical Dictionary of Napoleonic France,* 249. Kennedy's biography is *A Philosophe . . . Destutt de Tracy and the Origins of "Ideology,"* (Philadelphia: 1978).

4. Elizabeth Williams, *The Physical and the Moral: Anthropology, Physiology, and Philosophical Medicine in France, 1750–1850* (Cambridge: Cambridge University Press, 1994), 77–78. For some reason, her list of sixteen does not include any of the men Cabanis himself listed as most important in the preface to volume 3 of his *Oeuvres.* See note 2 above for his names.

5. Balthasar Richerand, "Discours sur Cabanis," *Séance Publique de la Faculté de Médecine de Paris,* 24 Novembre 1808, 4 (1807–1810): 13.

6. Ibid., 5.

7. Ibid., 8. This *femme de lettres* socialized with Dr. Benjamin Franklin. See: *Les Français vus par Eux-Mêmes–le XVIIIe Siècle; Anthologie des Mémoralistes du XVIIIe Siècle* (Paris: Éditions Robert Laffont, 1996), 365, 592–93, 609–11. Claude Adrien Helvétius (1715–71) was the son of a physician but became a wealthy tax farmer and radical philosopher. His hedonistic philosophy attacked the religious foundation of ethics. He claimed that everyone's sole motivation was self-interest. Because he argued that everyone is equally capable of learning, he argued with Rousseau's *Emile.* He produced two important works: in 1758, *De L'esprit,* which was condemned and burned; and posthumously in 1772, *De L'homme,* which said that through education people could solve all human problems.

Pressure from the Church caused Helvétius to recant three times so as not to share the same fate as his first book. He influenced the English Utilitarians.

8. Ibid.

9. Ibid., 7. Condorcet also advanced mathematics with the creation of a new theory of probability.

10. *Dictionnaire des Sciences Médicales, Biographie Médicale,* s.v. "Cabanis" (Paris: C. L. F. Pankoucke, 1822), 3: 99. Hippocrates was more popular among the eighteenth-century French medical community than Galen, the previous favorite.

11. Richerand, "Discours sur Cabanis," *Séance Publique de la Faculté de Médecine de Paris (1807–1810),* 4: 7.

12. Ibid., 4: 8, 13. *Dictionnaire des Sciences Médicales* is wrong when it says he never practiced medicine, 3: 103.

13. Elizabeth Williams, *The Physical and the Moral,* 76–85.

14. Richerand, "Discours sur Cabanis," *Séance Publique de la Faculté de Médecine de Paris (1807–1810),* 4: 8–9.

15. Preceding paragraph based on ibid., 4: 12–13. Furthermore, in a second eulogy presented by Richerand at the Faculty of Medicine on 24 November 1801, he likewise used the word *machine* to represent the body of Claude-Barthelme-Jean Leclerc, a professor of legal medicine who had headed the Hôpital Saint Antoine at the time of his death, but who formerly had been Corvisart's adjoint; later, Leclerc had replaced Professor Mahon when he died, vacating the Chair of Legal Medicine: ". . . le coeur était pâle et flêtre, comme si le miasme délétère avait spécialement dirigé son action contre ce ressort principal de la machine." Ibid., 4: 2.

16. See: Elizabeth Williams, *The Physical and the Moral: Anthropology, Physiology and Philosophical Medicine in France, 1750–1850*, 1–19. Older books on "the science of man" have seen the movement for anthropological and philosophical medicine as a briefer period ending with the ascendency of Bonaparte. As her subtitle suggests, she takes a longer view of the movement with its influence extending even beyond 1850 in the sense that after its composite disciplines veered off in separate directions, it continued to have effects on the new sciences. She credits the development of discourse analysis for making it possible to see the movement over this extended period. Williams disliked the sexist slant of the term, so she chose a different phrase as the title for her book on "the science of man," which concentrated on the physical and the moral.

17. Work cited, quoted from the book's dust jacket. Staum touched slightly upon Cabanis's explanation of the physical basis for sex roles in society, 213–17.

18. Cabanis, *Rapports*, 3: 296.

19. Ibid., 3: 40.

20. Ibid., 4: 297; 3: 40.

21. Ibid., 3: 14. He said the Scottish philosophers were the experts on sympathetic responses.

22. Ibid., 3: 40.

23. Ibid., 3: 296.

24. Ibid., 3: 293–95.

25. Ibid., 3: 297.

26. Ibid., 3: 219.

27. Ibid., 3: 297.

28. Ibid., 3: 299–300.

29. Ibid., 3: 300–01.

30. Ibid., 3: 309.

31. Ibid., 3: 317.

32. Ibid., 3: 311.

33. Ibid., 3: 310.

34. Ibid., 3: 309.

35. Ibid., 3: 301–02.

36. Ibid., 3: 142, n.1.

37. Ibid., 3: 302.

38. Ibid., 3: 318.

39. Ibid., 3: 303.

40. Ibid., 3: 312–13.

41. Ibid., 303–04.

42. Preceding paragraph based on ibid., 3: 336–38.

43. Ibid., 3: 327–28.

44. Ibid., 3: 347.

45. Ibid., 3: 348.

46. Ibid., 3: 348, n. 1; 349, n.1.

47. Ibid., 3: 336.

48. Ibid., 3: 352–54.

49. Ibid., 4: 111–12.

50. Madame Mère is shown in Jacques-Louis David's propagandistic painting, "The

Crowning of Josephine," which hangs in the Louvre, but she did not actually attend.

51. Williams, *The Physical and the Moral,* 105.

Chapter 7

1. A shorter version of this chapter and part of Chapter 9 were published together as "Human Rights Issues Affecting Women in Napoleonic Legal Medicine Textbooks," *History of European Ideas,* ed. Karen Offen. Vol. 8, no. 4/5 (1987): 427–33.

2. Matthew Ramsey, "Medicine," *Historical Dictionary of Napoleonic France,* ed. by Owen Connelly et al. (Westport, Conn.: Greenwood Press, 1985), 331–32.

3. "Médecine légale," *La Grande Encyclopédie* (Paris: H. Lamirault, 1886–1902), 23: 350.

4. See: Yvonne Knibiehler and Catherine Fouquet, *La Femme et les Médecins* (Paris: Hachette, 1983). Other pertinent literature includes: Pierre Darmon, *Damning the Innocent: A History of the Persecution of the Impotent in Pre-Revolutionary France* (New York: Viking, 1986); John T. Noonam Jr., *Contraception: A History of Its Treatment by the Catholic Theologians and Cannonists* (Cambridge, Mass.: Harvard University Press, 1965); William Schneider, "Toward the Improvement of the Human Race: the History of Eugenics in France," *Journal of Modern History* 54: (June 1982): 268–91.

5. "Jurisprudence Médecine légale," *Grand Dictionnaire Universel du XIXe siècle* (Paris, 1982) 10: 1418B.

6. "Médecine légale," *La Grande Encyclopédie,* 23: 350.

7. "Belloc, Jean-Jacques," *Dictionnaire de Biographie Française* (Paris: Librairie Letouzey, 1959), 4: 1366.

8. "Dubois, Antoine," ibid., 11: 923; and "Dubois, (Antoine, Baron)," *Biographie Universelle, Ancienne et Moderne,* ed. Nouvelle (Paris: Madame C. Desplaces, 1843–65), 2: 358. Chaussier was included by Elizabeth Williams in her list of sixteen in "Physicians Associated with Ideology during the Revolutionary Era," *The Physical and the Moral* (Cambridge: Cambridge University Press, 1994), 78.

9. "Chaussier, François," *Biographie Universelle, Ancienne et Moderne* (Paris, 1966), 8: 50–52; and M. Prevost and Roman d'Amat, *Dictionnaire de Biographie Française* (1959), 8: 885.

10. Work cited by P. A. O. Mahon with notes by M. Fautrel (Paris, year X).

11. "Mahon (Paul-Augustin-Olivier)," *Biographie Universelle Ancienne et Moderne* (1966), 26: 406. The work referred to is *Histoire de la Médecine Clinique et Recherches sur l'Existence, la Nature et la Communication des Maladies Syphilitiques dans les Femmes Enceinntes, les Nouveaux-nés et les Nourrices... Et Manière de Traiter les Maladies Syphilitiques dans les Femmes Enceintes, dans les Enfans Nouveaux-nés et dans les Nourrices; par Louis Lemauve* (Paris: Buisson, year XII [1804]).

12. "François-Emmanuel Fodéré," *Nouvelle Biographie Générale Depuis les Temps les plus Reculés Jusqu'à 1850–60* (Copenhagen, 1965), 17: 22–23; Archives Nationales F^17 20749; L. Ducros de Sixt, *Notice Historique sur la Vie et les Travaux du Docteur Fodéré* (Paris, 1845), 29; and Académie des Sciences-Procès-verbaux (Séance de 1 fructidor, an V), 1: 257 and (1802), 10: 193 Fodéré married the daughter of Dr. Moulard, thereby becoming the cousin-in-law of Julie and Desirée Clary, the wives of Joseph Bonaparte and Marshall Bernadotte, respectively.

13. Arturo Castiglioni, *A History of Medicine* (New York: 1975), 637.

14. Ibid.

15. François-E. Fodéré, *Traité de Médecine Légale et d'Hygiene Publique ou de Police de Santé Adapté aux Codes de l'Empire Française et aux Connaissances Actuelles,* 6 vols. (Paris: Mame, 1813), 1: 328.

16. P. A. O. Mahon, *Médecine légale, et police médicale,* 3 vols. (Paris: Buisson, year XII [1802]), 3: 43–44.

17. Ibid., 47.

18. Ibid., 49.

19. Ibid., 53.

20. Ibid., 89–100 passim; and J. J. Belloc, *Cours de Médecine Légale, Théorique et Pratique; Ouvrage Utile, Non-seulement aux Médecins, et aux Chirurgiens, Mais Encore aux Juges et Jurisconsultes,* 2nd ed. (Paris: Méquignon l'aîné, 1811), 37. For an overview of leprosy see: June K. Burton, "The Revolution in Health: Leprosy and Society by the French Revolution Era," *Consortium on Revolutionary Europe 1750–1850: Selected Papers 1994* (Tallahassee: Florida State University Press, 1995), 189–96.

21. Fodéré, *Traité de Médecine Légale,* 1: 351.

22. Although Belloc did not say, the surgery to which he was referring must have been cesarean delivery.

23. Belloc, *Cours de Médecine Légale,* 37–39.

24. Mahon also believed that deformed people should be banished from public gardens and walkways so as not to frighten pregnant women who might thereupon miscarry. *Médecine Légale,* 3: 37–39.

25. Ibid., 1: 268 and 2: 102.

26. Fodéré, *Traité de Médecine Légale,* 1: 5–8. Canon law, of course, originally set seven years of age as the "age of reason" when one technically could begin to sin and, therefore, needed the sacraments for salvation. But the glosses on Gratian shifted emphasis from reasoning ability to physical capacity. Thus fertility and virility became necessary for marriage to be permissible. Noonan, *Power to Dissolve–Marriages in the Courts of the Roman Curia* (Cambridge, Mass.: Harvard University Press, 1972) 6.

27. Mahon, *Médecine Légale,* 3: 131.

28. Belloc, *Cours de Médecine Légale,* 36.

29. Preceding paragraph based largely on Fodéré, *Traité de Médecine Légale,* 4: 359–61.

30. Belloc made a special point of accepting neighbor's testimony because they knew the person. *Cours de Médecine Légale,* p. xv.

31. This notion can be traced back to Hebrew law.

32. Fodéré, *Traité de Médecine Légale,* 4: 340–42.

33. Ibid., 4: 369.

34. Code penal, liv. 3, tit. 2, chap. 1, sec. 4. Cited by ibid., 4: 328–29.

35. *Jurisprudence de la Cour de Cassation* (25 April 1806) in *Recueil Général des Lois et des Arrêts . . . (1re Série, 1791–1830),* ed. by L.-M. Devilleneuve and A. A. Carette. 2: 237–38.

36. Fodéré, *Traité de Médecine Légale,* 1: 497.

37. Ibid., 1: 500.

38. Mahon, *Médecine Légale,* 1: 161.

39. See: Noonan, *Contraception,* chapters 1–13 passim.

40. Mahon, *Médecine Légale,* 1: 214–17.

41. Fodéré, *Traité de Médecine Légale,* 4: 385–86.

42. Ibid., 4: 387.

43. Mahon, *Médecine Légale,* 1: 234–36; and Fodéré, *Traité de Médecine Légale,* 2: 61–64.

44. Ibid., 2: 63.

45. Chester Bradley, "Les Opinions de Napoléon sur les Complications de l'Accouchement," *Réalités* (December 1969), 21–25.

46. Mahon, *Médecine Légale,* 2: 381–84 passim.

47. Ibid., 2: 418.

48. C.-M. Gardien, *Traité d'Accouchemens, de Maladies des Femmes, de l'Éducation Médicinale des Enfans, et des Maladies Propres à Cette Âge* (Paris: Crouchard, 1807), 1: 146.

Chapter 8

1. This phrase is borrowed from the title of Peter Hoffer and N. E. H. Hull's book, *Murdering Mothers: Infanticide in England and New England 1558–1803* (New York: New York University Press, 1981).

2. Pierre Sue, *Apperçu Général Appuyé de Quelques Faits, sur l'Origine et le Sujet de la Médecine Légale* (Paris: Société de Médecine, Year VIII), 25. Dr. Sue also was identified as an Ideologue (along with P. J. G. Cabanis and François Chausier) by Elizabeth Williams and included in her list of sixteen from the revolutionary era: *The Physical and the Moral* (Cambridge: Cambridge University Press, 1994), 78.

3. François-Emmanuel Fodéré, *Traité de Médecine Légale et d'Hygiène Publique ou de Police de Santé Adapté aux Codes de l'Empire Française, et aux Connaissances Actuelles* (Paris: Mame, 1813), 4: 395–97.

4. Code Penal, Sections 300 and 302, cited by Fodéré, *Traité de Médecine Légale,* 4: 398.

5. *Jurisprudence de la Cour de Cassation,* 25 November 1811, 3: 141.

6. P. A. O. Mahon, *Médecine Légale, et Police Médicale* (Paris: Buisson, 1801), 1: 227.

7. A. Lecieux, *Considérations sur l'Infanticide* (Paris: J.-B. Baillière, 1819), 3; Mahon, *Médicine légale,* 1: 381; and J.-L. Baudelocque, *L'Art des Accouchemens* (Paris: Méquinon, 1807), 1: 185. Fodéré also mentioned insertion of a long delicate needle into the brain, as a method sometimes used by midwives when only the head came out of the uterus. *Traité de Médecine Légale,* 4: 492.

8. Mahon, *Médecine Légale,* 2: 418.

9. Ibid., 2: 383 and 433.

10. Fodéré, *Traité de Médecine Légale,* 5: 29–30 and *Essai Historique et Moral sur la Pauvreté des Nations, le Population, la Mendicité, les Hôpitaux et les Enfans Trouvés* (Paris: Madame Huzard, 1825), 575.

11. Mahon, *Médecine Légale,* 3: 181–82.

12. Léon Milhaus, "Le Rétablissement des Tours," *La Revue Philanthropique* (Paris: 1897), 2: 20; and Archives Nationales F[17] 2456, Department d'Ain, 2 Frimaire An XIV.

13. Mahon, *Médecine Légale,* 1: 234–36, and Fodéré; *Traité de Médecine Légale,* 2: 61–64.

14. J. Capuron, *Cours Théorique et Pratique d'Accouchemens* (Paris: Croullebois, 1811), 514 and 587.

15. François-Emmanuel Fodéré, *Nouvel Examen des Questions Suivantes de Police*

Médical; Est-il des Cas ou, d'Après l'Expérience, l'Accouchement Prématuré Artificiel est Advantageux à la Mère. . . ? (Strasbourg: Levrault, s.d.), 2–17.

16. Capuron, *Cours Théorique,* 678.

17. Ibid., 618.

18. Mahon, *Médicine Légale,* 2: 386.

19. Ibid., 1: 166 and 225.

20. A. Richerand, *Des Erreurs Populaires Relatives à la Médecine,* 2nd ed. (Paris: Caille et Ravier, 1812), 244–46; and A. Lecieux, *Considérations sur l'Infanticide,* 44–45.

21. Roederer determined the weight of average full-term babies as 6–7 1/2 lbs. from reports compiled about births in Paris hospitals by Camus. These were printed in August 1803. The research was continued at the Hospice de la Maternité by Lecieux, who published his tables in 1819 in *Considérations sur l'Infanticide,* 9–13.

22. J. J. Belloc, *Cours de Médecine Légale, Théorique et Pratique,* 2nd ed. (Paris: Méquinon l'aîné, 1811), 72–82.

23. A. Lecieux, *Considérations sur l'Infanticide,* 68–77.

24. Fayolle, *Le Petit Magasin des Dames* (Paris: Solvet et Pichon, 1803) 1: 204–08. The following account is from this source.

25. L.-M. Devilleneuve and A. A. Carette, *Recueil Général des Lois et Arrêts,* 1st Series 1791–1830, 29 May 1806, 2: 250–51. This contains the *Jurisprudence de la Cour de Cassation."*

26. Lecieux, *Considérations sur l'Infanticide,* 68–77. The following report is based on this source.

27. The report supplied English as well as metric weights.

28. Clement-V.-F.-G. Prunelle, *De la Médecine Politique en Général et de Son Objet; De la Médecine-Légale en Particulier* (Montpellier: Jean Martel, 1814), 9.

29. Journal cited (Paris: Croullebois, 1810), 353–68. The following account is from this source.

30. One may well wonder why she took such pains to preserve the placenta. According to Matthew Ramsey, during the Old Regime superstitious country folks used afterbirths in witchcraft or magical rituals. *Professional and Popular Medicine in France, 1770–1830* (Cambridge: Cambridge University Press, 1988), 23. Recently, medical scientists have used stem cells from placentas to engineer the growth of new cells to correct medical problems, especially in children. Stem cell research holds great promise, although it has become a political issue because of the fear that abortions will be committed in order to harvest stem cells from the fetuses or that stem cells might be sold over the Internet.

31. Devilleneuve and Carette, *Recueil Général,* 25 October 1811, 3: 414.

32. Ibid., footnote (1).

33. *De la Médecine Politique,* 13.

34. Ibid., 15.

35. Devilleneuve and Carette, *Recueil Général,* 17 November 1814, 4: 630.

36. Anonymous, *L'Etat Conjual Consideré Sous Tous ses Rapports avec le Bonheur de l'Homme et de la Femme . . .* (Paris: Maugeret fils, 1809), 135–37.

37. *Considérations sur l'Infanticide,* 4.

38. *Traité d'Accouchemens de Maladies des Femmes, de l'Éducation Médicinale des Enfans et des Maladies Propres à Cette Âge* (Paris: Crouchard, 1807) 1: 146.

Chapter 9

1. Dr. Chauffard, *De la Loi Actuelle sur les Enfants-Trouvés et de la Nécessité de Rétablir les Tours* (Avignon, 1861), [3].

2. See: Chatagnier, *De l'Infanticide dans ses Rapports avec le Loi, la Morale, la Médicine Légale et les Mesures Administratives* (Paris, 1855), 246. The author was a judge from Bourg.

3. Bernard Mahieu, Marcel Candille, and Jacqueline Sonolet, *Saint Vincent de Paul et l'Hôpital* (Paris, 1960), 48.

4. Maternal bonding was a concept promoted by Jean-Jacques Rousseau. Today psychologists are treating the dysfunctional behavior of "unattached" children by putting them through bonding exercises. Rousseau, however, had no qualms about abandoning his own children in a foundling home.

5. Ambroise Tardieu, *Étude Médico-Légale sur l'Infanticide* (Paris, 1868), v–vi.

6. Jacques-André Millot, *Médecine Perfective, ou Code des Bonnes Mères*, 2 vols. (Paris, 1809), II: 159; François-Emmanuel Fodéré, *Essai Historique et Moral sur la Pauvreté des Nations, la Population, la Mendicité, les Hôpitaux et les Enfans Trouvés* (Paris, 1825), 575–76.

7. *Puerpéral* means "following childbirth." Childbed fever was explained by Semmelweis, who suggested thorough hand washing as prevention.

8. J. Capuron, *Cours Théorique et Pratique d'Accouchemens* (Paris, 1811), 519–26. Napoleon himself told the obstetrician to opt for Marie Louise during the troubled delivery of the King of Rome. See: Chapter 1.

9. Terra Ziporyn, *Nameless Diseases* (New Brunswick, N.J.: Rutgers University Press, 1992), 19–20.

10. Alphonse Esquiros, *Paris ou les Sciences, les Institutions et les Moeurs au XIXᵉ Siècle*, 2 vols. (Paris, 1847), 2: 135–37.

11. Fodéré, *Traité de Médecine Légale et d'Hygiene Publique ou de Police de Santé Adapté aux de l'Empire Français*, 6 vols. (Paris, 1813), 6: 403–08.

12. Chatagnier, *De l'Infanticide*, 15. Ironically, foundlings were then called "children of St. Louis"; that holy day was proposed as the day to farm them out to peasant households.

13. Ibid., 7.

14. Ibid., 19.

15. The footnotes to *Jurisprudence de la Cour de Cassation* contain useful discussions of ambiguities of language and application.

16. Chatagnier, *De l'Infanticide*, 20; Fodéré, *Traité de Médecine Légale*, 4: 321 and 398.

17. Abbé A. H. Gaillard, *Examen du Rapport de M. le Baron de Watteville sur les Tours, les Infanticides, etc.* (Paris, 1856), 9–10.

18. "Bulletin du mercredi 10 février 1808," no. 108, in Ernest d'Hauterive, *La Police Secrète du Premier Empire, Nouvelle Série 1808–1809* (Paris, 1963), 52–53.

19. Chatagnier, *De l'Infanticide*, 21.

20. Ibid., 23.

21. See: Anne Tychenne Case, 24 October 1811; Marie Patain Case, 17 November 1814; *Jurisprudence de la Cour de Cassation*, 3: 414 and 4: 630, respectively.

22. Figures differ on the exact number of *tours*. Chatagnier says shortly after 1811,

there were supposed to be 273 (one per hospice), but only 250 actually were constructed in seventy-seven *départements*. Another figure used is 269. See: June K. Burton, "Public Welfare," in Owen Connelly, General Editor; Harold T. Parker, Peter Becker, and June K. Burton, Associate Editors, *Historical Dictionary of Napoleonic France* (Westport, Conn.: Greenwood Press, 1985), 409.

23. Work cited (n.p., 1759), 424–31.

24. Work cited (Dijon, year 10), 26.

25. See: J. P. Maygrier, ed., *Annuaire Médicale* (Paris, 1809, 1810).

26. A. Lecieux, *Considérations sur l'Infanticide* (Paris: J. B. Ballière, 1819), 64–67.

27. Chatagnier, *De l'Infanticide*, 20.

28. Ibid., 23. During the Terror, Dr. Cabanis had demanded that the guillotine be abandoned as the instrument of judicial murder. Some of his friends went to see executions to test the medical theory of unitary consciousness of the body and the head. Nevertheless, Cabanis thought it was an inhuman instrument, although he did not think it could be verified that the body still felt pain after the head was severed. Others opposed the use of the guillotine merely because it stifled the victims' attempts to die like Stoic heros before the amassed people. But Cabanis also thought that the guillotine made the crowd become indifferent to judicial murder, which had taken longer under the Old Regime when an ax was used instead. In other words, the speed of the guillotine, and the fact that it was raised too high for those below to really see very much, sanitized death. Dorinda Outram, *The Body and the French Revolution: Sex, Class and Political Culture* (New Haven: Yale University Press, 1989), 111–120, passim.

29. Ibid., 26.

30. Code Pénal, art. 300–301. Association Henri Capitant, *Vocabulaire Juridique*, 2nd ed. (Paris, 1990).

31. Chatagnier, *De l'Infantiide*, 248.

32. Ibid., 246.

33. Rapet proved that Ramacles' earlier statistics were wrong. Cited in ibid., 248.

34. Gaillard, *Examen du Rapport*, 18–19.

35. Chatagnier, *De l'Infanticide*, 258.

36. Preceding paragraph based on Tardieu, *Étude Médico-Légale sur l'Infanticide*, 133.

37. Dr. Chauffard, *De la Loi Actuelle* 6–9; Anonymous, *Essai sur un Point Important de la Législation Pénale*, 46–51.

38. Chauffard, *De la Loi Actuelle sur les Enfans-Trouvés et de la Nécessité de Rétablir les Tours* (Avignon: Aubanel Frères, 1861), 13 and 16.

39. François Fodéré, *Essai Historique sur la Pauvreté des Nations, la Population, la Mendicité, les Hôpitaux et les Enfans Trouvés* (Paris: chez Madame Huzard, 1825), 74.

Chapter 10

1. "Fanny" was the *nom-de-plume* of Frances Burney, as well as the familiar name used by her family. While some excellent recent feminist scholarship consistently uses her Christian name instead, in this chapter about intimate family life I have opted frequently to use the name by which her contemporaries knew her.

2. Before his death La Grange was owned by Count René de Chambrun. He and the Fondation Josée et René de Chambrun allowed the Library of Congress in 1995–96 to microfilm many of the papers only discovered there in 1956; a duplicate of the micro-

films, which contain approximately 25,000 items on 64 reels, was acquired by Cleveland State University Library in 1998. Hereafter these microfilms will be referred to as LP LG. Before the Count's death, the late Mr. John Horton brought me an autographed copy of Monsieur Chambrun's *La Grange* (Paris: Dupont-Véro-Dodat, 1997), which is a guided tour with color photos of the restored château.

3. Joyce Hemlow et al, eds., *The Journals and Letters of Fanny Burney (Madame d'Arblay)*, 12 vols. (Oxford, 1975) 5: xlii. [Hereafter JLFB]. Hemlow has also written the authoritative biography: *The History of Fanny Burney* (1958).

4. For examples see: LP LG, Reel 3/Folder 31b, 42 and 43a. Although Adrienne proudly called herself "la femme de Lafayette," she signed her letters using her maiden name and her married name as a good public relations ploy since her seventeenth-century ancestor had been the Marshal de Noailles.

5. Ibid., Reel 4/Folder 45.

6. Judy Simon's introduction, Fanny Burney, *Cecilia or Memoirs of an Heiress* (London, 1986), viii.

Burney later published a fourth novel, *The Wanderer* (1814), depicting a penniless and unprotected spinster's efforts to earn her own living in England. All of Burney's novels involved plots about women's oppression in contemporary English society as well as displayed her enormous gift for depicting character. Her major works are discussed in J. M. Thompson, *The Popular Novel in England, 1770–1800* (1932); Lionel Stevenson, *The English Novel: A Panorama* (1960); and Ronald Paulson, *Satire and the Novel in Eighteenth Century England* (1967). Julia Epstein has presented painstaking and analytical research on the social and physical violence in Burney's novels as well as a literary deconstruction of her mastectomy letter in a short paper that was part of a session on the body and history at the 1986 Southern Historical Association; an article "Writing the Unspeakable: Fanny Burney's Mastectomy and the Fictive Body," *Reflections,* 16 (Fall 1986): 131–65; and a monograph, *The Iron Pen: Frances Burney and the Politics of Women's Writing* (University of Wisconsin Press, 1989).

7. Hemlow, JLFB, 5: 303.

8. Ibid., 5: 302.

9. Anastasie Lafayette De Lasteyrie, *Life of Madame de Lafayette by Mme De Lasteyrie* (Paris, 1872), 358.

10. Constance Wright, *Madame de Lafayette* (New York, 1959): 260.

11. JLFB, V: xliii and 303–04.

12. Jules Cloquet, M.D., *Recollections of the Private Life of General Lafayette* (New York, 1836): 34–41.

13. Burney claimed that it would take her an entire volume just to tell about all the members of the Noailles-Lafayette family whom she had met. JLFB, 5: 282.

14. Emilie's father, Comte and Dr. A. L. C. Destutt de Tracy, filled Dr. Cabanis's vacant place in the Institut de France following the latter's death in 1808, and delivered his eulogy. Elizabeth Williams told us that Tracy believed in vitalism-sensationalism, epistemological psychology, and a naturalistic approach to the body-mind problem, which he wrote in *Éléments de l'Idéologie*. Tracy associated with Cabanis. *The Physical and the Moral* (Cambridge: Cambridge University Press, 1994), 108, 111 and 134. He also was a good friend of the Lafayettes. General Lafayette wrote letters to Tracy, which are in the microfilms from La Grange at Cleveland State University Library.

15. Cloquet, *Recollections,* 59.

16. Dr. Prévost was mentioned in passing by Lobinhes in a letter to Anastasie, 7 October 1807, LP LG, Reel 3/Folder 44. Six letters from Lobinhes either to Adrienne or Anastasie written during the final illness exist in this file. All further references to Lobinhes's treatment are based on this series of correspondence, not all are dated.

17. See: ibid., Reel 4/folder 45.

18. The long, undated letter Lafayette wrote to his close friend La Tour-Maubourg in early January 1808 gives all the details of Adrienne's final illness. The original is in LP LG, Reel 4/Folder 48 and also printed elsewhere, but edited, sometimes omitting critical phrases. Maurois followed the letter carefully, however.

19. Jean-Nicolas Corvisart (1755–1821) presided over the medical service of the Napoleonic court. His credentials include teaching anatomy, surgery, pharmacy, pathology, and obstetrics at the Faculty of Medicine; member of the Légion of Honor; member of the Institut; and Baron of the Empire.

20. George Washington Lafayette was born December 24, 1779, so this was his twenty-seventh birthday.

21. To La Tour-Maubourg, Mme de Staël, and Mme de Grammont in LP LG, Reel 4/Folder 48.

22. Mme de Lasteyrie, *Life of Mme de Lafayette,* especially 392 and 395–96.

23. Reel 4/Folder 45. I am grateful to Dr. J. Leon Lichtin, Ph.D., Professor Emeritus of Pharmacology at the University of Cincinnatti, for his invaluable conversations about the possible uses of lead cerates and compounds, and many kindnesses. Note: the word for leaded substances used in these bills for Adrienne's prescriptions is *saturne* or a derivative, not *plomb.*

24. Lafayette to La Tour-Maubourg, previously cited.

25. Robert, "Saturne," *Dictionnaire Alphabétique et Analogique de la Langue Française* (1973) 6: 147.

26. Born Frances Burney on 13 June 1752 to Dr. Charles Burney (1726–1814), a noted musicologist, and Esther Sleepe at King's Lynn. Her mother, who was the granddaughter of a French refugee named Dubois, died in 1761, soon after the birth of her ninth child. Dr. Burney received his doctor of music Oxon in 1770. He traveled to the continent publishing his traveler's journals as *The Present State of Music in France and Italy* (London: 1771, 2nd edition 1773); and *The Present State of Music in Germany, the Netherlands, etc.* (1772–73, 2nd edition 1775). His four-volume *General History of Music* was published 1776–1789, and is still considered worth consulting. Frances Burney d'Arblay edited the *Memoirs of Dr. Burney, arranged by his daughter* (1832), a title that modestly shows her deference to her father by omitting her own name. Her adventurous brother, Admiral James Burney (1750–1824), wrote accounts of his voyages and about the game of whist. He accompanied Captain Cook on his last two voyages, and replaced him as captain of the *Discovery.*

27. Judy Simons, *Cecilia,* ix.

28. Mrs. Elizabeth Allen, whom Dr. Burney had secretly married in October 1767, when Fanny was about fifteen. Allen so disapproved of a writing career for women that Fanny destroyed all her "scribblings." When her father remarried, all plans to send Fanny abroad to be educated with her sisters were abandoned.

29. D'Arblay descended from the Bazille family of Joigny, France.

30. Note the British spelling in contrast to his father's Christian name. He became a priest in the Church of England, a vocation both parents promoted because it provided financial security—something that General d'Arblay had sought unsuccessfully for most of his life and for which Fanny Burney also struggled as a female writer.

31. "Dress and Adornment," *Encyclopedia Britannica CD,* 1999 Standard Edition.

32. All events in this paragraph are described in JLFB, V. It is noteworthy that as General d'Arblay's wife, Burney could live in Passy and Paris even though she was British. After the Peace of Amiens was broken in 1803, British gentlemen between the ages of eighteen and sixty traveling in France were detained as P.O.W.s as an act of reprisal. James Forbes, *Letters from France Written in the Years 1803 & 1804, Including a Particular Account of Verdun and the Situation of the British Captives in That City,* 2 vols. (London: J. White, 1806). This was another reason Burney prudently shied away from social contact with "politically incorrect" women whose acquaintance might jeopardize her husband's somewhat dubious economic prospects.

33. JLFB, 6: 553.

34. Readers will recall from Chapter 4 that Dubois (1756–1837), a military surgeon who had been with the Institut d'Egypte but had left Egypt for France without Bonaparte's order, later became a professor of the Paris medical faculty and teacher at La Maternité. Also, after the untimely death of J.-L. Baudelocque, Corvisart overcame Napoleon's reluctance to make Dubois Empress Marie Louise's official accoucheur. After the difficult birthing of the King of Rome, Napoleon conferred the Légion of Honor and the title of Baron of the Empire on Dubois, which made him financially secure. Burney does not say that he is a relative, although his surname is the same as that of her maternal great-grandfather. Moreau de la Sarthe (1771–1826) was also a military surgeon and author of *Histoire naturelle de la femme,* 3 vols. (Paris: Duprat, 1803). In 1805–09 Moreau edited and annotated a ten-volume edition of Levater to which he added a historical introduction on physiognomy since the Renaissance.

35. Léon Pérel, "Conception Pathogénique et Traitement du Cancer du Sein au 18ième Siècle," in International Congress for the History of Medicine, *Actes du Congrès, Proceedings: XXVe Congrès, Quèbec, 21–28 Août, 1976,* 1073–80. He said he quoted from the 8th posthumous ed. (1777) of Dionis's *Cours d'Opérations de Chirurgie . . . ,* although the *Bibliothèque Nationale Catalogue* says this appeared in 1767 and gives no later example.

36. François-Emmanuel Fodéré, *Médecine Légale* (1813 ed.), 6: 450–51.

37. Elizabeth Williams, *The Physical and the Moral,* 72.

38. François Ribe (1774–1847), a pupil of Savateur, in 1805 became surgeon in the Emperor's Household, which meant that he was supposed to stay close to Napoleon in case the emperor was wounded; however, he was far away when Napoleon was wounded at Ratisbonne.

39. Elizabeth Williams, *The Physical and the Moral,* 78. Moreau de la Sarthe was critical of the anatomist Dr. Franz-Joseph Gall's theorizing of twenty-two places on the brain where certain faculties are produced. Ibid., 109. Gall said that the vicera produced the passions separately from the brain.

40. For the best medical analysis of the contents of her journals and letters see: Anthony R. Moore, "Pre-Anesthetic Mastectomy: A Patient's Experiences," *Surgery* 83, no. 2 (February 1978): 200–05. Moore thinks Burney's case is a lesson in what surgeons

ought to avoid doing to heighten patients' discomfort, such as overly reassuring them, making them wait beyond the appointed time, not telling them what to expect or partial truths, and treating women childishly. Nowadays "informed consent" policies force surgeons to avoid some of their errors while better medical education about male-female power relationships should help avoid others.

41. For comparison, see the classic: Harold T. Parker, *Three Napoleonic Battles*. (Durham, N.C.: Duke University Press, 1944, 1983, and 1987).

42. JLFB, 6: 613.

43. "Writing the Unspeakable: Fanny Burney's Mastectomy and the Fictive Body," 150.

44. Ibid., 145–47; and JLFB, 6: 611.

45. JLFB, 6: 612–14.

46. The complete French text of "The Account of the Breast Operation drawn up by the chief Pupil of the Baron de Larrey who passed the Night by the side of the Nurse to watch the still dreadfully suffering Malade" as well as an English translation by Julia Epstein is found in her article, "Writing the Unspeakable," 150–51.

47. JLFB, 6: 615–16.

48. Ibid., 6: 596–616.

49. Scott's *Diary,* November 1826, quoted in "Frances Burney," *The American Whig,* New Series, vol. VII (1851): 270.

50. Emil Ludwig, *Napoleon* (New York, 1954), 598.

51. I am indebted to the late Harold T. Parker for calling this to my attention.

52. J. Christopher Herold, *The Mind of Napoleon* (New York, 1961), 137.

53. Herold also points out that in his last will, Napoleon called Larrey "the most virtuous man I have ever known." Ibid., 138.

Glossary

accoucheur: male midwife, obstetrician

afterbirth: placenta and fetal membranes expelled from the womb following childbirth since they are no longer needed to sustain and contain the fetus in utero

apothecary: category of healer who primarily prepared and sold herbals, medications, and drugs; the predecessor of the modern pharmacist

baptism: a Christian sacrament; in the Roman Catholic faith, cleansing away Original Sin of an infant by a priest applying holy water to the head while prayers are said for the saving of the child's soul; in an emergency when a fetus was stillborn or died after birth, a doctor or midwife could apply water with a syringe and recite the prayer for salvation

breech: instead of turning to exit the birth canal headfirst, sometimes a fetal presentation is across the cervix, and a shoulder, a thigh, or a buttock blocks its passage during labor; in such cases the infant either has to be turned or forceps applied to extract it; sometimes a C-section is necessary; occurrence of a breech delivery is why a midwife or obstetrician is needed to assist the mother who otherwise might die

cadaver: a corpse; used for dissection in the study of anatomy and practice of midwifery and surgical procedures before attempting them on live patients; because the Church forbade this, they usually were dug up and stolen from cemeteries at night, or were bodies of indigents or criminals (who could not be buried in holy ground anyhow). In order to reduce the odor, they were submerged in water for use

cesarean section: a "C-section"; so called because tradition has it that Roman Emperor Julius Caesar was delivered by this surgical procedure: cutting through the mother's abdominal and uterine walls to take the fetus before it dies from distress; a method for taking a fetus from a dead woman

cahiers de doléances: lists of grievances prepared by the local assemblies that elected deputies to the Estates General of 1789, held at Versailles where the French Revolution broke out; there were two kinds of lists: general *cahiers* (model lists copied by numerous local groups) and individual *cahiers;* more than 40,000 exist

capon: a castrated rooster fattened for eating

companionate marriage: a love match or personal choice of life partner; opposite of a traditional arranged marriage where each partner's family chooses who a person will marry

complementarity: the belief that a married man and woman together form one social unit; their masculinity and femininity "complement," fulfill, or complete each other; gender differences that form a whole; an element of relational feminism

elephantitis: a tropical disease making skin resemble elephant hide, which the French encountered in Egypt; characterized by massive swelling or "tumors" in the arms, legs, or genitalia, which then had to be carried in a sling in order to walk; Dr. Larrey established that it was not a form of leprosy as previously believed but an obstruction of lymphatic vessels

episiotomy: the cutting and wrapping or, later, stitching together of the tissue in the perineum, the area between the vagina and the anus, in order to facilitate delivery of a baby during labor without tearing the vaginal opening

"fine mind": a negative term used to describe the woman who wants to write poetry in the quarrel that started with a polemical poem written by Ponce Denis Echouchard Lebrun and was answered by Gabriel Legouvé and Constance Pipelet de Salme: can women possess knowledge and reason?

forceps: a wooden or metal two-pronged implement; tongs or pincers curved to fit the shape of a uterus, with scissor-like handles, used to deliver an infant that cannot free itself from the womb by the natural process; forceps might crush the infant, especially the head, if the user is unskilled

gardien/gardienne: French terms for a man or woman who cares for the sick; a keeper or caretaker

Hôtel Dieu: a charity institution in each city, traditionally run by nuns, where medical care was administered; patients were used for teaching interns in medicine and midwifery; in Paris, it was located on Ile de la Cité

école de santé: a national school of health, so named in 1794 legislation

hospice: traditionally, a shelter or place for indigents to die while receiving prayer and comfort to make death more humane; also, a maternity home before the medicalization of childbirth changed this natural process into a "disease"

hospital: a public institution where patients received medical and surgical care; proximity of patients often made them sites of great epidemics

labor: parturition; the normal muscular contractions culminating pregnancy, which expel the fetus from the uterus via the birth canal

leprosy: Hansen's bacillus; a bacterial contagious disease feared since ancient times and which reappeared as an epidemic in late-nineteenth-century Europe, especially Scandinavia; characterized by damaged nerves, tumors, and the loss of extremities, hence the flattened "lion face" with the nose eroded; fingers, toes, and genitals also atrophied; blindness was a common result

lumpectomy: the removal of a "lump," that is, a piece of cancerous tissue, from the breast, leaving the breast looking normal

maîtresse sage-femme: French term for a midwife who had earned the degree of mastership; a certified teacher of midwifery

manikin: anatomical model made from cloth, leather, plaster, or other material, for the purpose of teaching surgery or midwifery

mastectomy: breast removal surgery; in total mastectomy an elliptical incision is made to remove the entire breast, extending into the armpit along with its lymph nodes; once the breast tissue is removed, all bleeding vessels are tied off, a drain is inserted before the wound is closed to heal; performed today under general anesthesia

meconium: thick, sticky, greenish-black feces passed by infants during the first two days of life; poisonous substance found in the mouth of a newborn infant that has experienced fetal distress whereby it inhaled meconium from the amniotic fluid; it must be removed to enable the infant to breathe

nourrice: a wet-nurse

officier de santé: a third category of less-educated healers who were regulated in 1803 by the Napoleonic regime but given permission to practice only in one department after being examined by its *jury médical;* practiced medicine in the countryside since military conscription created a shortage of highly qualified surgeons and physicians; they served as public health officials during epidemics and practiced legal medicine

pap: baby food, hence the popular American brand name "Pablum" for finely ground, prepared baby cereals; sometimes French peasants made it by mixing raw flour (instead of baked bread crumbs) with water or milk to form a soft paste that filled up a hungry baby but soured its stomach and made it sick; the first food given after breast milk no longer satisfied an infant's appetite or it had too many teeth to continue to nurse without biting

physician: a doctor who practiced internal medicine; normally possessed more of a philosophical and humanistic education and training than a surgeon, whose craft historically had been considered less prestigious until the nineteenth century

placenta: organ within the uterus, connected to the fetus by the umbilical cord; it serves as the structure through which the fetus receives nourishment from the mother's circulatory system as well as how it eliminates its waste matter

puerperal sepsis: "childbed fever"; an infection originating in the genital tract within ten days after childbirth, miscarriage, or abortion and spreading to the uterus; an epidemic that struck lying-in hospitals; symptoms are fever, offensive-smelling vaginal discharge, headache, chills, and pain in the lower abdomen; can cause infertility, peritonitis, and septicemia, which is fatal

la querelle: French term for the discourse initiated by Sylvain Maréchal in the 1790s; he stated there should be a law against women being taught how to read; women lack the ability to use reason that men have, so they belong in the home to rear children. Maréchal was answered by Mme de Gacon-Dufour and Mme Clémery-Hémery

sage-femme: French term, literally a wise woman, midwife

"science of man": medical doctrine that lasted from 1750 to 1850, which joined physiology, anatomy, anthropology, and psychology; adherents believed that medicine should be used to solve social problems; how the mind orders the body to work is explained by sensationalism (*sensibilité*); holistic medicine that tended to study human types according to sex, race, age, climate, and geography

sponge: a flexible, plantlike sea animal whose skeleton softens when wet and absorbs many times its own weight in water; used for nipples on baby bottles

surgeon: a doctor with less humanistic philosophical education and more practical training and scientific education who performed operations; successor of barbers; used in the military to amputate limbs and remove bullets on the battlefields

syphilis: a venereal disease caused by a spirochete, usually transmitted by sexual intercourse or acquired congenitally from one's mother, producing sores on the genitals, skin lesions, and possibly infections and disablements of bone, muscle, and nerve tissues; treated with mercury

toucher: an internal prenatal exam performed digitally by a midwife or obstetrician to explore the pelvic area enabling him or her to examine and determine the size and position of a fetus and the cord, before labor begins

umbilical cord: cord connecting the navel of a fetus to the placenta of the mother, which is cut after birth and tied to prevent hemorhage; the knotted stub becomes the child's "belly button"

vitalism: a medical doctrine that originated at Montpellier and explained the mystery of human existence; embraced the notion of a basic force, metaphysical idea, or "vital principle" or spirit that animates the physical body to make it exist in a state of life; in death a body has lost the vital principle, yet the vital principle cannot exist alone without the soul and body of humans; founded by Théophile de Bordeu and Paul-Joseph Barthez

wet-nurse: woman who had recently given birth who breast-fed the infants of aristocratic women or mothers whose milk failed; often done by poor women for a fee before knowledge of sterilization of baby bottles and the pasteurization of milk made artificial feeding practical; a nineteenth-century civil-service occupation serving foundlings and orphans whose mothers had died in childbirth

Chronology of Primary Sources

1759–

[Riquetti, Victor, Marquis de Mirabeau and François Quesnay]. *L'Ami des Hommes ou Traité de la Population.* Nouvelle éd. augmentée d'une quatriéme Partie & de Sommaires.

1778–

Burney, Fanny (Frances). *Evelina or a Young Lady's Entrance into the World.*

1780s

Burney, Fanny (Frances). *Cecilia or Memoirs of an Heiress,* 1782.
Tenon, Jacobus R. *Mémoire sur les Hôpitaux de Paris,* 1788.

1790s–

Burney, Fanny (Frances). *Camilla or a Picture of Youth,* 1796.
Journal des Dames et des Modes. Lamésengère, 1796–1800.
Journal Général de la Littérature de France ou Répertoire Méthodique des Livres Nouveaux, Cartes Géographiques, Estampes et Oeuvres de Musique Qui Paraissent Successivement en France, Accompagné de Notes Analytiques et Critiques, 44 vols., 1798–1841.
Fréville, A. F. J. *Vie des Enfans Célèbres ou les Modèles du Jeune âge, suivis des plus beaux Traits de Piété Filiale,* 2 vols., Year VI.

1800–

Fodéré, François-Emmanuel. *Les Lois Éclaires par les Sciences Physiques; ou Traité de Médecine-Légale et d'Hygiène Publique,* 3 vols., Year VII.
Fourcroy, M. de. *Les Enfans Élevés dans l'Ordre de la Nature, ou Abrégé de l'Histoire Naturelle des Enfans du Premier Âge: à l'Usage des Pères et Mères de Famille,* Nouvelle ed.
Legroing-La Maisonneuve, Antoinette. *Essai sur le Genre d'Instruction Qui Paroît le plus Analogue à la Destination des Femmes.*

1801–

Agrippa, C. *De l'Excellence et de la Supériorité de la Femme; Ouvrage Traduit du Latin de C. Agrippa, avec les Commentaires de Roétitg.*

Gacon-Dufour, Marie-A.-J. *Contre le Projet de Loi de S*** M**** [Sylvain Maréchal] *Portant Défense d'Apprendre à Lire aux Femmes, par une Femme Qui ne se Pique Point d'Être Femme de Lettres,* Year IX (September 1801).

Guilloutet, A. L. *Nouvelle Théorie de la Vie.*

Landais. *Dissertation sur les Avantages de l'Allaitment des Enfans par les Mères.*

Planchon, Antoine. *Traité Complet de l'Opération Césarienne.*

[Raoul, Fanny], *Opinion d'une Femme sur les Femmes par F. R****. Giguet, 1801.

Robert, Louis Joseph Marie. *Essai sur la Mégalanthropogénésie ou l'Art de Faire des Enfans d'Esprit, Qui Deviennent de Grands-Hommes: Suivi des Traits Physiognomiques, Propres à les Faire Reconnaître, d'Écrits par Lavater, et du Meilleur Mode de Génération.*

Rollin. *Les Études des Enfans,* Nouvelle ed.

Société de la Charité maternelle. *Prospectus.*

Sue, Pierre. *Apperçu Général Appuyé de Quelque Faits, sur l'Origine et le Sujet de la Médecine Légale,* Year VIII.

Vigarous, Joseph-Marie-Joachim. *Cours Élémentaire de Maladies des Femmes, ou Essai sur une Nouvelle Méthode pour Étudier et pour Classer les Maladies de Ce Sexe,* 2 vols.

Wandelcourt, Hubert. *Plan d'Education.*

1802–

Chaussier, François. *Table Synoptique du Plan Général, des Divisions et Sous-Divisions du Cours d'Anatomie,* Year IX.

Dubroca, Louis. *Les Femmes Célèbres de la Révolution.*

Mahon, P. A. O. *Médecine Légale, et Police Médicale avec Quelques Notes de M. Fautrel, Ancien Officier de Santé des Armées,* 3 vols., Year X.

Millot, Jacques André. *L'Art de Procréer les Sexes à Volonté,* 3rd ed.

Necker, Suzanne, *Réflexions sur le Divorce,* Nouvelle ed.

Nougarède, André. *De la Législation sur le Mariage et sur le Divorce.*

Royer-Collard, A. A. *L'Essai sur l'Aménorrhée, ou Suppression du Flux Menstruel.*

Sacombe, Dr. Jean-François. *Élémens de la Science des Accouchemens, avec un Traité des Maladies des Femmes et des Enfans.*

1803–

Amalric, François de Sales. *Cours de Morale à l'Usage des Jeunes Demoiselles.*

Blanchard, Abbé Pierre. *Précepts pour l'Éducation des Deux Sexes à l'Usage des Familles Chrétiennes . . . Redigés et Mis en Ordre, d'Après son Manuscrit, par Bruyset Âiné, l'Académie de Lyon, de la Société d'Agriculture et des Arts de la Même Ville,* 2 vols.

Essai sur un Point Important de la Législation Pénale à l'Occasion d'une Case d'Infanticide Jugée à Dijon le 29 Pluviôse An 10.

Fayolle, ed. *Le Petit Magasin des Dames*, 1803–1807.

Gabet, Gabriel. *Avis aux Femmes Enceintes*, Year X.

Médecine Portative ou Guide de Santé à l'Usage de Toute le Monde, Year XI.

Moreau, Jacques L. *Histoire Naturelle de la Femme*, 3 vols.

Nougarède, André. *Histoire des Lois sur le Mariage et sur le Divorce*, 2 vols.

Roussel, Pierre. *Système Physique et Moral de la Femme*, Nouvelle ed.

Ségur, Joseph-Alphonse. *Les Femmes, Leur Condition et Leur Influence dans l'Ordre Social chez Différents Peuples Anciens et Modernes*, 3 vols. [1st ed. 1803], 1813. (Went through many editions Year XI [1803]–1836.)

St. Martin, Felicité Gueriot. *La Paix*, Year X.

1804–

Annales de Chimie [J.-A. Chaptal was an author and co-proprietor in 1804.]

Buchan, William. *Le Conservation de la Santé des Mères et des Enfans.* Trans. Thomas Duverne de Prailes.

Gacon-Dufour, Marie-A.-J. *Recueil Pratique d'Économie Rurale et Domestique.*

Gasc, Charles. *La Fièvre puerpérale.* Trans. P. F. Briot. (Bound as second part of G. G. Stein. *L'Art d'Accoucher,* starting on page 188.)

Jouard, G. *Nouvel Essai sur la Femme Considérée Comparativement à l'Homme Sous les Rapports Moral, Physique, Philosophique, etc.*

Mahon, P. A. O. *Histoire de la Médecine Clinique, Depuis son Origine Jusqu'à Nos Jours et Recherches Importantes, sur l'Existence, la Nature et la Communication des Maladies Syphilitiques dans les Femmes Enceintes, dans les Enfans Nouveaux-nés et dans les Nourrices . . . et Manière de Traiter les Maladies Syphilitiques dans les Femmes Enceintes, dans les Enfans Nouveaux-nés et dans les Nourrices; par Louis Lemauve,* Year XII.

Pastoret, Claude Emmanuel. *Rapport Fait au Conseil Général des Hospices . . . Depuis le 1er Janvier 1804 Jusqu'à 1er Janvier 1814.*

Sacombe, Dr., ed. *Lucine Française, ou Recueil Périodique d'Observations Médicales, Chirurgicales, Pharmaceutiques, Historiques, Critiques et Littéraires, Relative à la Science des Accouchemens,* Year XI–XIII.

Stein, Georges, Wilhelm. *L'Art d'Accoucher.*

Verdier-Heurtin. *Discours et Essai Aphoristique sur l'Allaitement et l'Éducation Physique des Enfans.*

Vitet, Louis. *Maladies des Femmes—Accouchemens,* Vol. XI of *Le Médecin du Peuple ou Traité Complet des Maladies Dont le Peuple Est Communement Affecté— Ouvrage Composé avant la Révolution Français.*

1805–

Esquirol, Jean-Etienne Dominque. *Des Passions, Considérées Comme Causes, Symptômes et Moyens Curatifs de l'Aliénation Mentale: Thèse.*

Gacon-Dufour, Marie-A.-J. *De la Nécessité de l'Instruction pour les Femmes.*

Gacon-Dufour, Marie-A.-J. *Manuel de la Ménagère, à la Ville et à la Campagne, et* de la Femme de Basse-Cour: Ouvrage dans Lequel on Trouve des Remèdes Eprouvés pour la Guerison des Bestiaux, 2 vols.

Guyton de Morveau, Louis-B. Traité des Moyens de Désinfecter l'Air, de Prévenir la Contagion, en d'En Arrêter les Progrès, 3rd ed.

Morlanne, Pierre, ed. Journal d'Accouchemens ou Recueil Périodique d'Observations sur les Accouchemens, Year XII–XIII. (Appeared monthly.)

1806–

L'Ami des Jeunes Femmes, ou Les Devoirs du Mariage et de la Maternité, 2nd ed.

Baigniéres and Perral. Traité des Maladies des Femmes Enceintes, des Femmes en Couche et des Enfans Nouveaux-nés, . . . Redigé sur les Leçons d'Antoine Petit.

Baudelocque, Jean-Louis. Principes sur l'Art des Accouchemens par Demandes et par Réponses, en Faveur des Élèves Sages-Femmes, 3rd rev. ed., May 1806 and 1811. Also, 4th ed., 1812.

Gacon-Dufour, Marie-A.-J. Moyens de Conserver la Santé des Habitans des Campagnes et de Leur Préserver des Maladies dans Leur Maisons et les Champs.

Girard de Propriac, Catherine-Joseph-Ferdinand. Le Plutarque des Jeunes Demoiselles, ou Abrégé des Vies des Femmes Illustres de Tous les Pays avec des Leçons Explicatives de Leurs Actions et de Leurs Ouvrages. Ouvrage Élémentaire Destiné à l'Usage des Jeunes Personnes, 2 vols.

Harmand de Montgarny, J.-P. Félébriologie ou Dissertation Physique, Morale, Politique, Médicale, sur l'Allaitement des Enfan Nouveau-nés; Contenant la Méthode d'Allaitement Artificiel avec le Lait des Animaux Orgé et Froid, 3rd ed.

[Marie de Saint-Urban, P. J.] L'Ami des Femmes, ou Lettres d'un Médecin, Concernant l'Influence de l'Habillement des Femmes sur Leurs Moeurs et Leur Santé; et la Nécessité de l'Usage Habituel des Bains, en Conservant Leur Costume Actuel; Suivi d'Un Appendice Contenant des Recettes Cosmétiques et une Thérapeutique Appropriée au Goût, 2nd ed.

Petit, Marc-Antoine. Essai sur la Médecine du Coeur; Auquel on a Joint les Principaux Discours Prononcés à l'Ouverture des Cours d'Anatomie, d'Opérations et de Chirurgie Clinique de l'Hôtel-Dieu de Lyon, Savoir: 1º sur l'Influence de la Révolution sur la Santé Publique; 2º sur la Manière d'Exercer la Bienfaisance dans les Hôpitaux; 3º sur la Douleur; 4º sur les Maladies Observées dans l'Hôtel-Dieu de Lyon Pendant Neuf Années; 5º l'Éloge de Desaut. (A 2nd ed. published 1823, 1826, and 1828.)

Renneville, Mme Sophie de. Lettres d'Octavie, Jeune Pensionnaire de la Maison de Ste-Clair; ou Essai sur l'Éducation des Demoiselles.

Schweighaeuser, Jacques-Frédéric. Tablettes Chronologiques de l'Histoire de la Médecine Puerpérale.

Warchouf, Stephanie. Velocifère Grammatical ou la Langue Française, et l'Orthographe Apprises en Chantant, Ouvrage Très-Élémentaire, Unique en son Genre, mis en Vaudévilles, et Dédié aux Demoiselles.

1807–

Baudelocque, Jean-Louis. *L'Art des Accouchemens,* 2 vols., 4th ed.

Gardien, C.-M. *Traité d'Accouchemens, des Maladies des Femmes, de l'Éducation Médicinale des Enfans, et des Maladies Propres à cette Âge,* 3 vols.

Millot, Jacques André. *Le Nestor Français ou Guide Moral et Physiologique,* 3 vols.

Montain, J.-F.-Fréderik l'aîné. *Le Guide des Bonnes Mères.*

Pelissot, F. *Observations sur les Laits Répandus.*

1808–

De Senacour, P. *De l'Amour Considéré dans les Lois Réelles et dans les Formes Sociales de l'Union des Sexes,* 2nd ed.

Gazette de Santé. 1808–13. (Published every 10 days.)

Gacon-Dufour, Marie-A.-J. *Dictionnaire Rural Raisonné,* 2 vols.

Gacon-Dufour, Marie-A.-J. *Supplément au Recueil Pratique d'Économie Rurale et Domestique.*

Hombron. *Mémoire Historique et Instructif sur la Maternité.*

Hucherard, Sausseret, and Girault. *Mémoire Historique et Instructif sur l'Hospice de la Maternité.*

Jullien, Marc-Antoine. *Essai Général d'Éducation Physique, Morale, et Intellectuel.*

Montain, G. Alph. Claudius. *Du Lait Considéré Comme Cause des Maladies des Femmes en Couche.*

Renneville, Mme Sophie de, and Pierre Blanchard. *Amusemens de l'Adolescence ou Lectures Agréables et Instructions à l'Usage des Deux Sexes.*

1809–

Costard. *L'État Conjugal Considéré Sous Tous ses Rapports avec le Bonheur de l'Homme et de la Femme.*

Ligne, Charles-Joseph prince de. *Oeuvres et Pensées du Prince de Ligne,* 2 vols.

Loiseau. *Dictionnaire des Arrêts Modernes,* 2 vols.

Maygrier, J., ed. *Annuaire Médical,* 1809–1810.

Millot, Jacques André. *Discours tel au'il Devait Être Prononcé à la Séance Publique de la Société Académique des Sciences du 18 Décembre 1808.*

Millot, Jacques-André. *Médecine Perfective, ou Code des Bonnes Mères,* 2 vols.

Schweigger, August Friedrich. *Les Hôpitaux et Institutions Charitables de Paris.*

1810–

Boivin, Marie-Anne Victoire Gillain. "Lettre à l'Éditeur." *Gazette de Santé,* no. 33 (21 November 1810): 260–61.

Bret. *Mémoire sur l'Éducation Physique des Enfans: Couronné en 1784 par la Société Royale de Médecine de Paris.*

Chaveau de la Militière, Mme. *Rapport Fait à l'Athénée des Arts sur les Farines de Pommes-de-terre; Brevet d'Invention Pâtes de Pommes-de-terre, Riz, Sagou, Semoule de la Dame Vᵉ Chaveau et Dufour.* (A 4-page pamphlet from a séance on July 1, 1810.)

Choiseul-Meuse, Felicité. *Recréations Morales et Amusantes à l'Usage des Jeunes Demoiselles Qui Entrent dans le Monde.*

Dard, H. J. B. *Instruction Facile sur les Contrats de Mariage Selon les Principes du Code Napoléon.*

Daubanton, A. G. *Traité Complet des Droits des Époux l'un Envers l'Autre et à l'Égard de Leurs Enfans.*

Daubanton, A. G. *Traité Pratique de Toutes Espèces de Conventions, Contrats, Obligations et Engagemens Qu'il Est Permis de Passer Sous Seings Privés,* 2nd ed.

Gasc, J.-P. *Discours sur l'Éducation des Femmes.*

Richerand, Balthalsar-Anthelme. *Des Erreurs Populaires Relatives à la Médecine,* 2nd ed., 1810 and 1812.

Richerand, Balthalsar-Anthelme. "Discours sur Cabanis." In *Séance de la Faculté de Médecine de Paris,* 24 Novembre 1808, 5–13.

Rougeron, P. N. *L'Historien des Jeunes Demoiselles.*

Sacombe, Dr. Jean-François. *La Luciniade Poëme en Dix Chants sur l'Art des Accouchemens,* 3rd aug. ed., Year VII.

1811–

Ansiaux fils. *Dissertation sur l'Opération Césarienne et la Section de la Symphyse des Pubis.*

Belloc, J. J. *Cours de Médecine Légale, Théorique et Pratique, Ouvrage Utile, Non-Seulement aux Médecins et aux Chirurgiens, Mais Encore aux Juges et aux Jurisconsultes,* 2nd ed.

Capuron, J. *Cours Théorique et Pratique d'Accouchemens.*

De l'Éducation Chrétienne des Jeunes Gens et des Jeunes Demoiselles.

Dufay, Pierre. *Essai sur la Théorie et la Pratique des Accouchemens.*

Guizot, François, and Pauline de Meulan, eds. *Annales de l'Éducation,* 4 vols., 1811–14.

Journal de Médecine, Chirurgie, Pharmacie, etc. 1811–13. (Eds. are Corvisart, Leroux, and Boyer.)

La Perrière, J. B. *L'Arithmétique des Demoiselles, Appliquée au Nouveau Système Métrique.*

Lagneau, L. V. *Exposé des Symptômes de la Maladie Venérienne.*

Lagneau, L. V. *Exposé des Diverses Méthodes de Traiter la Maladie Vénérienne,* Nouvelle ed.

Lalande, Jérôme de. *Astronomie des Dames.* In *Bibliothèque Universelle des Dames,* 154 vols., 4th ed.

Leroy, Dr. Alphonse. *De la Conservation des Femmes: Ouvrage Utile à la Population.*

Loiseau. *Traité des Enfans Naturels, Adultérins, Incestueux et Abandonnés.*

Réglement Général pour l'École d'Accouchement Établie à l'Hospice de la Maternité, à Paris.

1812–

Boivin, Marie-Anne Victoire Gillain. *Mémorial de l'Art des Accouchemens . . . Dédié à Mme La Chapelle.*

Bouilly, J. N. *Conseils à Ma Fille.*

Boyveau-Laffecteur. *Traité des Maladies Physiques et Morales des Femmes,* 4th ed.

Dubuisson, J. R. J. *Tableau de l'Amour Conjugal,* 4 vols.

Etrennes de Charité pour l'Année 1812, Contenant les Règlements et la Première Liste des Dames de la Société Maternelle du Conseil Général et du Comité Central avec une Notice sur les Établissements de Bienfaisance Publics et Particuliers et sur les Sociétés de Charité de la Ville de Paris.

Fothergill, Dr. *Conseils aux Femmes de Quarante-Cinq à Cinquante Ans ou Conduite à Tenir Lors de la Cessation des Règles,* 3rd ed.

Gastellier, René-Georges. *Des Maladies Aiguës de Femmes en Couche.*

Hocquart. *Le Lavater des Dames,* 4th ed.

Lemaire, Joseph. *Le Dentiste des Dames.*

Petit-Radel. *Cours de Maladies Syphilitiques; Fait aux Écoles de Médecine de Paris en 1809,* 2 vols.

Schweighaeuser, Jacques-Frédéric. *Sur Quelques Points de Physiologie Relatifs à la Conception et l'Économie Organique de Foetus.*

Wigand, Dr. J.-H. *Hamburgisches Magazin für die Geburtshilfe (Magazine Hambourgeois pour l'Art des Accouchemens).*

1813–

Capuron, J. *Traité des Maladies des Enfans Jusqu'à la Puberté.*

Fodéré, François-Emmanuel. *Traité de Médecine Légale et d'Hygiène Publique ou De Police de Santé Adapté aux Codes de l'Empire Français et aux Connaissances Actuelles,* 6 vols.

Renneville, Mme Sophie de. *Conversations d'Une Petite Fille avec sa Poupée.*

Renneville, Mme Sophie de. *Le Retour des Vendanges; Contes Variés à la Portée des Enfans de Différens Âges,* 3 vols.

Renneville, Mme Sophie de. *Les Deux Éducations ou le Pouvoir de l'Example.*

Robert, J. B. M. *Jurisprudence sur la Capacité Personnelle et sur l'Effet des Contrats des Femmes Mariées ou Ayant des Biens Situés Tant dans les Ci-devant Pays de Droit Écrit Que dans Quelques Coutumes Principalement dans le Ci-devant Normandie, Avant et Après la Loi du 17 Ventôse, an II (6 Janvier 1794).*

1814–

Burney, Fanny (Frances). *The Wanderer.*

Grégoire, Abbé Henri-Baptiste. *De la Domesticité Chez les Peuples Anciens et Modernes.*

Lebrun, Isidore. *De l'Instruction Publique sous Napoléon et de l'Université.*

Maygrier, J. P. *Nouveaux Elémens de la Science et l'Art des Accouchemens.*

Nougarède, André. *Lois de Familles ou Essais sur l'Histoire de la Puissance Paternelle et sur le Divorce,* 2nd ed.

Prunelle, Clément-V.-F.-G. *De la Médecine Politique en Général et de son Objet; De la Médecine-Légale en Particular.* . . .

Rendu, Ambroise. *Reflexions sur Quelques Parties de Notre Législation Civile.*

Salgues, Ad.-V. *L'Ami des Mères de Familles, ou Traité d'Éducation Physique et Morale des Enfans.*

1815–

Chaussier, François. *Table Synoptique de l'Accouchement.* (An approximately 2' × 3' wall chart suitable for teaching pupils in the classroom.)

Cross, John. *Sketches of the Medical Schools of Paris.*

Fodéré, François-Emmanuel. *Manuel du Garde-Malade, des Gardes des Femmes en Couche et des Enfans au Berceau . . . Publié par Ordre de Feu M. de Lezay-Marnésia.*

Lagneau, L. V. *Exposé des Diverses Méthodes de Traiter la Maladie Vénérienne,* Nouvelle ed. Paris: Méquignon, 4th ed. rev et aug.

Scott, John. *Visit to Paris in 1814.*

1816–

Berthollet, Cte C. L. *Institut Royal de France. Funerailles de M. le Baron Guyton-Morveau, le 4 Janvier 1816.*

1819–

Grégoire, Abbé Henri-Baptiste. *Des Gardes-Malades, et la Nécessité d'Établir pour Elles des Cours d'Instruction.*

Lecieux, A. *Considérations Médico-Légale sur l'Infanticide.* . . . (Edition intended for medical students)

Lecieux, A. *Médecine Légale; ou Considérations sur l'Infanticide. Thèse.*

1820–

Campe. *Elise ou Entretiens d'un Père avec sa Fille sur la Destination des Femmes dans la Société,* 2 vols.

1821–

Grégoire, Abbé Henri-Baptiste. *De l'Influence du Christianisme sur la Condition de la Femme.*

Lachapelle, Marie-Louise Dugès. *Pratique des Accouchemens, ou Mémoires, et Observations Choisies, sur les Points les Plus Importants de l'Art,* 3 vols., 1821–25.

1822–

Ratier, M. S. *De la Condition et de l'Influence des Femmes, sous l'Empire, et Depuis la Restauration.*

1823–

Chaussier, François. *Notice Historique sur la Vie et les Écrits de Mme Lachapelle.*

1824–

Cabanis, Pierre-Jean-Georges. *Oeuvres de Cabanis . . . Accompagnées d'une Notice sur sa Vie et ses Ouvrages,* 4 vols. (Vols. 3 and 4 are entitled *Rapports du Physique et du Moral de l'Homme.*)

1825–

Fodéré, François-Emmanuel. *Essai Historique et Moral sur la Pauvreté des Nations, la Population, la Mendicité, les Hôpitaux et les Enfans Trouvés.*

1826–

Alhoy, Louis-François. *Promenades Poétiques dans les Hospices et Hôpitaux de Paris.*

1832–

Thénard. *Institut de France, Académie Royale de Sciences. Funérailles de M. le Cte Chaptal. 1 Août 1832.*

1834–

Delacoux, A. *Biographie des Sages-Femmes Célèbres, etc.*

1836–

Cloquet, Jules, M.D. *Recollections of the Private Life of General Lafayette.*

1837–

Lee, Edwin. *Observations on the Principal Medical Institutions and Practices of France, Italy, and Germany.*

1839–

De Gérando. *De la Bienfaisance Publique.* 4 vols.

1845–

Dubois d'Amiens, E.-Fréd. *Éloges lus dans les Séances Publiques de l'Académie de Médecine (1845–1863). Tableau du Mouvement de la Science et des Progrès de l'Art.*
Rapet, Jean-Jacques. *De l'Influence de la Suppression des Tours dans les Hospices d'Enfants Trouvés sur le Nombre des Infanticides.*

1847–

Tucker, David Hunter. *Elements of the Principles and Practice of Obtetrics.*

1848–

Tucker, David Hunter. *Elements of the Principles and Practice of Midwifery.*

1855–

Chatagnier, Juge à Bourg. *De l'Infanticide dans ses Rapports avec la Loi, la Morale, la Médecine Légale et les Mesures Administratives.*

1856–

Gaillard, Abbé A. H. *Examen du Rapport de M. le Baron de Watteville sur les Tours, les Infanticides, etc.*

Marque, Jules de la. "Rapport à son Excellence le Ministre de l'Intérieur sur les Tours, les Abandons, les Infanticides, les Mort-nés, par le Baron de Watteville." *Annales de la Charité,* no. 12 (1856): 422–27.

1861–

Chauffard, Dr. *De la Loi Actuelle sur les Enfants-Trouvés et de la Necessité de Rétablir les Tours.*

1862–

La Maternité: École d'Accouchement en 1862. Paris: Guillaumin et Cie and E. Dentu, 1862. (Anonymous notes from courses taught by Mme Lachapelle and Mme Alliot, midwife-in-chief.)

1866–

Bechamp, J. A. *Éloge Historique de J.-A. Chaptal.*

1868–

Tardieu, Ambroise. *Étude Médico-Légale sur l'Infanticide.*

1872–

De Lasteyrie, Anastasie Lafayette. *Life of Madame de Lafayette.*

1883–

Bonde, Amédée. *Étude sur l'Infanticide.*

1956–

Tinthoin, Robert. "Preface." In *Bicentenaire de la Naissance de Chaptal.* (Exhibit organized by the Ministry of National Education and the Archives départementales de la Lozère, published by the Imprimerie Chaptal at Mende.)

Bibliography

Official Records

Almanach Impérial de France. Paris: Testu, 1804–14. [Succeeds *Almanach National de France.*]

Archives de l'Assistance Publique. Paris. *Notice Historique sur l'Object de la Société de Charité Maternelle et sur les Résultats de ses Travaux Pendant 30 Ans,* 1831.

Archives Nationales, Paris.

    Fonds Roederer 29 AP 75.

    BB^1 200–211.

    F^{15} 444, 1863, 2740.

    F^{17} 2456–2473.

Bibliothèque Historique de la Ville de Paris. "La Maternité: Pièces Administratives, 1803–21." Manuscrit Nouvelles acq. 479, fol. 310.

"Bulletin du mercredi 10 fevrier 1808," no. 108. In *La Police Secrète du Premier Empire, Nouvelle Série 1808–1809,* ed. by Ernest d'Hauterive. Paris, 1963.

Cleveland State University Library Archives, USA. The Marquis de Lafayette Microfilm Collection [of papers discovered at La Grange in 1956], 64 reels.

Dictionnaire des Médecins, Chirurgiens et Pharmaciens Français, Légalement Reçus avant et Depuis la Fondation de la République Français, Publié sous les Auspices du Gouvernement. Paris: Moreau, Year X.

Generallandesarchiv Karlsruhe, Germany.

    Bestand 205 Universität Heidelberg, Nr. 404.

    Bestand 213.

"Jurisprudence de la Cour de Cassation." In *Recueil Général des Lois et des Arrêts . . .* (1st Series, 1791–1830), ed. by L.-M. Devilleneuve and A. A. Carette. 10 vols. [Vol. 2 (1806–08), 3 (1809–11), and 4 (1812–14)] Paris: M. Pouleur, 1843.

Hucherard, Sausseret, and Girault. *Mémoire Historique et Instructif sur l'Hospice de la Maternité.* Paris: Imprimerie des Hospices Civils, 1808.

Napoleon I, Emperor. *Correspondance de Napoléon Ier Publiée par Ordre de l'Empereur Napoléon III.* 32 vols. Paris: Henri Plon, 1858–70.

Pastoret, Claude Emmanuel. *Rapport Fait au Conseil Général des Hospices . . . Depuis 1er Janvier 1804 Jusqu'à 1er Janvier 1814.* Paris: Imprimerie de Madame Hazard, 1816.

Règlement Général pour l'École d'Accouchement Établie à l'Hospice de la Maternité, à Paris. Paris: Imprimerie des Hospices Civils de Paris, 1811.

Ruprecht-Karls-Universität Heidelberg, Universitätsarchiv. Signatur: A-557/1–6.

Imperial Journals

Annales de Chimie [J.-A. Chaptal was an author and co-proprietor in 1804.]

Bibliographie de la France; ou Journal Général de l'Imprimerie et de la Librairie, [*annual*]. Paris: Au Cercle de la librairie, November 1811–1929.

Fayolle, ed. *Le Petit Magasin des Dames,* Paris: Solvent et Pichon, 1803–07.

Gazette de Santé. 1808–13. [Published every 10 days]

Guizot, François, and Pauline de Meulan, eds. *Annales de l'Éducation,* 4 vols. Paris: Le Normant, 1811–14.

Journal de Médecine, Chirurgie, Pharmacie, etc. 1811–13. [Eds. are Corvisart, Leroux, and Boyer.]

Journal des Dames et des Modes. Lamésengère, 1796–1800.

Journal Général de la Littérature de France ou Répertoire Méthodique des Livres Nouveaux, Cartes Géographiques, Estampes et Oeuvres de Musique Qui Paraissent Successivement en France, Accompagné de Notes Analytiques et Critiques, 44 vols. Strasbourg: Treuttel et Würtz, 1798–1841.

Maygrier, J., ed. *Annuaire Médical,* Paris: Crouille, 1809–10.

Morlanne, Pierre, ed. *Journal d'Accouchemens ou Recueil Périodique d'Observations sur les Accouchemens,* Paris: Belin; Metz: Devilly, Year XII–XIII. [Appeared monthly.]

Sacombe, Dr., ed. *Lucine Française, ou Recueil Périodique d'Observations Médicales, Chirurgicales, Pharmaceutiques, Historiques, Critiques et Littéraires, Relative à la Science des Accouchemens,* Paris: Lefebvre, Year XI–XIII.

Wigand, Dr. J.-H. *Hamburgisches Magazin für die Geburtshilfe (Magazine Hambourgeois pour l'Art des Accouchemens),* Hambourg: F. Perthes, 1812.

Other Primary Sources

Agrippa, C. *De l'Excellence et de la Supériorité de la Femme; Ouvrage Traduit du Latin de C. Agrippa, avec les Commentaires de Roétitg.* Paris: Louis, 1801.

Alhoy, Louis-François. *Promenades Poétiques dans les Hospices et Hôpitaux de Paris.* Paris: C.-J. Trouve, 1826.

Amalric, François de Sales. *Cours de Morale à l'Usage des Jeunes Demoiselles.* Paris: Bernard, 1803.

Ansiaux fils. *Dissertation sur l'Opération Césarienne et la Section de la Symphyse des Pubis.* Paris: Gabon, 1811.

Baigniéres and Perral. *Traité des Maladies des Femmes Enceintes, des Femmes en Couche et des Enfans Nouveaux-nés, . . . Redigé sur les Leçons d'Antoine Petit.* Paris: Pillot, 1806.

Baudelocque, Jean-Louis. *L'Art des Accouchemens,* 2 vols., 4th ed. Paris: Méquignon, 1807.

———. *Principes sur l'Art des Accouchemens par Demandes et par Réponses, en*

Faveur des Élèves Sage-Femmes. 3rd rev. ed. Paris: Méquignon l'aîné, May 1806 and 1811. Also, 4th ed., Paris: Méquignon l'aîné père, 1812.

Bechamp, J. A. *Éloge Historique de J.-A. Chaptal.* Paris: P. Asselin, 1866.

Belloc, J. J. *Cours de Médecine Légale, Théorique et Pratique, Ouvrage Utile, Non-Seulement aux Médecins et aux Chirurgiens, Mais Encore aux Juges et aux Jurisconsultes,* 2nd ed. Paris: Méquignon l'aîné, 1811.

Berthollet, Cte C. L. *Institut Royal de France. Funerailles de M. le Baron Guyton-Morveau, le 4 Janvier 1816.* Paris: 1816.

Blanchard, Abbé Pierre. *Précepts pour l'Éducation des Deux Sexes à l'Usage des Familles Chrétiennes . . . Redigés et Mis en Ordre, d'Après son Manuscrit, par Bruyset âiné, l'Académie de Lyon, de la Société d'Agriculture et des Arts de la Même Ville,* 2 vols. Lyon: chez Bruysset aîné et Cie, 1803.

Boivin, Marie-Anne Victoire Gillain. "Lettre à l'éditeur." *Gazette de Santé,* no. 33 (21 November 1810): 260–61.

———. *Mémorial de l'Art des Accouchemens . . . Dédié à Mme La Chapelle.* Paris: Méquignon père, 1812.

Bourgery and W. H. Jacob. *Traité Complet de l'Anatomie de l'Homme Comprenant: La Médecine Opératoire par le Docteur Bourgery avec Planches Lithographiées d'Après Nature par W. H. Jacob.* Vol. VII Atlas. Paris: C. Delaunay, 1840.

Bouilly, J. N. *Conseils à Ma Fille.* Paris: Rosa, 1812.

Boyveau-Laffecteur. *Traité des Maladies Physiques et Morales des Femmes,* 4th ed. Paris: chez l'auteur, 1812.

Bret. *Mémoire sur l'Éducation Physique des Enfans: Couronné en 1784 par la Société Royale de Médecine de Paris.* Arles: Gaspard Mesnier, 1810.

Buchan, William. *Le Conservation de la Santé des Mères et des Enfans.* Trans. Thomas Duverne de Prailes. Paris: Métier, 1804.

Burney, Fanny (Frances). *Cecilia or Memoirs of an Heiress.* Introduction by Judy Simon. London, 1986.

———. *The Wanderer.* London, 1814.

Cabanis, Pierre-Jean-Georges. *Oeuvres Complètes de Cabanis . . . Accompagnées d'une Notice sur sa Vie et ses Ouvrages,* 4 vols. Paris: Bossange Frères, February 1824. Volume 2 contains his *Coup d'Oeil sur les Révolutions et les Réformes de la Médecine* (1804): 65–254. Volumes 3 and 4 are entitled *Rapports du Physique et du Moral de l'Homme.*

Campe, Joachim Heinrich. *Elise, ou Entretiens d'un Père avec sa Fille sur la Destination des Femmes dans la Société,* 2 vols. Paris: 1820. [The B.N. lacks the 1st ed.]

Capuron, J. *Cours Théorique et Pratique d'Accouchemens.* Paris: Croullebois, 1811.

———. *Traité des Maladies des Femmes.* Paris: Croullebois, 1812.

———. *Traité des Maladies des Enfans Jusqu'à la Puberté.* Paris: Croullebois, 1813.

Chaptal, Jean-Antoine. *Mes Souvenirs sur Napoléon.* Paris: Librairie Plon, 1893.

Chatagnier, Juge à Bourg. *De l'Infanticide dans ses Rapports avec la Loi, la Morale, la Médecine Légale et les Mesures Administratives.* Paris: Cosse, 1855.

Chauffard, Dr. *De la Loi Actuelle sur les Enfants-Trouvés et de la Nécessité de Rétablir les Tours.* Avignon: Aubanel Frères, 1861.

Chaussier, François. *Notice Historique sur la Vie et les Écrits de Mme Lachapelle.* Paris: Madame Huzard, 1823.

———. *Table Synoptique de l'Accouchement.* Paris: Théophile Barrois, 1815. (An approximately 2' × 3' wall chart or poster suitable for teaching pupils in the classroom.)

———. *Table Synoptique du Plan Général, des Divisions et Sous-Divisions du Cours d'anatomie.* Paris: Barrois, Year IX.

Chaveau de la Militière, Madame. *Rapport Fait à l'Athénée des Arts sur les Farines de Pommes-de-terre; Brevet d'Invention Pâtes de Pommes-de-terre, Riz, Sagou, Semoule de la Dame Ve Chaveau et Dufour.* Paris: 1810. [A four-page pamphlet from a séance on July 1, 1810.]

Choiseul-Meuse, Felicité. *Recréations Morales et Amusantes à l'Usage des Jeunes Demoiselles Qui Entrent dans le Monde.* Paris: Blanchard, 1810.

Cloquet, Jules, M.D. *Recollections of the Private Life of General Lafayette.* New York, 1836.

Costard. *L'Etat Conjugal Considéré Sous Tous ses Rapports avec le Bonheur de l'Homme et de la Femme.* Paris: Maugeret, 1809.

Cross, John. *Sketches of the Medical Schools of Paris.* London: J. Callow, Medical Bookseller, 1815.

Cutler, William. *The Life of Lafayette.* Boston: Sanborn, Carter Bazin & Co., 1849.

Dansette, Adrien, ed. *Napoléon, Pensées Politiques et Sociales.* Paris: Flammarion, 1969.

Dard, H. J. B. *Instruction Facile sur les Contrats de Mariage Selon les Principes du Code Napoléon.* Paris: Garnery, 1810.

Daubanton, A. G. *Traité Complet des Droits des Époux l'un Envers l'Autre et à l'Égard de leurs Enfans.* Paris: Crapart, 1810.

———. *Traité Pratique de Toutes Espèces de Conventions, Contrats, Obligations et Engagemens Qu'il Est Permis de Passer Sous Seings Privés.* 2d ed. Paris: Buisson, 1810.

De Gérando. *De la Bienfaisance Publique.* 4 vols. Paris: 1839.

Delacoux, A. *Biographie des Sages-Femmes Célèbres, etc.* Paris: 1834.

De Lasteyrie, Anastasie Lafayette. *Life of Madame de Lafayette by Mme De Lasteyrie.* Paris: 1872.

De l'Éducation Chrétienne des Jeunes Gens et des Jeunes Demoiselles. Paris: Cretté, 1811.

De Senacour, P. *De l'Amours Considéré dans les Lois Réelles et dans les Formes Sociales de l'Union des Sexes,* 2nd ed. Paris: Capelle et Renand, 1808.

Devilleneuve, L.-M., and A. A. Carette. *Recueil Général des Lois et Arrêts,* 1st Series 1791–1830, 29 May 1806, Vol 2.

Dubois d'Amiens, E.-Fréd. *Éloges lus dans les Séances Publiques de l'Académie de Médecine (1845–1863). Tableau du Mouvement de la Science et des Progrès de l'Art.* Paris: Didier, 1864.

Dubroca, Louis. *Les Femmes Célèbres de la Révolution.* Paris: Bonneville, 1802.

Dubuisson, J. R. J. *Tableau de l'Amour Conjugal,* 4 vols. Paris: Duprat-Duverger, 1812.

Dufay, Pierre. *Essai sur la Théorie et la Pratique des Accouchemens.* Paris: de l'imprimerie de Hocquet et Cie, 1811.

Esquirol, Jean-Etienne Dominque. *Des Passions, Considerées Comme Causes, Symptômes et Moyens Curatifs de l'Aliénation Mentale: Thèse.* Paris: Didot jeune, 1805.

Essai sur un Point Important de la Législation Pénale à l'Occasion d'une Cause d'Infanticide Jugée à Dijon le 29 Pluviôse An 10. Dijon: chez Bernard-Defay, Year X.

Etrennes de Charité pour l'Année 1812, Contenant les Règlements et la Première Liste des Dames de la Société Maternelle du Conseil Général et du Comité Central avec une Notice sur les Établissements de Bienfaisance Publics et Particuliers et sur les Sociétés de Charité de la Ville de Paris. Paris: Petit, 1812.

Fodéré, François-Emmanuel. *Essai Historique et Moral sur la Pauvreté des Nations, la Population, la Mendicité, les Hôpitaux et les Enfans Trouvés.* Paris: Madame Huzard, 1825.

———. *Les Lois Éclairées par les Sciences Physiques, ou Traité de Médecine-Légale et d'Hygiène Publique,* 3 vols. Paris: Croullebois & Deterville, Year VII.

———. *Manuel du Garde-Malade, des Gardes des Femmes en Couche et des Enfans au Berceau . . . Publié par Ordre de Feu M. de Lezay-Marnésia.* Strasbourg: Levrault, 1815.

———. *Nouvel Examen des Questions Suivantes de Police Médical: Est-it des Cas où, d'Après l'Expérience, l'Accouchement Prémature Artificiel est Avantageux à la Mère. . . . ?* Strasbourg: Levrault, n.d.

———. *Traité de Médecine Légale et d'Hygiène Publique ou De Police de Santé adapté aux Codes de l'Empire Français et aux Connaissances Actuelles,* 6 vols. Paris: Mame, 1813.

Fothergill, Dr. *Conseils aux Femmes de Quarante-Cinq à Cinquante Ans ou Conduite à Tenir Lors de la Cessation des Règles,* 3rd ed. Paris: Méquignon-Marvis, 1812.

Fourcroy. *Les Enfans Élevés dans l'Ordre de la Nature, ou Abrégé de l'Histoire Naturelle des Enfans du Premier Âge: à l'Usage des Pères et Mères de Famille.* Nouvelle ed. Paris: Delalain fils, 1800.

Fréville, A. F. J. *Vie des Enfans Célèbres ou les Modèles du Jeune Âge, Suivis des Plus Beaux Traits de Piété Filiale,* 2 vols. Paris: A. J. Dugour et Durand, Year VI.

Gabet, Gabriel. *Avis aux Femmes Enceintes.* Strasbourg: Levrault, Year X.

Gacon-Dufour, Marie-A.-J. *Contre le Projet de Loi de S*** M*** [Sylvain Maréchal] Portant Défense d'Apprendre à Lire aux Femmes, par une Femme Qui ne se Pique Point d'Être Femme de Lettres.* Paris: Ouvrier et Barba, Year IX (September 1801).

———. *De la Nécessité de l'Instruction pour les Femmes.* Paris: Buisson et Delaunay, 1805.

———. *Dictionnaire Rural Raisonné,* 2 vols. Paris: Collin, 1808.

———. *Manuel de la Ménagère, à la Ville et à la Campagne, et de la Femme de Bassecour: Ouvrage dans Lequel on Trouve des Remèdes Eprouvés pour la Guerison des Bestiaux,* 2 vols. Paris: Buisson, 1805.

———. *Moyens de Conserver la Santé des Habitans des Campagnes et de leur Préserver des Maladies dans leur Maisons et les Champs.* 1806.

———. *Recueil Pratique d'Économie Rurale et Domestique.* Paris: Buisson, 1804.

———. *Supplément au Recueil Pratique d'Économie Rurale et Domestique.* Paris: Arthus-Bertrand, 1808.

Gaillard, Abbé A. H. *Examen du Rapport de M. le Baron de Watteville sur les Tours, les Infanticides, etc.* Paris: Parent-Desbarres; Poitiers: Henri Oudin, 1856.

Gardien, C.-M. *Traité d'Accouchemens, des Maladies des Femmes, de l'Éducation Médicinale des Enfans, et des Maladies Propres à Cette Âge,* 3 vols. Paris: Crouchard, 1807.

Gasc, Charles. *La Fièvre Puerpérale.* Trans. by P. F. Briot. Paris: n.p. 1804. Bound as second part of G. G. Stein. *L'Art d'Accoucher,* starting on page 188.

Gasc, J.-P. *Discours sur l'Éducation des Femmes.* Paris: Lebel et guitel, 1810.

Gastellier, René-Georges. *Des Maladies Aiguës de Femmes en Couche.* Paris: Crapart et Le Normant, 1812.

Girard de Propriac, Catherine-Joseph-Ferdinand. *Le Plutarque des Jeunes Demoiselles, ou Abrégé des Vies des Femmes Illustres de Tous les Pays avec des Leçons Explicatives de leurs Actions et de leurs Ouvrages. Ouvrage Élémentaire Destiné à l'Usage des Jeunes Personnes,* 2 vols. Paris: Gérard, 1806.

Grégoire, Abbé Henri-Baptiste. *De la Domesticité chez les Peuples Anciens et Modernes.* Paris: A. Egron, 1814.

———. *De l'Influence du Christianisme sur la Condition de la Femme.* Paris: Baudouin frères, 1821.

———. *Des Gardes-malades, et la Nécessité d'Établir pour Elles des Cours d'Instruction.* Paris: Baudouin fils, 1819.

Guilloutet, A. L. *Nouvelle Théorie de la Vie.* Paris: Arthus Bertrand, 1801.

Guinan-Laoureins, J.-B. pseud John-Baptiste Reinolds. *Le Classique des Dames, ou Cahiers Élémentaires d'Histoire, de Geographie, d'Histoire Naturelle, de Mythologie, de Langues Française, Italienne et Anglaise, et de Morale Universelle.* Paris: Planzoles, Year XI [1803].

Guyton de Morveau, Louis-B. *Traité des Moyens de Désinfecter l'Air, de Prévenir la Contagion, en d'en Arrêter les Progrès,* 3rd ed. Paris: Bernard, 1805.

Harmand de Montgarny, J.-P. *Félébriologie ou Dissertation Physique, Morale, Politique, Médicale, sur l'Allaitement des Enfans Nouveau-nés; Contenant la Méthode d'Allaitement Artificiel avec le Lait des Animaux Orgé et Froid,* 3rd ed. Châlons-sur-Marne: Martin, 1806.

Hemlow, Joyce et al, eds. *The Journals and Letters of Fanny Burney (Madame d'Arblay),* 12 vols. Oxford, 1975.

Herold, J. Christopher. *The Mind of Napoleon.* New York: 1961.

Hocquart. *Le Lavater des Dames,* 4th ed. Paris: Saintin, 1812.

Hombron. *Mémoire Historique et Instructif sur la Maternité.* Paris: 1808.

Hunter, William. *Traité d'Accouchemens de Maladies des Femmes, de l'Éducation Médicinale des Enfans et des Maladies Propres à Cette Âge.* Paris: Crouchard, 1807.

Jouard, G. *Nouvel Essai sur la Femme Considérée Comparativement à l'Homme sous les Rapports Moral, Physique, Philosophique, etc.* Paris: chez l'auteur, 1804.

Jullien, Marc-Antoine. *Essai Général d'Éducation Physique, Morale, et Intellectuel.* Paris: Firmin Didot, 1808.

La Perrière, J. B. *L'Arithmétique des Demoiselles, Appliquée au Nouveau Système Métrique.* Paris: Didot, 1811.

Lachapelle, Marie-Louise Dugès. *Pratique des Accouchemens, ou Mémoires, et Observations Choisies, sur les Points les Plus Importants de l'Art,* 3 vols. Paris: J. B. Baillière, 1821–25.

Lagneau, L. V. *Exposé des Symptômes de la Maladie Venérienne.* Paris: Méquignon, 1811.

————. *Exposé des Diverses Méthodes de Traiter la Maladie Vénérienne,* Nouvelle ed. Paris: Méquignon, 1811; 4th ed. rev et aug., Paris: Gabon, 1815.

Lalande, Jérôme de. "Astronomie des Dames." In *Bibliothèque Universelle des Dames,* 154 vols., 4th ed. Paris: Ménard et Desenne fils, 1811.

Landais. *Dissertation sur les Avantages de l'Allaitement des Enfans par les Mères.* Paris: Méquignon l'aîné, 1801.

Las Cases, Emmanuel de. *Las Cases, le Mémorialiste de Napoléon.* Paris: Librairie Arthème Fayard, 1959.

Lebrun, Isidore. *De l'Instruction Publique sous Napoléon et de l'Université.* Paris: Gide fils, 1814.

Lecestre, Léon, ed. *Lettres Inédites de Napoléon Ier,* 2nd ed. Paris: Plon, 1897.

Lecieux, A. *Considérations Médico-Légale sur l'Infanticide . . . .* Paris: J.-B. Baillière, 1819. (Edition intended for medical students.)

————. *Médecine Légale; ou Considérations sur l'Infanticide. Thèse.* Paris: J.-B. Baillière, 1819.

Lee, Edwin. *Observations on the Principal Medical Institutions and Practices of France, Italy and Germany.* Philadelphia: Haswell, 1837.

Legroing-La Maisonneuve, Antoinette. *Essai sur le Genre d'Instruction Qui Paraît le plus Analogue à la Destination des Femmes.* Paris: Pougens, 1800.

Lemaire, Joseph. *Le Dentiste des Dames.* Paris: Foucault, 1812.

Leroy, Dr. Alphonse. *De la Conservation des Femmes: Ouvrage Utile à la Population.* Paris: Méquignon l'aîné, 1811.

Ligne, Charles-Joseph prince de. *Oeuvres et Pensées du Prince de Ligne,* 2 vols. Geneva: J. J. Paschoud; Paris: J. Chaumerot, 1809.

Loiseau. *Dictionnaire des Arrêts Modernes,* 2 vols. Paris: Clament frères, 1809.

————. *Traité des Enfans Naturels, Adultérins, Incestueux et Abandonnés.* Paris: J. Antoine, 1811.

Mahon, P. A. O. *Histoire de la Médecine Clinique, Depuis son Origine Jusqu'à nos Jours et Recherches Importantes, sur l'Existence, la Nature et la Communication des Maladies Syphilitiques dans les Femmes Enceintes, dans les Enfans Nouveaux-nés et dans les Nourrices . . . et Manière de Traiter les Maladies Syphilitiques dans les Femmes Enceintes, dans les Enfans Nouveaux-nés et dans les Nourrices; par Louis Lemauve.* Paris: Buisson, Year XII (1804).

————. *Médecine Légale, et Police Médicale avec Quelques Notes de M. Fautrel, Ancien Officier de Santé des Armées,* 3 vols. Paris: Buisson, Year X (1802).

[Marie de Saint-Urban, P. J.]. *L'Ami des Femmes, ou Lettres d'un Médecin, Concernant l'Influence de l'Habillement des Femmes sur leurs Moeurs et leur Santé; et la Nécessité de l'Usage Habituel des Bains, en Conservant leur Costume Actuel; Suivi d'un Appendice Contenant des Recettes Cosmetiques et une Thérapeutique Appro-*

priée au Goût, 2nd ed. Paris: Lenormand, 1806. The 2nd edition was also published by Genets jeune, 1806.

Marque, Jules de la. "Rapport à son Excellence le Ministre de l'Intérieur sur les Tours, les Abandons, les Infanticides, les Mort-nés, par le Baron de Watteville." *Annales de la Charité,* no. 12 (1856): 422–27.

La Maternité: École d'Accouchement en 1862. Paris: Guillaumin et Cie and E. Dentu, 1862. [Anonymous notes from courses taught by Mme Lachapelle and Mme Alliot, midwife-in-chief.]

Maygrier, J. P. *Nouveaux Élémens de la Science et l'Art des Accouchemens.* Paris: Audibert, 1814.

Médecine Portative, ou Guide de Santé à l'Usage de Toute le Monde. Paris: Pironnet, Year XI (1803).

Millot, Jacques-André. *L'Art de Procréer les Sexes à Volonté,* 3rd ed. Paris: Migneret et Pernier, 1802.

———. *Discours Tel au'il Devait Être Prononcé à la Séance Publique de la Société Académique des Sciences du 18 Décembre 1808.* Paris: 1809.

———. *Médecine Perfective, ou Code des Bonnes Mères,* 2 vols. Paris: Léopold Collin, 1809.

———. *Le Nestor Français, ou Guide Moral et Physiologique,* 3 vols. Paris: Buisson, 1807.

Montain, G. Alph. Claudius. *Du Lait Considéré Comme Cause des Maladies des Femmes en Couche.* Paris: Brunot-Labbe, 1808.

Montain, J.-F.-Fréderik l'aîné. *Le Guide des Bonnes Mères.* Lyon: J.-M. Barret, 1807.

Moreau, Jacques L. *Histoire Naturelle de la Femme,* 3 vols. Paris: Duprat, 1803.

Napoléon Ier, Emperor. *Vues Politiques.* Foreword by Adrien Dansette. Paris: Librairie Arthème Fayard, 1939.

Necker, Suzanne. *Réflexions sur le Divorce,* Nouvelle ed. Paris: Ch. Pougens, 1802.

Nougarède, André. *De la Législation sur le Mariage et sur le Divorce.* Paris: Le Normant, 1802.

———. *Histoire des Lois sur le Mariage et sur le Divorce,* 2 vols. Paris: Le Normant, 1803.

———. *Lois de Familles ou Essais sur l'Histoire de la Puissance Paternelle et sur le Divorce,* 2nd ed. Paris: Le Normant, 1814.

Pelissot, F. *Observations sur les Laits Répandus.* Paris: l'auteur, 1807.

Petit, Marc-Antoine. *Essai sur la Médecine du Coeur; Auquel on a Joint les Principaux Discours Prononcés à l'Ouverture des Cours d'Anatomie, d'Opérations et de Chirurgie Clinique de l'Hôtel-Dieu de Lyon, Savoir: 1º sur l'Influence de la Révolution sur la Santé Publique; 2º sur la Manière d'Exercer la Bienfaisance dans les Hôpitaux; 3º sur la Douleur; 4º sur les Maladies Observées dans l'Hôtel-Dieu de Lyon Pendant Neuf Années; 5º l'Éloge de Desaut.* Lyon: Garnier, 1806. (A 2nd ed. published 1823, 1826, and 1828.)

Petit-Radel. *Cours de Maladies Syphilitiques, Fait aux Écoles de Médecine de Paris en 1809,* 2 vols. Paris: Chanson et Fournier, 1812.

Planchon, Antoine. *Traité Complet de l'Opération Césarienne.* Paris: l'auteur, 1801.

Prunelle, Clément-V.-F.-G. *De la Médecine Politique en Général et de son Objet; De la Médecine-Légale en Particular. . . .* Montpellier: Jean Martel, 1814.

[Raoul, Fanny]. *Opinion d'une Femme sur les Femmes par F. R***.* Giguet, 1801.

Rapet, Jean-Jacques. *De l'Influence de la Suppression des Tours dans les Hospices d'Enfans Trouvés sur le Nombre des Infanticides.* Paris: 1845.

Ratier, M. S. *De la Condition et de l'Influence des Femmes, sous l'Empire, et Depuis la Restauration.* Paris: Thiériot et Belin, 1822.

Rendu, Ambroise. *Reflexions sur Quelques Parties de Notre Législation Civile.* Paris: Nicolle, 1814.

Renneville, Mme Sophie de. *Conversations d'une Petite Fille avec sa Poupée.* Paris: Billois, 1813.

———. *Correspondance de Deux Petites Filles.* Paris: Belin fils, 1811.

———. *Élémens de la Lecture à l'Usage des Enfans.* Paris: Blanchard et Eymery, 1812.

———. *La Fée Bienfaisante ou la Mère Ingénieuse.* Paris: Eymery, 1814.

———. *La Mère Gouvernante ou Principe de Politesse Fondés sur les Qualités du Coeur.* Paris: Belin-Le Prieur, 1812.

———. *Le Retour des Vendanges; Contes Variés à la Portée des Enfans de Différens Âges,* 3 vols. Paris: Genet, 1813.

———. *Les Deux Éducations ou le Pouvoir de l'Example.* Paris: Eymery, 1813.

———. *Lettres d'Octavie, Jeune Pensionnaire de la Maison de Ste-Clair; ou Essai sur l'Éducation des Demoiselles.* Paris: Leprieur, 1806.

Renneville, Mme Sophie de, and Pierre Blanchard. *Amusemens de l'Adolescence ou Lectures Agréables et Instructions à l'Usage des Deux Sexes.* Paris: 1808.

Richerand, Balthalsar-Anthelme. *Des Erreurs Populaires Relatives à la Médecine,* 2nd ed. Paris: Caille et Ravier, 1810 and 1812.

———. "Discours sur Cabanis." In *Séance de la Faculté de Médecine de Paris, 24 novembre 1808,* 5–13. Paris: Bibliothèque interuniversitaire de Médecine, 1810.

[Riquetti, Victor, Marquis de Mirabeau and François Quesnay]. *L'Ami des Hommes, ou Traité de la Population.* Nouvelle éd. Augmentée d'une Quatrième Partie & de Sommaires. 1759.

Robert, Louis Joseph Marie. *Essai sur la Mégalanthropogénésie ou l'Art de Faire des Enfans d'Esprit, Qui Deviennent de Grands-Hommes: Suivi des Traits Physiognomiques, Propres à les Faire Reconnaître, Décrits par Lavater, et du Meilleur Mode de Génération.* Paris: Debray et Bailleul, 1801.

Robert, J. B. M. *Jurisprudence sur la Capacité Personnelle et sur l'Effet des Contrats des Femmes Mariées ou Ayant des Biens Situés Tant dans les Ci-devant Pays de Droit Écrit Que dans Quelques Coutumes Principalement dans le Ci-devant Normandie, avant et après la Loi du 17 Ventôse an II (6 Janvier 1794).* Paris: Arthus Bertrand, 1813.

Rollin. *Les Études des Enfans,* Nouvelle ed. Paris: Madame Lamy, 1801.

Rougeron, P. N. *L'Historien des Jeunes Demoiselles.* Paris: Ancelle, 1810.

Roussel, Pierre. *Système Physique et Moral de la Femme,* Nouvelle ed. Paris: Crapart, Caille et Ravier, 1803.

Royer-Collard, A. A. *L'Essai sur l'Aménorrhée, ou Suppression du Flux Menstruel.* Paris: Gabon, 1802.

Sacombe, Dr. Jean-François. *Élémens de la Science des Accouchemens, avec un Traité des Maladies des Femmes et des Enfans.* Paris: Courcier, 1802.

———. *La Luciniade: Poëme en Dix Chants sur l'Art des Accouchemens,* 3rd aug. ed. Paris: Courcier, Year VII.

Saint-Martin, Felicité Gueriot. *La Paix.* Paris: Year X.

Salgues, Ad.-V. *L'Ami des Mères de Familles, ou, Traité d'Éducation Physique et Morale des Enfans.* Paris: Dentu, 1814.

Schweigger, August Friedrich. *Les Hôpitaux et Institutions Charitables de Paris.* Bayreuth: Johann Andreas Lübecks Erben, 1809.

Schweighaeuser, Jacques-Frédéric. *Sur Quelques Points de Physiologie Relatifs à la Conception et l'Économie Organique de Foetus.* Strasbourg: Louis Eck, 1812.

———. *Tablettes Chronologiques de l'Histoire de la Médecine Puerpérale.* Strasbourg, 1806.

Scott, John. *Visit to Paris in 1814.* London: Longman, Hurst, Rees, Orme and Brown, 1815.

Ségur, Joseph-Alphonse. *Les Femmes, Leur Condition et Leur Influence dans l'Ordre Social Chez Différents Peuples Anciens et Modernes,* 3 vols. Paris: Didot jeune, 1813. (Went through many editions Year XI [1803]–1836.)

Société de la Charité maternelle. *Prospectus.* Paris: Cordier, 1801.

Stein, Georges, Wilhelm. *L'Art d'Accoucher.* Paris: Croullebois, 1804.

Sue, Pierre. *Apperçu Général Appuyé de Quelque Faits, sur l'Origine et le Sujet de la Médecine Légale.* Paris: Imprimerie de la Société de Médecine, Year VIII.

Tardieu, Ambroise. *Étude Médico-Légale sur l'Infanticide.* Paris: J.-B. Baillièra, 1868.

Tenon, Jacobus R. *Mémoire sur les Hôpitaux de Paris.* Paris: Imprimerie de Ph.-D. Pierres, 1788.

Thénard. *Institut de France, Académie Royale de Sciences. Funérailles de M. le Cte Chaptal. 1 Août 1832.* Paris: Institut de France, 1832.

Tinthoin, Robert. *Bicentenaire de la Naissance de Chaptal.* Mende: Imprimerie Chaptal, 1956. [Exhibit organized by the Ministry of National Education and the Archives départementales de la Lozère.]

Tucker, David Hunter. *Eléments of the Principles and Practice of Obstetrics.* Philadelphia: Lindsay & Blakiston, 1847.

———. *Eléments of the Principles and Practice of Midwifery.* Philadelphia: Lindsay & Blakiston, 1848.

Tulard, Jean, ed. *Cambacérès: Lettres Inédites à Napoléon 1802–1814,* 2 vols. Paris: Editions Klincksieck, 1973.

Verdier-Heurtin. *Discours et Essai Aphoristique sur l'Allaitement et l'Éducation Physique des Enfans.* Paris: chez l'auteur, 1804.

Vigarous, Joseph-Marie-Joachim. *Cours Élémentaire de Maladies des Femmes, ou Essai sur une Nouvelle Méthode pour Étudier et pour Classer les Maladies de ce Sexe,* 2 vols. Paris: Deterville, 1801.

Vitet, Louis. *Maladies des Femmes—Accouchemens,* Vol. XI of *Le Médecin du Peuple, ou Traité Complet des Maladies Dont le Peuple Est Communement Affecté—Ouvrage Composé avant la Révolution Français.* Lyon: chez les Frères Peressi, 1804.

Wandelcourt, Hubert. *Plan d'Education.* Paris: Fournier, 1801.

Warchouf, Stephanie. *Velocifère Grammatical ou la Langue Française, et l'Orthographe Apprises en Chantant Ouvrage Très-élémentaire, Unique en son Genre, Mis en Vaudévilles, et Dédié aux Demoiselles.* Paris: Le Normant, 1806.

Wigand, Dr. J.-H. *Hamburgisches Magazin für die Geburtshilfe (Magazine Hambourgeois pour l'Art des Accouchemens).* Hambourg: F. Perthes, 1812.

Secondary Sources

Ackerknecht, Erwin H. *The Paris Hospital.* 1967.

———. *Therapeutics from the Primitive to the 20th Century.* New York: Hafner Press, 1973.

Adams, Christine. "Constructing Mothers and Families: The Society for Maternal Charity of Bordeaux, 1805–1860." *French Historical Studies* 22, no. 1 (Winter 1999): 65–86.

———. "Maternal Societies in France Private Charity Before the Welfare State," *Journal of Women's History* 17, no. 1 (Spring 2005): 87–205.

Akkerman, Tjitske, and Siep Stuurman, eds. *Perspectives on Feminist Political Thought in European History from the Middle Ages to the Present.* London and New York: Routledge, 1998.

Antoine, Marie-Elizabeth, and Jean Waquet. "La Médecine Civile en France à l'Époque Napoléonienne et le Legs du XVIIIe Siècle: Étude d'un Recruitement Professionnel." *Revue de l'Institut Napoléon* 132 (1976): 7–89.

Aronson, Theo. *Napoleon and Josephine.* London: John Murray, 1990.

"Assistance Publique." *La Grande Encyclopédie* 2: 264–82.

Aubert, Françoise. "Les Femmes Doivent-elles Apprendre à Lire? Une Polémique en 1801," 1: 76–97. In *Studi sull'uguaglianza contributi alla Storia,* 2 vols., ed. Corrado Rosso. Pise: Gollardica, 1973.

Aveling, James Hobson. *English Midwives, Their History and Prospects.* London: 1872.

Barsky, Hannah K. *Guillaume Dupuytren: A Surgeon in His Place and Time.* New York: Vantage Press, 1984.

Bartel, Paul. *La Jeunesse Inédite de Napoléon d'Après de Nombreux Documents.* Paris: Amiot-Dumont, 1954.

Bass, G. *Die Gerichtsmedizin als Spezialfach in Paris von 1800 bis 1815.* Zurich: 1964.

Bazy, Pierre. *Les Biographies Médicales.* Paris: Librairie J.-B. Baillière et fils, 1932.

Benassis, Dr. "La Maternité." *La Revue Thérapeutique des Alcaloïdes* (extracts from April, May, June, and July 1938): 23–31.

Block, Maurice. *Dictionnaire de l'Administration Française.* 2nd ed. Paris: Berger-Levrault et Cie, 1878.

"Boivin, Marie-Anne Victoire Gillain, femme." In *Biographie Universelle, Ancienne et Moderne,* Nouvelle ed. Edited by Michaud. 1843. 4: 612–13.

Boivin, Marie-Anne Gillain. *Chirurgie Utérine.* 1830.

Bonde, Amédée. *Étude sur l'Infanticide.* Paris: Alphonse Derenne, 1883.

Boucé, Paul-Gabriel, ed. *Sexuality in Eighteenth-Century Britain.* Manchester: Manchester University Press, 1982.

Bouchard, Georges. *Guyton-Morveau, Chemiste et Conventionnel (1737–1816).* Paris: Librairie Académique Perrin, 1938.

Bourgoin, Eduard. "Chaptal." *La Grand Encyclopédie,* 10: 577.

Bradley, Chester. "Les Opinions de Napoléon sur les Complications de l'Accouchement." *Realités* (December 1969): 21–25.

Buck, Albert H. *The Dawn of Modern Medicine.* New Haven, Conn.: Yale University Press, 1920.

Burton, June K. "Adrienne Noilles Lafayette and Frances Burney d'Arblay: Better Halves in the Worst of Times." *The Consortium on Revolutionary Europe 1750–1850, Selected Papers 1999,* 83–92. Tallahassee: Florida State University Press, 2002.

———. *Adrienne Noailles Lafayette (1759–1807) as Medical Patient: Lafayette's "Better Half" in the Worst of Times.* Easton, Penn.: The American Friends of Lafayette, 1999.

———. "The Contents of Humanistic Manuals of Home Economics and Sex during the Napoleonic Era." *The Consortium on Revolutionary Europe Proceedings, 1983,* 681–96. Athens: University of Georgia Press, 1985.

———. "Human Rights Issues Affecting Women in Napoleonic Legal Medicine Textbooks." *History of European Ideas* 8, nos. 4/5 (1987): 427–34.

———. *Napoleon and Clio: Historical Writing, Teaching and Thinking during the First Empire.* Durham, N.C.: Carolina Academic Press, 1979.

———. "Napoleon Savior or Child Abuser?: The 19th-century Controversy Surrounding Abolition of the *Tours.*" *The Consortium on Revolutionary Europe 1750–1850, Selected Papers, 1997,* 234–41. Tallahassee: Florida State University Press, 1997.

———. "The Revolution in Health: Leprosy and Society by the French Revolutionary Era," *The Consortium on Revolutionary Europe 1750–1850: Selected Papers, 1994,* 189–96. Tallahassee: Florida State University Press, 1995.

Carrier, Henrietta. *Origines de la Maternité de Paris–Les Maîtresses Sages-Femmes et l'Office des Accouchées de l'Ancien Hôtel-Dieu (1378–1796).* Paris: Georges Steinheil, 1888.

Carrington, Dorothy. "Corsica and Napoleon: How Dorothy Carrington Discovered Corsican Culture and History, and Became a Napoleonic Scholar," *Napoleon* 9 (September 1997): 36–50.

———. *Napoleon and His Parents: On the Threshold of History.* London, Viking Press, 1988; New York: Dutton, 1990.

———. "La Premier Ascension Sociale des Bonaparte." *Revue d'Institut Napoléon* no. 155 (1990–II): 11–23.

———. *Portrait de Charles Bonaparte d'Après ses Écrits de sa Jeunesse et ses Mémoires.* Ajaccio: Alain Piazzola, 2002.

Carter, Richard B. *Descartes' Medical Philosophy: The Organic Solution to the Mind-*

Body Problem. Baltimore: The Johns Hopkins Press, 1983.

Cassagne, Hélène. "Le Malade, le Médecin et le Guérisseur au XIXe Siècle." *L'Histoire* no. 20 (February 1980): 80–81.

Castiglioni, Arturo. *A History of Medicine.* Translated from the Italian and edited by E. B. Krumbhaar. New York: J. Aronson, 1975.

"Chaussier, François." *Biographie Universelle, Ancienne et Moderne,* Nouvelle ed. Edited by Michaud. 8 (1854): 50–52.

"Chaussier, François." *Dictionnaire de Biographie Française* 8 (1959): 886.

Chevillet, Georges. *Les Enfans Assistés à Travers l'Histoire.* Paris and Nancy: Berger-Levrault et Cie, 1903.

Chuquet, Arthur. *La Jeunesse de Napoléon.* 2 vols. Paris: Armand Colin, 1897.

———. "Wenceslas Jacquemont." *Feuilles d'Histoire* no. 2 (July-Dec., 1909): 120–32.

Cianfrani, Theodore. *A Short History of Obstetrics.* Springfield, Ill: Charles C. Thomas, 1960.

Cole, Joshua. *The Power of Large Numbers: Population, Politics, and Gender in Nineteenth-Century France.* Ithaca, N.Y.: Cornell University Press, 2000.

Cutter, Irving S., and Henry R. Viets. *A Short History of Midwifery.* Philadelphia: Saunders, 1964.

Darmon, Pierre. *Damning the Innocent: A History of the Persecution of the Impotent in Pre-Revolutionary France.* New York: Viking, 1986.

Defranceschi, Jean. *La Jeunesse de Napoléon: Les Dessous de l'Histoire* Paris: Lettrage, 2001.

Delaunay, Paul. *La Maternité de Paris.* Paris: Jules Rousset, 1909.

———. "Les Enfants Trouvés à l'Hospice de la Maternité (1795–1814)." *La France médicale* (1907): 337–42.

———. *L'Obstétrique dans le Maine au XVIIIe et au XIXe Siècle: Les Cours de Sages-Femmes sous l'Ancien Régime; la Maternité de l'Hôpital du Mans.* Le Mans: Imprimerie Mennoyer, 1911.

Delon, Michael. "Combats Philosophiques, Préjugés Masculins et Fiction Romanesque sous le Consulat." *Raison présente* no. 67 (1983): 67–76.

Devilliers. "De l'Assistance des Enfants Abandonnés du Premier Âge et, en Particulier, de l'Institution des Tours." *Annales d'Hygiène Publique et Médecine Légale* 2 (3rd series, 1879): 174–76.

The Diary and Letters of Frances Burney, Madame d'Arblay, revised and edited by Sarah Chauncey Woolsey (pseud. Susan Coolidge). Vol. 1. Boston: Roberts Brothers, 1880.

Dinet, Dominique. "Statistiques de Mortalité Infantile sous le Consulat et l'Empire." In *Hommage à Marcel Reinhard sur la Population Français au XVIIIe et au XIXe Siècles,* 215–30. Paris: Société de Démographie Historique, 1973.

Donnison, Jean. *Midwives and Medical Men: A History of Inter-Professional Rivalries and Women's Rights.* New York: Schocken, 1977.

Ducamp, Maxime. *Paris, ses Organes, ses Fonctions et sa Vie dans la Seconde Moitié du XIXe Siècle.* 4 vols. Paris: Hachette, 1873.

Du Chatenat. *Les Savants Célèbres.* Limoges: Eugene Ardant.

Ducros de Sixt, L. *Notice Historique sur la Vie et les Travaux du Docteur Fodéré.* Paris: 1845.

Dupin, Baron. *Histoire de l'Administration des Secours Publics.* Paris: Alexis Eymery, 1821.

"Enfans Trouvés." *Extrait du Dictionnaire des Sciences Médicales* 1818: 267–94.

Englund, Steven. *Napoleon: A Political Life.* New York: Scribner's, 2004.

Epstein, Julia. *The Iron Pen: Frances Burney and the Politics of Women's Writing.* Madison: University of Wisconsin Press, 1989.

———. "Writing the Unspeakable: Fanny Burney's Mastectomy and the Fictive Body." *Reflections* 16 (Fall 1986): 131–65.

Erickson, Carolly. *Josephine: A Life of the Empress.* New York: St. Martin's Press, 2000.

Fäy-Sallois, Fanny. *Les Nourrices à Paris au XIXᵉ Siècle.* Paris: Payot, 1980.

Findley, Palmer. *Priest to Lucina: The Story of Obstetrics.* Boston: 1939.

Fosseyeux, Marcel. *Les Sages-Femmes et Nourrices à Paris au XVIIIe Siècle. Extrait de la Revue de Paris du 1ᵉʳ Octobre 1921.* Paris: 1921.

———. "Port Royal de Paris et la Maternité (1625–1928)." *La Semaine des Hôpitaux de Paris* no. 15 (15 October 1928): 455–62.

Fowler, O. S. *Maternity.* New York: 1868.

Fraisse, Geneviève. *La Raison des Femmes.* Paris: Plon, 1992.

———. *Muse de la Raison: La Démocracie Exclusive et la Différence des Sexes.* Aix-en-Provence: Édition Alinéa, 1989.

———. "Preface." In *Opinions de Femmes: De la Veille au Lendemain de la Révolution Française.* Paris: Côté-femmes, 1989.

———. *Reason's Muse: Sexual Difference and the Birth of Democracy.* Chicago: University of Chicago Press, 1994.

Fraisse, Geneviève, and Michelle Perrot, eds. *A History of Women in the West,* IV. *Emerging Feminism from Revolution to World War.* Cambridge, Mass.: Harvard University Press, 1993.

"Frochot (Nicolas-Thérèse-Benoît, comte)." *La Grande Encyclopédie* 18: 187.

Fuchs, Rachel G. *Poor & Pregnant in Paris: Strategies for Survival in the Nineteenth Century.* New Brunswick, N.J.: Rutgers University Press, 1992.

Furet, François. *Revolutionary France 1777–1870.* Translated by Antonia Nevill. Oxford: Blackwell Publishers, Inc., 1992.

Gaillard, l'Abbé A.-H. *Recherches Administratives, Statistiques et Morales sur les Enfans Trouvés, les Enfans Naturels et les Orphelins en France et dans Plusieurs Autres Pays d'Europe.* Paris: Th. Leclerc, 1837.

Galerie Adminstrative ou Biographie des Préfets Depuis l'Organisation des Préfectures Jusqu'à ce Jour. Aurillac: 1839.

Ganière, Paul. *L'Académie de Médecine, ses Origines et son Histoire.* Paris: Editions Moline, 1964.

Gelbart, Nina Ratner. *The King's Midwife: A History and Mystery of Madame du Coudray.* Berkeley: University of California Press, 1998.

Gélis, Jacques, Mireille Laget, and Marie-France Morel. *Entrer dans la Vie: Naissances et Enfances dans la France Traditionnelle.* Paris: Editions Gaillimard-Julliard, 1978.

Georger-Vogt, Hélène. "François-Emmanuel Fodéré: Père de la Médecine Légale." *Alsace Historique,* nos. 7–8 (1977): 218–23 and 266–68.

Gille, F. *La Société de Charité maternelle de Paris.* Paris: V. Goupy et Jourdan, 1887.

Godechot, Jacques. *Les Institutions de la France sous la Révolution et l'Empire.* 2nd rev. ed. Paris: Presses Universitaires de France, 1968.

Goldsmith, Elizabeth, and Dena Goodman, eds. *Going Public: Women and Publishing in Early Modern France.* Ithaca, N.Y.: Cornell University Press, 1995.

Gosset, Dr. Pol. *Les Sages-Femmes du Pays Rémois au XVIIe et au XVIIIe Siècle.* Reims: Matot-Braine, 1909.

Guerber, H. A. *Empresses of France.* New York: Dodd Mead & Co., 1901.

Guillois, Antoine. *Le Salon de Madame Helvétius: Cabanis et les Idéologues,* 2nd ed. Paris: Calmann Levy Editeur, 1894.

Gutwirth, Madelyn. *The Twilight of the Goddesses: Women and Representation in the French Revolutionary Era.* New Brunswick, N.J.: Rutgers University Press, 1992.

Haeger, Knut. *The Illustrated History of Surgery.* New York: Bell Publishing, 1988.

Hampson, Norman. *The First European Revolution 1776–1815.* New York: W. W. Norton, 1969.

Hazlitt, William. *The Life of Napoleon.* Vol. 1. London: Grolier Society, 1830.

Hesse, Carla. Alison. *The Other Enlightenment: How French Women Became Modern.* Princeton, N.J.: Princeton University Press, 2001.

———. *Publishing and Cultural Politics in Revolutionary Paris, 1789–1810.* Berkeley: University of California Press, 1991.

Hoffer, Peter C., and N. E. H. Hull. *Murdering Mothers: Infanticide in England and New England 1558–1803.* New York: New York University Press, 1981.

Huard, Pierre. *Science, Médecine, Pharmacie de la Révolution à l'Empire 1789–1815.* Paris: Editions Roger Dacosta, 1970.

Hunt, Lynn. "Foreword." In *Re-creating Authority in Revolutionary France.* Edited by Bryant T. Ragan Jr. and Elizabeth A. Williams. New Brunswick, N.J.: Rutgers University Press, 1992.

Hurd-Mead, Kate Campbell, M.D. *A History of Women in Medicine from the Earliest Times to the Beginning of the Nineteenth Century.* Haddam, Conn.: The Haddam Press, 1938.

Husson, Armand. *Étude sur les Hôpitaux.* Paris: Paul Dupont, 1867.

Imbert, Jean. *Le Droit Hospitalier de la Révolution et de l'Empire.* Paris: Recueil Sirey, 1954.

"Jacquemont (Victor)." *La Grande Encyclopédie.* 20: 1169.

"Jacquemont, Victor." *Larousse Grand Dictionnaire Universel du XIXe Siècle.* Paris: 1873. 9: 870.

Joerger, Muriel. "The Structure of the Hospital System in France in the Ancien Régime." In *Medicine and Society in France, Selections from the Annales Economies, Sociétés, Civilisations.* Edited by Robert Forster and Orest Ranum,

104–36. Baltimore, Md.: The Johns Hopkins University Press, 1980.

Joret-Desclosières. "Biographies des grands inventeurs." *L'Investigateur* 40, no. 1 (January 1874): 1–10. (Biography of Guyton de Morveau.)

Knibiehler, Yvonne, and Catherine Fouquet. *La Femme et les Médecins.* Paris: Hachette, 1983.

"Lachapelle, Marie-Louise Dugès." In *Biographie Universelle, Ancienne et Moderne,* Nouvelle ed. Edited by Michaud. Paris: C. Desplaces, 1854. 22: 353–54.

"Lachapelle, Marie-Louise Dugès." In *Nouvelle Biographie Générale.* 27 (1958): 510–11.

Laget, Mireille. "Childbirth in Seventeenth- and Eighteenth-Century France: Obstetrical Practices and Collective Attitudes." In *Medicine and Society in France, Selections from the Annales Economies, Sociétés, Civilisations.* Ed. by Robert Forster and Orest Ranum, 137–76. Baltimore, Md.: The Johns Hopkins University Press, 1980.

Lallemand, Léon. *Histoire de la Charité.* Paris: Picard, 1912.

———. *Histoire des Enfans Abandonnés et Délaissés.* Paris: Picard, 1885.

———. *La Question des Enfans Abandonnés et Délaisses au XIXe Siècle.* Paris: Alphonse Picard, 1885.

Landes, Joan B. *Women in the Public Sphere in the Age of the French Revolution.* Ithaca, N.Y.: Cornell University Press, 1988.

Lee, Vera. *The Reign of Women in Eighteenth-Century France.* Cambridge, Mass.: Schenkman Publishing Co., 1975.

Legrand, Hubert. "Madame de Fougeret, Fondateur de la Société de Charité Maternelle (1746–1813)." *Presse Médicale,* Annex no. 69 (30 August 1905): 553–54.

Léonard, Jacques. "Women, Religion, and Medicine." In *Medicine and Society in France, Selections from the Annales Economies, Sociétés, Civilisations.* Ed. by Robert Forster and Orest Ranum, 24–47. Baltimore, Md.: The Johns Hopkins University Press, 1980.

Lesch, John E. *Science and Medicine in France the Emergence of Experimental Physiology, 1790–1855.* Cambridge, Mass.: Harvard University Press, 1984.

Ludwig, Emil. *Napoleon.* New York: 1954.

Mahieu, Bernard, Marcel Candille, and Jacqueline Sonolet. *Saint Vincent de Paul et l'hôpital.* Paris, 1960. (Catalogue of an exhibit at La Salpétrière.)

Masson, Frédéric. *Napoleon: Lover and Husband.* New York: Merriam Co., 1894.

Mathiez, Albert. *La Théophilanthropie et le Culte Décadaire 1796–1801.* Thèse. Faculté des Lettres, Université de Paris. Paris: Felix Alcan, 1903.

Matignon, Camille. *Inauguration du Monument Élevé à la Mémoire de Jean Chaptal à Mende, Lozère, 21 août 1932.* Paris: Palais de l'Institute, 1932.

Maurepas, Arnaud de, and Florent Bagard. *Les Français vus par Eux-mêmes—le XVIIIe Siècle; Anthologie des Mémorialistes du XVIIIe Siècle.* Paris: Editions Robert Laffront, 1996.

McMillan, Sally. "Mothers' Sacred Duty: Breast-Feeding Patterns among Middle- and Upper-Class Women in the Antebellum South." *Journal of Southern History* 51, no. 3 (August 1985): 333–56.

Memoirs of Madame Junot (Duchesse d'Abrantès). Vol. 5. London: The Grolier Society, no date.

Milhaud, Léon. "Le Rétablissement des Tours." *La Revue Philanthropique* 2 (1897): 17–24.

"Miollis, Honoré-Gabriel-Henri, Baron de." In *Nouvelle Biographie Générale*. Vols. 35/36, column 617. Paris: Firmin Didot Frères, 1968.

Moi, Toril. *French Feminist Thought: A Reader*. Oxford, U.K.: Basil Blackwell, 1987.

Monnier, A. *Histoire de l'Assistance Publique,* 3rd ed. Paris: 1866.

Moore, Anthony R. "Pre-Anesthetic Mastectomy: A Patient's Experience," *Surgery* 83, no. 2 (February 1978): 200–05.

Morel, Marie-France. "City and Country in Eighteenth-Century Medical Discussions about Early Childhood." In *Medicine and Society in France, Selections from the Annales Economies, Sociétés, Civilisations*. Edited by Robert Forster and Orest Ranum, 48–65. Baltimore, Md.: The Johns Hopkins University Press, 1980.

Naphys, George H. *The Physical Life of Women*. Philadelphia: 1880.

Noonan, John T., Jr. *Contraception: A History of Its Treatment by the Catholic Theologians and Cannonists*. Cambridge, Mass.: Harvard University Press, 1965.

———. *Power to Dissolve—Marriages in the Courts of the Roman Curia*. Cambridge, Mass.: Harvard University Press, 1972.

Offen, Karen. *European Feminisms 1700–1950: A Political History*. Stanford, Cal.: Stanford University Press, 2000.

———. "Reclaiming the European Enlightenment for Feminism or Prologomena to Any Further History of Eighteenth-Century Europe." *Signs Journal of women in Culture and Society* 14, no. 1 (Autumn 1988): 119–57.

———. "Was Mary Wollstonecraft a Feminist? A Contextual Re-reading of *A Vindication of the Rights of Woman,* 1792–1992." In *Quilting a New Canon: Stitching Women's Words*. Edited by Uma Parameswaran. Toronto: Sister Vision Press, 1996.

Outram, Dorinda. *The Body and the French Revolution: Sex, Class and Political Culture*. New Haven, Conn.: Yale University Press, 1989.

Parker, Harold T. *Three Napoleonic Battles*. Durham, N.C.: Duke University Press, 1944, 1983, and 1987.

———. "Two Administrative Bureaux under the Directory and Napoleon." *French Historical Studies* 4, no. 2 (September 1965): 150–69.

Pérel, Léon. "Conception Pathogénique et Traitement du Cancer du Sein au 18-ième Siècle." In International Congress for the History of Medicine, *Actes du Congrès, Proceedings: XXVe Congrès, Quèbec, 21–28 Août, 1976*. 1073–80.

Perrot, Michelle, ed. *A History of Private Life, Vol IV: From the Fires of Revolution to the Great War*. Philippe Ariès and Georges Duby, general eds. Cambridge, Mass.: Harvard University Press, 1990.

Pieuchot, Serge. "Les Enfans Trouvés et Abandonnés à Toulon au XIXᵉ Siècle." Mémoire for the Maîtrise, Faculté des Lettres et Sciences, Aix-en-Provence, 1970.

Radcliffe, Walter. *Milestones in Midwifery*. Bristol, England: 1967.

Ramsey, Matthew. *Professional and Popular Medicine in France, 1770–1830: The Social World of Medical Practice.* Cambridge: Cambridge University Press, 1988.

Regnier, J. *Les Préfets du Consulat et de l'Empire.* Paris: 1907.

Remacle, Bernard-Benoit. *Des Hospices des Enfans-Trouvés en Europe et Principalement en France Depuis leur Origine Jusqu'à nos Jours.* Paris: Crapelet, 1838.

Reval, Gabrielle. *Madame Campan, Assistante de Napoléon.* Paris: Albin Michel Editeur, 1931.

Richardson, Robert G. *Larrey: Surgeon to Napoleon's Imperial Guard.* London: John Murray, 1974.

Risler, Marcelle. "La Condition des Enfans Assistés en France de 1818 à 1850. Etude d'Administration Sociale," Thèse compl. doct. ès lettres. Paris: dact. [Archives d' Assistance Publique C-617].

Rogers, Rebecca. *Les Demoiselles de la Légion d'Honneur: Les Maisons d'Éducation de la Légion d'Honneur au XIXe Siècle.* Paris: Plon, 1992.

Rosenberg, C. E., ed. *The Family in History.* Philadelphia: University of Pennsylvania Press, 1975.

Rousseau, G. S. and Roy Porter, eds. *Sexual Underworlds of the Enlightenment.* Chapel Hill: University of North Carolina Press, 1988.

Savant, Jean. *Les Préfets de Napoléon.* Paris: Hachette, 1958.

———. *Les Ministres de Napoléon.* Paris: Hachette, 1959.

Schiebinger, Londa. *The Mind Has No Sex?* Cambridge, Mass.: Harvard University Press, 1989.

———. *Nature's Body.* Boston: Beacon Press, 1993.

Schneider, Rachel R. "Jean Pierre and Marie Madeleine Blanchard: Foremost Pioneers in Ballooning." Masters thesis, University of Akron, 1977.

Schneider, William. "Toward the Improvement of the Human Race: The History of Eugenics in France." *The Journal of Modern History* 54 (June 1982): 268–91.

Scholten, Catherine M. "On the Importance of the Obstetrick Art: Changing Customs of Childbirth in America." *The William and Mary Quarterly* 34, 3rd series, no. 3 (July 1977): 426–45.

Scott, Barbara. "Madame Campan." *History Today* 23, no. 10 (October 1973): 683–90.

Shapiro, Gilbert, and John Markoff. *Revolutionary Demands: A Content Analysis of the Cahiers de Doléances of 1789.* Palo Alto, Calif.: Stanford University Press, 1998.

Sicard de Plauzoles, J-J-E. *La Maternité et la Défense Nationale contre la Dépopulation.* Paris: V. Giard & E. Brière, 1909.

Speert, Harold. *Obstetric and Gynecologic Milestones: Essays in Eponymy.* New York: Macmillan, 1958.

Staum, Martin S. *Cabanis: Enlightenment and Medical Philosophy in the French Revolution.* Princeton, N.J.: Princeton University Press, 1980.

Stolberg, Michael. "A Woman Down to Her Bones: The Anatomy of Sexual Difference in the Sixteenth and Early Seventeenth Centuries." *Isis* 94 (2003): 274–99.

Stübler, Eberhard, M.D. *Geschichte der medizinischen Fakultät der Universität Hei-*

delberg 1386–1925. Heidelberg: Carl Winters Universitätsbuchhandlung, 1926.

Sullerot, Evelyne. *La Presse Féminine,* 2nd. Paris: Armand Colin, 1966.

Sussman, George D. *Selling Mother's Milk: The Wet-Nursing Business in France 1715–1914.* Urbana, Ill.: University of Illinois Press, 1982.

Taillandier, M. A. *Documents Biographiques sur P. C. R. Daunou.* Paris: Firmin Didot Frères, 1841.

Terson, Henri. *Origines et Évolution du Ministère de l'Intérieur. Thèse pour le Doctorat ès Sciences Politique et Economique.* Montpellier: Imprimerie Firmin et Montane, 1913.

Thoms, Herbert. *Chapters in American Obstetrics.* Springfield, Ill.: Thomas, 1933.

———. *Our Obstetric Heritage.* Hamden, Conn.: Shoestring Press, 1960.

Tomiche, Nada. *Napoléon Écrivain.* Paris: Librairie Armand Collin, 1952.

Trébuchet. "Statistique des Décès dans la Ville de Paris Depuis 1809." *Annales d'Hygiène Publique et de Médecine Légale* 40 (1850): 1–49.

Trumbach, Randolph. *The Rise of the Egalitarian Family.* New York: Academic Press, 1878.

Tuckerman, Bayard. *Life of General Lafayette,* 2 vols. New York: Dodd, Mead & Co., 1889.

Vallery-Radot, Pierre. *Deux Siècles d'Histoire Hospitalière de Henri IV à Louis-Philippe (1602–1836).* Paris: Editions Paul Dupont, 1947.

Vartanian, Aram, ed. *La Mettrie's* L'Homme Machine: *A Study in the Origins of an Idea.* Princeton, N.J.: Princeton University Press, 1960.

Vedette, Henri. *L'Art de Vaincre les Allemands.* Auxerre: Imprimerie A. Laulanie, 1906.

Vidal, Charles. *Notice sur les Hôpitaux de Castres.* Castres: Imprimerie Abeilhou, 1904.

Vissière, Isabelle, ed. *Procès des Femmes au Temps des Philosophes, ou La Violence Masculine au XVIIIᵉ Siècle.* Paris: Les Femmes, 1985.

Webb, Gerald B. *René Théophile Hyacinthe Laennec: A Memoir.* New York: Paul B. Hoeber Inc., 1928.

Weber, Eugen. "Intimations of Bucolic Bliss." *Times Literary Supplement* (14 July 1978): 801–02.

Wellman, Kathleen. *La Mettrie: Medicine, Philosophy, and Enlightenment.* Durham, N.C.: Duke University Press, 1992.

Whitcomb, Edward A. "Napoleon's Prefects." *American Historical Review* 79, no. 4 (October 1974): 1089–1118.

Wintle, Justin, ed. *Makers of Nineteenth Century Culture 1800–1914.* London: Routledge & Kegan Paul, 1982.

Williams, Elizabeth A. *The Physical and the Moral Anthropology: Physiology and Philosophical Medicine in France, 1750–1850.* Cambridge: Cambridge University Press, 1994.

Wright, Constance. *Madame de Lafayette.* New York: 1959.

Ziporyn, Terra. *Nameless Diseases.* New Brunswick, N.J.: Rutgers University Press, 1992.

Reference Works

Association Henri Capitant. *Vocabulaire Juridique,* 2nd ed. Paris: Presses Universitaires de France, 1990.

Biographie Universelle, Ancienne et Moderne. Paris: Michaud, 1811–62.

Biographie Universelle, Ancienne et Moderne par J. Fr. Michaud, Nouvelle ed. Paris: Madame C. Desplaces, 1843–65.

Biographie Universelle, Ancienne et Moderne par J. Fr. Michaud. Graz: Akademische Druck-u. Verlagstalt, 1966.

Biographies des Grands Hommes et des Personnages Remarquables Qui ont Veçu sous l'Empire. Paris: Eugène et Victor Penaud Frères, 1852.

Clozet, E. *Répertoire des Sources Manuscrites de l'Histoire de Paris.* Series directed by Marcel Poëte. Paris: Leroux, 1915.

Code Pénal Annoté d'Après la Doctrine et la Jurisprudence, 63rd ed. Paris: Jurisprudence Générale Dalloz, 1966.

Connelly, Owen, Peter Becker, Harold T. Parker, and June K. Burton eds. *Historical Dictionary of Napoleonic France.* Westport, Conn.: Greenwood Press, 1985.

Dictionnaire de Biographie Française. Paris: Librairie Letouzey et Ané, 1959.

Dictionnaire de Droit, 2nd ed. Paris: Librairie Dalloz, 1966.

Dictionnaire des Sciences Médicales. Biographie Médicale. Paris: C. L. F. Pankoucke, 1822.

Encyclopedia Britannica CD, 1999 Standard Edition.

Gillespie, Charles, ed. *Dictionary of Scientific Biography.* New York: Charles Schribner's Sons, 1970.

Le Grand Dictionnaire Universel du XIXe Siècle par Pierre Larousse. Paris: Administration du grand dictionnaire universel, 1873.

Le Grand Dictionnaire Universel du XIXe Siècle. Paris: 1982.

La Grande Encyclopédie. Paris: H. Lamirault, 1886–1902.

Isambert, Decresy, and Taillamdrier. *Recueil Général des Anciennes Lois Françaises depuis l'An 420 Jusqu'à la Révolution de 1789 Table.* Paris: Belin-Leprieur & Verdière, 1833.

Monglond, André. *La France Révolutionnaire et Impériale.* Grenoble: Editions b. Arthaud, 1930.

Nouvelle Biographie Générale. Paris: Firmin Didot Frères, 1958.

Nouvelle Biographie Générale depuis les Temps les Plus Reculés Jusqu'à 1850–60. Copenhagen, 1965.

Quérard, Joseph-Marie. *La France Littéraire. . . .* Paris: F. Didot père et fils, 1827–39.

Table Générale par Ordre Alphabétique de Matières des Lois, Sénatus-Consultes, Decrés, Arrêtés, avis du Conseil d'Etat etc. Publiée dans Le Bulletin des Lois et les Collections Officielles. . . . Paris: Rondonneau et Decle, 1816.

Wickersheimer, Ernest. *Index Chronologique des Périodiques Médicaux de la France (1679–1856)* [extract from *Bibliographie Moderne,* 1908, nos. 1–3]. Paris: A. Moline, 1910.

Index